MW00527627

# Birds of the West Indies

## SECOND EDITION

Herbert A. Raffaele, James W. Wiley,
Orlando H. Garrido, Allan R. Keith & Janis I. Raffaele

Principal Illustrators:
Dale Dyer, Tracy Taylor, and Kristin Williams

Supporting Illustrators:
Cynthie Fisher and Bart Rulon

**Princeton University Press**

**Princeton and Oxford**

Copyright © 2020 by Princeton University Press

Plates and illustrations copyright © 2020, 2003, 1998 by Herbert Raffaele, James Wiley, Orlando Garrido, Allan Keith, Janis Raffaele, Dale Dyer, Tracy Taylor, Kristin Williams, Cynthie Fisher, Bart Rulon

Requests for permission to reproduce material from this work should be sent to permissions@press.princeton.edu

Published by Princeton University Press
41 William Street, Princeton, New Jersey 08540
6 Oxford Street, Woodstock, Oxfordshire OX20 1TR

press.princeton.edu

LCCN 2019025312 (print)
LCCN 2019025313 (ebook)
ISBN 9780691180519 (paperback)
ISBN 9780691199931 (ebook)

**British Library Cataloging-in-Publication Data is available**

Editorial: Robert Kirk and Kristin Zodrow
Production Editorial: Ellen Foos
Cover Design: Lorraine Doneker
Production: Steven Sears
Publicity: Matthew Taylor and Julia Hall
Copyeditor: Laurel Anderton

Cover art by Dale Dyer

This book has been composed in ITC Galliard (main text) and Avenir (headings)

Printed on acid-free paper. ∞

Typeset and designed by D & N Publishing, Wiltshire, UK

Printed in Hong Kong

10 9 8 7 6 5 4 3 2 1

# CONTENTS

4

# DEDICATION

To the people of the Caribbean Islands and the conservation of the unique avifauna that is their heritage.

# ACKNOWLEDGMENTS

The authors, artists, and publishers would like to express their gratitude to the following organizations for providing sponsorship and support in the production of this book: World Wildlife Fund U.S., National Fish and Wildlife Foundation, U.S. Fish and Wildlife Service, and U.S. Forest Service.

# ARTIST CREDITS

**Tracy Taylor (Pedersen):** 1–3, 10, 11 (exc. Purple Heron), 12–13, 14 (exc. Southern Lapwing), 15, 17 (Wood Sandpiper), 19 (Curlew Sandpiper, Common Greenshank), 25–26, 27 (exc. grebes), 29 (exc. Muscovy Duck), 30 (exc. Eurasian form of Green-winged Teal), 31–32, 44 (Least Pauraque), 45–49, 50, 56, 57 (exc. wrens), 60 (exc. Inagua Woodstar), 61–64, 65 (exc. Yellow-crowned Parrot), 66, 67 (Green-rumped Parrotlet, Budgerigar), 70 (Western Kingbird, Giant Kingbird), 71 (Gray Kingbird), 72, 73 (exc. Hispaniolan Elaenia), 74 (exc. Olive-sided Flycatcher), 76 (exc. Mangrove Vireo), 77, 78 (exc. Yellow-green Vireo), 79, 94–95, 96 (exc. solitaires), 102 (exc. Eastern Meadowlark), 103 (exc. Cuban Oriole), 104 (Yellow-headed Blackbird), 106 (Tawny-shouldered Blackbird, Yellow-shouldered Blackbird), 107, 112, 114 (exc. Common Waxbill), 115 (exc. White-headed Munia, Chestnut Munia, Chestnut-bellied Seed-Finch), 118 (Dovekie, Black Noddy), 120 (Western Reef-Heron dark phase), 121 (Pacific Golden-Plover, Northern Lapwing), 122 (Orinoco Goose), 123 (Canvasback swimming, Bufflehead swimming, American Black Duck swimming, White-faced Whistling-Duck swimming), 125 (Least Flycatcher, Euler's Flycatcher, Tropical Kingbird), 126 (Alpine Swift, Eastern Bluebird), 127 (Hooded Oriole, Eastern Whip-poor-will), 128 (Swamp Sparrow), 129 (Jamaican Petrel, Jamaican Pauraque, Ivory-billed Woodpecker)

**Dale Dyer:** 11 (Purple Heron), 14 (Southern Lapwing), 19 (Western Willet), 22 (Eurasian form of Whimbrel), 29 (Muscovy Duck), 30 (Eurasian form of Green-winged Teal), 36 (Short-tailed Hawk), 37 (Mississippi Kite), 38 (Swainson's Hawk), 39 (Cooper's Hawk, Gundlach's Hawk), 40 (Cuban Black Hawk), 51 (White-fronted Quail-Dove), 55 (Ringed Turtle-Dove, Pied Imperial Pigeon), 60 (Inagua Woodstar), 65 (Yellow-crowned Parrot), 67 (exc. Green-rumped Parrotlet, Budgerigar), 68–69, 70 (Rufous-tailed Flycatcher, Great Crested Flycatcher), 71 (exc. Gray Kingbird), 73 (Hispaniolan Elaenia), 74 (Olive-sided Flycatcher), 76 (Mangrove Vireo), 78 (Yellow-green Vireo), 80–93, 103 (Cuban Oriole), 105 (Boat-tailed Grackle, Great-tailed Grackle), 108 (Cayman Bullfinch), 109 (Lesser Antillean Bullfinch, Barbados Bullfinch), 114 (Common Waxbill), 115 (White-headed Munia, Chestnut Munia, Chestnut-bellied Seed-Finch), 118 (exc. Dovekie, Black Noddy), 119 (exc. Whiskered Tern, White-winged Tern), 120 (exc. Western Reef-Heron dark phase), 121 (Spotted Crake, Common Ringed Plover), 122 (Little Stint, Brant, Long-billed Curlew), 123 (Tufted Duck, Garganey), 124, 125 (Townsend's Warbler), 126 (Common House-Martin, Common Cuckoo, Lazuli Bunting), 127 (Greater Ani, Fish Crow, House Crow), 128 (Vesper Sparrow, Horned Lark), 129 (Bachman's Warbler, Semper's Warbler, St Kitts Bullfinch)

**Kristin Williams:** 4–9, 27 (grebes), 28, 36 (exc. Short-tailed Hawk), 37 (exc. Mississippi Kite), 38 (Northern Harrier, Red-tailed Hawk), 39 (Broad-winged Hawk, Sharp-shinned Hawk), 40 (exc. Cuban Black Hawk), 41–43, 44 (exc. Least Pauraque), 51 (exc. White-fronted Quail-Dove), 52–54, 55 (Rock Pigeon, Eurasian Collared-Dove), 57 (wrens), 58–59, 75, 96 (solitaires), 97–101, 102 (Eastern Meadowlark), 104 (exc. Yellow-headed Blackbird), 105 (Greater Antillean Grackle, Carib Grackle), 106 (exc. Tawny-shouldered Blackbird, Yellow-shouldered Blackbird), 108 (exc. Cayman Bullfinch), 109 (St Lucia Black Finch, Blue-black Grassquit), 110–111, 113, 116–117, 119 (Whiskered Tern, White-winged Tern), 122 (Tundra Swan, Greater White-fronted Goose), 128 (Lark Sparrow, Dark-eyed Junco, American Goldfinch), 129 (Grand Cayman Thrush)

**Cynthie Fisher:** 16, 17 (exc. Wood Sandpiper), 18, 19 (exc. Curlew Sandpiper, Common Greenshank, Western Willet), 20–21, 22 (exc. Eurasian form of Whimbrel), 23–24, 122 (Spotted Redshank), 129 (Eskimo Curlew)

**Bart Rulon:** 33–35, 123 (Canvasback flying, Bufflehead flying, American Black Duck flying, White-faced Whistling-Duck flying)

"Impressive" hardly describes Caribbean bird evolution over the brief 17 years since publication of this book's first edition. Of course, I am referring to "bird evolution" not in a literal sense but in a figurative one—the evolution of bird study as a hobby and the growth of sundry local organizations that support it. What was the realm of a handful of resident enthusiasts has skyrocketed into one with numerous conscientious observers scattered among the islands. Needless to say, this stands as a most positive development that we hope bodes well for increased conservation initiatives throughout the West Indies. The efforts of BirdsCaribbean to promote bird study and conservation within the region deserve special recognition in this regard. That organization has made a priority of promoting bird study in both school classrooms and informal settings. And it is paying off!

More observers mean more discoveries—and there have been many!

Perhaps the most startling is that four species of hawks previously not known to occur in the West Indies actually migrate in numbers along Cuba's northwest coast in transit to Mexico's Yucatán Peninsula. The Swainson's Hawk, Short-tailed Hawk, Mississippi Kite, and Cooper's Hawk all fit this bill. Add the Swallow-tailed Kite, which was known from Cuba but not nearly in the numbers now documented to occur, and that makes five extraordinary new ecological discoveries.

Comparable to the hawk discovery is that of a major seabird migration off Guadeloupe, an event that has transformed our understanding of seabird occurrence in the Caribbean. The Manx Shearwater, a species unknown from the West Indies not long ago, and still considered "rare" until recently, has been observed in numbers over 1,500 in a single hour! The five species of jaegers and skuas, other scarcely recorded seabirds, have now all been observed in a single day. The Arctic Tern, the farthest-migrating bird in the world and not long ago a vagrant in the West Indies, is frequently observed from Guadeloupe during April and May. We can hope that local observers will soon determine whether this seabird phenomenon observed from Pointe des Châteaux at Guadeloupe's eastern tip is observable from promontories on other Lesser Antillean islands or whether it occurs too far offshore to be detected from land.

Then, there are all the new vagrants that have been spotted straying to the region. Some, like the Horned Lark and Olive-sided Flycatcher, are species from eastern North America that have simply strayed too far, but a surprising number of others, beginning to represent a pattern, are Old World species that have wandered far across the Atlantic. The Eurasian Kestrel, Western Marsh Harrier, Purple Heron, and Black Kite are but a few of these. All told, over 30 new vagrants have been added to the tally of West Indian birds these past few years—and that is after applying fairly stringent conditions on what qualifies a species to be placed in this category.

These impressive discoveries do not likely reflect a change in the migratory patterns of these hawks and seabirds or many of the vagrants being detected. Rather, they almost certainly are the consequence of many more observers throughout the region scanning remote places more intensively. And clearly this is a good thing. The more people out watching birds, the more who care about their survival and want to protect them.

A bit less surprising than the hawks and seabirds, but more spectacular in impact, is the introduction of approximately 17 new exotic species from various parts of the world that are now breeding in the wild and established in the West Indies. Who would have thought but a few years ago that toucans, lovebirds, and macaws would become part of the West Indian landscape! Though these introduced species are not yet common, it remains to be seen how extensively they colonize the region. One that has spread dramatically since the first edition of this book is the Eurasian Collared-Dove, now widespread throughout the Caribbean. Such success across the region is not likely for these new introductions, but some may become common on the island where they were introduced.

The success of these exotic birds, despite their beauty, should not be viewed as anything but a failure from an ecological perspective. Introducing foreign species has caused countless woes all over the world, particularly on islands, not the least of which has been the transmission of diseases or competition with native species. The establishment of so many exotic species in the West Indies is a major warning sign that island governments are not taking seriously the numerous negative impacts such introductions forebode, one being the potentially serious threat to the survival of their extraordinary native avifauna.

The West Indies has long been recognized as housing two unique families of birds—families in the taxonomic sense. (One or more species of birds may belong to one genus, and one or more genera make up a taxonomic family. The 10,000 or so bird species in the world are thus divided among 2,000-plus genera, and these into approximately 200 families.) These two West Indian families are represented by the Palmchat of Hispaniola and the five species of todies in the Greater Antilles. These two unique families once served to highlight the antiquity of the region's birds, since many millions of years must have been required to produce such distinctive local families, or to cause their isolation on remote oceanic islands.

Such is the case no longer. Detailed genetic analyses have revealed five additional bird families unique to the West Indies. These include the Cuban warblers (Teretistridae), Puerto Rican Tanager (Nesospingidae), chat-tanagers (Calyptophilidae), palm-tanagers (Phaenicophilidae), and spindalis tanagers (Spindalidae). The significance of this new taxonomic revision confirms much more definitively the incredibly long time the islands of the Caribbean have been isolated from the mainland. Such isolation has led to more highly distinct animals than ever imagined. Now with seven unique bird families, the West Indies advances dramatically as a center for biodiversity on a global scale.

This new edition has been modified in several ways. Most significantly, all the vagrants, over 60 species, have been moved to the back of the book to avoid having them clutter up pages illustrating birds far more likely to be encountered. Relatedly, the order of birds in the book has been modified for better comparison of birds from shared habitats and similar-looking species. For example, birds in the book are presented from the sea landward—ocean, coastal waters, seashore, marshes, and finally upland. Also, most of the land birds with black plumages or thick bills have been placed near one another rather than being dispersed within the book in line with taxonomic sequence. Following taxonomic sequence is fine for experts, but terrible as a tool when it comes to field identification, which is what this book is for. One exception is that birds of the same family have been kept together. This precluded, for example, moving the Smooth-billed Ani to be placed with other black land birds. Another improvement is the color marking of the various endemic species by island or island group. We felt that these especially important birds should be more easily singled out. You will also find some excellent new artwork and less congested plates that allow for larger images and expanded text. Numerous maps have also been added, as well as weights for each bird.

On the flip side, the passing of James Wiley, a longtime friend and coauthor of this and other books, was particularly distressing. Jim's legacy to bird conservation in the West Indies is vast, and he will be sorely missed throughout the region, particularly in Cuba, where he dedicated the later years of his brilliant career toward assisting Cuban ornithologists with training, research, and their careers.

We hope that this book will help stimulate the next generation of Jim Wileys to ensure a bright future for the Caribbean's birds for generations to come.

## ACKNOWLEDGMENTS

Undertaking a project covering an expanse as vast and diverse as the West Indies cannot be achieved effectively without expert input from throughout the region. I have been fortunate to receive such support from a wide array of friends and associates who dedicated substantial time and effort to improving the quality of this book. Salient among these is Anthony Lavesque, who critiqued the manuscript at various stages of completion, and each time in fine detail. Anthony's knowledge of and discoveries on Guadeloupe, not to mention other Lesser Antillean islands along with the little-known San Andrés and Providencia, provided important new updates to our knowledge of the region's avifauna. Other important contributors, too numerous for me to elaborate on their specific contributions, include Patricia Bradley (Cayman Islands), Sergio Colon (Puerto Rico), Jeff Gerbacht (eBird—Cornell Lab of Ornithology), Bruce Hallett (Bahamas), Lyndon John (St Lucia), Steve Latta (National Aviary and Dominican Republic), Catherine Levy (Jamaica), Eddie Massiah (Barbados), Alcides Morales (Puerto Rico), Nils Navarro (Cuba), Clive Petrovic (British Virgin Islands), Jose Salguero (Puerto Rico), and Joe Wunderle (West Indies).

Complementing the updated text is extraordinary new art by Dale Dyer, who upgraded some of the older work and contributed all the illustrations of new species. Not only is Dale's art of the highest quality in terms of both beauty and accuracy, but Dale was amazingly efficient, thorough, timely, and a pleasure to work with through the entire process. Those who provided valuable support to Dale include curators and staff at the American Museum of Natural History's Ornithology Department—George Barrowclough, Joel Cracraft, Paul Sweet, and Brian Tilston Smith—as well as Steve Cardiff and Van Remsen at Louisiana State University's Museum of Zoology, Nate Rice at the Academy of Natural Sciences of Drexel University, and Jeremiah Trimble at the Harvard Museum of Comparative Zoology.

To all these individuals and their institutions—a hearty THANKS!

Herb Raffaele

## GOAL

The primary goal of this guide is to promote an interest in birds among the local people of the Caribbean islands. It is only when people appreciate and respect their birdlife that they ever come to protect it. The book also aims to facilitate the enjoyment and study of West Indian birds by both novice and professional alike.

## GEOGRAPHIC COVERAGE

The West Indies is taken to include all islands of the Bahamas, Greater Antilles, Virgin Islands, Cayman Islands, Lesser Antilles, San Andrés, and Providencia. Omitted are Trinidad and Tobago and other islands off the north coast of South America. Though Trinidad and Tobago appear contiguous to the Lesser Antilles, their origins, and consequently their birdlife, are entirely different. This is because those islands were formerly attached by a land bridge to South America during the Pleistocene epoch. As a consequence, their avifauna is much more representative of South America than it is of the West Indies.

The West Indies includes two islands that are divided politically between two nations. One is Hispaniola, which includes the countries of Haiti and the Dominican Republic, and the second is St Martin, half of which belongs to France (Saint-Martin), and the other half to the Netherlands (Sint Maarten). In most cases we treat each island as a single entity, though in a few instances where the status of a bird differs greatly between the two countries, this is pointed out. Regrettably, however, Haiti has received less coverage as a result, exacerbated by the small amount of ornithological activity reported from there.

A similar circumstance arises when clusters of small islands are divided between nations. One case is the Bahamas archipelago, which is encompassed primarily by the nation of that name—the Commonwealth of the Bahamas—but also includes a small cluster of islands at the southern tip of the archipelago that is a British Overseas Territory known as Turks and Caicos. A second case is that of the Virgin Islands, which are divided between Great Britain and the United States. As in the previous instance, the two entities are treated as one in this book except in unusual cases; consequently, reference to the "Bahamas" includes Turks and Caicos, while reference to the "Virgin Islands" includes both the U.S. and British islands. In a few instances, the distinction is made. The Lesser Antilles too fall into this category, except that they are divided into a much more complicated political mosaic. Generally, if a bird has pretty much the same status among the islands, that status is given for the Lesser Antilles. If a bird's status differs among these islands, to the extent practical the status is given island by island.

Finally, there are several cases of a number of islands belonging to a single country. This is so for the Bahamas, Cayman Islands, and St Vincent and the Grenadines, among others, and the status of each bird is generally given to represent the entire group of islands. Where this is not the case, it is so stated. Obviously, since smaller islands usually have more limited habitat than their larger counterparts, their birdlife is often less diverse and abundant. Regrettably, because of space limitations and the need to be concise, the status of birds on the smaller islands is less accurately represented.

## SPECIES COVERAGE

The text presents accounts of 614 bird species known to occur with reasonable frequency in the West Indies. To that end, native species included in the book are those for which there is a minimum of either two specimens or photographs from the region, or six separate sight records by reliable observers. Had looser criteria been used, such as one definitive photograph, or fewer verified sight records, numerous other bird species would have been added to this book—many dozens. The Black-footed Albatross, Aplomado Falcon, and Ruby-topaz Hummingbird would have been a few of these dazzlers. But this approach would have resulted in the book containing far too many species that most observers would never see. In balance, we thought such an approach would detract from the book's value as a field guide—its basic purpose.

The book also includes an increased number of introduced species. These are the result of pet birds brought from other regions of the world either escaping or being released by their owners. Now flying free at an accelerating rate, these escaped birds more readily find mates, thus increasing their potential to become established. Only those exotic species considered to be established and breeding are presented, with three exceptions—the Ringed Turtle-Dove, Budgerigar, and Cockatiel. These are so regularly seen that they are important for birders to recognize, and their numbers suggest they have a strong potential to become established at some point. Dozens of other introduced species observed in the wild, but not believed to be established, have been excluded. Again, this was done to avoid overwhelming book users with birds unlikely to be seen. At the same time, five introduced species have been removed from this edition. Those are the Crested Bobwhite, Spotted Dove, Yellow-headed Parrot, Black-hooded Parrot, and Hill Myna. All had established wild populations at some point, but these appear to have failed.

The last plate of the book includes eight species widely thought to have become extinct in the region sometime since 1900. These are included for two reasons. First, there is always a chance that a bird thought to be extinct might be rediscovered after many years of going undetected. The Puerto Rican Nightjar is one example. Collected in 1888, the species went undetected for 73 years until being rediscovered in 1961. We can only hope that this will also be the case for the Jamaican Petrel, which occupies remote precipices and is entirely nocturnal during its brief stint on land. Second, it is important to remember what we have lost, or are about to lose. Our hope is that this book will encourage a greater appreciation of what we still have, an awareness of its fragility, and a wider recognition that extinction is irreversible. Numerous other bird species have become extinct in the West Indies during historical time. At least 15 species of parrots alone fall into this category. These birds are not included in this book.

## TAXONOMY

The taxonomy of birds is in upheaval. This is due to the amazing insights the new techniques of genetic analyses provide us, insights that were virtually impossible to derive but a few decades ago. Prior to the application of genetic analyses, bird taxonomists had to depend primarily on visible plumage and anatomical characteristics of birds, along with differences in vocalizations, to distinguish one species from another. With the development of genetic techniques, taxonomists now use differences in genetic makeup as a major character to determine species uniqueness. The result? Numerous new bird species are being described at an astonishing rate. Basically, many birds that look relatively similar and were formerly divided into subspecies are being found through genetic analyses to be much more distinct from one another than simple visual examination can detect. For that reason, some birds are regularly being split off into new species, which, when nearly identical in appearance, are widely referred to as sibling species. To take an example from the West Indies, relatively recent studies have revised the West Indian genus *Spindalis*. From what was formerly considered to be one very variable species, the Stripe-headed Tanager, four distinct ones have been described: Jamaican Spindalis, Hispaniolan Spindalis, Puerto Rican Spindalis, and Western Spindalis. It has been speculated that when genetic characteristics are applied to all of the world's birds, the number of species could grow from its present number on the order of 10,500 to as many as 18,000.

Not only are new species being described hand over fist, but the relationships among different groups of birds are undergoing major revision as well. Grebes, a family of diving water birds, was formerly thought to be closely related to loons, another diving bird. Not so. Turns out they are more closely related to sandgrouse.

A particularly exciting outcome of this new taxonomic revolution has been the splitting of not only bird species, but even bird genera and families. This has confirmed that the birds of the West Indies are, in fact, substantially more unique and distinctive than previously realized. For the longest time, it was believed that the Caribbean housed only two families of birds endemic to the region. One is the Palmchat, a noisy and gregarious bird that builds communal nests and is found only on Hispaniola. The second is the delightful tody family, of which there are five species inhabiting the Greater Antilles.

Now, however, five new West Indian bird families have been recognized. These include the single Puerto Rican Tanager (Nesospingidae) endemic to that island, the two chat-tanagers (Calyptophilidae) found only on Hispaniola, the four palm-tanagers (Phaenico-philidae) endemic to that island as well, the two Cuban warblers (Teretistridae), and the four spindalis tanagers (Spindalidae) that span the Greater Antilles and some of the Bahamas. That the Caribbean islands are now known to house seven endemic families speaks volumes regarding the richness and long-standing isolation of these islands, major factors supporting their biological importance.

In general, for the purpose of this guide, we followed the taxonomy and common names proposed in the American Ornithologists' Union (AOU) Checklist of North American Birds (1998) and its supplements. There are a few exceptions. We have veered from that taxonomy when research, sometimes by one or more of the authors, has suggested otherwise. We hope that at some point the AOU's classification and nomenclature committee will adopt these revisions.

A few English common names were also changed to better represent certain species. An example is the substitution of the name Rose-throated Parrot for the long-standing, but inaccurate, Cuban Parrot. This change eliminates the implication that this parrot is unique to Cuba, when in fact it is a flagship species of the Bahamas and Cayman Islands. Efforts to conserve these parrots are not enhanced by such a misnomer. Similar changes were not made for species such as the Bahama Mockingbird, which also happens to occur in Jamaica. This was in deference to the general conservativeness of the ornithological community.

## USING THE GUIDE
### Species Accounts
Each account has been kept brief in order to fit opposite its complementary bird illustrations, as well as to keep the book to a reasonable length for easy use in the field. In most instances, accounts are grouped by bird family. While this may not be the best approach for bird identification, it has been followed in deference to the traditions of bird guides and ornithological traditionalists. However, in some cases, particularly among marine and aquatic birds, species have been grouped according to similarity of appearance to help facilitate comparison.

While the taxonomic relationships of birds are fascinating to some, the order in which bird families evolved is of no value for identification purposes. Consequently, though birds are generally grouped by family, the sequence in which the families are presented does not follow the AOU's taxonomic order. The reason is simple—this is a guide for identifying birds, for amateur and professional alike. It is not a taxonomic treatise.

The birds have been sequenced beginning with those that occur at sea, to those found inland. Families of inland birds are sequenced somewhat for comparison of similar-looking birds. For example, families of birds that are primarily black (crows and orioles) are placed near one another, as are various families of thick-billed finch-like birds.

Importantly, all 60-plus vagrant species, birds that occur less than once every 10 years, have been placed at the back of the book. This simplifies the identification of regularly occurring species. We felt that inserting so many vagrants into the main text would add unnecessary confusion and complexity to everyday bird identification. In the few instances where a species is very rare in the West Indies as a whole but is a vagrant on any given island, such species have been included in the main text.

Not all islands are birded with equal intensity. The small islands of Guadeloupe and Grand Cayman are relatively heavily birded. The large island of Hispaniola, and the country of Haiti in particular, have very little activity. This is not meant as a judgment, but rather to indicate that the status of birds presented in the book reflects what we know today based on relatively limited observations in some places. Over time, these gaps should be filled. Such gaps are particularly noticeable for marine birds, since few birders have the opportunity to travel far

## DESCRIPTIVE PARTS OF A BIRD

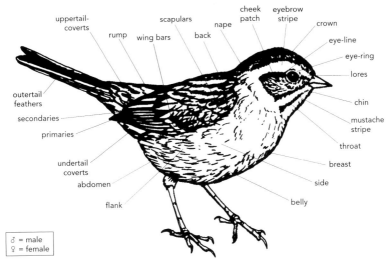

♂ = male
♀ = female

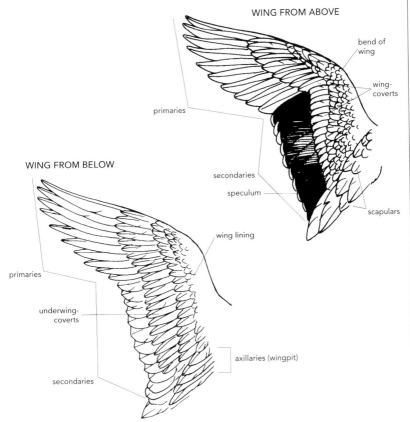

WING FROM ABOVE

WING FROM BELOW

offshore. To adjust for this, in a few cases, such as the South Polar Skua, we have speculated on the broader status of birds within the West Indies based on extrapolation from well-studied areas. We have noted such cases, of which there are few. In others, such as the Masked Booby, data are presented placing the bird in the seas virtually surrounding Cuba, but not near the island itself. Can the Masked Booby somehow not sustain itself in coastal Cuban waters for some ecological reason (similar to the case of the Bananaquit unable to colonize the land)? Or is this simply an artifact of limited birders in the field? Only time will tell.

## Identification

**BIRD NAME** The common and scientific names of each species are presented. In cases where a bird is commonly known by more than one name, a second is presented in parentheses. Endemic species unique to particular islands are color coded for quick recognition. The codes and colours are:

**C**—Found only in Cuba

**H**—Found only in Hispaniola

**J**—Found only in Jamaica

**P**—Found only in Puerto Rico

**S**—Found only on one island other than the four listed above

**M**—Found on more than one island, but not outside of the Caribbean

**SIZE** The body length and weight of each species are listed immediately after its name to offer a sense of the bird's size. In some cases, as for sea birds and raptors, which are often seen soaring, wingspan measurements are also provided. In many cases a range of lengths or weights is displayed, particularly when these measurements vary substantially because of sexual size differences or just basic size variation within the species. Even in cases where only a single length or weight is provided, it should be recognized that this represents an average for the species and that there will be variation from this figure. On each plate every effort has been made to present species in proper size proportion to one another. However, that has proven impossible in some cases, which are noted on the plates.

**BEHAVIOR** Unusual behaviors or attributes of birds that aid in identification are included in this section. They are placed early in the write-up because they are often of great importance in identification.

**DESCRIPTION** Only salient field marks are presented. These are key features to look for when identifying the bird. No attempt is made to describe the species comprehensively, since this is better discerned via the illustrations and would occupy too much space. Plumages that vary by age, sex, or season are differentiated. So are variations when a species differs substantially among islands. For species that occur in the West Indies for only a portion of the year, the plumage most likely to be seen is presented first, with the least likely plumage presented last. For example, of the various gull species that occur in the West Indies but do not breed, immature birds occur much more regularly than adults. Consequently, the subadult plumages are described before those of the adults. For species that do not breed in the West Indies and that rarely occur, the breeding plumage may not be illustrated in every case. If a bird belongs to an endemic genus or family, making it that much more unique from an evolutionary standpoint, such is indicated.

**FLIGHT** This is described when it is a specific asset to identification.

**VOICE** The calls, songs, and notes as known in the West Indies are described when useful for identification.

**STATUS AND RANGE** The extent to which the bird depends on the West Indies during its life cycle is presented. Some species reside on a single island during their entire lives. Others may pass through the islands only during certain migratory periods.

The following terms are used to represent the overall status of each species:

*Endemic*: A species that is native to a limited geographic range (island or small group of islands) and occurs nowhere else in the world. Example: Arrowhead Warbler.

*Permanent resident*: A species that spends its entire life cycle on a particular island or group of islands regardless of any environmental fluctuations from year to year. Example: Cuban Bullfinch.

*Year-round resident*: A species that spends its entire life cycle on a particular island or island group as long as environmental conditions are adequate, but flies elsewhere when conditions deteriorate. Example: Glossy Ibis.

*Breeding resident*: A species that breeds on a particular island or group of islands and then migrates elsewhere during the non-breeding season. Example: Cuban Martin.

*Non-breeding resident*: A species that breeds elsewhere but occurs on a particular island or group of islands during the non-breeding season. Sometimes referred to as a "visitor" or "visitant." Other bird guides often refer to such birds as "winter visitors." This term has been deliberately avoided in this work since "winter" is not a term used on all islands, so it would represent a bird's status from a North American perspective. Example: Lesser Yellowlegs.

*Migrant*: A species that migrates between islands or to areas outside the West Indies on a seasonal basis. Sometimes referred to as a "transient." Example: Swallow-tailed Kite.

*Visitor or wanderer*: A species that moves between islands at irregular intervals. Example: Little Egret.

The terms used to describe the likelihood of observing a given species are defined below:

*Common*: Five or more individuals likely to be seen daily. (Occurs in high densities.) This does not apply to species such as raptors, which, because of large territories, are sighted less frequently.

*Fairly common*: One to four individuals likely to be seen daily. (Occurs in moderate densities.)

*Uncommon*: Not likely to be seen on every trip but can be expected at least twice per year. (Occurs in low densities.)

*Rare*: Fewer than two records per year; at least one occurrence every five years. (Occurs in very low densities.)

*Very rare*: Occurs once every five to ten years. (Usually not present.)

*Vagrant*: Occurs less than once every ten years.

These categories are based on a skilled observer seeking the bird in the right place at the right time. In some cases, this means visiting a very specific habitat, such as a particular freshwater pond during the migration season. For birds that roost or breed communally (e.g., herons and terns), the status given represents the likelihood of encountering the species under more general field conditions and does not include flocks flying to or from a roost.

Needless to say, some species are substantially more detectable than others. For example, every Snowy Egret in a small swamp can be located easily. However, a single Yellow-breasted Crake in that same swamp would be inordinately more difficult to detect. This would be the case even if crakes were substantially more abundant than egrets. To address this, we have tried to indicate species that are particularly difficult to detect. This is either stated in the text or implied in the description of the bird's habitat, which might be "at sea." Our intent, however, is to reflect a bird's true status, thus presuming detection of the bird by an experienced observer using appropriate techniques. We considered providing a "detectability index" but felt this would be very subjective, especially considering the wide use of tape recordings in the field, an increasingly widespread practice that we seriously frown upon under most circumstances.

This issue of detectability is particularly important regarding endangered species. The critically endangered Yellow-shouldered Blackbird might be seen during every trip to its roosting or feeding areas in Puerto Rico, thus classifying it as "locally common." This is not to say that the total population size of the species is large. We have tried to indicate, at least for threatened and endangered species, cases where a species is classified as locally common, but in fact its population is small.

Misconceptions can be created by these terms when applied to small islands. A small island with a small pond may sustain only one pair of Pied-billed Grebes or a single Great Blue Heron. Yet these birds might be observed on every birding trip and are thus "common." Similarly, if that particular pond is full only seasonally, grebes may be present whenever it has water but will be absent when it is dry. We leave it to your common sense to determine how circumstances such as these apply to any particular species or island.

Detectability also has to do with being in the right place at the right time. For all intents and purposes, the Manx Shearwater very rarely if ever occurs in Guadeloupe—but it sure may be plentiful if you have a field scope and are looking out to sea from Pointe des Châteaux in April or May. The same is true for migratory hawks in Cuba. The place to be is Cape San Antonio on the Guanahacabibes Peninsula at Cuba's far western tip. Hawks never seen elsewhere on the island sometimes show up in numbers at this important migratory staging area. Among the exciting discoveries yet to be made on many islands are these special places where unusual birds occur in numbers previously not thought possible. Thinking more like tired, long-traveling birds facing a seemingly endless ocean should help launch some of these discoveries.

Migratory species, a group that predominates in the West Indies, create other complexities regarding status designation. Because such species are so dependent on and affected by weather conditions, they may occur frequently one year and be rare or absent the next. They may also move in aggregates, with large numbers of birds occurring at one moment and then disappearing shortly thereafter. Also, migration patterns of southbound birds sometimes differ when the birds return northward. Consequently, a species might be more abundant as a southbound migrant and less frequent or absent as a northbound one. To complicate matters further, a species might be more common as a southbound migrant in one part of the Caribbean but more frequent as a northbound migrant in another. We have tried to indicate this where apparent.

**HABITAT** This is the specific environment in which the bird is likely to be found. When there are many, we have tried to list the preferred habitats first. It should always be kept in mind that the status designations of "common," "rare," and so on depend on the extent to which a bird's habitat requirements are met. For example, if an island has only one major freshwater wetland, and that wetland usually has a fair number of Least Grebes, then the bird will be described as "locally common" on the island. This implies that over most of the island the bird will not be found at all.

## Maps

Each map displays the range of a species within the West Indies. Maps are included only in cases where they can be helpful in portraying the distribution of a species at a glance. Maps are omitted for species that occur throughout the West Indies or that inhabit only one or two islands. Islands where species occur only as vagrants are not indicated as part of the range on the maps.

*Green*: Permanent or year-round resident. Some species may move periodically among islands. Example: White-cheeked Pintail.

*Maroon*: Occurs only a portion of the year and migrates elsewhere to breed. Includes migrants and non-breeding residents. Example: Tree Swallow.

*Orange*: Breeds in the West Indies but migrates elsewhere during the non-breeding season. Example: Caribbean Martin. There are very few species in this category.

## Plates

The color plates depict every species for which there is an account in the text. The plumage of some birds differs noticeably from island to island, for example the ubiquitous Banana-quit. In such cases, various island forms are illustrated. Variations in plumage between male and female, adult and immature, and breeding and non-breeding birds are also depicted if important for identification. For species that do not breed in the West Indies, the breeding plumage may not be illustrated. Or if it is, it may be rendered in a smaller size. Overall, the plumage most likely to be encountered at any given time in the West Indies is featured. In a few cases, such as the gulls, hawks, and warblers, birds may be illustrated on several plates for comparison. Birds on each plate are rendered in appropriate relative size to one another unless indicated otherwise.

# CONSERVATION

## The Problem

The growth of human populations and extensive changes in land-use practices have resulted in major impacts on the earth's biological resources, especially its birdlife. Directly as a result of these human impacts, several hundred species and subspecies of birds have become extinct worldwide over recent centuries. Of particular conservation concern to the West Indies is that most of these extinct species were island forms.

Island species are particularly vulnerable for two reasons. First, most species occupy very limited ranges, leaving few areas to serve as safe havens where small populations might manage to survive. Second, island species have generally evolved in the absence of terrestrial predators such as cats, dogs, pigs, mongooses, and humans. Consequently, they often lack appropriate mechanisms with which to defend themselves and their young.

Endangerment and extinction can be part of the natural evolutionary process. However, this is considered to be the case only when naturally occurring events, such as hurricanes, are the cause of the decline. Bulldozing the last remaining stand of trees sheltering a species, or releasing exotic animals that prey on the young of ground-nesting birds, are hardly natural events. Not surprisingly, given the extensive development of the Caribbean over the past few centuries, virtually every bird species presently considered endangered or threatened in the West Indies has become so as the result of human-induced causes.

## Principal Causes of Endangerment and Extinction

HABITAT DESTRUCTION AND DISTURBANCE  Every natural habitat known to the West Indies has been significantly altered by humans. Some of these alterations are obvious, such as the cutting of lowland forest and its replacement with cattle pastures or housing developments. Others are less so, for example the channelization of wetlands as a means of mosquito control. Some might argue that our most remote mountain forests are unaltered, but this too can be challenged. Puerto Rico's uncut Luquillo rain forest is infested with feral cats and rats that prey on native birds, including the young of the endangered Puerto Rican Parrot. St Christopher's Mount Misery has suffered the affliction of the African green monkey (*Cercopithecus aethiops*) for centuries. In fact, it is often these insidious, inconspicuous changes we inflict on our environment that are the most threatening because their impacts often go so long undetected.

Given the extent of development in the West Indies, it is not surprising that habitat destruction and disturbance are by far the primary causes of endangerment to West Indian birds. Unless a serious attempt is made to manage these development trends wisely, through integrated planning efforts focused on each ecosystem as a whole, the list of endangered and threatened species in the West Indies will continue to grow.

Heavy deforestation in the West Indies began soon after European colonization. Lowland forests were the first to disappear, followed by those of the foothills and lower mountain slopes. Timber extraction for house construction, fuelwood, and furniture, along with clearing for agriculture and cattle production, quickly took a heavy toll on the native vegetation. Flat islands were denuded most rapidly, and those with precipitous mountains or otherwise remote localities more slowly. Nevertheless, by the late 1800s most forests of the West Indies had either been felled by ax or saw, or cleared by ox or fire. The twentieth century brought the bulldozer and chain saw as new threats to native forests along with the expansion of roads into previously inaccessible areas. Fortunately, this has been counteracted on some islands by natural forest regeneration resulting from the replacement of charcoal by gas and electricity, and by the abandonment of marginal agricultural lands and the resulting shift of rural populations to cities.

The forests of some West Indian islands are in better shape now than they were a century ago, but others are decidedly worse off. Considering the ever-increasing threat of the chain saw, population growth, and expansive development, increased care must be taken to ensure that habitat destruction and disturbance do not continue to be the greatest threats to West Indian birdlife.

**HUNTING** Historically, hunting was a traditional pastime on most islands of the West Indies. It was widely practiced without adequate attention to the biology of the game species hunted, or to controls regarding the numbers of birds taken. Also, hunting protocols devised in the United States were transferred to the Caribbean without considering the region's vastly different ecological conditions. These factors have resulted in dramatic declines of formerly common species, particularly among pigeons, doves, and waterfowl. This is one area in which carefully conceived conservation measures can benefit all involved, including hunters, bird aficionados, and the birds themselves.

**HARVEST AND TRADE** Capturing wild birds for house pets or for the international bird trade has reduced native parrot numbers particularly. As parrots have become more endangered, they have also become more valuable. Illegal take is exacerbated by the cutting down of nesting trees to acquire the birds and take the fledglings. Nesting trees on many islands are relatively scarce; consequently, not only are individual birds lost but so is the capacity for future pairs to obtain adequate nest sites. Harvesting has also affected colorful birds like the Painted Bunting, Antillean Euphonia, and Cuban Grassquit, as well as birds with enticing songs such as the Northern Mockingbird and Cuban Bullfinch. The collecting of bird eggs for food has been detrimental to flamingos and a number of colonial nesting seabirds. On some islands, eggs of a few species such as the Sooty Tern are considered aphrodisiacs and are heavily harvested.

**INTRODUCED PREDATORS** Prior to colonization of the West Indies by either Amerindians or Europeans, the avifauna evolved on most islands in the absence of mammalian predators. Human colonization dramatically altered that situation with the introduction of black and brown rats, cats, dogs, pigs, and mongooses, among others. These nonindigenous creatures have doubtless had dramatic effects on many local bird species, particularly ground nesters. Various seabirds, ducks, rails, doves, owls, goatsuckers, and songbirds that nest on or near the ground have suffered significantly as a result of such predation. Tree nesters have doubtless also suffered, but to a lesser extent. It is difficult to know precisely how much these introduced predators have affected local species, but it appears likely that they played major roles in the serious decline of several rail and goatsucker species.

**OTHER CAUSES** Various other factors have negative impacts on the avifauna of the West Indies. The killing of birds considered to be pests has affected parrots and several other species. The Shiny Cowbird, a parasite on the nests of other birds and a recent arrival from South America, is wreaking havoc with several native orioles and other species. Introduced bird species, primarily parrots and finches, may compete with native relatives for food or nest sites. Such exotics also pose the serious threat of unknowingly introducing foreign diseases that can decimate native bird species unadapted to them. Local folklore can have a major impact on birds. On several islands, for example, owls are considered a bad omen and are killed as a result. Chemical pollutants, ranging from agricultural pesticides and herbicides to industrial and chemical wastes, have notoriously negative impacts on birds. Though reports of such impacts are rare in the West Indies, this does not mean damage has not occurred. The near absence of insect-eating birds on New Providence in the Bahamas may well be the result of intensive spraying for mosquito control. While none of these factors individually has been proven to be a major reason for the decline of the West Indian avifauna, each is, or has the potential to be, important in species declines. They all warrant the attention of decision makers and natural resource managers.

### Island Conservation Needs

The salient need facing the Caribbean, as is the case worldwide, is a set of environmental values that guide societal behavior. Without such values, and the appropriate behaviors and norms to accompany them, bird conservation, or any other important societal goal, is but a pipe dream. What are these values? How are they established? In what ways are they adopted? Those are topics outside the scope of this book. Nevertheless, societal values are the silver bullet that determines success or failure in conservation or anything else. We will say that to address conservation values we must focus on society as a collection of constituencies and what drives them rather than concentrate on particular bird species and the problems they face. Solving the latter can be achieved only by properly addressing the former.

Related to this is the need for public outreach at all levels—to schools, to the general public, and to decision makers. This remains true even though several Lesser Antillean islands have undertaken some of the most comprehensive bird conservation outreach campaigns, built around the development of local pride, conducted anywhere in the world. Most of these campaigns have been impressively successful, as demonstrated by the remarkable recovery of the St Lucia Parrot. The Lesser Antilles is also where the use of radio soap operas to promote conservation values was conceived and effectively implemented, particularly regarding sea turtle conservation. These advances show the importance of expanding such outreach programs if local conservation objectives are to have any hope of being achieved.

"Outreach" does not apply only to dispersing technical information. To be effective, it must also include identifying and promoting societal conservation values and behaviors.

Clearly, there are many other priorities before bird conservation can be effectively achieved. It is important to keep in mind, however, that none of these can be accomplished without first addressing the underlying matter of societal values.

One need is more effective implementation of existing legislation. Most of the islands, if not all, have conservation laws to protect birds. Developing a conservation ethic and the institutional capacity to implement these statutes would contribute significantly to conservation on the islands. Some islands need to update their local laws and regulations.

Setting aside protected areas—conserving habitat—is decidedly important, but perhaps wise land-use planning is even more so. This is especially the case because of the difficulty in determining how climate change will affect each island over time. Consequently, wisely managing all lands is more important than carefully protecting a few. While habitat destruction and deterioration are clearly the most important factors threatening the Caribbean's birdlife, saving it directly is not the most essential conservation measure. It seems that Caribbean islanders believe that what is in the hearts and minds of the people is more important than what is set aside by decree, fiat, or legal mandate. They lead most other nations in advancing this concept.

The list goes on. But we believe the point has been made. First conservation values, then behavior change, and finally everything else falls into place.

### Endangered Species List

The tables overleaf list birds considered to be (1) critically endangered, (2) endangered, or (3) threatened in the West Indies. Listed birds represent either endemic species, or any species that is threatened or endangered throughout all or the greater portion of its range in the West Indies. The latter category may include birds not threatened in other portions of their range outside the West Indies. An example is the Hook-billed Kite, which is critically endangered in Grenada but quite abundant in Mexico, Central America, and South America. Species in this category are designated as such. The tables also identify what are believed to be the primary causes of endangerment, including both past and present impacts.

## Critically Endangered

**Definition**—Species that have declined dramatically to such low population levels that their continued survival is in serious jeopardy. Active steps must be taken to ensure their survival.

| | Habitat loss | Hunting | Harvest or trade | Introduced predators | Other |
|---|---|---|---|---|---|
| | | | **Causes** | | |
| Black-capped Petrel | X | | X | X | |
| Hook-billed Kite (Grenada) | | | | | |
|   (WI subspecies)[1] | X | X | | | |
| Cuban Kite | X | X | | | |
| Ridgway's Hawk | X | X | | | |
| Spotted Rail[1] | X | | | ? | |
| Zapata Rail | X | | | ? | |
| Grenada Dove | X | ? | | X | |
| Puerto Rican Parrot | X | X | X | X | X[3] |
| St Vincent Parrot | X | X | X | | |
| Imperial Parrot | X | X | X | | |
| Brown-headed Nuthatch | | | | | |
|   (WI subspecies)[1] | X | | | | |
| White-breasted Thrasher | X | | | X | |
| Western Chat-Tanager | X | | | | |
| Eastern Chat-Tanager | X | | | | |
| Yellow-shouldered Blackbird | X | | | | X[2] |
| Bahama Oriole | X | | | X | X[2] |

1. Stable population occurs outside West Indies
2. Brood parasitism by Shiny Cowbird
3. Competition with introduced species and egg predation by Pearly-eyed Thrasher

## Endangered

**Definition**—Species that have declined significantly to such low population levels that unless this trend is halted in the immediate future, the survival of the species will be in jeopardy.

| | Habitat loss | Hunting | Harvest or trade | Introduced predators | Other |
|---|---|---|---|---|---|
| | | | **Causes** | | |
| Piping Plover | X | | | | |
| Gundlach's Hawk | X | X | | | |
| Sharp-shinned Hawk | | | | | |
|   (WI subspecies)[1] | X | | | X | X[2] |
| Plain Pigeon | X | X | | X | |
| White-fronted Quail-Dove | X | X | | X | |
| Blue-headed Quail-Dove | X | X | | X | |
| Red-necked Parrot | X | X | X | | |
| St Lucia Parrot | X | X | X | | |
| Cuban Parakeet | X | X | X | | |
| Stygian Owl | | | | | |
|   (Cuban subspecies) | X | | | | |
| Bay-breasted Cuckoo | X | X | | | |
| Puerto Rican Nightjar | X | | | X | |
| Rufous Nightjar | | | | | |
|   (WI subspecies)[1] | X | | | X | |

## Endangered *continued*

| | Habitat loss | | | |
|---|---|---|---|---|
| Fernandina's Flicker | X | | | |
| Zapata Wren | X | | | |
| Giant Kingbird | X | | | |
| Golden Swallow | X | | | |
| Cuban Palm Crow | Unknown | | | |
| La Selle Thrush | X | | | |
| Kirtland's Warbler | X | | | X[3] |
| Hispaniolan Highland-Tanager | X | | | |
| Montserrat Oriole | X | | | X[2,3] |
| St Lucia Black Finch | | X | | X |
| Hispaniolan Crossbill | X | | | |
| Zapata Sparrow | | | | X[4] |

1. Stable population occurs outside West Indies
2. Brood parasitism by Shiny Cowbird
3. Volcanic eruption
4. Small, local populations

## Threatened

**Definition**—Species that have experienced moderate declines or face imminent threats, thus warranting specific conservation measures.

| | Causes | | | | |
|---|---|---|---|---|---|
| | Habitat loss | Hunting | Harvest or trade | Introduced predators | Other |
| West Indian Whistling-Duck | X | X | X | X | |
| White-cheeked Pintail[1] | X | X | | X | |
| Sandhill Crane[1] | X | X | | X | |
| Double-striped Thick-knee[1] | X | X | | | |
| Roseate Tern | X | | X | X | |
| White-crowned Pigeon | X | X | X | X | |
| Ring-tailed Pigeon | X | X | | | |
| Gray-fronted Quail-Dove | X | X | | X | |
| Hispaniolan Parakeet | X | X | | | |
| Rose-throated Parrot | X | | X | | |
| Yellow-billed Parrot | X | | X | | |
| Black-billed Parrot | X | | X | | |
| Hispaniolan Parrot | X | X | X | | |
| Stygian Owl (Hispaniolan subspecies)[1] | X | X | X | | |
| Least Pauraque | X | | | X | |
| White-tailed Nightjar[1] | X | | | X | |
| Bee Hummingbird | X | | | | |
| Hispaniolan Trogon | X | | | | |
| White-necked Crow | X | X | | | |
| Bicknell's Thrush | X | | | | |
| Forest Thrush | X | | | | |
| Cuban Solitaire | X | | | | |
| Elfin-Woods Warbler | X | | | | |
| Whistling Warbler | X | | | | |
| Gray-crowned Palm-Tanager | X | | | | |
| Jamaican Blackbird | X | | | | |
| Martinique Oriole | X | | | | X[2] |
| St Lucia Oriole | X | | | | X[2,3] |

1. Stable population occurs outside West Indies
2. Brood parasitism by Shiny Cowbird
3. Pesticide spraying

**Shearwaters:** Generally far out at sea. Distinctive flight is gliding on long, narrow wings low over waves with periodic shallow flaps.

**GREAT SHEARWATER (GREATER SHEARWATER)** *Ardenna gravis* 48cm (19in); wingspan 105–122cm (3.5–4ft); 850g. One of two large shearwaters in West Indies; noticeable white bands on hindneck and rump contrast with black cap and dark grayish-brown upperparts. (Black-capped Petrel has more extensive white on upperparts, especially on forehead; mantle blacker.) **FLIGHT** Much slower wingbeats than Manx and Audubon's Shearwaters and Black-capped Petrel. **STATUS AND RANGE** Fairly common migrant off Guadeloupe primarily May–July, but can occur any month. Uncommon among Bahamas and off Puerto Rico. Likely rare through Lesser Antilles during these months. Very rare or vagrant elsewhere in West Indies. **HABITAT** At sea.

**CORY'S SHEARWATER** *Calonectris diomedea* 46–53cm (18–21in); wingspan 100–126 cm (3.3–4.2ft); 560–1060g. Large shearwater, appears featureless at distance. Pale yellowish bill, white uppertail-coverts variable in extent; coloration of cheek and neck blend with underparts. (Great Shearwater has dark bill, sharply defined black cap, more defined white uppertail-coverts, and more purposeful flight.) **FLIGHT** Leisurely on broad, loosely held wings, noticeably angled at wrist. **STATUS AND RANGE** Fairly common migrant among Bahamas and off Guadeloupe primarily May and June, but until December. Rare in rest of West Indies; likely transits off most Lesser Antilles. **HABITAT** At sea.

**BLACK-CAPPED PETREL** *Pterodroma hasitata* 35–40cm (14–16in); wingspan 96cm (3.2ft); 280g. **BEHAVIOR** Nocturnal at nesting cliffs. **DESCRIPTION** Upperparts blackish except for white rump, hindneck, and forehead. Extent of white variable. (*See* Great Shearwater.) **FLIGHT** Black front edge of underwing. Wrist more bent than shearwater's and flight more erratic. **VOICE** Calls only at night around nesting colonies. Drawn out *aaa-aw, eek,* or *ooow, eek*; and yelps like hurt puppy. **STATUS AND RANGE** Rare and very local breeding resident in West Indies primarily November–June. Breeds in high mountains of southern Haiti (Massif de la Selle and Massif de la Hotte), southern Dominican Republic (Sierra de Bahoruco), and Dominica. May breed in Cuba (Sierra Maestra). These islands comprise entire breeding range. Rare at sea off southeastern Guadeloupe. Critically endangered. **HABITAT** At sea except when breeding in mountain cliffs.

**SOOTY SHEARWATER** *Ardenna grisea* 40–46cm (16–18in); wingspan 94–110cm (3.2–3.6ft); 800g. Medium-sized, blackish overall with whitish underwings. Wings long and narrow. **FLIGHT** Swift and direct, with rapid flapping ascents and long glides usually close to water surface. **STATUS AND RANGE** Apparently rare visitor in West Indies primarily late May–July, but some through November. Might be expected any month. **HABITAT** At sea.

**MANX SHEARWATER** *Puffinus puffinus* 30–38cm (12–15in); wingspan 76–89cm (2.5–3ft); 400g. Medium-sized; short tail. Blackish above and white below, including wing linings and undertail-coverts. (Audubon's Shearwater slightly smaller, with short-winged long-tailed appearance and dark undertail-coverts. Manx has long-winged short-tailed appearance and white undertail-coverts.) **FLIGHT** Four or five distinctive snappy wingbeats and a rocking glide in light winds or flat seas. **STATUS AND RANGE** Common visitor off Guadeloupe and likely of regular occurrence at sea off southern Lesser Antilles primarily February–May, though few records to date. Very rare or vagrant elsewhere in West Indies. **HABITAT** At sea.

**AUDUBON'S SHEARWATER** *Puffinus lherminieri* 30cm (12in); wingspan 64–72cm (2–2.3ft); 200g. **BEHAVIOR** Nocturnal at nesting cliffs. **DESCRIPTION** Relatively small, long-tailed shearwater, blackish-brown above and white below, but with dark undertail-coverts. (*See* Manx Shearwater.) **VOICE** Mournful, cat-like cries at night in flight around nests. **STATUS AND RANGE** The most regularly encountered shearwater in West Indies. In Bahamas, a common breeding resident primarily March–July; uncommon in other months. Locally common in Virgin Islands. Elsewhere in West Indies generally uncommon to rare and very local breeding resident on offshore islands, decidedly rarer outside breeding season. Very rare in Cuba and Jamaica. Very few recent records from Cayman Islands, though bred there before settlement. **HABITAT** At sea except when breeding on offshore islands.

GREAT SHEARWATER

CORY'S SHEARWATER

BLACK-CAPPED PETREL

SOOTY SHEARWATER

MANX SHEARWATER

AUDUBON'S SHEARWATER

**Pelicans:** Use huge throat pouches to catch fish.
**Storm-Petrels:** Far out at sea. Swoop and flutter low over ocean, sometimes pattering surface.

**MAGNIFICENT FRIGATEBIRD** *Fregata magnificens* 89–114cm (35–45in); wingspan 2.2–2.5m (7–8ft); 1.3kg. **BEHAVIOR** Chases other seabirds to rob prey. Does not land on sea surface. **DESCRIPTION** Long, forked tail; long, slender, pointed wings sharply bent at wrist; floats motionless in air. **ADULT MALE** Black. During courtship, inflatable throat pouch bright red. **ADULT FEMALE** Blackish, with white breast. **IMMATURE** Blackish; head and breast white. **FLIGHT** Frequently soars motionless. **STATUS AND RANGE** Common but somewhat local year-round resident throughout West Indies. **HABITAT** Bays, inshore waters, and offshore cays where it roosts and breeds.

**AMERICAN WHITE PELICAN** *Pelecanus erythrorhynchos* 125–165cm (4–5.4ft); wingspan 2.4–3m (8–10ft); 5–9kg. Huge size, massive bill, white coloration. Black primaries and outer secondaries. **BREEDING ADULT** Bill orange-yellow, knob on upper mandible; hindcrown and hindneck tan. **NON-BREEDING ADULT** Bill orange-yellow; hindcrown and hindneck gray. **IMMATURE** Bill gray. **STATUS AND RANGE** Irregular locally common migrant and non-breeding resident in Cuba, where numbers increasing. Very rare in Puerto Rico. Vagrant elsewhere in West Indies. May occur in any month. **HABITAT** Freshwater lakes and coastal bays.

**BROWN PELICAN** *Pelecanus occidentalis* 107–137cm (3.5–4.5ft); wingspan 2–2.3m (6.8–7.6ft); 3–4kg. **BEHAVIOR** Plunges into sea from substantial height. **DESCRIPTION** Large size, massive bill, dark coloration. **BREEDING ADULT** Reddish-brown hindneck and back of head, though infrequently the hindneck remains white. **NON-BREEDING ADULT** White hindneck and back of head. **IMMATURE** Overall grayish-brown; paler below. **STATUS AND RANGE** Common year-round resident in southern Bahamas, Greater Antilles, and locally in northern Lesser Antilles south to Guadeloupe. Generally uncommon to rare through rest of West Indies. Migrants augment local numbers November–February. **HABITAT** Bays, lagoons, other calm coastal waters.

 **BAND-RUMPED STORM-PETREL** *Hydrobates castro* 19–21cm (7.5–8in); wingspan 43–46cm (17–18in); 47g. Medium-sized; black head and upperparts. Conspicuous narrow white rump band contrasts with blackish tail and underparts; square tail. **FLIGHT** Buoyant and direct, though sometimes erratic and shearwater-like with deep wingbeats. Feet do not extend beyond tail. Readily approaches boats. (Wilson's is smaller, has yellow webbing on feet, which protrude past tail.) **STATUS AND RANGE** Very rare visitor off Bahamas, Cuba, Antigua, Martinique, and probably all of the Lesser Antilles. Expected primarily May–August. Status in West Indies poorly known. **HABITAT** At sea.

**LEACH'S STORM-PETREL** *Hydrobates leucorhous* 20cm (8in); wingspan 43–48cm (17–19in); 35g. A small, brownish-black seabird with white rump. Has slightly forked tail, pale brown wing band, and white rump patch appearing divided at close range. **FLIGHT** Feet do not extend beyond tail. Flight more erratic and wingbeats deeper than Wilson's. **STATUS AND RANGE** Decidedly rare migrant and non-breeding resident through most of West Indies primarily November–June, but sometimes occurs in other months. Not expected to occur in Jamaica, Cayman Islands, San Andrés, and Providencia. **HABITAT** At sea.

 **WILSON'S STORM-PETREL** *Oceanites oceanicus* 18–19cm (7–7.5in); wingspan 38–42cm (15–16.5in); 34g. Small, dark brownish-black seabird with white rump. Blacker, wings shorter, broader, and more rounded with less angled wrists than Leach's Storm-Petrel, also tail more square. **FLIGHT** Feet, with yellow toe-webbing, extend beyond tail. Regularly follows boats, swooping over wake and touching sea with feet. **STATUS AND RANGE** Fairly common migrant off Guadeloupe primarily May and June, uncommon among Bahamas, and rare off Cuba, Hispaniola, Puerto Rico, Virgin Islands, and remaining Lesser Antilles. **HABITAT** At sea.

MAGNIFICENT
FRIGATEBIRD

adult ♂

adult ♀

adult ♂

imm

non-br adult

AMERICAN WHITE PELICAN

BROWN PELICAN

non-br
adult

br

imm

BAND-RUMPED
STORM-PETREL

LEACH'S
STORM-PETREL

WILSON'S
STORM-PETREL

Plate not to scale

**Tropicbirds:** Feed at sea, diving on prey from substantial heights.
**Boobies and Gannet:** Feed at sea by diving for prey from substantial heights.

**WHITE-TAILED TROPICBIRD** *Phaethon lepturus* 81cm (32in) (with plumes), 37–40cm (15–16in) (without plumes); wingspan 89–96cm (3–3.2ft); 350g. ADULT White overall; long tail feathers; heavy black stripes on upperwing and outer primaries. Bill yellow or orange. IMMATURE Barred back; short central tail feathers. Bill yellowish, ringed with black. (Immature differs from immature Red-billed due to coarser black barring on upperparts and lack of black band across hindneck.) VOICE Raspy *crick-et*. STATUS AND RANGE Widespread; very locally common breeding resident in West Indies primarily March–June (through October in Bahamas). The typical tropicbird of Bahamas, Greater Antilles, and Cayman Islands; also common in Virgin Islands, St Bartholomew, Saba, St Vincent, and Grenadines, where it overlaps more with Red-billed Tropicbird. Generally, scarcer in other Lesser Antilles. HABITAT At sea except when breeding in sea cliffs.

**RED-BILLED TROPICBIRD** *Phaethon aethereus* 91–107cm (36–42in) (with plumes), 46–51cm (18–20in) (without plumes); wingspan 1–1.1m (3.2–3.5ft); 750g. ADULT White overall; black barred back; long tail plumes; red bill. IMMATURE Similar to White-tailed, but back less boldly barred, darker black band across hindneck. VOICE Long, harsh, raspy *keé-arrr*. STATUS AND RANGE Fairly common and local in Virgin Islands and uncommon and very local year-round resident throughout Lesser Antilles and on Culebra off Puerto Rico. Vagrant elsewhere in West Indies. HABITAT At sea except when breeding on offshore islands.

**RED-FOOTED BOOBY** *Sula sula* 66–76cm (26–30in); wingspan 1m (3.3ft); 1kg. ADULT Brown phase—Brown, with white hindparts and tail. White phase—All white, with black primaries and secondaries. IMMATURE Sooty brown; paler below, sometimes slightly darker breast band. VOICE Guttural *ga-ga-ga-ga*, of variable length—trails off. Also distinctive squawk. STATUS AND RANGE Widespread, but very local year-round resident in West Indies. Abundant near remote roosting and nesting islands. Most frequent in Little Cayman (Cayman Islands), U.S. Virgin Islands, Lesser Antilles, and islands off western Puerto Rico. Uncommon very locally in Hispaniola, rare in Bahamas, and very rare in Cuba and Jamaica. Not often seen from shore. HABITAT At sea except when breeding and roosting on remote islands.

**BROWN BOOBY** *Sula leucogaster* 71–76cm (28–30in); wingspan 1.5m (5ft); 1.3kg. ADULT Entirely brown head sharply demarcated from white belly and abdomen. IMMATURE Light brown belly and abdomen. (Immature Masked Booby has white hindneck and lacks brown on upper breast.) VOICE Hoarse *kak*. STATUS AND RANGE Fairly common but local year-round resident offshore throughout West Indies; locally abundant near breeding grounds. HABITAT Bays, coastal areas, and at sea. Roosts and breeds on offshore islands.

**MASKED BOOBY** *Sula dactylatra* 81–91cm (32–36in); wingspan 1.6–1.7m (5.2–5.5ft); 1.2–2.2kg. ADULT Primarily white; black tail, primaries, and secondaries. SUBADULT Similar to adult, but upperparts brown on head and rump; brown flecks on wing-coverts. (White phase Red-footed Booby has white tail.) IMMATURE Head and upperparts brown with white hindneck. Underparts white except throat, undertail, and flight feathers. STATUS AND RANGE Common year-round resident very locally around offshore breeding islets but very rare and local generally through much of West Indies. Breeds on islets off Jamaica, Puerto Rico, Virgin Islands (Cockroach Cay, Sula Cay), Anguilla (Dog Island), Antigua (Redondo Island), and Grenadines. Vagrant in Cuba and Cayman Islands. Threatened. HABITAT At sea. Roosts and breeds on offshore islands.

**NORTHERN GANNET** *Morus bassanus* 1m (3.3ft); wingspan 1.7–1.8m (5.5–6ft); 2.3–3.6kg. IMMATURE Dark gray above, flecked white on wings and mantle. Paler below. (Immature Masked Booby has yellowish rather than dark bill.) ADULT White with tan crown and black wingtips. Immatures are most likely in West Indies. STATUS AND RANGE Rare visitor in Bahamas September–May. Vagrant elsewhere. HABITAT At sea.

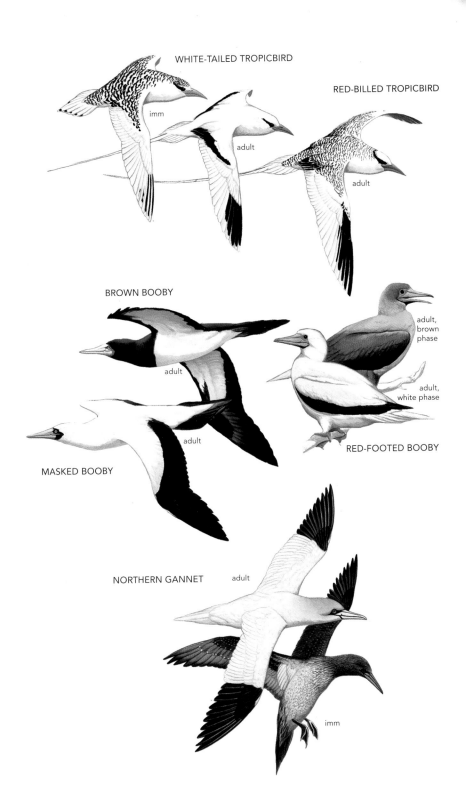

WHITE-TAILED TROPICBIRD

imm

RED-BILLED TROPICBIRD

adult

adult

BROWN BOOBY

adult

adult, brown phase

adult, white phase

adult

RED-FOOTED BOOBY

MASKED BOOBY

NORTHERN GANNET

adult

imm

**Skuas and Jaegers:** Chase other seabirds to rob their prey.

**GREAT SKUA** *Stercorarius skua* 51–66cm (20–26in); wingspan 1.3–1.4m (4–4.5ft); 1.3–1.4kg. Large, bulky, powerful, gull-like. Extremely similar to South Polar Skua. Dark brown; reddish-brown highlights; golden or reddish-brown streaks on head and neck. Underparts paler. Indistinct dark cap. **FLIGHT** White wing patch. **STATUS AND RANGE** Likely occurs through West Indies at low frequencies primarily November–May. **HABITAT** Well out at sea.

**SOUTH POLAR SKUA** *Stercorarius maccormicki* 53cm (21in); wingspan 1.3–1.4m (4–4.5ft); 1–1.4kg. Extremely similar to Great Skua but slightly smaller. Three color phases. Dark phase—As above, but darker underparts and lacks reddish tones. Intermediate phase—Light brown head, neck, and underparts, light hindneck, may have dark cap. Light phase—Pale gray underparts, head, and neck. **FLIGHT** White wing patch. **STATUS AND RANGE** Rare off Guadeloupe, but likely occurs through West Indies at lower frequencies migrating northbound primarily April–June. **HABITAT** Well out at sea.

**PARASITIC JAEGER** *Stercorarius parasiticus* 46–67cm (18–26.5in); wingspan 1.1–1.3m (3.5–4ft); male 400g, female 500g. Small jaeger. **ADULT** Light phase—Dark brownish-gray above, whitish below; grayish-brown cap; narrow, dark upper breast band. Dark phase—Dark brown overall. **SUBADULT** Finely barred below; often reddish cast to plumage. Pointed tips to central tail feathers. (Pomarine Jaeger is decidedly larger, with more labored flight and heavily barred sides. Long-tailed Jaegers without long central tail feathers cannot be distinguished reliably.) **FLIGHT** Strong and direct, showing white patch on primaries. **STATUS AND RANGE** Generally an uncommon migrant and rare non-breeding resident in West Indies August–May, though common off Guadeloupe. **HABITAT** Well out at sea.

**POMARINE JAEGER** *Stercorarius pomarinus* 65–78cm (25.5–31in); wingspan 1.1–1.4m (3.6–4.5ft); male 650g, female 750g. Heavy-bodied; the largest jaeger. Two color phases with intermediate variation. **ADULT** Central tail feathers can be long but are usually twisted to give a spoon-like appearance. Light phase—Blackish cap and broad, dark band across breast. Dark phase—Less frequent; entirely dark ranging from brown to black. **SUBADULT AND IMMATURE** Usually heavily barred below, especially sides under the wings. Central tail feathers may not extend beyond rest of tail. (Parasitic Jaeger is smaller, has more buoyant flight, lacks heavy barring on sides. Long-tailed is smaller still, adults have very long pointed tail feathers, no breast band, and graceful tern-like flight.) **FLIGHT** White patch on primaries. **STATUS AND RANGE** Generally uncommon, but sometimes common, migrant and non-breeding resident October–May in West Indies, especially among Bahamas, off Hispaniola (east and south coasts), and during northbound migration off Lesser Antilles. **HABITAT** Well out at sea.

**LONG-TAILED JAEGER** *Stercorarius longicaudus* 50–58cm (19.5–23in), including tail 15–25cm (6–10in); wingspan 1–1.2m (3.3–3.8ft); male 250g, female 350g. The smallest jaeger. **ADULT** Long central tail feathers; grayish-brown cap; no breast band; back and secondaries grayish contrasting with darker primaries. **SUBADULT** Dark phase—Uniform grayish-brown; darker cap; tail feathers not extended. Light phase—Finely barred below; fine white barring on back. Some have pale head and hindneck. Tail feathers short. **FLIGHT** Graceful, tern-like; small white wing patch. **STATUS AND RANGE** Uncommon migrant off Guadeloupe but very rare or vagrant through rest of West Indies primarily August–October and March–May. **HABITAT** Well out at sea.

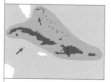

**BLACK SKIMMER** *Rynchops niger* 40–51cm (16–20in); wingspan 1.1–1.3m (3.5–4.2ft); male 350g, female 250g. **BEHAVIOR** Plows water surface with bill, often nocturnal. **DESCRIPTION** Unmistakable scissor-like black and orange bill with lower mandible longer than the upper. **STATUS AND RANGE** Uncommon migrant and non-breeding resident in Cuba primarily October–April. Very rare in Bahamas, Puerto Rico, Virgin Islands, and Cayman Islands. Vagrant elsewhere in West Indies. **HABITAT** Calm coastal bays and lagoons.

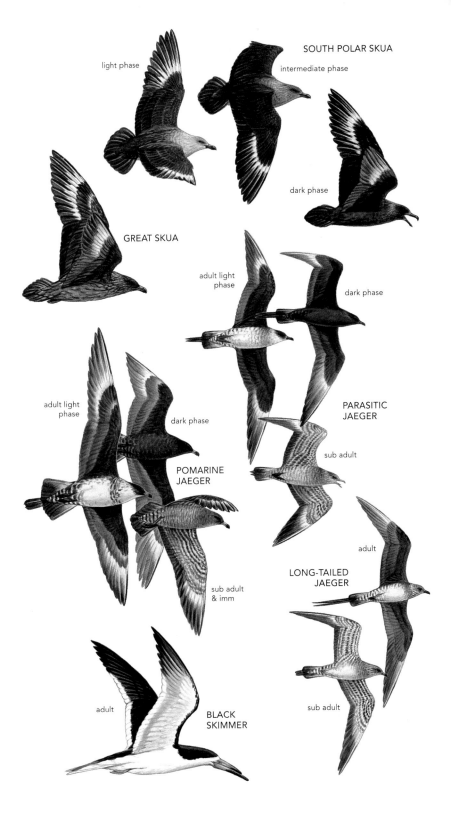

SOUTH POLAR SKUA

light phase

intermediate phase

dark phase

GREAT SKUA

adult light
phase

dark phase

PARASITIC
JAEGER

adult light
phase

dark phase

sub adult

POMARINE
JAEGER

adult

LONG-TAILED
JAEGER

sub adult
& imm

adult

BLACK
SKIMMER

sub adult

**GREAT BLACK-BACKED GULL** *Larus marinus* 69–79cm (27–31in); wingspan 1.5–1.7m (5–5.5ft); male 1.8kg, female 1.5kg. STATUS AND RANGE Uncommon visitor locally in northern Bahamas and Hispaniola October–April; rare in southern Bahamas and Puerto Rico; decidedly rare in Guadeloupe; very rare elsewhere in West Indies. Numbers are increasing. HABITAT Beaches and calm bays. (*See also* Plate 6.)

**LESSER BLACK-BACKED GULL** *Larus fuscus* 53–63cm (21–25in); wingspan 1.2–1.5m (4–5ft); male 825g, female 700g. STATUS AND RANGE Through much of West Indies, where fairly common visitor locally in northern Bahamas and uncommon and local in southern Bahamas, cays off north-central Cuba, Puerto Rico, and most of the larger Lesser Antilles October–April. Rare or very rare elsewhere in West Indies, but numbers increasing rapidly, particularly in Lesser Antilles. HABITAT Beaches, calm bays, and dumps. (*See also* Plate 6.)

**RING-BILLED GULL** *Larus delawarensis* 46–51cm (18–20in); wingspan 1.1–1.2m (3.6–4ft); male 550g, female 470g. STATUS AND RANGE Through most of West Indies, where fairly common but local visitor in northern Bahamas and Cuba; uncommon and local in southern Bahamas, Hispaniola, Puerto Rico, Cayman Islands; rare in Virgin Islands and Lesser Antilles south to Barbados. Occurs in all months, but primarily December–March. Numbers and range increasing. HABITAT Coastal harbors, lagoons, and open ground from parking lots to grassy fields. Often urban areas. (*See also* Plate 6.)

**HERRING GULL** *Larus argentatus* 56–66cm (22–26in); wingspan 1.4–1.5m (4.6–4.9ft); male 1.2kg, female 1kg. STATUS AND RANGE Generally uncommon and local visitor in Bahamas, Cuba, Hispaniola, and Cayman Islands September–May and rare June–August. Rare in Jamaica, Puerto Rico, and Virgin Islands; very rare to vagrant in Lesser Antilles October–March. Numbers increasing. HABITAT Coastal areas, harbors, and lagoons. (*See also* Plate 6.)

**BLACK-LEGGED KITTIWAKE** *Rissa tridactyla* 43cm (17in); wingspan 90cm (3ft); 400g. STATUS AND RANGE Very rare visitor in Bahamas December–March; vagrant elsewhere. HABITAT Far offshore. (*See also* Plate 7.)

**BLACK-HEADED GULL** *Chroicocephalus ridibundus* 39–43cm (15–17in); wingspan 1m (3.3ft); 200–320g. STATUS AND RANGE Rare and local visitor in Bahamas, Virgin Islands, Guadeloupe, and Barbados. Very rare visitor in Puerto Rico and vagrant elsewhere in West Indies. Occurs November–June. Numbers increasing. HABITAT Coastal harbors. (*See also* Plate 7.)

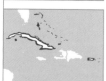

**BONAPARTE'S GULL** *Chroicocephalus philadelphia* 28–36cm (11–14in); wingspan 80–85cm (2.6–2.8ft); 180–225g. STATUS AND RANGE Decidedly uncommon visitor locally in Bahamas August–April. Rare in Cuba and Puerto Rico. Vagrant elsewhere but occurring more frequently. HABITAT Coastal harbors, lagoons, and at sea. (*See also* Plate 7.)

**LAUGHING GULL** *Leucophaeus atricilla* 38–43cm (15–17in); wingspan 1–1.1m (3.3–3.6ft); male 330g, female 290g. STATUS AND RANGE Widespread resident in West Indies, but breeds only locally. Generally common April–September; irregular and rare through most of West Indies remainder of year. HABITAT Calm bays, coastal waters, and islets. (*See also* Plate 7.)

2nd-year

LESSER BLACK-
BACKED GULL

2nd-year

non-br adult

non-br adult

GREAT BLACK-
BACKED GULL

non-br adult

RING-BILLED GULL

non-br adult

HERRING GULL

non-br
adult

BLACK-HEADED GULL

BLACK-LEGGED
KITTIWAKE

non-br adult

non-br adult

BONAPARTE'S
GULL

immature

non-br
adult

LAUGHING GULL

**GREAT BLACK-BACKED GULL** *Larus marinus* 69–79cm (27–31in); wingspan 1.5–1.7m (5–5.5ft); male 1.8kg, female 1.5kg. Very large, with massive bill. **FIRST YEAR** Mottled grayish-brown; head white with pale flecks on rear and hindneck; bill black; tail with broad black band. **SECOND YEAR** Bill pinkish with large black band near tip, rump white, mantle with black blotches. **NON-BREEDING ADULT** Black mantle, pink legs, pale flecks on head, bill yellow with red spot near tip. **BREEDING ADULT** Head white. (*See also* Plate 5.)

**LESSER BLACK-BACKED GULL** *Larus fuscus* 53–63cm (21–25in); wingspan 1.2–1.5m (4–5ft); male 825g, female 700g. Large, with large bill. **FIRST YEAR** Mottled grayish; head brownish in contrast. **SECOND YEAR** Bill pinkish with large black band near tip. Broad black tail band; white rump; brownish-gray wings with no white spots at tip. **NON-BREEDING ADULT** Dark grayish-black mantle, pale yellow legs, yellow bill with red spot near tip. **BREEDING ADULT** Head and neck white. (Great Black-backed Gull larger; bill more massive. Winter adult has decidedly less dark feathering on head and hindneck. Adult Herring Gull has paler mantle and pink legs; first and second year birds have less pronounced white rump patch.) (*See also* Plate 5.)

**HERRING GULL** *Larus argentatus* 56–66cm (22–26in); wingspan 1.4–1.5m (4.6–4.9ft); male 1.2kg, female 1kg. Large, with large bill. **FIRST YEAR** Back and wings heavily streaked grayish-brown, bill pinkish at base, tipped black; tail lacks clear band; legs pink. **SECOND YEAR** Variable gray on back and wings; outer primaries black; bill pinkish with pale gray band beyond nostril. **THIRD YEAR** Tail white with broad black band; bill yellowish with dark band. **NON-BREEDING ADULT** Heavy yellow bill with red spot near tip of lower mandible; head and underparts white; legs pink. **BREEDING ADULT** Head and underparts white. (*See also* Plate 5.)

**RING-BILLED GULL** *Larus delawarensis* 46–51cm (18–20in); wingspan 1.1–1.2m (3.6–4ft); male 550g, female 470g. Fairly large, with medium-sized bill. **FIRST YEAR** Mottled grayish-brown wings; gray back. Broad black tail band; bill pinkish, tipped black. **SECOND YEAR** Upperparts and mantle mostly gray; black primaries with white spot at tip. **NON-BREEDING ADULT** Bill yellowish with black band; legs yellowish-green. **BREEDING ADULT** White head and underparts. Smaller than Herring Gull, more delicate head and bill, yellowish-green or grayish-green legs. (Herring Gull lacks bill-ring and has pink legs.) (*See also* Plate 5.)

GREAT BLACK-BACKED GULL

br

1st-year

LESSER BLACK-
BACKED GULL

br

1st-year

HERRING
GULL

br

1st-year

br

1st-year

RING-BILLED GULL

**LAUGHING GULL** *Leucophaeus atricilla* 38–43cm (15–17in); wingspan 1–1.1m (39–43in); male 330g, female 290g. **BREEDING ADULT** Black head; dark gray mantle; black wingtips; reddish bill. **NON-BREEDING ADULT** Similar, but diffuse gray mark on rear of white head; bill black. **IMMATURE** Mottled gray-brown; belly whitish. **FIRST YEAR** White rump; gray sides and back; broad black tail band. **SECOND YEAR** Partial hood; spotting on tail; mantle gray. **VOICE** Squawky, variable *caw* and *caw-aw*. Also laugh-like *ka-ka-ka-ka-ka-ka-ka-kaa-kaa-kaaa-kaaa*. (*See also* Plate 5.)

**BLACK-LEGGED KITTIWAKE** *Rissa tridactyla* 43cm (17in); wingspan 90cm (3ft); 400g. **FIRST YEAR** White head; black ear-spot, bill, and terminal tail band. **NON-BREEDING ADULT** Yellow bill; white head, black mark behind eye; gray mantle; black wingtips with no white. **BREEDING ADULT** Head entirely white. First year distinguished from Bonaparte's Gull by black half collar on hindneck and white trailing edge of secondaries. **FLIGHT** In first year birds wings and mantle marked with contrasting "W." (*See also* Plate 7.)

**BLACK-HEADED GULL** *Chroicocephalus ridibundus* 39–43cm (15–17in); wingspan 1m (3.3ft); 200–320g. **FIRST YEAR** Black ear-spot; two-toned bill; narrow, black tail band; gray undersides to primaries. **NON-BREEDING ADULT** Bill reddish, black-tipped; mantle pale gray; outer primaries white, black-tipped. **BREEDING ADULT** Head black; bill red. (Bonaparte's Gull lacks pale gray undersides to primaries.) (*See also* Plate 5.)

**BONAPARTE'S GULL** *Chroicocephalus philadelphia* 28–36cm (11–14in); wingspan 80–85cm (2.6–2.8ft); 180–225g. **FIRST YEAR** Black ear-spot; thin black bill; narrow black tail band; whitish undersides to primaries. **NON-BREEDING ADULT** Mantle pale gray, tail and outer primaries white; legs red. **BREEDING ADULT** Head black. (Black-headed Gull has gray undersides to primaries.) (*See also* Plate 5.)

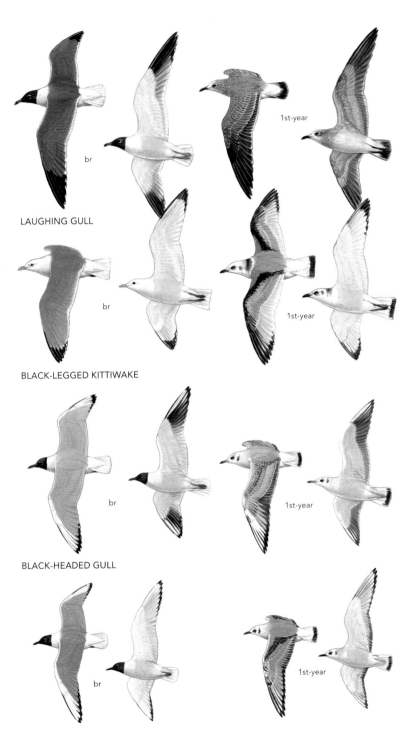

LAUGHING GULL br 1st-year

BLACK-LEGGED KITTIWAKE br 1st-year

BLACK-HEADED GULL br 1st-year

BONAPARTE'S GULL br 1st-year

**Terns:** Slim birds of graceful flight. Hover well above water surface, then dive for prey.

**CASPIAN TERN** *Hydroprogne caspia* 48–58cm (19–23in); wingspan 1.3m (50in); 660g. Large, with long, stout, red bill; black crest; dark gray underside to primaries. **NON-BREEDING ADULT** Crest flecked white. **BREEDING ADULT** Crest black. (Royal Tern smaller, bill orange-yellow, underside of primaries pale; forehead white in non-breeding plumage.) **STATUS AND RANGE** Fairly common very locally and may breed in Cuba, as occurs year-round. Rare non-breeding resident locally in Bahamas, Jamaica, Hispaniola, and Cayman Islands October–March. Very rare in Puerto Rico and Virgin Islands. Vagrant elsewhere. **HABITAT** Lagoons.

**ROYAL TERN** *Thalasseus maximus* 46–53cm (18–21in); wingspan 104cm (41in); 470g. Large, with orange-yellow bill. **BREEDING ADULT** Crown black. **NON-BREEDING ADULT AND IMMATURE** Forehead white. **VOICE** Harsh, high-pitched *kri-i-ik*. **STATUS AND RANGE** Through West Indies, where common, but local year-round resident in Bahamas, Greater Antilles, Virgin and Cayman Islands; generally fairly common in Lesser Antilles. **HABITAT** Lagoons.

**SANDWICH TERN** *Thalasseus sandvicensis* 41–46cm (16–18in); wingspan 86cm (34in); 200g. Relatively large. **BREEDING ADULT** Shaggy black crest; slender black bill tipped yellow. Sometimes bill patched or entirely dull yellow. **NON-BREEDING ADULT** Crown white, flecked black. **STATUS AND RANGE** Common year-round resident in Bahamas, Cuba, and Anegada (Virgin Islands); uncommon in Puerto Rico, other Virgin Islands, and possibly Sombrero Island (Anguilla). Non-breeding birds range to other islands, where common on Jamaica, St Bartholomew, and Antigua primarily October–March; uncommon on Hispaniola, St Martin, Guadeloupe, Martinique, and St Lucia; rare to very rare elsewhere. **HABITAT** Coastal lagoons.

**GULL-BILLED TERN** *Gelochelidon nilotica* 33–38cm (13–15in); wingspan 86cm (34in); 170g. Chunky, gull-like. Heavy black bill; broad wings; shallow fork to tail. **BREEDING ADULT** Black crown and hindneck. **NON-BREEDING ADULT** Crown whitish with pale gray flecks; gray spot behind eye. **VOICE** Raspy two- to three-syllable *za-za-za*, or *kay-wek, kay-wek*. **STATUS AND RANGE** Uncommon and local breeding resident in Bahamas and Hispaniola; rare in larger Virgin Islands (particularly Anegada) April–August. Uncommon and local migrant in Puerto Rico, Cayman Islands, and Sombrero Island (Anguilla) September–October and April–May, but may occur in any month. Rare to vagrant among other Lesser Antilles September–March. **HABITAT** Ponds, lagoons, fields.

**ARCTIC TERN** *Sterna paradisaea* 35–43cm (14–17in); wingspan 79cm (31in); 85–125g. **NON-BREEDING ADULT** Blackish line along trailing edge of primaries; short black bill; short red legs. **BREEDING ADULT** Bill entirely blood-red; underparts gray; cheek patch white. **IMMATURE** Incomplete black cap and indistinct shoulder bar; tail shorter than adult's. **FLIGHT** "Neckless" appearance, upperwing uniformly gray. **STATUS AND RANGE** Uncommon northbound migrant off east coast of Guadeloupe April–May and apparently so for most of Lesser Antilles. Rare off Puerto Rico June–October. Very rare or vagrant elsewhere in West Indies. **HABITAT** Generally far out at sea.

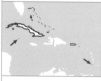

**FORSTER'S TERN** *Sterna forsteri* 35–42cm (14–16.5in); wingspan 79cm (31in); 160g. **NON-BREEDING ADULT** Silvery-white primaries; large black spot enclosing eye; forked tail extends beyond folded wings. (Non-breeding Roseate, Common, and Arctic terns lack distinctive black eye patch. Black on their heads extends around hindneck. Roseate Tern has much faster wingbeats.) **BREEDING ADULT** Bill orange with black tip. **STATUS AND RANGE** Decidedly rare migrant and non-breeding resident in Bahamas, Cuba, Cayman Islands, and Grenadines November–April. Very rare in Puerto Rico and Virgin Islands. Vagrant elsewhere. **HABITAT** Lagoons.

CASPIAN TERN

non-br adult

br

ROYAL TERN

non-br adult
and imm

br

SANDWICH TERN

Cayenne race

non-br adult

br

br

GULL-BILLED TERN

non-br
adult

br

br

ARCTIC TERN

non-br
adult

imm

FORSTER'S TERN

br

non-br adult

**COMMON TERN** *Sterna hirundo* 33–40cm (13–16in); wingspan 76cm (30in); 120g. BREEDING ADULT Black cap; red bill with black tip; partly black outer primaries; tail does not extend beyond tips of folded wings. NON-BREEDING ADULT Bill blackish; shoulder with dark bar; forehead white past eye. VOICE Strong *kee-arr-r*. STATUS AND RANGE Uncommon to rare migrant throughout West Indies. Occurs February–June and August–November, but primarily in March and September. HABITAT Coastal lagoons.

**ROSEATE TERN** *Sterna dougallii* 35–41cm (14–16in); wingspan 74cm (29in); 110g. Very long, deeply forked tail; pale gray mantle and primaries; tail extends well beyond wingtips; underside of primary feather tips white with little or no blackish. BREEDING ADULT Bill black with some red (much more red than in North American birds); cap black. NON-BREEDING ADULT Bill blackish; indistinct dark marking on shoulder; forehead white past eye. IMMATURE Dark forehead and crown; bill blackish; back mottled; shoulder with indistinct marks. (Adult Common Tern's mantle darker gray and primary wing feathers with noticeable blackish on underside. Immature Common Tern has distinct black shoulder mark.) VOICE Raspy *krek* and soft two-syllable *tu-ick*. STATUS AND RANGE Widespread, but generally uncommon to rare and very local breeding resident in West Indies primarily April–September. Common only in Virgin Islands, where widely dispersed but local. Threatened. HABITAT Coastal bays.

**LEAST TERN** *Sternula antillarum* 21.5–24cm (8.5–9.5in); wingspan 51cm (20in); 45g. Smallest West Indies tern. BREEDING ADULT Black crown; V-shaped white forecrown; pale yellow bill with black tip. STATUS AND RANGE Generally common, but local breeding resident in Bahamas, Greater Antilles, Virgin and Cayman Islands, St Martin, Antigua, Barbuda, and Guadeloupe primarily May–August. Migrants occur September–March through West Indies, where uncommon to very rare. Breeding declining. HABITAT Lagoons.

**SOOTY TERN** *Onychoprion fuscatus* 38–43cm (15–17in); wingspan 81cm (32in); 200g. ADULT Blackish above and white below; tail deeply forked; white outertail feathers; white of forehead extends only to eye. (Bridled Tern has white line from forehead to behind eye, white hindneck, and browner upperparts.) IMMATURE Dark brown with whitish spots on mantle and wings; tail less deeply forked. VOICE Distinctive, plaintive *wide-a-wake* or *wacky-wack*. STATUS AND RANGE Generally a common breeding resident throughout West Indies May–August. Rare in other months. Vagrant on Cayman Islands, San Andrés, and Providencia. HABITAT Far offshore, except when breeding on offshore islands.

**BRIDLED TERN** *Onychoprion anaethetus* 38cm (15in); wingspan 76cm (30in); 100g. ADULT Grayish-brown above and white below; white hindneck, and white line above and behind eye. (Sooty Tern is blacker above, lacks white hindneck, and white on forehead does not extend behind eye.) IMMATURE Upperparts flecked pale gray. VOICE Puppy-like *yep* or whining *yerk*. Also continuous *ah-ah-ah* … STATUS AND RANGE Generally fairly common but local breeding resident throughout West Indies April–August. Infrequent in other months. HABITAT Far offshore except when breeding on offshore islands.

**BLACK TERN** *Chlidonias niger* 23–26cm (9–10in); wingspan 61cm (24in); 65g. NON-BREEDING ADULT Gray above; forecrown, hindneck, and underparts white except dark patches on sides of breast. Dark patch behind eye. BREEDING ADULT Head, breast, and belly black. IMMATURE Upperparts washed brownish, sides washed grayish. FLIGHT Buoyant and slightly erratic. Often hovers. STATUS AND RANGE Fairly common migrant in Jamaica and Puerto Rico. Uncommon in Hispaniola, Cayman Islands, Antigua, and Barbados. Uncommon to rare locally in Cuba. Rare in most of Bahamas, Virgin Islands (Anegada), and Guadeloupe. Very rare or absent elsewhere in West Indies. Occurs primarily August–October and April–June. HABITAT Fresh and brackish ponds and rice fields.

**BROWN NODDY** *Anous stolidus* 38–40cm (15–16in); wingspan 81cm (32in); 200g. ADULT Entirely dark brown except silvery-white forecrown fading to brown on hindneck. VOICE Harsh *karrk*. STATUS AND RANGE Locally common and widespread year-round resident throughout Bahamas, Greater Antilles, Virgin Islands, and Lesser Antilles. A few probably breed in Cayman Islands. Away from breeding islets, usually seen only at sea. HABITAT Far offshore, except when breeding on offshore islands.

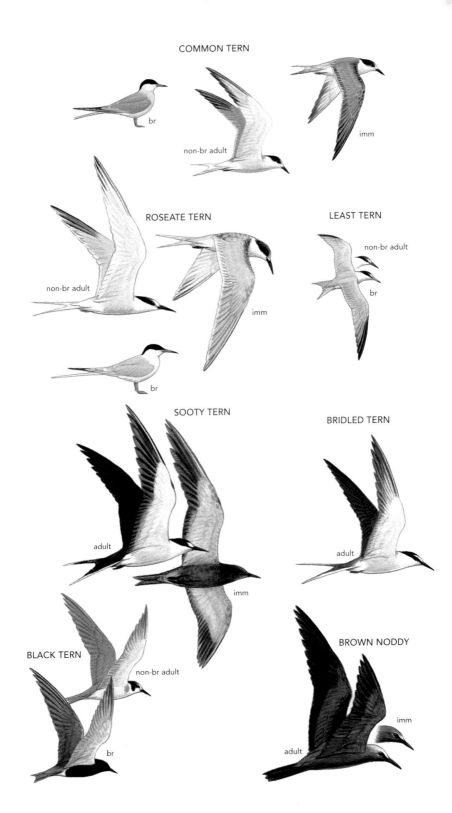

COMMON TERN

br

non-br adult

imm

ROSEATE TERN

LEAST TERN

non-br adult

non-br adult

imm

br

br

SOOTY TERN

BRIDLED TERN

adult

adult

imm

BLACK TERN

non-br adult

BROWN NODDY

imm

br

adult

**Herons:** Most wade in shallow water and hunt prey by stealth.

**LITTLE BLUE HERON** *Egretta caerulea* 56–71cm (22–28in); wingspan 1m (3.3ft); 340g. Medium size; bill grayish, tipped black. **ADULT** Dark gray. **IMMATURE** Initially white; later mottled with dark feathers. **VOICE** Croaking, very throaty *gruuh.* **STATUS AND RANGE** Common year-round resident throughout West Indies. Migrants augment local numbers October–March. **HABITAT** Calm, shallow freshwater and saltwater areas; swift-flowing rivers and streams.

**TRICOLORED HERON** *Egretta tricolor* 61–71cm (24–28in); wingspan 90cm (3ft); 420g. **ADULT** Gray with white belly and undertail-coverts. **IMMATURE** Browner. **STATUS AND RANGE** Common year-round resident in Bahamas, Greater Antilles, Cayman Islands, and San Andrés. Uncommon in Virgin Islands. Generally rare in Lesser Antilles. Migrants augment local numbers October–March. **HABITAT** Mangrove swamps and saltwater lagoons, infrequently freshwater wetlands.

**LITTLE EGRET** *Egretta garzetta* 55–65cm (22–25.5in); wingspan 90cm (3ft); 500g. **BEHAVIOR** Gregarious. **BREEDING ADULT** White phase—White; usually two long head plumes; bill and legs black, feet yellow; lores reddish. Dark phase—Gray; sometimes white chin and throat. **NON-BREEDING** Gray-green lores. (Differs from Snowy Egret primarily by long head plumes, which are less distinctive in breeding and absent in nonbreeding Snowy. Little Egret has slightly longer bill. Also facial skin reddish during breeding and bluish-gray or greenish-gray in non-breeding compared to bright yellow or greenish-yellow in Snowy.) **STATUS AND RANGE** Uncommon breeding resident in Barbados and Antigua. Uncommon wanderer or non-breeding resident in Guadeloupe and St Lucia. Rare or very rare in other Lesser Antilles and very rare elsewhere in West Indies, but range and numbers increasing. **HABITAT** Coastal ponds and lagoons.

**SNOWY EGRET** *Egretta thula* 51–71cm (20–28in); wingspan 1.1m (3.5ft); 370g. **BEHAVIOR** Gregarious. **ADULT** Legs black; feet and lores yellow; bill thin and black. **IMMATURE** Legs dark in front and greenish-yellow in back. **VOICE** Guttural *guarr,* higher pitched and more raspy than Great Egret. **STATUS AND RANGE** Occurs throughout West Indies where common year-round resident in Bahamas, Greater Antilles, Virgin and Cayman Islands, Antigua, Guadeloupe, and Barbados. Generally uncommon non-breeding resident or transient elsewhere in Lesser Antilles, though breeds on St Martin and Guadeloupe. Uncommon on San Andrés. **HABITAT** Freshwater swamps, but also river banks and saltwater lagoons.

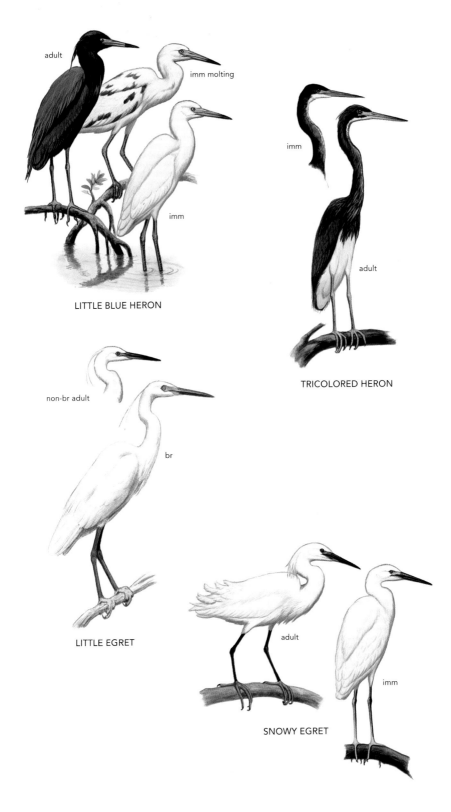

adult

imm molting

imm

LITTLE BLUE HERON

imm

adult

TRICOLORED HERON

non-br adult

br

LITTLE EGRET

adult

imm

SNOWY EGRET

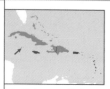

**REDDISH EGRET** *Egretta rufescens* 69–81cm (27–32in); wing-span 1.2m (4ft); 450g. **BEHAVIOR** Dances in water. **ADULT** Black-tipped bill, pinkish at base; ruffled neck feathers. Dark phase—Grayish; head and neck reddish-brown. White phase—White overall. **IMMATURE** Bill entirely dark; neck feathers unruffled. **VOICE** Squawks and croaks. **STATUS AND RANGE** Locally common year-round resident in Bahamas, Cuba, and Hispaniola; uncommon and very local migrant and non-breeding visitor in Jamaica and Cayman Islands, but increasing in Caymans. Decidedly rare wanderer to Puerto Rico, and very rare in Lesser Antilles and San Andrés. **HABITAT** Shallow, protected coastal waters, also swamp edges.

**GREAT BLUE HERON** *Ardea herodias* 107–132cm (42–52in); wingspan 1.8m (6ft); 2.4kg. Very large. Dark phase—Primarily gray; large, straight bill; black eyebrow stripe. White phase—White overall; yellow bill and legs. **VOICE** Deep, throaty croak like large frog, *guarr*. **STATUS AND RANGE** Common migrant and non-breeding resident in Bahamas, Greater Antilles, Virgin and Cayman Islands primarily October–April. Uncommon in Lesser Antilles. Decidedly uncommon in other months, during which known to breed in Cuba, Hispaniola, and Virgin Islands. White phase extremely rare in West Indies. **HABITAT** Ponds and lagoons.

**GRAY HERON** *Ardea cinerea* 90–98cm (35–38in); wingspan 1.8m (6ft); 1.5kg. Very large; gray upperparts; white neck; white thighs in all plumages. (Great Blue Heron darker, particularly on neck and abdomen; thighs reddish-brown.) **STATUS AND RANGE** Rare visitor to Guadeloupe and Barbados; very rare on Montserrat and Martinique. Vagrant elsewhere in West Indies. Numbers increasing. **HABITAT** Ponds and lagoons.

**GREAT EGRET** *Ardea alba* 89–107cm (35–42in); wingspan 1.3m (4.3ft); 870g. **BEHAVIOR** Gregarious. **DESCRIPTION** Very large, with yellow bill and black legs. **VOICE** Hoarse, throaty croak. **STATUS AND RANGE** Common year-round resident in Bahamas, Greater Antilles, Antigua, and Guadeloupe; uncommon in Virgin Islands. Common migrant and non-breeding resident to these islands and in Cayman Islands, St Bartholomew, and Barbados; uncommon visitor elsewhere in Lesser Antilles September–April. Uncommon on San Andrés and Providencia. **HABITAT** Large freshwater and saltwater swamps, grassy marshes, river banks, and shallows behind reefs. Sometimes open areas such as grasslands and golf courses.

**PURPLE HERON** *Ardea purpurea* 78–90cm (31–36in); wingspan 1.2–1.5m (4–5ft); 1kg. Medium-sized heron. Dark bodied with black crown, yellowish bill, and striped rufous and black on neck. **STATUS AND RANGE** Decidedly rare on Barbados, occurring nearly every year but in very small numbers, perhaps only one or a few individuals. May occur on other islands. Questionable whether increase in occurrence will be sustained. **HABITAT** Dense vegetation along water bodies.

**CATTLE EGRET** *Bubulcus ibis* 48–64cm (19–25in); wingspan 90cm (3ft); 340g. **BEHAVIOR** Flocks. Prefers uplands. **DESCRIPTION** Small, with short, thick, yellowish bill. **BREEDING** Reddish legs and eyes; reddish-tinted bill. Tan wash on crown, breast, and upper back. **NON-BREEDING** Black legs and yellow bill. Tan wash reduced. (Great Egret much larger and aquatic, not away from water.) **STATUS AND RANGE** Common year-round resident throughout West Indies. **HABITAT** Pastures and fields. Roosts in mangroves or dense woods.

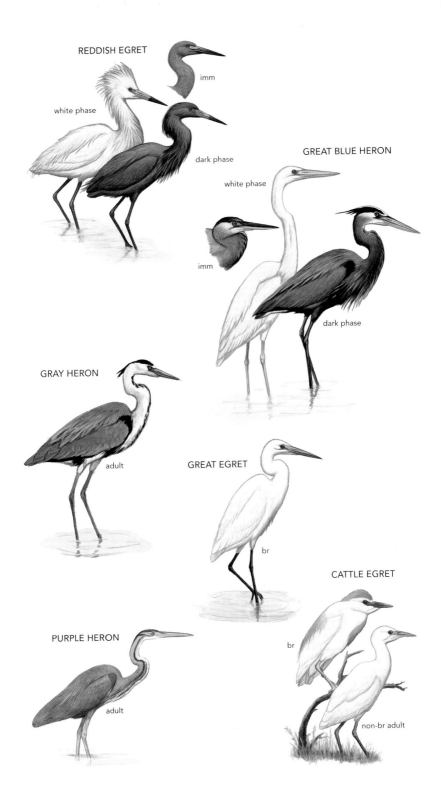

REDDISH EGRET

imm

white phase

dark phase

GREAT BLUE HERON

white phase

imm

dark phase

GRAY HERON

adult

GREAT EGRET

br

CATTLE EGRET

br

PURPLE HERON

adult

non-br adult

**AMERICAN BITTERN** *Botaurus lentiginosus* 58–61cm (23–24in); wingspan 1.1m (3.5ft); 700g. **BEHAVIOR** Often points bill upward. **DESCRIPTION** Mottled brown overall with black neck mark. **FLIGHT** Blackish wingtips. (Immature night-herons darker and lack black on neck and wingtips.) **VOICE** Peculiar pumping sound, *oong-ka-chunk*! **STATUS AND RANGE** Migrant and non-breeding resident in West Indies primarily October–March. Uncommon and local on larger islands of Bahamas and in Cuba; very rare in Jamaica, Hispaniola, Puerto Rico, and Virgin and Cayman Islands. Vagrant elsewhere in West Indies. **HABITAT** Dense vegetation of freshwater swamps.

**LEAST BITTERN** *Ixobrychus exilis* 28–35cm (11–14in); wingspan 45cm (1.5ft); 90g. Small, reddish-yellow, with cream-colored patch on upperwing. **VOICE** *Koo-koo-koo-koo*, almost a *coo*, first syllable often higher, call accelerates slightly. Also loud, harsh *kack*, sometimes in series. **STATUS AND RANGE** Common year-round resident in Cuba and Jamaica; fairly common in Hispaniola and Puerto Rico; uncommon in Cayman Islands and Guadeloupe; uncommon to rare in Bahamas and Dominica; rare in Virgin Islands. **HABITAT** Dense vegetation of freshwater swamps, often with cattails; also mangroves.

**YELLOW-CROWNED NIGHT-HERON** *Nyctanassa violacea* 56–71cm (22–28in); wingspan 1.1m (3.5ft); 690g. Nocturnal. Medium-sized, with chunky appearance. **ADULT** Gray underparts, black-and-white head markings. **IMMATURE** Grayish-brown with white flecks. **VOICE** Distinctive *quark*. **STATUS AND RANGE** Through West Indies, where common year-round resident in Bahamas, Greater Antilles, Virgin Islands, and generally so in Lesser Antilles, San Andrés, and Providencia. Uncommon migrant and resident in Cayman Islands. **HABITAT** Mangroves, but also freshwater areas, mud flats, and dry thickets.

**BLACK-CROWNED NIGHT-HERON** *Nycticorax nycticorax* 58–71cm (23–28in); wingspan 1.1m (3.5ft); 880g. Nocturnal. Medium-sized, with chunky appearance. **ADULT** Black crown and back; white face, underparts, and head plumes. **IMMATURE** Brown with white flecks. **FLIGHT** Only feet extend beyond tail. (Browner, with larger white flecks on wings and upperparts, a thinner bill, and shorter legs than immature Yellow-crowned Night-Heron.) **VOICE** Distinctive *quark*. **STATUS AND RANGE** Through West Indies, where locally common year-round resident in Cuba, Puerto Rico, St Croix (Virgin Islands), St Martin, Guadeloupe, Martinique, St Lucia, and Barbados. Uncommon and local resident in Bahamas, Jamaica, Hispaniola, remaining Virgin Islands, Antigua, and Grenada. Uncommon migrant and non-breeding resident in Cayman Islands, and uncommon to rare visitor and non-breeding resident in remaining Lesser Antilles October–April. **HABITAT** Freshwater swamps; also brackish lagoons and salt ponds.

**LIMPKIN** *Aramus guarauna* 69cm (27in); wingspan 1.1m (3.5ft); 1kg. Primarily nocturnal; wades among vegetation in search of snails. Large, long-legged, long-necked wading bird, brown with white streaks. Long, slightly down-curved bill. **VOICE** Loud, piercing *carrao*. **STATUS AND RANGE** Common permanent resident on some northern Bahamas islands, Cuba, and locally in Jamaica; rare, local resident in Hispaniola and Puerto Rico; rare visitor to other islands of Bahamas. Vagrant elsewhere. **HABITAT** Grassy freshwater wetlands, wooded floodplains, upland forests.

**GREEN HERON** *Butorides virescens* 40–48cm (16–19in); wingspan 65cm (2ft); 210g. Small, with short neck, dark coloration, and greenish-yellow to orangish legs. **BREEDING ADULT** Legs bright orange. **IMMATURE** Heavily streaked below. (Vagrant Striated Heron has pale gray cheeks and sides of neck.) **VOICE** Distinctive, piercing *skyow* when flushed; softer series of *kek*, *kak*, or *que* notes when undisturbed. **STATUS AND RANGE** Common year-round resident throughout West Indies. Migrants augment local numbers. **HABITAT** All water bodies. Sometimes inland in Bahamas.

AMERICAN
BITTERN

LEAST BITTERN

imm

adult

YELLOW-
CROWNED
NIGHT-HERON

imm

adult

BLACK-CROWNED
NIGHT-HERON

imm

adult

imm

adult

imm

LIMPKIN

adult

BLACK-CROWNED
NIGHT-HERON

GREEN HERON

adult

imm

**WHITE IBIS** *Eudocimus albus* 56–71cm (22–28in); wingspan 90cm (3ft); male 1040g, female 760g. BEHAVIOR Flocks. ADULT White; long, down-curved, reddish bill. IMMATURE Brown; belly and rump white. FLIGHT Outstretched neck, wingtips black. STATUS AND RANGE Common year-round resident in Cuba and Hispaniola; uncommon and local resident in Jamaica and Puerto Rico. In Bahamas breeds on Bimini, but rare non-breeding resident elsewhere. Rare wanderer in Cayman Islands. Introduced on Necker Island (Virgin Islands). HABITAT Freshwater swamps, rice fields, and saltwater lagoons.

**GLOSSY IBIS** *Plegadis falcinellus* 56–64cm (22–25in); wingspan 90cm (3ft); 500–1000g. BEHAVIOR Flocks. ADULT Very dark, with long, down-curved bill. IMMATURE Lighter. STATUS AND RANGE Common year-round resident in Puerto Rico along coast; locally common in Hispaniola; uncommon and local in Cuba and Jamaica. Uncommon visitor in Bahamas, where may breed; very local and irregular visitor to Cayman Islands, primarily Grand Cayman; rare or vagrant elsewhere. HABITAT Mud flats, marshy savannas, and rice fields.

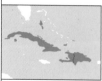

**ROSEATE SPOONBILL** *Platalea ajaja* 66–81cm (26–32in); wingspan 1.3m (4ft); 1.5kg. BEHAVIOR Flocks. Waves bill through water to feed. ADULT Pink, with spatula-like bill. IMMATURE White, some pink. STATUS AND RANGE Locally common year-round resident in Cuba and Hispaniola. In Bahamas, common year-round resident on Great Inagua, uncommon on Andros and rare on Caicos. Vagrant elsewhere. HABITAT Shallow saltwater lagoons and edges of mud flats.

**SCARLET IBIS** *Eudocimus ruber* 58.5cm (23in); wingspan 90cm (3ft); 1.2kg. BEHAVIOR Flocks. ADULT Unmistakable scarlet plumage; black wingtips. NON-BREEDING Bill pinkish. BREEDING Bill blackish. IMMATURE White below; brownish above; pale back and rump tinged pinkish-gray. STATUS AND RANGE Very rare wanderer to Grenada primarily January–June. Vagrant elsewhere. Introduced on Necker Islands (Virgin Islands). HABITAT Coastal swamps, lagoons, and mangroves.

**WOOD STORK** *Mycteria americana* 1m (3.3ft); wingspan 1.5m (5ft); 2.1–2.6kg. Large, with long legs. White coloration, black on wings, head dark. Bill large, down-curved at tip. ADULT Head bald and blackish, bill black. IMMATURE Head feathered and brownish, bill yellowish. FLIGHT Black trailing edge of wing; feet trail beyond tail. STATUS AND RANGE Rare year-round resident in Cuba; extirpated from Hispaniola. Vagrant elsewhere. HABITAT Swamps, mangroves, coastal mud flats, rice fields, ponds, and inland water bodies.

**AMERICAN FLAMINGO** *Phoenicopterus ruber* 1.1–1.2m(42–48in); wingspan 1.5m (5ft); 2.5kg. BEHAVIOR Flocks. Feeds with head upside down. ADULT Orangish-pink coloration; long legs and neck; strangely curved bill. IMMATURE Much paler. FLIGHT Head and neck outstretched and drooping; flight feathers black. VOICE Goose-like honks. STATUS AND RANGE Abundant breeding resident on Great Inagua and regular visitor to nearby islands in Bahamas. Common but very local year-round resident in Cuba and Hispaniola. Uncommon and local visitor in Jamaica. Rare and very local visitor in Puerto Rico. Numbers increasing. Reintroduced in British Virgin Islands, where breeding now well established on Necker Island and Anegada. Vagrant elsewhere. HABITAT Shallow lagoons and coastal estuaries.

**SANDHILL CRANE** *Antigone canadensis* 1m (40in); wingspan 1.8–2.3m (6–7.5ft); 4–4.5kg. BEHAVIOR Flocks. DESCRIPTION Very large, with long legs and long neck. ADULT Gray; bare red crown. IMMATURE Head and neck brownish; body gray mottled with brown. VOICE High-pitched trumpet-like call. STATUS AND RANGE Rare and very local permanent resident in Cuba. Vagrant in Bahamas. Cuban race threatened. HABITAT Marshes with emergent vegetation, swamp borders, edges of pine barrens, and natural savannas.

WHITE IBIS

adult

adult

imm

GLOSSY IBIS

adult

imm

ROSEATE SPOONBILL

imm

adult

adult

adult

SCARLET IBIS

non-br adult

imm

WOOD STORK

imm

adult

GREATER
FLAMINGO

adult

adult

imm

SANDHILL CRANE

adult

adult

**Plovers:** All West Indies species except Killdeer and lapwings frequent water edges, where they are surface feeders. All in region have neck or breast markings.

**SEMIPALMATED PLOVER** *Charadrius semipalmatus* 18.5cm (7.25in); 50g. **BEHAVIOR** Flocks. **DESCRIPTION** Brown upperparts; dark breast band; stubby bill; orange legs. Sometimes breast band shows only as bars on either side of breast. (Piping Plover much paler above. Wilson's is larger, with much larger bill and pinkish legs. Collared is smaller, with more slender bill, reddish-brown hindneck and back of head, and lacks white wing stripe in flight.) **NON-BREEDING** Bill dark and may lack orange at base. **BREEDING** Base of bill orange. **VOICE** Plaintive *weet*. **STATUS AND RANGE** Generally uncommon to common migrant and non-breeding resident throughout West Indies August–May, but occurs year-round. Most frequent September and October. **HABITAT** Tidal flats and sometimes beaches.

**WILSON'S PLOVER** *Charadrius wilsonia* 18–20cm (7–8in); 60g. Broad breast band; long, thick, black bill. **ADULT MALE** Breast band black. **ADULT FEMALE AND IMMATURE** Breast band brown. **VOICE** Emphatic, raspy whistles, or quick *ki-ki-ki*. **STATUS AND RANGE** Common year-round resident in Bahamas, Greater Antilles, Virgin Islands, and some northern Lesser Antilles. Uncommon in Guadeloupe, Grenada, and Grenadines. Locally fairly common to uncommon migrant and non-breeding resident in Cayman Islands. Rare or very rare elsewhere in West Indies. **HABITAT** Salt pond borders and undisturbed sandy beaches.

**COLLARED PLOVER** *Charadrius collaris* 15cm (5.75in); 35g. **ADULT MALE** Reddish-brown hindcrown and hindneck; white forehead, throat, and underparts; black band across breast. **ADULT FEMALE** Thinner breast band; less reddish-brown. **IMMATURE** Breast band limited to sides of neck; no black on crown; only hint of reddish-brown. **FLIGHT** No wing stripe. **VOICE** Sharp, metallic *peet* or *peep-peep* and *chitit*. **STATUS AND RANGE** Rare and irregular wanderer to Guadeloupe and Barbados primarily May–August, but occurs in other months. Very rare visitor to Grenada and Grenadines. Vagrant elsewhere. **HABITAT** Salt flats, coasts, and river banks.

**KILLDEER** *Charadrius vociferus* 25cm (9.75in); 100g. Two black bands on breast. **FLIGHT** Reddish-brown rump. **VOICE** Plaintive, high-pitched *kee* and *dee-de*. **STATUS AND RANGE** Common year-round resident in Bahamas, Greater Antilles, and Virgin Islands. Migrants augment local numbers primarily September–March. Irregular, varying yearly from very uncommon to fairly common migrant and non-breeding resident in Cayman Islands, northern Lesser Antilles, Barbados, and San Andrés. Rare to vagrant elsewhere in Lesser Antilles. **HABITAT** Wet fields, short grass, mud holes, and freshwater pond edges.

**SOUTHERN LAPWING** *Vanellus chilensis* 33–35cm (13–14in); wingspan 32–38cm (1–1.3ft); 250–425g. Large, crested plover with broad black breast band. Head brownish-gray with black forehead, chin, and center of throat. (Northern Lapwing has paler face, darker upperparts, and black on forehead extending to tip of crest.) **FLIGHT** Wingbeats slow and floppy, showing broad white bars on upperwing and white base of tail. **VOICE** A loud *kleek, kleek*. **STATUS AND RANGE** Previously a vagrant but now rare and breeding on Grenada. Formerly bred on Barbados, where numbers now very low. **HABITAT** Short-grass meadows, usually near water.

SEMIPALMATED
PLOVER

br

non-br

WILSON'S PLOVER

♀

♂

imm

adult ♂

COLLARED PLOVER

adult

KILLDEER

adult

SOUTHERN LAPWING

**PIPING PLOVER** *Charadrius melodus* 18cm (7in); 60g. Pale gray upperparts; short stubby bill; orange legs. **NON-BREEDING** Bill black; breast band may be partial or absent. **BREEDING** Base of bill orange; breast band may be partial or complete. **FLIGHT** White uppertail-coverts and black spot near tip of tail. **VOICE** Thin, whistled *peep* and *pee-lo*. **STATUS AND RANGE** Fairly common non-breeding resident in northern Bahamas; uncommon and local in Cuba; rare elsewhere in Bahamas, Jamaica, Hispaniola, Puerto Rico, and Virgin Islands (St Croix, Anegada) primarily late August–March. Vagrant elsewhere in West Indies. Endangered. **HABITAT** Dredged spoils and sandy water edges.

**SNOWY PLOVER** *Charadrius nivosus* 14–15cm (5.5–5.75in); 40g. Tiny, pale, slender, with black bill, dark neck marks, and blackish or dark legs. **BREEDING** Black ear patch. **NON-BREEDING** Lacks black markings. **VOICE** Weak whistle, like calling someone's attention. **STATUS AND RANGE** Common year-round resident in southern Bahamas, Hispaniola, and Anguilla. Uncommon and local year-round resident in Cuba, Virgin Islands (Anegada), and St Bartholomew. Rare and very local year-round resident in Puerto Rico (Cabo Rojo). Vagrant elsewhere. Threatened on several islands. **HABITAT** Beaches and lagoon borders with extensive salt flats.

**BLACK-BELLIED PLOVER** *Pluvialis squatarola* 26–34cm (10–13.5in); 220g. **BEHAVIOR** Flocks. **DESCRIPTION** Large, stocky, with short bill. **NON-BREEDING** Light mottled gray; indistinct contrast between gray crown and whitish eyebrow stripe. **BREEDING** Black underparts. **FLIGHT ABOVE** White uppertail-coverts, white tail with dark bars and distinct white wing stripe. **FLIGHT BELOW** Black wingpits. **VOICE** Plaintive *klee* or *klee-a-lee*. **STATUS AND RANGE** Generally common migrant and non-breeding resident throughout West Indies August–May; occurs in all months. **HABITAT** Tidal mud flats, sandy beaches, and other coastal water edges.

**AMERICAN GOLDEN-PLOVER** *Pluvialis dominica* 26cm (10in); 150g. **BEHAVIOR** Flocks, prefers uplands. **DESCRIPTION** Fairly large and stocky, with short bill. **NON-BREEDING** Mottled gray; contrast between dark crown and whitish eyebrow stripe. **BREEDING** Black underparts; broad white patch edging breast; golden cast on mottled upperparts. (Black-bellied Plover is larger, has larger bill, and is grayer in non-breeding plumage. In breeding plumage has light crown and hindneck, and white rather than dark undertail coverts.) **FLIGHT ABOVE** Dark tail and uppertail-coverts; lacks white wing stripe. **FLIGHT BELOW** Lacks black wingpits. **VOICE** Loud whistle and soft, warbled *chee-dle-wur*, sometimes as loud whistle. **STATUS AND RANGE** Common on Barbados and Guadeloupe, uncommon on Puerto Rico, but generally rare southbound migrant throughout West Indies August–November and very rare northbound March–April. Less frequent in other months. **HABITAT** Fields and golf courses; also tidal flats.

br

non-br

PIPING PLOVER

non-br

br

SNOWY PLOVER

non-br

non-br

br

non-br

BLACK-BELLIED PLOVER

non-br

non-br

non-br

br

AMERICAN GOLDEN-PLOVER

**Shorebirds:** A composite of many bird families characterized by long legs and necks, and usually long, thin, pointed bills. Most wade in shallow water or on tidal flats, where they probe for invertebrates. Almost all are highly gregarious and often occur in mixed feeding assemblages. In the West Indies the vast majority are migratory and so are seen in non-breeding plumage.

**BLACK-NECKED STILT** *Himantopus mexicanus* 34–39cm (13.5–15.5in); 170g. **BEHAVIOR** Flocks. **DESCRIPTION** Large, with long pink legs, black upperparts, and white underparts. **FLIGHT** Black wings; white underparts, tail, and lower back, extending as "V" on back. **VOICE** Loud, raucous *wit, wit, wit, wit, wit*. **STATUS AND RANGE** Widespread throughout West Indies. Common breeding resident March–October in southern and central Bahamas, Greater Antilles, and Virgin and Cayman Islands. Uncommon to rare breeding resident in northernmost Bahamas; uncommon in northern Lesser Antilles south to Guadeloupe; rare to very rare elsewhere. **HABITAT** Mud flats, salt ponds, and open mangrove swamps.

**AMERICAN AVOCET** *Recurvirostra americana* 40–51cm (16–20in); 300g. **BEHAVIOR** Flocks. **DESCRIPTION** Large, black and white, with sharply upturned bill. **NON-BREEDING** Head and neck gray. **BREEDING** Head and neck cinnamon. **VOICE** High-pitched, melodious *klee*. **STATUS AND RANGE** Uncommon and local resident in Cuba, where known to breed, but usually occurs as migrant or non-breeding resident; very rare non-breeding resident in Bahamas, Jamaica, Puerto Rico, and Cayman Islands primarily July–January and in April. Vagrant elsewhere. **HABITAT** Shallow wetland borders.

**DOUBLE-STRIPED THICK-KNEE** *Burhinus bistriatus* 38–43cm (15–17in); 800g. **BEHAVIOR** Primarily nocturnal and terrestrial. **DESCRIPTION** Large, plover-like, with large yellow eye, whitish eyebrow stripe, striped breast. **FLIGHT** Conspicuous white wing patches. **VOICE** Loud, rattling *ca-ca-ca-ca* ... rising in volume then fading away. **STATUS AND RANGE** Uncommon and local year-round resident in Hispaniola and Great Inagua (Bahamas). Threatened in West Indies. **HABITAT** Semi-arid open country, savannas, plantations, and rice fields.

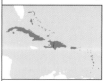

**AMERICAN OYSTERCATCHER** *Haematopus palliatus* 43–54cm (17–21in); 600g. Large, with black hood and long, heavy bill. **ADULT** Orange-red bill; pinkish legs. **IMMATURE** Dull pinkish bill, dark at tip. Gray legs. **FLIGHT** Broad white wing stripe and uppertail. **VOICE** Emphatic, coarsely whistled *wheep*. **STATUS AND RANGE** Fairly common but very local year-round resident in southern and central Bahamas, Puerto Rico, Virgin Islands, and Guadeloupe (Petite Terre); rare and local year-round in Cuba, while rare and local primarily outside breeding season in northernmost Bahamas, Hispaniola, Cayman Islands, and Lesser Antilles. **HABITAT** Rocky headlands, stony beaches, offshore islands, and cays.

BLACK-NECKED STILT

AMERICAN AVOCET

br

non-br

DOUBLE-STRIPED
THICK-KNEE

adult

AMERICAN OYSTERCATCHER

**SOLITARY SANDPIPER** *Tringa solitaria* 19–23cm (7.5–9in); 50g. **BEHAVIOR** Bobs body frequently; often solitary. **DESCRIPTION** White eye-ring, dark upperparts with white spots, black barring of outertail feathers; dark greenish legs; black mark down center of rump with white on either side. **VOICE** Series of emphatic whistles. **STATUS AND RANGE** Varies yearly but generally uncommon southbound migrant throughout West Indies September–October; less frequent northbound March–April; some occur as non-breeding resident November–February. **HABITAT** Freshwater edges. (*See also* Plate 24.)

**WOOD SANDPIPER** *Tringa glareola* 20cm (8in); 60g. Medium-sized, slender, with entirely white rump. Pale yellow or greenish-yellow legs; white eyebrow stripe especially before eye. (Solitary Sandpiper and both yellowlegs lack conspicuous eyebrow stripe.) **FLIGHT** Pale gray underwings. **VOICE** High-pitched *pip, pip, pip.* **STATUS AND RANGE** Rare visitor in Barbados and Guadeloupe. **HABITAT** Primarily freshwater edges.

**WILSON'S SNIPE** *Gallinago delicata* 27–29cm (10.5–11.5in); 100g. Long bill, striped head and back, reddish-brown tail. (Similar to dowitchers, but has more prominently striped head and back, lacks white rump patch.) **VOICE** Guttural squawk when flushed. **STATUS AND RANGE** Irregular, but generally fairly common migrant and non-breeding resident in Bahamas, Cuba, and Hispaniola; uncommon in Jamaica, Puerto Rico, Virgin Islands, Cayman Islands, Guadeloupe, and Barbados; rare through other Lesser Antilles. Occurs primarily October–April. **HABITAT** Grassy freshwater edges and grassy or muddy savannas. (*See also* Plate 24.)

**STILT SANDPIPER** *Calidris himantopus* 20–22cm (8–8.5in); 60g. **BEHAVIOR** Flocks. **DESCRIPTION** Dull greenish legs; whitish eyebrow stripe. Long bill, thick at base, slightly drooped at tip (dowitchers have longer, straighter bills). **NON-BREEDING** Grayish above, whitish below; pale eyebrow stripe. **BREEDING** Reddish-brown ear-patch and heavily barred underparts. **VOICE** Very soft, unmusical, and unabrasive *cue.* **STATUS AND RANGE** Generally uncommon migrant in West Indies, though common locally in Cuba, Hispaniola, Puerto Rico, Virgin Islands, Antigua, and Guadeloupe primarily late August–early November. Generally rare in Lesser Antilles from Dominica south except Barbados, where uncommon. Occurs in all months. **HABITAT** Mud flats and shallow lagoons. (*See also* Plate 23.)

**SHORT-BILLED DOWITCHER** *Limnodromus griseus* 26–30cm (10–12in); 100g. **BEHAVIOR** Flocks. Feeds with vertical bill thrusts. **DESCRIPTION** Very long, straight bill. **NON-BREEDING** Gray above, whitish below, pale gray breast, white eyebrow stripe. **BREEDING** Variable. Pale reddish-brown head and breast blending to white on belly. Breast finely barred, flanks heavily barred. **VOICE** In flight, soft, rapid whistle, *tu-tu-tu,* harsher when alarmed. Similar to Lesser Yellowlegs. **STATUS AND RANGE** Fairly common but local migrant and non-breeding resident in Bahamas, Greater Antilles, Virgin Islands, Cayman Islands, Guadeloupe, and Barbados August–April, and rarely May–July. Uncommon to rare in Lesser Antilles. **HABITAT** Tidal mud flats. (*See also* Plate 23.)

**LONG-BILLED DOWITCHER** *Limnodromus scolopaceus* 28–32cm (11–12.5in); 100g. **BEHAVIOR** Flocks. Feeds with vertical bill thrusts. **DESCRIPTION** Very long, straight bill. (Very similar to Short-billed Dowitcher; best distinguished by call.) **NON-BREEDING** Gray above, paler below, with white eyebrow stripe. **BREEDING** Reddish breast, belly, and abdomen. Breast finely barred, flanks moderately barred. **FLIGHT** White rump patch extends well up back. **VOICE** Thin, high-pitched *keek,* singly or in series. When flushed issues a rapid twitter. **STATUS AND RANGE** Status uncertain due to similarity with more frequent Short-billed. Apparently a rare migrant and very rare non-breeding resident through West Indies. **HABITAT** Primarily shallow fresh and brackish water, also tidal mud flats.

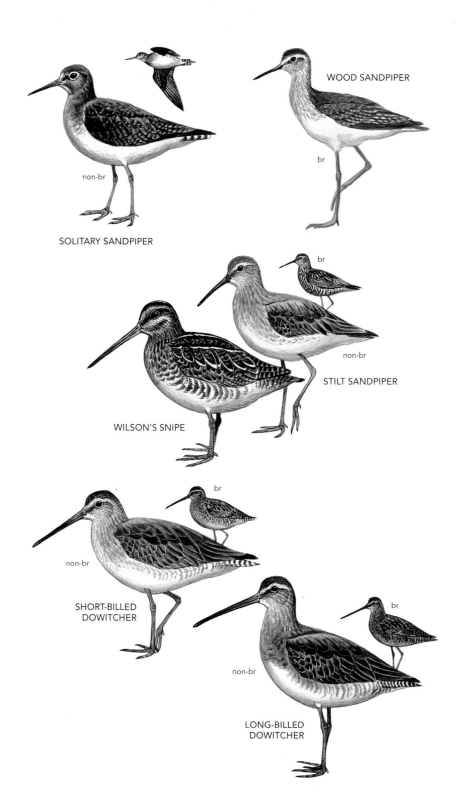

SOLITARY SANDPIPER

non-br

WOOD SANDPIPER

br

WILSON'S SNIPE

STILT SANDPIPER

br

non-br

SHORT-BILLED
DOWITCHER

non-br

br

LONG-BILLED
DOWITCHER

non-br

br

**SEMIPALMATED SANDPIPER** *Calidris pusilla* 14–16.5cm (5.5–6.5in); 26g. **BEHAVIOR** Flocks. **DESCRIPTION** Small, with black legs. Medium-length black bill slightly longer and more drooped at tip in female than in male. The principal small sandpiper to know well. **NON-BREEDING** Grayish-brown above; whitish below. **BREEDING** Finely barred upper breast; reddish-brown tints on upperparts. **VOICE** Soft chatter; also fairly deep, hoarse *cherk*. **STATUS AND RANGE** Generally common southbound migrant throughout West Indies August–October. Less frequent northbound April–May, except on Jamaica and Cayman Islands, where most frequent April–May. Generally uncommon non-breeding resident November–March. Occurs in every month. **HABITAT** Mud flats; still water edges from puddles to salt ponds. (*See also* Plate 23.)

**WESTERN SANDPIPER** *Calidris mauri* 15–18cm (5.75–7in); 27g. **BEHAVIOR** Flocks. **DESCRIPTION** Bill relatively long, heavy at base, narrower and drooping at tip. (Bill characters overlap with very similar Semipalmated Sandpiper. Best distinguished by voice and in breeding plumage.) **NON-BREEDING** Grayish-brown above; whitish below. **BREEDING** Reddish-brown crown, ear-patch, and scapulars. **VOICE** *Kreep*, coarser and more scratchy than Semipalmated Sandpiper. **STATUS AND RANGE** Fairly common to uncommon migrant and non-breeding resident throughout West Indies August–March, but most frequent during southbound migration August–October. Overlooked due to similarity to other sandpipers. **HABITAT** Primarily mud flats.

**LEAST SANDPIPER** *Calidris minutilla* 12.5–16.5cm (5–6.5in); 21g. **BEHAVIOR** Flocks. **DESCRIPTION** Tiny; brown with streaked breast. Yellowish-green legs distinguish it from all other small sandpipers. Thin bill has slightly drooping tip. **NON-BREEDING** Brown above and on breast; white belly and abdomen. **BREEDING** Plumage more mottled with reddish-brown tints. **VOICE** Thin, soft whistle, *wi-wi-wit*. Also whinny-like trill dropping in pitch and volume, *tr-tr-tr-tr* … **STATUS AND RANGE** Generally common migrant throughout West Indies August–October and April–May; uncommon to rare non-breeding resident November–March. **HABITAT** Mud flats and still water borders. (*See also* Plate 23.)

**WHITE-RUMPED SANDPIPER** *Calidris fuscicollis* 18–20cm (7–8in); 44g. **BEHAVIOR** Flocks. **DESCRIPTION** White rump. Easily overlooked. (Larger than Semipalmated and Western; darker gray in non-breeding plumage and darker brown in breeding plumage; breast more heavily streaked.) **NON-BREEDING** Brownish-gray above and on upper breast, appearing hooded. **BREEDING** Browner; reddish-brown tints on crown, upper back, and ear-patch. **VOICE** Mouse-like squeak, *peet* or *jeet*. Also thin, high-pitched trill. **STATUS AND RANGE** Irregular, but generally uncommon to rare southbound migrant through West Indies August–November; rarer northbound migrant March–May. In Cayman Islands most frequent April–June, when locally abundant in some years. Generally arrives later and leaves later than other sandpipers. **HABITAT** Rice fields, mud flats, and borders of still water. (*See also* Plate 23.)

**BAIRD'S SANDPIPER** *Calidris bairdii* 18–19cm (7–7.5in); 38g. **BEHAVIOR** Picks food rather than probes; tends to feed on drier substrate than similar sandpipers; occurs singly or in small groups. **DESCRIPTION** Long wings give streamlined appearance. (Larger than Semipalmated and Western, and wings extend beyond tail. Browner than White-rumped Sandpiper, but best separated in flight; white on rump of Baird's divided by dark central stripe.) **NON-BREEDING** Brownish-gray above and on breast. **BREEDING** Browner, with faint reddish-brown tints. **VOICE** Frequently a musical, rolling trill in flight. **STATUS AND RANGE** Very rare migrant in West Indies. Occurs primarily September and October. Status poorly known due to similarity to other sandpipers. Likely more frequent than records indicate. **HABITAT** Damp grasslands and edges of inland wetlands. Often some distance from water.

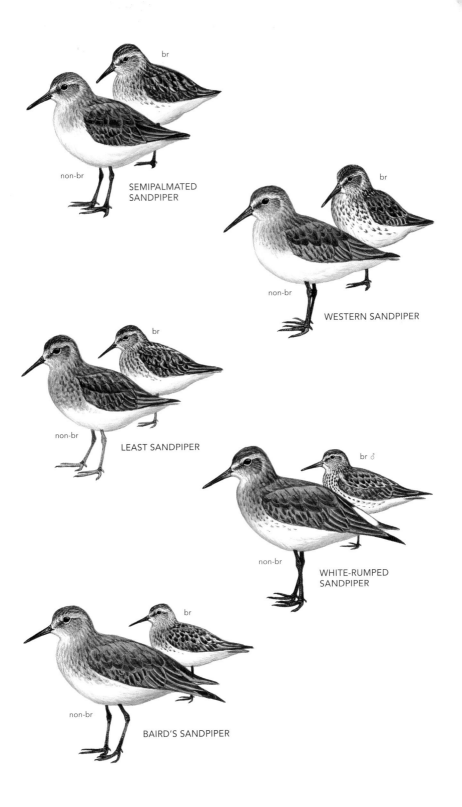

br

non-br

SEMIPALMATED
SANDPIPER

br

non-br

WESTERN SANDPIPER

br

non-br

LEAST SANDPIPER

br ♂

non-br

WHITE-RUMPED
SANDPIPER

br

non-br

BAIRD'S SANDPIPER

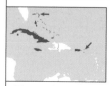

**DUNLIN** *Calidris alpina* 20–23cm (8–9in); 55g. **BEHAVIOR** Flocks. **DESCRIPTION** Heavy bill, distinctively drooping at tip; short-necked; hunched appearance. **NON-BREEDING** Gray wash on breast, head, and upperparts. **BREEDING** Black belly and reddish back. **VOICE** Distinctive harsh, nasal *tzeep*. **STATUS AND RANGE** Rare migrant and non-breeding resident in Bahamas and Cuba; very rare in Jamaica, Puerto Rico, and Virgin Islands; vagrant elsewhere. Sometimes present in numbers. Occurs late August–April. **HABITAT** Borders of still water, particularly mud flats. (*See also* Plate 23.)

**CURLEW SANDPIPER** *Calidris ferruginea* 18–23cm (7–9in); 60g. Bill slightly down-curved throughout its length. **FLIGHT** White rump. (Dunlin white rump divided by black bar, and bill down-curved only at tip.) **NON-BREEDING ADULT** Upperparts brownish-gray; underparts white. **BREEDING MALE** Reddish-brown. **BREEDING FEMALE** Duller. **VOICE** A soft *chirrup*. **STATUS AND RANGE** Very rare and irregular southbound migrant in Barbados September–October and much less frequently April–June. Vagrant elsewhere in West Indies. **HABITAT** Mud flats, marshes, and beaches.

**GREATER YELLOWLEGS** *Tringa melanoleuca* 33–38cm (13–15in); 170g. **BEHAVIOR** Flocks. **DESCRIPTION** Large, with orangish-yellow legs. Long, straight bill often appears slightly upturned and two-toned. (That of Lesser Yellowlegs is relatively shorter, thinner and darker at base.) **FLIGHT** Dark above; white uppertail-coverts. Similar to Lesser Yellowlegs. **VOICE** Loud, raspy, three- or four-note whistle, *cu-cu-cu*, or *klee-klee-cu*. **STATUS AND RANGE** Common migrant and non-breeding resident throughout West Indies. Most frequent migrating August–October and February–April, but also common non-breeding resident November–January. Occurs in all months. **HABITAT** Mud flats and other water edges.

**LESSER YELLOWLEGS** *Tringa flavipes* 25–28cm (9.75–11in); 80g. **BEHAVIOR** Flocks. **DESCRIPTION** Medium-sized, with orangish-yellow legs and thin, straight bill. **VOICE** One- or two-note *cu-cu*, softer and more nasal than Greater Yellowlegs. **STATUS AND RANGE** Common migrant and non-breeding resident throughout West Indies. Most frequent migrating August–October and March–May, but occurs in all months. **HABITAT** Mud flats and other water edges. (*See also* Plate 23.)

**COMMON GREENSHANK** *Tringa nebularia* 30–35cm (12–14in); 125–300g. Large, with slightly upturned bill, thicker at base. **NON-BREEDING** Greenish or yellowish legs. **BREEDING** Breast heavily flecked with black. **FLIGHT** White "V" extends from uppertail-coverts onto back. (Greater Yellowlegs lacks this white "V.") **VOICE** Three short flute-like notes, *teu-teu-teu*. **STATUS AND RANGE** An increase in recent records indicates it is very rare in Barbados. Vagrant elsewhere in West Indies. **HABITAT** Mud flats.

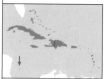

**EASTERN WILLET** *Tringa semipalmata* 38–40cm (15–16in); 200g. Large, light gray, with gray legs and thick bill. **BREEDING** Fine black stripes on head, neck, and breast. **NON-BREEDING** More uniformly gray. **FLIGHT** Black-and-white wing pattern. **VOICE** Sharp *will willet, will willet* repeated several times; also sharp whistles. **STATUS AND RANGE** Common but local breeding resident and migrant in Bahamas, Greater Antilles, Virgin Islands (Anegada), and Cayman Islands, where most frequent August–November, but occurs year-round. Likely to migrate to South America after breeding. Common migrant in Guadeloupe. Uncommon to rare elsewhere in West Indies. **HABITAT** Tidal flats; also borders of saltwater and freshwater bodies.

**WESTERN WILLET** *Tringa inornata* 38–43cm (15–17in); 250g. Very similar to Eastern Willet but slightly larger, with longer neck, legs, and bill. **NON-BREEDING** Pale gray overall, lighter below. **BREEDING** Fine black stripes on head, neck, and breast. **FLIGHT** Black-and-white wing pattern. **VOICE** Same as Eastern Willet. **STATUS AND RANGE** Unclear due to similarity to Eastern Willet. Fairly common to uncommon migrant and non-breeding resident in Cayman Islands and likely of similar status widely in West Indies, particularly in Bahamas and Greater Antilles. May be predominant willet in Caribbean November–March. Some consider willets one species. **HABITAT** Borders of saltwater and freshwater bodies.

non-br

br

DUNLIN

non-br

CURLEW SANDPIPER

GREATER
YELLOWLEGS

LESSER
YELLOWLEGS

non-br

br

COMMON
GREENSHANK

non-br

WESTERN WILLET
(Eastern nearly identical)

br

non-br

imm

EASTERN WILLET
(Western nearly identical)

**HUDSONIAN GODWIT** *Limosa haemastica* 33–40cm (13–16in); male 220g, female 290g. Long, slightly upturned bill, pinkish at base; black tail with white base. **NON-BREEDING** Gray overall, paler below; white eyebrow stripe. **BREEDING** Dark reddish-brown below, heavily barred. Female paler. **FLIGHT ABOVE** White wing stripe and base of tail. **FLIGHT BELOW** Blackish wing linings and white wing stripe. **VOICE** *Ta-wit*, but rarely calls in West Indies. **STATUS AND RANGE** Very rare migrant through most of West Indies primarily September and October. **HABITAT** Grassy freshwater pond edges and mud flats.

**MARBLED GODWIT** *Limosa fedoa* 40–51cm (16–20in); male 320g, female 420g. Large, with no white on rump. Long, slightly upturned bill. **NON-BREEDING** Pale tan underparts. **BREEDING** Reddish-brown underparts barred black. **FLIGHT ABOVE** Cinnamon-colored; blackish primary wing-coverts. **FLIGHT BELOW** Cinnamon-colored wing linings with paler flight feathers. **STATUS AND RANGE** Very rare migrant to West Indies primarily late August–early April, occurring as vagrant on most islands. **HABITAT** Mud flats and marshes.

**SANDERLING** *Calidris alba* 18–22cm (7–8.5in); 50g. **BEHAVIOR** Flocks; typically advances and retreats with waves at tideline. **NON-BREEDING** The lightest-colored sandpiper; white underparts and light gray upperparts. Black mark on bend of wing. **BREEDING** Reddish-brown head and breast. **VOICE** Distinctive *whit*. **STATUS AND RANGE** Irregular, but generally fairly common migrant and non-breeding resident in Bahamas, Greater Antilles, Cayman Islands, St Christopher, Guadeloupe, Barbados, and San Andrés September–April. A few occur May–August. It is uncommon to rare in Virgin Islands and other Lesser Antilles. **HABITAT** Sandy beaches. (*See also* Plate 24.)

**SPOTTED SANDPIPER** *Actitis macularius* 18–20cm (7–8in); 40g. **BEHAVIOR** Distinctive teetering walk. **NON-BREEDING** White underparts; dark patches on sides of breast; orangish base of bill. **BREEDING** Dark spots on underparts; orange bill with black tip. **VOICE** Whistled *we-weet*. **STATUS AND RANGE** Generally common migrant and non-breeding resident throughout West Indies August–May, less common other months. **HABITAT** Water edges of mangroves, coastlines, and streams. (*See also* Plate 24.)

**RED KNOT** *Calidris canutus* 25–28cm (9.75–11in); 140g. **BEHAVIOR** Flocks. **DESCRIPTION** Medium-sized, with chunky build, usually greenish legs, and relatively short bill. **NON-BREEDING** Gray above; white below. **BREEDING** Orangish-red face and underparts. **STATUS AND RANGE** Generally rare southbound migrant through West Indies September and October, less frequent northbound March and April. Rarer still as non-breeding resident November–February. Uncommon in Guadeloupe and Barbados, but generally very rare or vagrant from Dominica south in Lesser Antilles. Sometimes occurs in numbers. **HABITAT** Sandy tidal flats, mangrove lagoon edges. (*See also* Plate 23.)

HUDSONIAN
GODWIT

non-br

br

non-br

SANDERLING

br

non-br

MARBLED GODWIT

br

non-br

RED KNOT

br

SPOTTED SANDPIPER

non-br

non-br

**PECTORAL SANDPIPER** *Calidris melanotos* 20–24cm (8–9.5in); 100g. Yellowish-green bill and legs; sharp demarcation between heavily streaked breast and white belly. **NON-BREEDING** Gray-brown upperparts, head, and breast. **BREEDING MALE** More mottled; breast heavily streaked with black. **VOICE** Low, harsh *krip*. **STATUS AND RANGE** Irregular, but some years locally common in Puerto Rico, Cayman Islands, Guadeloupe, and Barbados during southbound migration August–early November. Generally uncommon through rest of West Indies during these months. Rare during northbound migration March and April. **HABITAT** Wet meadows, grassy areas after rains. (*See also* Plate 23.)

**RUFF** *Calidris pugnax* Male 30cm (12in), female 23–28cm (9–11in); female 100g, male 180g. **BEHAVIOR** Feeds sluggishly. **NON-BREEDING** Fairly chunky; erect posture; whitish around base of bill; pale gray breast, sometimes scaled; relatively short and slightly drooped bill. Legs often pale, varying from dull yellow to orange, green, or brown. **BREEDING MALE** Extremely variable, but all have elaborate breast and head feathers. **BREEDING FEMALE** Variable. Similar to non-breeding, but darker. **FLIGHT** Long, oval white patches at base of tail. **STATUS AND RANGE** Rare but regular migrant on Guadeloupe and Barbados; very rare or vagrant elsewhere in West Indies. Occurs primarily September and October. **HABITAT** Mud flats and borders of ponds and lagoons.

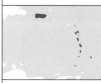

**BUFF-BREASTED SANDPIPER** *Calidris subruficollis* 19–22cm (7.5–8.5in); 70g. **BEHAVIOR** Favors grasslands. **ADULT** Upperparts with scaled look. Large dark eye framed by pale eye-ring on clean reddish-tan face; thin black bill. Underparts pale tan with spots on sides; yellow legs and feet; short tail not extending beyond folded wings at rest. (Upland Sandpiper larger, with longer neck, legs, and bill; streaked below.) **FLIGHT** White wing linings. **STATUS AND RANGE** Rare migrant in Puerto Rico, Guadeloupe, and Barbados and very rare in most other Lesser Antilles primarily late August–October. Vagrant elsewhere in West Indies. **HABITAT** Fields, pastures, short grass.

**UPLAND SANDPIPER** *Bartramia longicauda* 28–32cm (11–12.5in); 150g. **BEHAVIOR** Favors grasslands. **DESCRIPTION** Orangish-yellow legs; thin, relatively short bill; small head; long, slender neck; long tail. **FLIGHT** Dark primaries; long tail; stiff, shallow wingbeats. **STATUS AND RANGE** Irregular, but generally rare southbound migrant in Bahamas, Cuba, Puerto Rico, Virgin and Cayman Islands, Barbados, and Guadeloupe, primarily southbound August–early October, less frequent northbound April–May. Very rare or vagrant elsewhere in West Indies. Sometimes occurs in numbers. **HABITAT** Grasslands, pastures, and savannas.

br

PECTORAL SANDPIPER

non-br

non-br

br ♂

br ♀

non-br

RUFF
(FEMALE: REEVE)

adult

BUFF-BREASTED SANDPIPER

UPLAND SANDPIPER

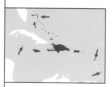

**WILSON'S PHALAROPE** *Phalaropus tricolor* 23cm (9in); 50g. BEHAVIOR Spins on water surface to feed. DESCRIPTION Thin, straight black bill. NON-BREEDING White breast; thin dark gray mark through eye. BREEDING MALE Reddish-tan wash on neck. BREEDING FEMALE Dark reddish-brown band from shoulder blending to black behind eye. STATUS AND RANGE Rare and local migrant and less frequently non-breeding resident August–May in Hispaniola, Puerto Rico, Guadeloupe, and Barbados; very rare in Bahamas, Jamaica, Virgin and Cayman Islands. Vagrant elsewhere. HABITAT Shallow ponds and lagoons. (*See also* Plate 24.)

**RED-NECKED PHALAROPE** *Phalaropus lobatus* 18cm (7in); 35g. BEHAVIOR Spins on water surface to feed. DESCRIPTION Thin, straight black bill. NON-BREEDING ADULT Black cap; white forehead; broad black bar through eye and ear-coverts. (Non-breeding Wilson's Phalarope has thin gray eye-stripe and longer bill.) BREEDING FEMALE Black cap, dark back streaked white or pale gray, pale reddish-brown neck, golden wing-coverts. BREEDING MALE Duller than female. (Wilson's Phalarope lacks white stripes on back.) STATUS AND RANGE Rare migrant to Puerto Rico in October and very rare non-breeding resident November–February. Very rare migrant in Bahamas. Vagrant in other islands. HABITAT Usually out at sea; sometimes ponds and lagoons. (*See also* Plate 24).

**RED PHALAROPE** *Phalaropus fulicarius* 21cm (8in); 50g. BEHAVIOR Spins on water surface to feed. DESCRIPTION Bill stout and black except for yellow spot at base of lower mandible. NON-BREEDING ADULT Unstreaked pale gray above, underparts white. Hindcrown blackish; broad black bar through eye to ear-coverts. BREEDING FEMALE Entirely dark reddish-brown below with a conspicuous white facial patch. BREEDING MALE Dull orangish-brown below with less distinct whitish facial patch. (Red is stockier than other phalaropes, with shorter and thicker bill, no stripes on back in any plumage, and noticeable wing stripe in flight.) STATUS AND RANGE Very rare migrant in West Indies October–January, but vagrant on any particular island. HABITAT Usually out at sea; sometimes ponds and lagoons. (*See also* Plate 24.)

**RUDDY TURNSTONE** *Arenaria interpres* 21–23cm (8–9in); 120g. BEHAVIOR Flocks. NON-BREEDING Dark breast markings; orange legs. BREEDING Unusual black-and-white facial markings; reddish-orange back. FLIGHT Distinctive white pattern on upperwings, back, and tail. VOICE Loud, nasal *cuck-cuck-cuck*, increasing in volume. STATUS AND RANGE Common migrant and non-breeding resident throughout West Indies in all months except June and July, when uncommon. HABITAT Mud flats, pond edges, sandy and rocky coasts.

**WHIMBREL** *Numenius phaeopus* 38–46cm (15–18in); male 360g, female 400g. BEHAVIOR Flocks. DESCRIPTION Relatively large, with striped crown and long, down-curved bill. FLIGHT Underwings barred, without cinnamon color. A very rare subspecies from Eurasia displays white rump and lower back. VOICE Harsh, rapid whistle, *whip-whip-whip-whip*. STATUS AND RANGE Generally uncommon to rare, but regular migrant throughout West Indies, primarily September, may remain as non-breeding resident. Occurs in all months. HABITAT Ponds, mangroves, swamps, and marshes. Frequents areas with fiddler crabs.

br ♀

non-br

WILSON'S PHALAROPE

non-br

RED-NECKED PHALAROPE

br ♀

br ♀

non-br

non-br

RED PHALAROPE

br

non-br

RUDDY TURNSTONE

non-br

hudsonicus

phaeopus

WHIMBREL
(not to scale)

**LESSER YELLOWLEGS** *Tringa flavipes* 25–28cm (9.75–11in). Dark above; white uppertail-coverts. (*See also* Plate 19.)

**STILT SANDPIPER** *Calidris himantopus* 20–22cm (8–8.5in). White rump; whitish tail. (*See also* Plate 17.)

**SHORT-BILLED DOWITCHER** *Limnodromus griseus* 26–30cm (10–12in). White rump patch extends well up back. Distinguished from Long-billed Dowitcher by voice. (Wilson's Snipe more prominently striped on head and back; lacks white rump patch.) (*See also* Plate 17.)

**RED KNOT** *Calidris canutus* 25–28cm (9.75–11in). Barred above; pale gray rump; white wing stripe; pale gray wing linings. (*See also* Plate 20.)

**DUNLIN** *Calidris alpina* 20–23cm (8–9in). White wing stripe; white rump divided by black bar. (*See also* Plate 19.)

**SEMIPALMATED SANDPIPER** *Calidris pusilla* 14–16.5cm (5.5–6.5in). Fine white wing stripe; white rump divided by black bar. (*See also* Plate 18.)

**LEAST SANDPIPER** *Calidris minutilla* 12.5–16.5cm (5–6.5in). Dark above; very faint wing stripe. (*See also* Plate 18.)

**PECTORAL SANDPIPER** *Calidris melanotos* 20–24cm (8–9.5in). Sharp breast demarcation; fine white wing stripe; white rump divided by black bar. (*See also* Plate 21.)

**WHITE-RUMPED SANDPIPER** *Calidris fuscicollis* 18–20cm (7–8in). White rump. Fine white wing stripe. (*See also* Plate 18.)

LESSER YELLOWLEGS

STILT SANDPIPER
non-br

SHORT-BILLED
DOWITCHER

non-br

RED KNOT
non-br

DUNLIN
non-br

SEMIPALMATED
SANDPIPER
non-br

PECTORAL
SANDPIPER
non-br

LEAST SANDPIPER
non-br

WHITE-RUMPED
SANDPIPER
non-br

**SPOTTED SANDPIPER** *Actitis macularius* 18–20cm (7–8in). Shallow, rapid wingbeats; white wing stripe. (*See also* Plate 20.)

**SANDERLING** *Calidris alba* 18–22cm (7–8.5in). White wing stripe; pale gray upperparts. (*See also* Plate 20.)

**SOLITARY SANDPIPER** *Tringa solitaria* 19–23cm (7.5–9in). Dark above; bars on white-edged tail; underwings dark. Wingbeats deep; erratic flight. (*See also* Plate 17.)

**WILSON'S SNIPE** *Gallinago delicata* 27–29cm (10.5–11.5in). Zig-zag flight while uttering call note. (*See also* Plate 17.)

**RED-NECKED PHALAROPE** *Phalaropus lobatus* 18cm (7in). White wing stripe; white stripes on back. (*See also* Plate 22.)

**WILSON'S PHALAROPE** *Phalaropus tricolor* 23cm (9in). White rump; dark upperparts. (*See also* Plate 22.)

**RED PHALAROPE** *Phalaropus fulicarius* 21cm (8in). Unstreaked pale gray above; white wing stripe. (*See also* Plate 22.)

non-br

SPOTTED SANDPIPER

non-br

SOLITARY SANDPIPER

non-br

SANDERLING

WILSON'S SNIPE

non-br

RED-NECKED PHALAROPE

non-br

WILSON'S PHALAROPE

non-br

RED PHALAROPE

**Rails:** Chicken-like marsh-dwelling birds. They are secretive, primarily nocturnal, and much more frequently heard than seen. Rails rarely flush, preferring to run for cover. Flight is labored, with legs dangling conspicuously.

 **ZAPATA RAIL** *Cyanolimnas cerverai* 29cm (11.5in). Very difficult to detect. Medium-sized; almost without stripes or spots. Long green bill, red at base; red legs and eyes. **VOICE** Not definitively known. **STATUS AND RANGE** Endemic to Cuba; very rare, confined to Zapata Swamp area. Critically endangered. Genus also endemic to Cuba. **HABITAT** Sawgrass savannas with tussocks.

**KING RAIL** *Rallus elegans* 38–48cm (15–19in); 290g. Difficult to detect. Chicken-like; bill long and slender. Flanks strongly banded black and white. **ADULT** Throat, breast, and wing-coverts reddish-brown. **IMMATURE** Grayer; lacks reddish-brown. (Clapper Rail less reddish, especially wings and neck; less distinct barring on flanks; occurs primarily in mangroves.) **VOICE** Shorter, more musical than Clapper Rail. **STATUS AND RANGE** Common permanent resident in Cuba. Vagrant to Jamaica. **HABITAT** Freshwater wetlands with tall, dense vegetation. Sometimes brackish marshes.

 **CLAPPER RAIL** *Rallus crepitans* 32–41cm (12.5–16in); male 320g, female 270g. Difficult to detect. Gray, chicken-like, with long, slender bill. Stalks among mangroves. Most active dawn and dusk. **VOICE** Loud, grating cackle, *kek-kek-kek-kek* ... , slowing at end. **STATUS AND RANGE** Common permanent resident in Bahamas, Cuba, and Puerto Rico; locally so in Jamaica, Hispaniola, Virgin Islands, and Barbuda; rare and local in St Christopher and Guadeloupe. Vagrant elsewhere. **HABITAT** Salt marshes and mangroves.

**VIRGINIA RAIL** *Rallus limicola* 23cm (9in); 65–95g. Difficult to detect. **ADULT** Breast, belly, and wing-coverts reddish-brown. Cheek gray; bill long, reddish. (King and Clapper Rails are about twice as large, with bill and wings usually less red.) **IMMATURE** Mottled gray or blackish below; bill dark. **VOICE** Metallic *kid-ik* or *ticket-ticket*. **STATUS AND RANGE** Rare migrant and non-breeding resident September–April on Grand Bahama (Bahamas). Vagrant elsewhere. **HABITAT** Primarily freshwater marshes with dense vegetation, also brackish and saltwater wetlands.

ZAPATA RAIL

KING RAIL

CLAPPER RAIL

VIRGINIA RAIL

imm

adult

**SORA** *Porzana carolina* 22cm (8.5in); 75g. Difficult to detect. Small, brownish-gray, with stubby yellow bill. **ADULT** Blackish face, throat, and center of breast. **IMMATURE** Brown face and breast. **VOICE** Clear, descending whinny and plaintive, rising whistle, *ker-wee*. **STATUS AND RANGE** Migrant and non-breeding resident throughout West Indies primarily October–April. Common in Cuba; fairly common in Bahamas; uncommon and local in Jamaica, Hispaniola, Puerto Rico, Virgin and Cayman Islands, and Guadeloupe; rare in rest of Lesser Antilles. **HABITAT** Rice fields, dense vegetation of freshwater swamps; sometimes saltwater ponds and mangroves.

**SPOTTED RAIL** *Pardirallus maculatus* 28cm (11in); 170g. Difficult to detect. Medium-sized, with long red legs. Long, greenish-yellow bill, red at base. **ADULT** Spotted, barred black and white. **IMMATURE** Browner, less spotting. **VOICE** Accelerating *tuk-tuk-tuk-tuk* ... a bit like a bouncing ball; also a peculiar high, guttural grunt much like a pig. **STATUS AND RANGE** Uncommon and local permanent resident in western Cuba and rare in Hispaniola. Very rare and local in Jamaica. Critically endangered in West Indies. **HABITAT** Freshwater swamps with emergent vegetation. Also rice fields.

**BLACK RAIL** *Laterallus jamaicensis* 14cm (5.5in); 35g. Very difficult to detect. **BEHAVIOR** Nocturnal. **DESCRIPTION** Tiny, with short black bill, white spots on back, dark reddish-brown hindneck. (Downy young gallinules, coots, and rails are black but lack these marks.) **VOICE** Whistled *ki-ki-kurr*, last note lower. **STATUS AND RANGE** Rare and very local non-breeding resident in Cuba and Hispaniola, though may breed on these islands; very rare and local in Bahamas and Jamaica primarily October–March. Vagrant elsewhere in West Indies. **HABITAT** Wet grassy marsh edges, saline and fresh.

**YELLOW-BREASTED CRAKE** *Hapalocrex flaviventer* 14cm (5.5in); 25g. Difficult to detect. Tiny, pale yellowish-brown, with blackish crown and white eyebrow stripe. **VOICE** Medium-pitched *tuck* and high-pitched, whistled *peep*. **STATUS AND RANGE** Uncommon and local permanent resident in Cuba, Jamaica, and Puerto Rico; rare in Hispaniola. **HABITAT** Short vegetation of swamps and canals.

imm

adult

SORA

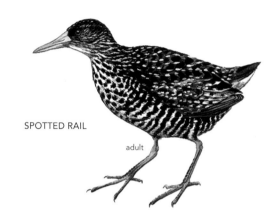

SPOTTED RAIL

adult

BLACK RAIL

YELLOW-BREASTED CRAKE

**NORTHERN JACANA** *Jacana spinosa* 19–23cm (7.5–9in); male 80g, female 140g. **BEHAVIOR** Wades over floating vegetation with huge toes. **DESCRIPTION** Chicken-like, with large yellow wing patches and extremely long, slender, greenish toes. **ADULT** Deep reddish-brown; blackish head and neck. Bill and forehead shield yellow. **IMMATURE** Whitish below; white eyebrow stripe. **FLIGHT** Low over water with shallow wingbeats and dangling legs. **VOICE** Sharp, repeated cackle. **STATUS AND RANGE** Common permanent resident in Cuba, Jamaica, and Hispaniola. Vagrant elsewhere in West Indies. **HABITAT** Freshwater bodies with large-leaved floating vegetation.

**AMERICAN COOT (CARIBBEAN COOT)** *Fulica americana* 38–40cm (15–16in); male 720g, female 550g. **BEHAVIOR** Swims with bobbing head; dives; flocks. **DESCRIPTION** Duck-like. **ADULT** Grayish-black; bill and undertail-coverts white. **IMMATURE** Paler. Caribbean Coot now a subspecies of American Coot. **STATUS AND RANGE** Uncommon breeding resident in Bahamas, Greater Antilles, and Cayman Islands, primarily May–August. Migrants augment numbers September–April, making it common throughout these islands and San Andrés during these months. Uncommon and occasionally breeds in Virgin Islands; generally rare to Lesser Antilles, but breeds on several islands (Antigua, Guadeloupe, and Martinique). **HABITAT** Open fresh water.

**PURPLE GALLINULE** *Porphyrio martinicus* 33cm (13in); 240g. **BEHAVIOR** Wades among dense swamp vegetation. **ADULT** Bluish-purple; yellow legs; bluish-white frontal shield. **IMMATURE** Golden-brown, bluish wings. **VOICE** High-pitched, melodious *klee-klee*. **STATUS AND RANGE** Common but local permanent resident in Cuba, Jamaica, and Hispaniola; uncommon in Puerto Rico, the Cayman Islands, and San Andrés. In Bahamas, uncommon migrant on larger northern islands August–October and March–May; rare and local on remainder. Rare year-round resident on St Bartholomew, Montserrat, Guadeloupe, Martinique, Barbados, and Grenadines. Very rare elsewhere. **HABITAT** Freshwater bodies with dense vegetation.

**COMMON GALLINULE** *Gallinula galeata* 34cm (13.5in); 300g. **BEHAVIOR** Swims with bobbing head. **DESCRIPTION** Duck-like. **ADULT** Red bill tipped yellow, red frontal shield; white line down flank. **IMMATURE** Gray and brown; bill lacks red. **VOICE** Piercing, laugh-like cackle, slowing at end: *ki-ki-ki-ki-ka, kaa, kaaa*. **STATUS AND RANGE** Generally common year-round resident throughout West Indies. Rare on St Vincent and a few smaller islands lacking wetlands. **HABITAT** Most wetlands with water plants.

**LEAST GREBE** *Tachybaptus dominicus* 23–26cm (9–10in); 120g. **BEHAVIOR** Excellent diver. **DESCRIPTION** Small, blackish, with thin bill and yellow-orange eye. White wing patch not always visible. **VOICE** Rising, reed-like *week*. **STATUS AND RANGE** Common year-round resident in Bahamas, Cuba, and Jamaica; uncommon and local in Hispaniola, Puerto Rico, and Virgin Islands. Very rare visitor or vagrant elsewhere in West Indies. **HABITAT** Primarily freshwater cattail swamps and small ponds with plant cover.

**PIED-BILLED GREBE** *Podilymbus podiceps* 30–38cm (12–15in); 440g. **BEHAVIOR** Excellent diver. **DESCRIPTION** Grayish-brown, duck-like, with conical bill. **BREEDING ADULT** Black throat; bill with black band. **NON-BREEDING ADULT** White throat; bill lacks black band. **IMMATURE** Head mottled brown and white. **VOICE** Harsh cackle breaking into distinctive *kowp, kowp, kowp*, slowing at end. **STATUS AND RANGE** Throughout West Indies. Common year-round resident on Bahamas, Greater Antilles, Virgin Islands (uncommon and local on British islands), Cayman Islands, and northern Lesser Antilles south to Guadeloupe. Uncommon to rare in southern Lesser Antilles. Generally very rare or absent on smallest islands of West Indies. **HABITAT** Primarily fresh water, but also brackish and hypersaline lagoons.

NORTHERN JACANA

imm

adult

N American race

adult

AMERICAN COOT

adult

imm

Caribbean race

PURPLE GALLINULE

adult

imm

COMMON GALLINULE

adult

LEAST GREBE

non-br adult

br

PIED-BILL GREBE

non-br adult

imm

br

TDP

**COMMON LOON** *Gavia immer* 70–100cm (27–40in); 3–4kg. **BEHAVIOR** Excellent diver. **DESCRIPTION** Large water bird, similar to goose in size. Bill long, straight. **NON-BREEDING** Dark above, light below. **BREEDING** Dark head; upperparts with large white flecks. **FLIGHT** Head lower than body, legs extending beyond tail. **STATUS AND RANGE** Very rare migrant in Cuba late November–December. **HABITAT** Coastal wetlands.

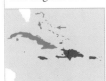

**DOUBLE-CRESTED CORMORANT** *Phalacrocorax auritus* 74–89cm (29–35in); 1.7kg. **BEHAVIOR** Sits with wings spread, dives, flocks. **DESCRIPTION** Large, with long neck and hooked bill. (Shorter tail than Neotropic Cormorant, especially noticeable in flight. Also decidedly smaller bulk and thinner bill.) **BREEDING ADULT** Black. Yellowish-orange skin at bill base and chin; small ear-tufts sometimes visible. **NON-BREEDING ADULT** Skin at bill base and chin paler orange; lacks ear-tufts. **IMMATURE** Brown; paler below; skin at bill base and chin pale yellowish-orange. **STATUS AND RANGE** Common year-round resident in Cuba and northern Bahamas. Uncommon non-breeding resident locally elsewhere in Bahamas and Hispaniola. Rare wanderer to Cayman Islands and Puerto Rico, occurring any month. Very rare wanderer to Jamaica and Virgin Islands. Vagrant to Lesser Antilles. Expanding range in region. **HABITAT** Inland and calm coastal waters. Frequents saltwater more than Neotropic Cormorant.

**NEOTROPIC CORMORANT** *Phalacrocorax brasilianus* 63–69cm (25–27in); 1.2kg. **BEHAVIOR** Sits with wings spread, dives, flocks. **DESCRIPTION** Large, black, with long neck and hooked bill. **BREEDING ADULT** Orangish-yellow base of bill and chin edged white. **NON-BREEDING ADULT** Base of bill yellowish, and white edge reduced or absent. **IMMATURE** Brown, paler below; base of bill pale yellow. **STATUS AND RANGE** Common year-round resident in Cuba, and locally in Bahamas. Non-breeding birds range more broadly, but generally very rare or vagrant elsewhere in West Indies. **HABITAT** Inland and calm coastal waters. Frequents fresh water more than Double-crested.

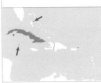

**ANHINGA** *Anhinga anhinga* 85cm (34in); 1.2kg. **BEHAVIOR** Sits with wings spread, dives. **DESCRIPTION** Large, with long neck, long tail, pointed bill, large whitish patches on back and upperwing. **ADULT MALE** Glossy black. **ADULT FEMALE** Head to breast light brown. **IMMATURE** Brown above; tan below. Resembles cormorant, but neck more snake-like, tail longer, and bill longer and pointed. **VOICE** Guttural croaking and clicking sounds. **STATUS AND RANGE** Common year-round resident in Cuba. Irregular visitor to Grand Cayman (Cayman Islands); a few birds on New Providence (Bahamas); very rare or vagrant elsewhere in West Indies. **HABITAT** Shallow calm waters.

**SNOW GOOSE** *Anser caerulescens* 58–71cm (23–28in); 2.5kg. **BEHAVIOR** Often grazes; flocks. **ADULT** Two color phases. White phase—Entirely white; black primaries; pink bill and legs. Dark phase—Bluish-gray; white head and upper neck; pink bill and legs. **STATUS AND RANGE** Rare migrant in northern Bahamas October–March. Very rare in Cuba and vagrant elsewhere in West Indies. Numbers increasing. **HABITAT** Borders of freshwater ponds and swamps, flooded uplands, croplands.

**CANADA GOOSE** *Branta canadensis* 64–110cm (25–43in); wingspan 1.2–1.8m (4–6ft); 1.5–6kg. **BEHAVIOR** Surface feeder, often grazes, flocks. **DESCRIPTION** Distinctive black head and neck, with white band on cheeks and throat. **FLIGHT** Dark wings with white band across uppertail-coverts. **STATUS AND RANGE** Formerly a vagrant, now occurring with greater frequency and thus very rare in northern Bahamas October–April. Vagrant to southern Bahamas, Cuba, Jamaica, Hispaniola, Puerto Rico, and Cayman Islands. **HABITAT** Wetland borders and grassy areas.

NEOTROPIC CORMORANT

non-br adult

br

imm

COMMON LOON

non-br adult

br

br

non-br adult

imm

DOUBLE-CRESTED
CORMORANT

adult ♀

imm

ANHINGA

adult ♂

dark
phase

white
phase

imm

adult ♀

imm

SNOW GOOSE

CANADA GOOSE

**MUSCOVY DUCK** *Cairina moschata* Male 86cm (34in), female 64cm (25in); 3–5kg. **BEHAVIOR** Surface feeder. **DESCRIPTION** A very large duck, variable in coloration. Wild state—Black overall with green cast and large white wing patch. Domesticated varieties—Varying amounts of white in plumage, some entirely white; bare face patch often red. **STATUS AND RANGE** Introduced widely in West Indies, where escaped birds now feral or semi-feral. Fairly common in Cuba, uncommon and local in Puerto Rico, Beef Island (Virgin Islands), and Martinique. **HABITAT** Ponds, often near farms or towns.

**NORTHERN SHOVELER** *Spatula clypeata* 43–53cm (17–21in); 620g. **BEHAVIOR** Surface feeder. **DESCRIPTION** Unusually large bill. **MALE** Green head, white breast, reddish-brown sides and belly. **FEMALE** Mottled brown. **STATUS AND RANGE** Migrant and non-breeding resident throughout West Indies primarily October–May. Common in Cuba and Jamaica; uncommon and local in Bahamas, Hispaniola, Puerto Rico, and Cayman Islands; rare and local in Virgin Islands. Generally rare to vagrant in Lesser Antilles. **HABITAT** Shallow wetlands. (*See also* Plate 33.)

**NORTHERN PINTAIL** *Anas acuta* Male 69–74cm (27–29in), female 54–56cm (21–22in); male 1040g, female 990g. **BEHAVIOR** Surface feeder. **FEMALE AND NON-BREEDING MALE** Mottled brown; pointed tail; long, slender neck; gray bill. **BREEDING MALE** Brown head; white breast and neck stripe; long, pointed tail. **STATUS AND RANGE** Common migrant and non-breeding resident in Cuba; uncommon in Puerto Rico; rare in Bahamas, Jamaica, Hispaniola, Virgin Islands, St Bartholomew, Guadeloupe, and Barbados. Very rare in Cayman Islands and vagrant elsewhere in West Indies. Occurs September–April. **HABITAT** Shallow wetlands. (*See also* Plate 33.)

**MALLARD** *Anas platyrhynchos* 51–71cm (20–28in); 750–1500g. **BEHAVIOR** Surface feeder. **DESCRIPTION** Large, with blue speculum edged white. **NON-BREEDING MALE AND IMMATURE** Mottled brown overall, olive bill. **ADULT FEMALE** Bill orange with black markings. **BREEDING MALE** Green head, yellow bill, maroon breast. **STATUS AND RANGE** Very rare migrant and non-breeding resident October–April in northern Bahamas, Cuba, and Puerto Rico. Vagrant elsewhere in West Indies. **HABITAT** Calm, shallow waters. (*See also* Plate 33.)

**AMERICAN WIGEON** *Mareca americana* 46–56cm (18–22in); 500–1300g. **BEHAVIOR** Surface feeder. **MALE** White crown, light blue bill, green eye-patch. Brownish; gray head; light blue bill. **STATUS AND RANGE** Migrant and less frequent non-breeding resident throughout West Indies principally October–April. Common in Cuba; fairly common in Jamaica and Hispaniola; uncommon in Bahamas, Puerto Rico, Virgin and Cayman Islands; rare in Lesser Antilles south to Barbados; vagrant elsewhere in West Indies. **HABITAT** Shallow wetlands. (*See also* Plate 33.)

**EURASIAN WIGEON** *Mareca penelope* 42–52cm (16.5–20in); 500–1000g. **BEHAVIOR** Surface feeder. **MALE** Dark reddish-brown head; cream-colored crown stripe; pinkish breast. **FEMALE** Gray phase—Brownish; gray head; light blue bill. Red phase—Similar; reddish tint to head and neck. (Gray phase female similar to American Wigeon but head darker gray. Red phase female decidedly redder on head. Both Eurasian phases have blackish flecks in wingpits.) **STATUS AND RANGE** Very rare in West Indies October–February. **HABITAT** Freshwater ponds. (*See also* Plate 33.)

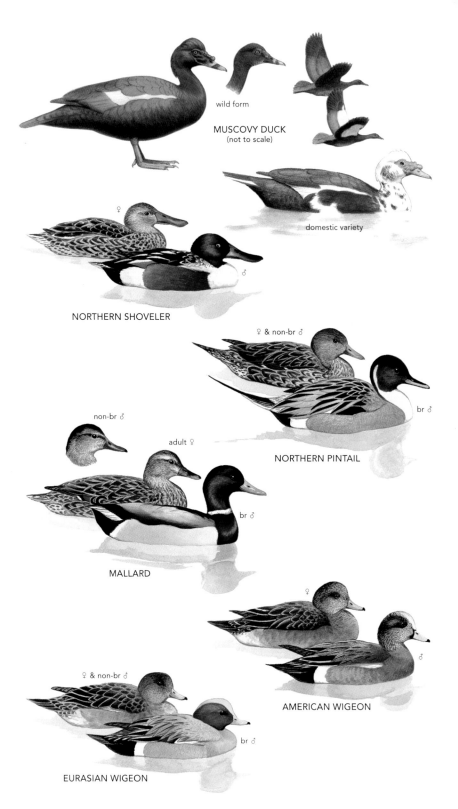

wild form

MUSCOVY DUCK
(not to scale)

domestic variety

♀

♂

NORTHERN SHOVELER

♀ & non-br ♂

br ♂

NORTHERN PINTAIL

non-br ♂

adult ♀

br ♂

MALLARD

♀

♂

AMERICAN WIGEON

♀ & non-br ♂

br ♂

EURASIAN WIGEON

**GADWALL** *Mareca strepera* 46–57cm (18–22.5in); 800–1000g. **BEHAVIOR** Surface feeder. **DESCRIPTION** White speculum. **MALE** Mottled gray; rump black; head dark brown. **FEMALE** Mottled brown; whitish belly; bill slightly orange with dark gray ridge. (Female Mallard has whitish tail and blue speculum. Female American Wigeon has light blue bill and green speculum.) **STATUS AND RANGE** Rare migrant and non-breeding resident in Bahamas; very rare in Cuba and Puerto Rico. Increasing in numbers. Occurs October–March. Vagrant elsewhere. **HABITAT** Freshwater wetlands. (*See also* Plate 33.)

**BLUE-WINGED TEAL** *Spatula discors* 38–40cm (15–16in); 300–400g. **BEHAVIOR** Surface feeder. **DESCRIPTION** Small, with blue forewing. **FEMALE AND NON-BREEDING MALE** Mottled brown; speculum green; very similar to female and non-breeding male Green-winged Teal, but Blue-winged has light spot on lores and a darker belly, lacks pale patch beneath tail, and has yellow legs. **BREEDING MALE** White face crescent. **STATUS AND RANGE** Most common migrant and non-breeding duck in West Indies, primarily October–April. Uncommon only on St Christopher, Montserrat, Dominica, St Vincent, and Grenada. **HABITAT** Shallow wetlands. (*See also* Plate 33.)

**CINNAMON TEAL** *Spatula cyanoptera* 38–40cm (15–16in); 400g. **BEHAVIOR** Surface feeder. **FEMALE AND NON-BREEDING MALE** Mottled brown; speculum green. (Very similar female and non-breeding male Blue-winged Teal have light spot on lores, dark line through eye, and smaller bill; lack reddish tint to plumage, most notably on face.) **BREEDING MALE** Cinnamon-colored head and underparts. **STATUS AND RANGE** Very rare in Puerto Rico and vagrant elsewhere in West Indies. **HABITAT** Shallow ponds. (*See also* Plate 33.)

**GREEN-WINGED TEAL** *Anas crecca* 33–39cm (13–15.5in); 300–400g. **BEHAVIOR** Surface feeder. **DESCRIPTION** Small, with green speculum; lacks blue in forewing. **FEMALE AND NON-BREEDING MALE** Mottled brown; dark lores; whitish belly; pale patch beneath tail; dark legs. (*See* Blue-winged Teal.) **BREEDING MALE** Green eye-patch and speculum; reddish-brown head; white vertical bar in front of wing. Vagrant European race (*crecca*) lacks vertical bar; has horizontal white stripe on wing edge. **STATUS AND RANGE** Uncommon and local migrant and non-breeding resident in northern Bahamas, Cuba, and Puerto Rico; rare in southern Bahamas, Jamaica, Virgin and Cayman Islands, Guadeloupe, and Barbados; very rare to vagrant in rest of Lesser Antilles and Hispaniola. Occurs October–March. **HABITAT** Shallow fresh water. (*See also* Plate 33.)

GADWALL

BLUE-WINGED TEAL

CINNAMON TEAL

GREEN-WINGED TEAL

**REDHEAD** *Aythya americana* 46–56cm (18–22in); 1kg. **BEHAVIOR** Dives, flocks. **DESCRIPTION** Steep forehead; blue bill tipped black. **MALE** Pale gray back and black neck contrast with rounded reddish head. Black breast and rump. **FEMALE** Dull brown. **STATUS AND RANGE** Very rare migrant and non-breeding resident in Bahamas and Cuba November–March. Vagrant elsewhere. **HABITAT** Ponds and lagoons. (*See also* Plate 34.)

**RING-NECKED DUCK** *Aythya collaris* 40–46cm (16–18in); 700g. **BEHAVIOR** Dives, flocks. **MALE** White bill-ring, black back, and white vertical bar in front of wing. **FEMALE** Light bill-ring and eye-ring, sometimes a trailing white streak between cheek and crown. **STATUS AND RANGE** Common migrant and non-breeding resident in Cuba, locally common in northern Bahamas; uncommon to locally common in Cayman Islands; uncommon in Jamaica, Puerto Rico, and Virgin Islands; rare in southern Bahamas, Hispaniola, Guadeloupe, Barbados, and San Andrés; vagrant elsewhere. Occurs October–March. **HABITAT** Open freshwater. (*See also* Plate 34.)

**GREATER SCAUP** *Aythya marila* 38–51cm (15–20in); 800–1300g. **BEHAVIOR** Dives, flocks. **MALE** Head iridescent green, appears black at distance, smoothly rounded or slightly flat-topped. Bill pale blue with wide black nail on tip. (Adult male Lesser Scaup has more peaked head profile, deep purple iridescence on head, a narrow black-tipped bill, and white confined to the secondaries in flight.) **FEMALE** White around base of bill reaches forehead. Dark brown sides and rump. **STATUS AND RANGE** Very rare southbound migrant in Bahamas and Virgin Islands (St Croix) September–February. Vagrant elsewhere. **HABITAT** Open bays. (*See also* Plate 34.)

**LESSER SCAUP** *Aythya affinis* 38–46cm (15–18in); 500–1000g. **BEHAVIOR** Dives, flocks. **MALE** Dark head, breast, and tail; whitish back and flanks. **FEMALE** Brown; large white mark behind bill. (Greater Scaup has rounder head and broader bill tip.) **STATUS AND RANGE** Through West Indies, where fairly common, but local migrant and non-breeding resident in Bahamas, Cuba, and Cayman Islands; uncommon and local in Jamaica, Hispaniola, and Puerto Rico. Rare in Virgin Islands, Anguilla, Guadeloupe, Barbados, and San Andrés; very rare in most of Lesser Antilles. Occurs November–March. **HABITAT** Open bays. (*See also* Plate 34.)

**HOODED MERGANSER** *Lophodytes cucullatus* 40–48cm (16–19in); 600g. **BEHAVIOR** Dives. **DESCRIPTION** Crest; slender, hooked bill. **MALE** Crest has large white patch. **FEMALE** Dark plumage and bill; bill dull orange near base. (Larger but similar female Red-breasted Merganser has darker face, bill, and back.) **STATUS AND RANGE** Decidedly rare migrant to northern Bahamas, particularly Grand Bahama, and to Cuba. Very rare in Puerto Rico. Vagrant elsewhere in West Indies. Occurs November–February. **HABITAT** Inland ponds, lagoons. (*See also* Plate 34.)

**RED-BREASTED MERGANSER** *Mergus serrator* 51–64cm (20–25in); 1kg. **BEHAVIOR** Dives. **DESCRIPTION** Crest; slender, hooked bill. **MALE** Green head, white collar, dark breast. **FEMALE** Reddish-brown head and bill; whitish chin, foreneck, and breast; gray back. Differs from Hooded Merganser by lighter face and back, reddish bill. **STATUS AND RANGE** Rare migrant in northern Bahamas and Cuba (locally common around north-central cays) November and March; decidedly rare and irregular in Cayman Islands and very rare in southern Bahamas and Puerto Rico. Vagrant elsewhere. **HABITAT** Open bays, ocean near shore, inland lagoons. (*See also* Plate 34.)

REDHEAD

RING-NECKED DUCK

GREATER SCAUP

LESSER SCAUP

HOODED MERGANSER

RED-BREASTED MERGANSER

**M** **WEST INDIAN WHISTLING-DUCK** *Dendrocygna arborea* 48–56cm (19–22in); 1.2kg.
**BEHAVIOR** Flocks, primarily nocturnal, surface feeder, often grazes. **DESCRIPTION** Deep
brown; white abdomen with black markings; erect stance. **VOICE** Shrill whistle, *chiriria*.
**STATUS AND RANGE** Locally common year-round resident in Cuba, Antigua, and Cayman
Islands; uncommon and local in Bahamas, Jamaica, Dominican Republic, Puerto Rico,
and Guadeloupe; rare and local visitor in U.S. Virgin Islands and Barbados. Vagrant
elsewhere. Threatened. These islands comprise entire range. **HABITAT** Mangroves, savannas,
wooded swamps, lagoons. (*See also* Plate 35.)

**FULVOUS WHISTLING-DUCK** *Dendrocygna bicolor* 46–51cm (18–20in); 700g.
**BEHAVIOR** Flocks, surface feeder, often grazes. **DESCRIPTION** Pale yellowish-brown with thin
white side stripe, white uppertail-coverts, erect stance. **VOICE** Squealing whistle, *puteow*.
**STATUS AND RANGE** Fairly common year-round resident in Cuba; uncommon and local in
Hispaniola. Rare and irregular migrant and non-breeding resident in Bahamas, Puerto Rico,
Cayman Islands, St Bartholomew, Antigua, and Barbados. Very rare wanderer or vagrant
elsewhere. Extending range eastward. **HABITAT** Fresh water with emergent plants, rice fields.
(*See also* Plate 35.)

**BLACK-BELLIED WHISTLING-DUCK** *Dendrocygna autumnalis* 46–53cm (18–21in);
850g. **BEHAVIOR** Fairly nocturnal, surface feeder, sometimes grazes, flocks. **ADULT** White
wing patch; black belly; reddish bill and legs. **VOICE** Shrill, chattering whistle. **STATUS AND
RANGE** Fairly common breeding resident on Barbados. Rare and very local year-round
resident on Cuba, where increasing. Rare visitor in northern Bahamas, Cayman Islands,
Antigua, Guadeloupe, and Grenada. A very rare wanderer or vagrant elsewhere, but range
and numbers expanding. **HABITAT** Freshwater and brackish lagoons. (*See also* Plate 35.)

**WHITE-CHEEKED PINTAIL** *Anas bahamensis* 38–48cm (15–19in); 550g. **BEHAVIOR**
Surface feeder, flocks. **DESCRIPTION** Red bill mark; white cheek. Speculum green, edged
tan. **STATUS AND RANGE** Locally common year-round resident in Bahamas, Cuba, Puerto
Rico, Virgin Islands, and Antigua; locally uncommon in Hispaniola and Guadeloupe;
uncommon to rare visitor in most northern Lesser Antilles and Barbados. Vagrant
elsewhere. Threatened in West Indies. **HABITAT** Calm, shallow waters. (*See also* Plate 35.)

**RUDDY DUCK** *Oxyura jamaicensis* 35–43cm (14–17in); 550g. **BEHAVIOR** Tail often erect,
dives, flocks. **MALE** Overall reddish-brown; white cheek patch; blue bill. **FEMALE AND
IMMATURE** Mostly brown; single brown stripe below eye. (Female Masked Duck has two
dark facial stripes.) **STATUS AND RANGE** Locally common year-round resident in New Providence (Bahamas), Jamaica, and Puerto Rico; uncommon and local year-round resident
elsewhere in Bahamas, Cuba, Hispaniola, and Virgin Islands. Irregular, generally uncommon visitor to Anguilla, St Martin, Antigua, and Guadeloupe; rare visitor to Cayman
Islands, Barbados, and Grenada. May breed on some of these islands. Very rare or vagrant
elsewhere. Often occurs in numbers. Migrants augment local populations October to
March. **HABITAT** Deep, open freshwater bodies; also brackish lagoons. (*See also* Plate 35.)

**MASKED DUCK** *Nomonyx dominicus* 30–36cm (12–14in); 370g. Difficult to detect.
**BEHAVIOR** Erect tail, dives. **DESCRIPTION** White wing patch. **BREEDING MALE** Black face;
reddish-brown coloration; blue bill. **NON-BREEDING MALE, FEMALE, AND IMMATURE** Two
brown facial stripes; white wing patch. **STATUS AND RANGE** Fairly common year-round
resident in Jamaica and Barbados; uncommon and local year-round resident in Cuba,
Hispaniola, and Puerto Rico; rare in Guadeloupe, Martinique, and Grand Anse in St Lucia.
Very rare or absent elsewhere. Threatened. **HABITAT** Dense vegetation of freshwater swamps
and rice fields. (*See also* Plate 35.)

**WOOD DUCK** *Aix sponsa* 43–51cm (17–20in); 650g. **BEHAVIOR** Surface feeder.
**DESCRIPTION** Crest. **MALE** Unusual facial pattern. **FEMALE** Asymmetrical eye-ring.
**VOICE** Male—Thin but emphatic *zweeeet!* increasing in intensity. Female—Squawking *oo-
eeek*, very unduck-like. **STATUS AND RANGE** Uncommon year-round resident in Cuba. Rare
migrant and non-breeding resident in northern Bahamas October–March. Vagrant
elsewhere. **HABITAT** Canals, lagoons, and impoundments. (*See also* Plate 35.)

WEST INDIAN
WHISTLING-DUCK

FULVOUS
WHISTLING-DUCK

BLACK-BELLIED
WHISTLING-DUCK

WHITE-CHEEKED PINTAIL

♀ & imm

non-br ♂

br ♂

RUDDY DUCK

non-br ♂
♀ & imm

br ♂

MASKED DUCK

♀

♂

WOOD DUCK

**NORTHERN SHOVELER** *Spatula clypeata* 43–53cm (17–21in); 620g. Large bill; green speculum; blue patch on forewing. **MALE** Green head; white breast; reddish-brown sides and belly. **FEMALE** Mottled brown. (*See also* Plate 29.)

**NORTHERN PINTAIL** *Anas acuta* Male 69–74cm (27–29in), female 54–56cm (21–22in); male 1040g, female 990g. Long, slender neck; pointed tail. **FEMALE AND NON-BREEDING MALE** White border on trailing edge of brown speculum; gray underwing contrasts with white belly. **BREEDING MALE** Greenish speculum, pale tan inner border; white trailing edge. (*See also* Plate 29.)

**MALLARD** *Anas platyrhynchos* 51–71cm (20–28in); 750–1500g. Blue speculum with white borders. **ADULT FEMALE** Mottled brown. **BREEDING MALE** Green head; maroon breast. (*See also* Plate 29.)

**EURASIAN WIGEON** *Mareca penelope* 42–52cm (16.5–20in); 500–1000g. White patches on forewing; green speculum; white belly; blackish flecks in wingpits. **MALE** Dark reddish-brown head; cream-colored crown stripe. **FEMALE** Brownish; gray or reddish head. (*See also* Plate 29.)

**AMERICAN WIGEON** *Mareca americana* 46–56cm (18–22in); 500–1300g. White patch on forewing; green speculum; white belly. (*See also* Plate 29.)

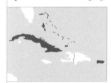

**GADWALL** *Mareca strepera* 46–57 cm (18–22.5in); 800–1000g. White speculum. **MALE** Mottled gray above; black rump; dark brown head. **FEMALE** Mottled brown; white belly. (*See also* Plate 30.)

**BLUE-WINGED TEAL** *Spatula discors* 38–40cm (15–16in); 300–400g. Small, with blue forewing; green speculum. **FEMALE AND NON-BREEDING MALE** Mottled brown; darkish belly. **BREEDING MALE** White crescent on face. (*See also* Plate 30.)

**CINNAMON TEAL** *Spatula cyanoptera* 38–40cm (15–16in); 400g. Light blue forewing; green speculum. **BREEDING MALE** Cinnamon head and underparts. **FEMALE AND NON-BREEDING MALE** Similar to female Blue-winged Teal (not illustrated). (*See also* Plate 30.)

**GREEN-WINGED TEAL** *Anas crecca* 33–39cm (13–15.5in); 300–400g. Small. Green speculum; lacks blue in forewing. **FEMALE AND NON-BREEDING MALE** Mottled brown; whitish belly. **BREEDING MALE** Green eye-patch; reddish-brown head; whitish belly. (*See also* Plate 30.)

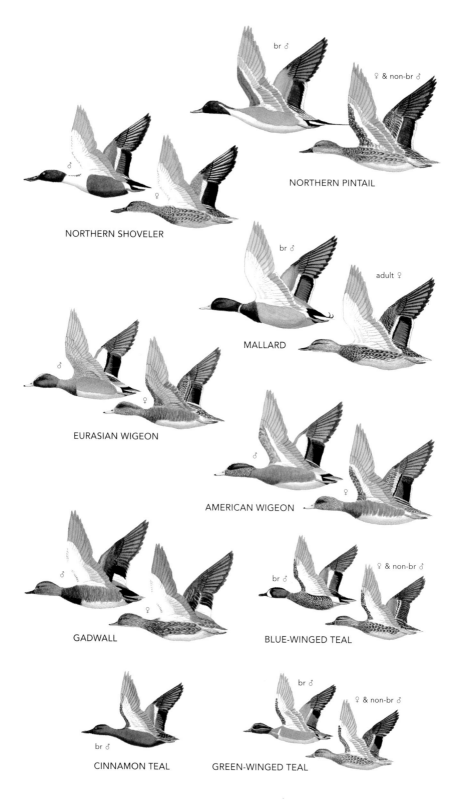

br ♂

♀ & non-br ♂

NORTHERN PINTAIL

♂

♀

NORTHERN SHOVELER

br ♂

adult ♀

MALLARD

♂

♀

EURASIAN WIGEON

♂

♀

AMERICAN WIGEON

♂

♀

GADWALL

br ♂

♀ & non-br ♂

BLUE-WINGED TEAL

br ♂

CINNAMON TEAL

br ♂

♀ & non-br ♂

GREEN-WINGED TEAL

**REDHEAD** *Aythya americana* 46–56cm (18–22in); 1kg. MALE Gray back and black neck contrast with reddish head. FEMALE Dull brown; white eye-ring; blue band around black-tipped bill. (*See also* Plate 31.)

**RING-NECKED DUCK** *Aythya collaris* 40–46cm (16–18in); 700g. Dark upperwing-coverts contrast with pale gray secondaries. MALE Underparts contrast black and white. FEMALE Underparts contrast brown and white. (*See also* Plate 31.)

**GREATER SCAUP** *Aythya marila* 38–51cm (15–20in); 800–1300g. White secondaries and inner primaries. White belly and abdomen. MALE White sides and flanks. FEMALE Brown sides and flanks. (*See also* Plate 31.)

**LESSER SCAUP** *Aythya affinis* 38–46cm (15–18in); 500–1000g. White secondaries and black primaries. White belly and abdomen. MALE White sides and flanks. FEMALE Brown sides and flanks. (*See also* Plate 31.)

**HOODED MERGANSER** *Lophodytes cucullatus* 40–48cm (16–19in); 600g. Crest; dark upperparts; small white patch on secondaries. MALE Pale forewing. (*See also* Plate 31.)

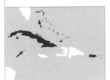

**RED-BREASTED MERGANSER** *Mergus serrator* 51–64cm (20–25in); 1kg. Crest. MALE White secondaries and forewing, crossed by two bars. FEMALE White secondaries, crossed by one bar. (*See also* Plate 31.)

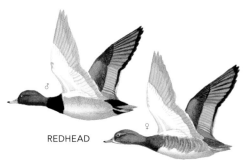

REDHEAD

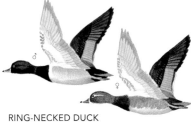

RING-NECKED DUCK

GREATER SCAUP

LESSER SCAUP

HOODED MERGANSER

RED-BREASTED MERGANSER

**BLACK-BELLIED WHISTLING-DUCK** *Dendrocygna autumnalis* 46–53cm (18–21in); 850g. Large white upperwing patch; black belly; reddish bill and legs. Head and feet droop; feet trail beyond tail. (*See also* Plate 32.)

**FULVOUS WHISTLING-DUCK** *Dendrocygna bicolor* 46–51cm (18–20in); 700g. Pale yellowish-brown; white stripe at wing base; white rump; dark wings; reddish-brown upperwing-coverts. Head and feet droop; feet extend beyond tail. (*See also* Plate 32.)

Ⓜ **WEST INDIAN WHISTLING-DUCK** *Dendrocygna arborea* 48–56cm (19–22in); 1.2kg. Dark overall; black-and-white abdomen; gray upperwing-coverts. Head and feet droop; feet extend beyond tail. (*See also* Plate 32.)

**WOOD DUCK** *Aix sponsa* 43–51cm (17–20in); 650g. Long, squared tail; large head; bill tilted down. MALE White throat. FEMALE White eye-patch. (*See also* Plate 32.)

**WHITE-CHEEKED PINTAIL** *Anas bahamensis* 38–48cm (15–19in); 550g. Red bill mark, white cheek; green speculum edged tan. (*See also* Plate 32.)

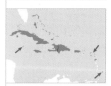

**RUDDY DUCK** *Oxyura jamaicensis* 35–43cm (14–17in); 550g. Chunky body; long tail; dark upperwings. BREEDING MALE White cheek. FEMALE AND IMMATURE Cheek stripe. (*See also* Plate 32.)

**MASKED DUCK** *Nomonyx dominicus* 30–36cm (12–14in); 370g. Chunky body; white wing patch; long tail. BREEDING MALE Reddish-brown, with black face. NON-BREEDING MALE, FEMALE, AND IMMATURE Brown; two dark stripes on face. (*See also* Plate 32.)

BLACK-BELLIED WHISTLING DUCK

FULVOUS WHISTLING DUCK

WEST INDIAN WHISTLING DUCK

WOOD DUCK

WHITE-CHEEKED PINTAIL

RUDDY DUCK

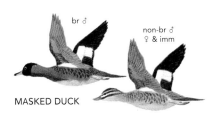

MASKED DUCK

**Falcons:** Possess slender, pointed wings and long, narrow tails. They are swift fliers and rarely soar.

**Hawks:** Possess broad wings with rounded tips. Those with relatively shorter, fan-shaped tails and broader wings tend to soar more frequently.

**[H] RIDGWAY'S HAWK** *Buteo ridgwayi* 36–41cm (14–16in); wingspan 50–66cm (20–26in); 280–450g. ADULT Dark brownish-gray upperparts; underparts gray washed with brownish-red; thighs reddish-brown; tail barred black and white. ADULT MALE Grayer than female, with bright reddish-brown bend of wing. ADULT FEMALE Browner overall; drab brown bend of wing; lighter breast with more barring, more heavily barred tail. (Broad-winged Hawk with wide, bold tail bands.) IMMATURE Pale tan below with heavy streaks. VOICE Whistled *kleeah*. STATUS AND RANGE Endemic to Hispaniola, where rare and very local. Most numerous in Los Haitises National Park and east. Extirpated from Haiti. Critically endangered. HABITAT Forested foothills, wet limestone forest, and mixed savanna-woodland-palm habitat. (*See also* Plate 42.)

**SHORT-TAILED HAWK** *Buteo brachyurus* 39cm (15.5in); wingspan 92cm (3ft); 425g. A small, chunky hawk with broad wings and a short, banded tail, fanned in flight. White phase—Entirely white underparts including wing linings. Dark phase—Entirely black underparts including wing linings. (Cuban Black Hawk is much larger and has much broader tail bands.) Often soars very high to hang motionless. STATUS AND RANGE An uncommon and very local migrant along coast of western Cuba, particularly extreme western tip (Cabo de San Antonio), September–October. HABITAT Occurs flying over coastal habitat regardless of type.

**MERLIN** *Falco columbarius* 25–34cm (10–13.5in); wingspan 64cm (2ft); male 160g, female 220g. Small falcon. Upperparts dark gray in male, dark brown in female. Underparts heavily streaked, tail barred black. Pale eyebrow stripe. FLIGHT Fast and agile. Pointed wings; long, narrow tail. STATUS AND RANGE Migrant throughout West Indies primarily in October. Somewhat scarcer as non-breeding resident until April. Common in Bahamas, Cuba, and Jamaica; fairly common in Cayman Islands; uncommon in Hispaniola, Puerto Rico, and Virgin Islands; rare in Lesser Antilles. HABITAT Coastal lakes and lagoons where shorebirds abound, also open and semi-open areas, woodlands, and forests.

**PEREGRINE FALCON** *Falco peregrinus* 36–58cm (14–23in); wingspan 75–120cm (29–47in); male 600g, female 1kg. Large, with pointed wings, long, narrow tail, and mask-like head pattern. ADULT Dark gray above; cream-colored with dark bars below. IMMATURE Brown above; underparts cream-colored with heavy brown streaks. FLIGHT Fast, powerful, and agile. Wings pointed and tail narrow. STATUS AND RANGE Generally uncommon to rare and local migrant and non-breeding resident through West Indies primarily October–April, but fairly common in Cayman Islands. A few breed in West Indies. HABITAT Offshore cays and rocks with seabirds, wetlands with shorebirds or waterfowl. Sometimes inland, including high buildings and church steeples.

**AMERICAN KESTREL** *Falco sparverius* 23–30cm (9–12in); wingspan 51–61in (20–24in); male 80–140g, female 85–165g. Small falcon, with reddish-brown back (except dark phase of Cuban race *F. s. sparveroides*, which is dark gray). Reddish tail with broad black terminal band; two black facial bars. Underparts vary between races from white to reddish-brown. ADULT MALE Blue-gray wings. ADULT FEMALE Reddish-brown wings. IMMATURE Dark breast streaks. FLIGHT Pointed wings; long, slender tail; hovers. VOICE High-pitched *killi-killi-killi*. STATUS AND RANGE Occurs through West Indies, where common permanent resident in Bahamas, Greater Antilles, Virgin Islands, and Lesser Antilles south to St Lucia. Rare to very rare farther south and on San Andrés. Migrants augment local numbers in Bahamas and Cuba October–April. An uncommon to fairly common migrant and non-breeding resident in Cayman Islands these months. HABITAT Dry, open lowlands with adequate perches and palm savannas. Also towns and forest edges in mountains.

RIDGEWAY'S HAWK

imm

adult ♂

dark phase imm

dark phase adult

white phase imm

SHORT-TAILED HAWK

white phase adult

white phase imm

MERLIN

♀

♂

PEREGRINE FALCON

imm

adult

adult ♀ Hispaniola race

AMERICAN KESTREL

adult ♀

adult ♂

Cuba, Bahamas, Jamaica race

Hispaniola race

**Kites:** A group of hawks with relatively narrow wings and tail. Several specialize on eating snails.

**HOOK-BILLED KITE** *Chondrohierax uncinatus* 38–43cm (15–17in); wingspan 90cm (3ft); 280g. Chunky. Bill large and deeply hooked; large oval wings prominently barred beneath; long, banded tail. Plumage variable. **ADULT MALE** Light phase—Dark gray; gray or finely gray-barred underparts. **ADULT FEMALE** Light phase—Dark brown; reddish-brown barring below; tan hindneck. **ADULT MALE AND FEMALE** Black phase—Solid black; tail with one broad white band. **IMMATURE** Light phase—White cheeks, hindneck, and underparts; breast, thighs, and tail barred. Black phase—Dark blue above, dark brown wings flecked white, streaked breast. **VOICE** Two to three whistled notes, also shrill scream. **STATUS AND RANGE** Uncommon and local permanent resident in southwest and northeast Grenada. Critically endangered in West Indies. **HABITAT** Dry forest. (*See also* Plate 42.)

C **CUBAN KITE** *Chondrohierax wilsonii* 38–43cm (15–17in). Large and robust, with massive, yellowish hooked bill and long, banded tail. **ADULT MALE** Typically dark gray with gray or finely gray-barred underparts. **ADULT FEMALE** Generally dark brown; underparts coarsely barred, reddish; tan hindneck. **IMMATURE** Bicolored black above, white below, white hindneck. **STATUS AND RANGE** Endemic to Cuba, where confined to northeast. Nearly extinct. Critically endangered. Some consider this a subspecies of Hook-billed Kite. **HABITAT** Tall trees of forests bordering rivers below 500m (1640ft). (*See also* Plate 42.)

**SWALLOW-TAILED KITE** *Elanoides forficatus* 51–66cm (20–26in); wingspan 1.2m (4ft); 440g. **BEHAVIOR** Flocks. **DESCRIPTION** Bicolored; long, deeply forked tail. White head and underparts contrast with black back, wings, and tail. **FLIGHT** When hunting glides slowly close to ground with steady wings but tail constantly balancing. **STATUS AND RANGE** Irregular year to year, but generally a common migrant locally along coast in Cuba, often in numbers; uncommon in Cayman Islands; rare in Jamaica and northern Bahamas; apparently rare in San Andrés and Providencia; very rare or vagrant elsewhere. Occurs primarily August–October, but a few birds remain to April. **HABITAT** Coastal swamps, savannas, and river mouths.

**SNAIL KITE** *Rostrhamus sociabilis* 43–48cm (17–19in); wingspan 1.1m (3.5ft); 430g. White rump; slender bill conspicuously hooked. Red legs, eyes, and lores. (Similar Northern Harrier has long, narrower wings and gliding, tilting flight.) **ADULT MALE** Blackish. **ADULT FEMALE** Brown above; white below, heavily streaked with brown; white eyebrow stripe. **VOICE** Raspy, ratchet-like *ge-ge-ge-ge*. **STATUS AND RANGE** Common permanent resident in Cuba. **HABITAT** Freshwater marshes, open swamps, reservoirs, rice fields, and canals. (*See also* Plate 41.)

**MISSISSIPPI KITE** *Ictinia mississippiensis* 30–37cm (12–15in); wingspan 80cm (31 in); 280g. **BEHAVIOR** Often flocks. **ADULT** Gray overall, paler below with very pale gray head. Tail black. **IMMATURE** Brownish above, heavily streaked below. Tail banded. **FLIGHT** Slender, pointed wings and long tail. Secondaries white from above. Captures and eats prey on the wing. **STATUS AND RANGE** A fairly common migrant very locally at the western tip of Cuba (San Antonio), where sometimes seen in numbers. Occurs July–December with peaks in July, and late September–October. Probably rare in San Andrés and Providencia, but status uncertain. A vagrant elsewhere in West Indies. **HABITAT** Lowland forests, savannas, and swamps.

HOOK-BILLED KITE

CUBAN KITE

♀

light phase
adult

light phase
adult

♂

adult ♂

adult ♀

SNAIL KITE

adult ♂

SWALLOW-TAILED KITE

adult ♀

imm

adult

adult

imm

MISSISSIPPI KITE

**NORTHERN HARRIER** *Circus hudsonius* 46–61cm (18–24in); wingspan 1–1.2m (3–4ft); male 360g, female 510g. Large, with long, slender wings and tail; white rump. **ADULT MALE** Grayish-blue. **ADULT FEMALE** Brown above; white below, heavily streaked with brown. **IMMATURE** Brown above; entirely reddish-brown below with dark brown streaks on breast. **FLIGHT** Low over ground with heavy flaps and distinctive tilting glides, wings held well above horizontal. **STATUS AND RANGE** Irregular, but occurs through most of West Indies. Generally an uncommon and local migrant and non-breeding resident primarily October–April in Bahamas and Cuba. Rare in Hispaniola, Puerto Rico, Virgin and Cayman Islands, and Lesser Antilles. Very rare and local in Jamaica. **HABITAT** Marshes, swamps, open savannas, and rice fields.

**RED-TAILED HAWK** *Buteo jamaicensis* 48–64cm (19–25in); wingspan 1.2m (4ft); male 1kg, female 1.2kg. Large. **ADULT** Dark brown above; pale below, dark belly stripes; tail reddish. **IMMATURE** Tail faintly barred grayish-brown; more heavily streaked underparts. **VOICE** Raspy *keeer-r-r-r*, slurring downward. **STATUS AND RANGE** Common permanent resident on larger islands of northern Bahamas, Greater Antilles, Virgin Islands, St Bartholomew, Saba, St Christopher, and Nevis; rare on St Eustatius. Vagrant elsewhere. **HABITAT** Open country, woodlands, forests, towns, at all elevations. (*See also* Plate 41.)

**SWAINSON'S HAWK** *Buteo swainsoni* 43–56cm (17–22in); wingspan 1.3m (4.3ft); male 900g, female 1070g. Large. Light phase—white below with broad, brown "bib" across breast. Banded tail has broader subterminal band. Vast majority of birds possess this coloration. Dark phase—partially or entirely dark brown, but tail similar to light phase. Intermediate phase—variable, between light and dark phases. **FLIGHT** Often soars. Wings fairly broad (less than Red-tailed) and tail fanned. Light phase—distinctive white wing linings contrast with dark flight feathers. Dark phase—partially or entirely dark below except for banded tail. **STATUS AND RANGE** An irregular and generally uncommon and local migrant in Cuba, primarily along western coast July–September, but also other coastal areas including Zapata Peninsula and Guantánamo Bay. Sometimes occurs in numbers. Vagrant elsewhere in West Indies. **HABITAT** Occurs flying over coastal habitat regardless of type.

adult ♂

adult ♀

adult ♂

NORTHERN HARRIER

RED-TAILED HAWK

adult

imm

intermediate
phase adult

light phase
adult

imm

dark phase adult

SWAINSON'S HAWK

imm

light
phase
adult

**BROAD-WINGED HAWK** *Buteo platypterus* 34–44cm (13–17in); wingspan 86cm (34in); male 420g, female 490g. Medium-sized, chunky. **ADULT** Tail boldly banded black and white; underparts barred reddish-brown. (Red-tailed Hawk much larger; white breast with dark belly streaks. Sharp-shinned and Gundlach's Hawks have similar color pattern but with long, narrow tail lacking bold bands.) **IMMATURE** Underparts white, streaked dark brown; tail bands more numerous, but less distinct. **VOICE** Thin, shrill squeal, *pweeeeeeeeee*. **STATUS AND RANGE** Common permanent resident in Cuba, Antigua, and Dominica south to Grenada, though absent in Barbados; generally rare and very local in Puerto Rico (though common in karst of Río Abajo). Uncommon on St Christopher, where likely migrant, and decidedly rare in Virgin Islands. Vagrant in Hispaniola. Migrants augment numbers in western Cuba August–May. Puerto Rico race threatened. **HABITAT** Dense broadleaf, mixed, and plantation forests at all elevations, less frequently open woodlands. Open woodlands and towns in Antigua. (*See also* Plate 42.)

**C GUNDLACH'S HAWK** *Accipiter gundlachi* 43–51cm (17–20in); wingspan 74–84 cm (29–33in); female 675g. Chunky, medium-sized forest hawk. Relatively short, rounded wings. Long, narrow tail, rounded at tip, boldly barred with black. **ADULT** Upperparts dark steel-blue; underparts barred reddish-brown on belly, becoming gray and ranging from unbarred to heavily barred on breast. Throat pale gray and only lightly streaked. **IMMATURE** Brown above; lighter and heavily streaked dark brown below. (*See* Cooper's Hawk.) **VOICE** Loud, harsh cackling, *kek-kek-kek-kek* … **STATUS AND RANGE** Endemic to Cuba, where rare but widely distributed. Endangered. **HABITAT** Forest borders, swamps, wooded coasts, and mountains below 800m (2600ft). (*See also* Plate 42.)

**COOPER'S HAWK** *Accipiter cooperii* Male 35–46cm (14–18in), female 42–50cm (17–20in); wingspan 74–94cm (29–37in); male 220–440g, female 330–700g. Medium-sized forest hawk. Relatively short, rounded wings; long, narrow tail barred with black and rounded at tip. Very similar to Cuba's endemic Gundlach's Hawk, which can be distinguished only at close range. There is some overlap in the following traits: Cooper's throat, breast, and abdomen have white background. Gundlach's has gray background. Cooper's has sharper demarcation between white of throat and gray on side of neck, while Gundlach's blends from pale gray to dark gray. Gundlach's is more densely reddish-brown on the underparts, especially its leg feathers. **IMMATURE** Background of Gundlach's underparts is pale tan rather than white with broader and bolder reddish breast streaks. Cooper's has whiter background and finer streaks. **FLIGHT** Flaps and glides, soars in spirals in thermal updrafts (kettles) when migrating, particularly along coast. Gundlach's Hawk does not do this. Its underwing coverts are not as red as in Gundlach's. **STATUS AND RANGE** Rare and local migrant in Cuba along west coast primarily August–September. Not yet documented, but some may remain as non-breeding residents through winter. Probably overlooked due to similarity to resident Gundlach's Hawk. **HABITAT** Semi-deciduous forests, mangroves, and sometimes rural areas.

**SHARP-SHINNED HAWK** *Accipiter striatus* Male 24–27cm (9.5–10.5in), female 29–34cm (11.5–13.5in); wingspan male 42–58 (17–23in), female 58–68 (23–27in); male 80–115g, female 150–220g. A small forest hawk. Short, rounded wings; small head; long, narrow, squared-off tail, boldly barred with black. (Gundlach's Hawk is much larger and more robust. Broad-winged Hawk is larger, chunkier, with shorter, broadly banded tail and broader wings.) **ADULT** Dark steel-blue above; narrow reddish bars below. **FEMALE** Larger than male. **IMMATURE** Brown above; whitish below, streaked dark brown. **VOICE** Leisurely, high-pitched *que-que-que-que* … **STATUS AND RANGE** Increasingly uncommon and local permanent resident in Hispaniola, rare and increasingly local permanent resident in Cuba and Puerto Rico. A few migrants occur in Bahamas, Cuba, Jamaica, and Virgin Islands February–April. Migrants likely occur in Hispaniola and Puerto Rico. All local races endangered. **HABITAT** Mature mountain forests; sometimes coastal forests in Cuba. (*See also* Plate 42.)

BROAD-WINGED HAWK

Puerto Rico race

adult

imm

adult

imm

imm

adult

COOPER'S HAWK

imm

GUNDLACH'S HAWK

adult

SHARP-SHINNED HAWK

Puerto Rico race

imm

adult

**COMMON BLACK HAWK** *Buteogallus anthracinus* 51–58cm (20–23in); wingspan 1.3m (4.2ft); 930g. Large, stocky, relatively inactive black hawk with broad wings. **ADULT** Single broad white tail band. **IMMATURE** Underparts whitish, heavily streaked with black; tail with several narrow pale bands. **VOICE** Loud whistles. **STATUS AND RANGE** Common permanent resident in mountains and foothills on southern half of St Vincent. **HABITAT** Humid, moist, and dry forests, particularly along streams. (*See also* Plate 41.)

**C CUBAN BLACK HAWK** *Buteogallus gundlachii* 51–58cm (20–23in); 650g. Large, stocky, relatively inactive dark chocolate-brown hawk with broad wings. **ADULT** Single broad white tail band. **IMMATURE** Underparts whitish, heavily streaked with black; tail with several narrow pale bands. **VOICE** Nasal, whistled *ba-tis-taa*, and a harsh *haaaah*. **STATUS AND RANGE** Endemic to Cuba, where fairly common and widely distributed. **HABITAT** Cays, coastal forests, and open areas near swamps and beaches. (*See also* Plate 41.)

**CRESTED CARACARA** *Caracara cheriway* 50–63cm (19.5–25in); wingspan 1.1–1.3m (42–51in); 800–1300g. **BEHAVIOR** Often on ground with vultures. **DESCRIPTION** Large, crested head; large beak with reddish facial skin. **ADULT** Breast whitish and barred. **IMMATURE** Browner overall, breast tanner and streaked rather than barred. **FLIGHT** Contrasting white patches near wingtips. Flies like a crow. Soars with wings flat. **VOICE** Harsh, rattling *ca-ca-ca-ca*. **STATUS AND RANGE** Cuba, where widespread permanent resident but common only locally. **HABITAT** Semi-arid open country, including palm savannas, cut-over areas, and pastures.

**BLACK VULTURE** *Coragyps atratus* 58–68cm (23–26.5in); wingspan 1.4–1.6m (4.5–5.3ft); 2–3kg. Large, black, with very short tail. **FLIGHT** Labored, rapid flapping alternating with brief glides. Wings held horizontal; white wing patches. (Turkey Vulture lacks white wing patches, has a longer tail, and rocks as it soars, flapping only occasionally, with wings held well above horizontal.) **STATUS AND RANGE** Year-round resident locally on Andros (Bahamas). Rare migrant to Cuba. Vagrant to Grenada. **HABITAT** Open lowlands; also urban areas, particularly dumps.

**TURKEY VULTURE** *Cathartes aura* 68–80cm (27–32in); wingspan 1.6–1.8m (5.3–6ft); 1–2.4kg. Large, blackish-brown, with small bare head. **FLIGHT** Soars. Dark two-toned wings held well above horizontal in broad "V." **STATUS AND RANGE** Common and widespread permanent resident in Cuba and Jamaica; common but local in large northern Bahamas islands (Grand Bahama, Abaco, and Andros), southwestern and eastern Hispaniola (where range expanding), and western Puerto Rico (expanding eastward to Arecibo and Guayama). Vagrant elsewhere in West Indies. **HABITAT** Open areas at all elevations.

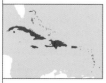

**OSPREY** *Pandion haliaetus* 53–61cm (21–24in); wingspan 1.5–1.8m (5–6ft); male 1.4kg, female 1.6kg. **BEHAVIOR** Hovers and dives for fish. **DESCRIPTION** Widespread migratory race (*P. h. carolinensis*)—White head, dark bar behind eye, contrast of primarily white underparts and dark upperparts. Resident race (*P. h. ridgwayi*)—Whiter head, only trace of eye-stripe. **FLIGHT** Wings characteristically bent at wrist, dark wrist patch. **VOICE** Piercing whistles. **STATUS AND RANGE** Resident race breeds commonly in southern Bahamas north to Exuma and Cat Islands, as well as on Cuba's offshore cays and in mangroves of Zapata Peninsula. Migrants and non-breeding residents occur throughout West Indies primarily September–April, though some remain throughout year. Common in Bahamas, Greater Antilles, and Virgin Islands; uncommon in Cayman Islands and Lesser Antilles. Migratory race breeds in Bahamas, Cuba, Puerto Rico, and St Lucia. Major migration through Cuba. **HABITAT** Margins of all calm freshwater or saltwater bodies.

adult

CUBAN BLACK HAWK

adult

imm

COMMON BLACK HAWK

CRESTED CARACARA

adult

BLACK VULTURE

OSPREY

imm

migratory race

TURKEY VULTURE

adult

resident race

**C** **CUBAN BLACK HAWK** *Buteogallus gundlachii* 51–58cm (20–23in); 930g. Large white patch at base of primaries; long legs dangle during flap-and-glide flight. Cuba. (*See also* Plate 40.)

**COMMON BLACK HAWK** *Buteogallus anthracinus* 51–58cm (20–23in); wingspan 1.3m (4.2ft); 930g. Large white patch at base of primaries; long legs dangle during flap-and-glide flight. St Vincent. (*See also* Plate 40.)

**SNAIL KITE** *Rostrhamus sociabilis* 43–48cm (17–19in); wingspan 1.1m (3.5ft); 430g. White rump; active, flapping flight passing slowly low to water. Cuba. (*See also* Plate 37.)

**RED-TAILED HAWK** *Buteo jamaicensis* 48–64cm (19–25in); wingspan 1.2m (4ft); male 1kg, female 1.2kg. Soars on broad, rounded wings and fanned tail. **ADULT** Reddish tail; pale underparts; dark belly band. **IMMATURE** Lightly barred tail; dark belly band less distinct. (*See also* Plate 38.)

adult

CUBAN BLACK HAWK

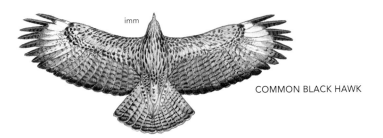

imm

COMMON BLACK HAWK

adult ♂

SNAIL KITE

adult ♀

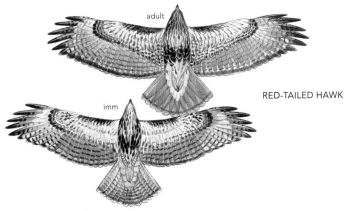

adult

RED-TAILED HAWK

imm

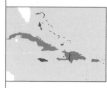

**SHARP-SHINNED HAWK** *Accipiter striatus* male 24–27cm (9.5–10.5in), female 29–34cm (11.5–13.5in); wingspan male 42–58cm (17–23in), female 58–68cm (23–27in); male 80–115g, female 150–220g. Short, rounded wings; long, narrow, squared-off tail. Flight rapid, alternately flapping and gliding, rarely soars. (*See also* Plate 39.)

**C GUNDLACH'S HAWK** *Accipiter gundlachi* 43–51cm (17–20in). Short, rounded wings; long, narrow tail, rounded at tip; flight rapid, alternating quick wingbeats with glides. (*See also* Plate 39.)

**H RIDGWAY'S HAWK** *Buteo ridgwayi* 36–41cm (14–16in); wingspan 50–66cm (20–26in); 280–450g. Broad, rounded wings; fan-shaped tail; soars; light "wing windows." Hispaniola. (*See also* Plate 36.)

**BROAD-WINGED HAWK** *Buteo platypterus* 34–44cm (13–17in); wingspan 86cm (34in); male 420g, female 490g. Alternates soaring and flapping on broad, rounded wings and fan-shaped tail. **ADULT** Boldly banded tail. **IMMATURE** Tail with finer bars; underparts streaked. (*See also* Plate 39.)

**C CUBAN KITE** *Chondrohierax wilsonii* 38–43cm (15–17in). Large, oval wings heavily barred beneath; long, banded tail. Cuba. (*See also* Plate 37.)

**HOOK-BILLED KITE** *Chondrohierax uncinatus* 38–43cm (15–17in); wingspan 90cm (3ft); 280g. Large, oval wings heavily barred beneath; long, banded tail. Several rapid flaps followed by tilting glide, soars infrequently. Grenada. (*See also* Plate 37.)

SHARP-SHINNED HAWK

GUNDLACH'S HAWK

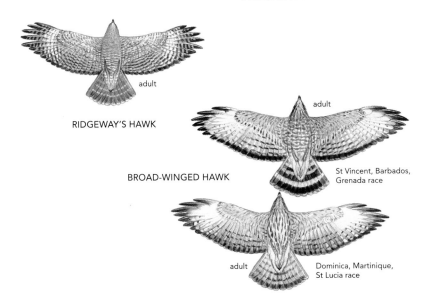

RIDGEWAY'S HAWK

BROAD-WINGED HAWK

adult

St Vincent, Barbados,
Grenada race

adult

Dominica, Martinique,
St Lucia race

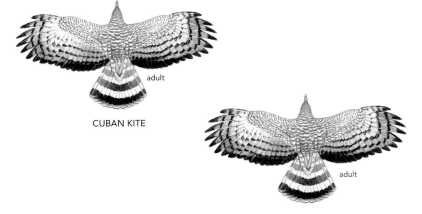

CUBAN KITE

HOOK-BILLED KITE

**Owls:** Birds of prey, most of which are nocturnal. They are characterized by a distinctive facial disk, a large head with eyes directed forward, and silent flight.

**H** **ASHY-FACED OWL** *Tyto glaucops* 35cm (14in); male 260–346g, female 465–535g. **BEHAVIOR** Nocturnal. **DESCRIPTION** Reddish-brown; long-legged; with silver-gray, heart-shaped face. **VOICE** Hissing, prefaced by high-pitched, ratchety clicks. **STATUS AND RANGE** Endemic to Hispaniola, where fairly widespread and common locally in Dominican Republic, particularly limestone cliffs south of Barahona and in Santo Domingo, Los Haitises National Park, Samaná Peninsula, and southeastern portion of island. Status in Haiti unknown. **HABITAT** Open woodlands, scrub, dry and moist forests from coast to high mountains.

**BARN OWL** *Tyto alba* 30–43cm (12–17in); 520g. **BEHAVIOR** Nocturnal. **DESCRIPTION** Large; with flat, heart-shaped face and large dark eyes. Greater Antilles birds paler. **VOICE** Loud, hissing screech, and loud clicking sounds. **STATUS AND RANGE** Common permanent resident in Cuba, Jamaica, Hispaniola, Dominica, St Vincent, Grenadines, and Grenada. Uncommon in Bahamas and Cayman Islands. Very rare in Puerto Rico, where now nesting. **HABITAT** In and around human settlements as well as relatively open areas from coast to mountains, including rice fields, sugarcane plantations, dry scrub, and open woodlands.

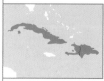

**STYGIAN OWL** *Asio stygius* 41–46cm (16–18in); 675g. **BEHAVIOR** Nocturnal. **DESCRIPTION** Large, very dark, with conspicuous ear-tufts. **VOICE** Generally silent; occasionally loud, abrupt *hu*! as if to scare someone. During breeding, male repeats low-pitched *fool* at intervals; female answers with higher-pitched *niek*. **STATUS AND RANGE** Uncommon but local permanent resident in Cuba. Threatened. Decidedly rare and local permanent resident in the Dominican Republic on Hispaniola, where endangered. Status in Haiti unknown but likely even rarer and critically endangered. Cuban and Hispaniolan birds are endemic subspecies. Other subspecies in Mesoamerica and South America. **HABITAT** Dense deciduous and pine forests, from semi-arid to humid, all elevations.

**SHORT-EARED OWL** *Asio flammeus* 35–43cm (14–17in); 350g. **BEHAVIOR** Most active dawn and dusk, perches on posts. **DESCRIPTION** Large owl, tan below, breast heavily streaked. Yellow eyes; distinct facial disk. **FLIGHT** Conspicuous black wrist patches on whitish underwings and large tan patches on upperwings. Flight erratic flaps and glides. **VOICE** Short, emphatic *bow-wow*. Also distinct wing clap. **STATUS AND RANGE** Locally common permanent resident in Cuba and Hispaniola. Uncommon and local in Puerto Rico, but increasing. Uncommon and irregular breeding resident in Cayman Islands. Rare resident in Virgin Islands. **HABITAT** Open lowlands.

ASHY-FACED OWL

Greater Antilles race

BARN OWL

Lesser Antilles race

STYGIAN OWL

Puerto Rico race

SHORT-EARED OWL

**⧉ BARE-LEGGED OWL (CUBAN SCREECH OWL)** *Margarobyas lawrencii* 20–23cm (8–9in); 80g. **BEHAVIOR** Nocturnal. **DESCRIPTION** Small, plump, with big head and large brown eyes. Beige eyebrow stripe; short tail; long, bare, greenish legs. Brownish overall, speckled with white. **VOICE** *Cu-cu-cu-cucucu*, in low and repeated sequence reminiscent of a bouncing ball. Sometimes harsh, plaintive screams. **STATUS AND RANGE** Endemic to Cuba; common and widespread at all elevations. Genus also endemic to Cuba. **HABITAT** Dense forests.

**⧉ CUBAN PYGMY-OWL** *Glaucidium siju* 17.5cm (7in); male 47–68g, female 66–102g. **BEHAVIOR** Active day and night. **DESCRIPTION** Small owl with big head and yellow eyes. Short, feathered, yellow feet; short tail often twitched sideways; two dark spots on back of head. **VOICE** Low, sporadically repeated *uh, uh, uh* … , syllables short and plaintive. Also *hui-hui-chiii-chiii-chi-chi-chi* … , increasing in strength. **STATUS AND RANGE** Endemic to Cuba; fairly common and widespread at all elevations. **HABITAT** Forests of all kinds, including tree plantations.

**BURROWING OWL** *Athene cunicularia* 23cm (9in); 150g. **BEHAVIOR** Active during day, bobs when approached. **DESCRIPTION** Small, with long legs. **ADULT** Underparts barred. **FLIGHT** Rapid and low to ground. Frequently hovers. **VOICE** Soft, high-pitched, two-note *coo-coooo*. Clucking chatter when alarmed. **STATUS AND RANGE** Generally uncommon and local permanent resident in Bahamas, population declining. Rare and very local permanent resident in Cuba, primarily in west. Locally common permanent resident in Haiti and western Dominican Republic. **HABITAT** Open scrub, sandy pine savannas, pastures, golf courses.

**⧉ PUERTO RICAN SCREECH-OWL** *Megascops nudipes* 23–25cm (9–10in); 103–154g. **BEHAVIOR** Nocturnal. **DESCRIPTION** Grayish to reddish-brown above, white below marked with heavy brown streaks. **VOICE** Tremulous trill; sometimes chatters, whoops, or maniacal laugh. **STATUS AND RANGE** The only small owl in Puerto Rico and Virgin Islands, which encompass entire range. Common in Puerto Rico. Likely extirpated from Virgin Islands. **HABITAT** Forests and wooded areas from coast to mountains, including coffee plantations and human settlements.

**⧉ JAMAICAN OWL** *Pseudoscops grammicus* 31–36cm (12–14in); 335g. **BEHAVIOR** Nocturnal. **DESCRIPTION** Medium-sized, with short ear-tufts. **ADULT** Mottled yellowish-brown above; paler with dark streaks below. **VOICE** Guttural *whogh*; occasionally high-pitched quivering *whoooo*. **STATUS AND RANGE** Endemic to Jamaica; common and widespread from coast to mid-elevations, infrequent in high mountains. **HABITAT** Forests, woodlands, forest edges, and gardens.

**Nightjars and allies:** These are nocturnal birds with large mouths that engulf flying insects on the wing. All have mottled plumages for camouflage. Some rest and nest on the ground.

**⧉ LEAST PAURAQUE (LEAST POORWILL)** *Siphonorhis brewsteri* 17–20cm (6.75–8in). **BEHAVIOR** Nocturnal. **DESCRIPTION** The smallest nightjar in the West Indies. Darkly mottled. **ADULT** White neck band; narrow white terminal band on tail. **FLIGHT** Erratic and floppy. **VOICE** Guttural, repeated *torico, torico*. Also rising whistle. **STATUS AND RANGE** Endemic to Hispaniola, where fairly common locally in southwestern Dominican Republic, generally from the coast to 300m (1000ft). In Haiti status unclear but occurs between Arcahaie and Montrouis north of Port-au-Prince. Numbers declining. Threatened. Genus endemic to West Indies. **HABITAT** Semi-arid cactus and thorn scrub often associated with pine forests.

BARE-LEGGED OWL

CUBAN PYGMY OWL

BURROWING OWL

PUERTO RICAN SCREECH-OWL

JAMAICAN OWL

LEAST PAURAQUE

**WHITE-TAILED NIGHTJAR** *Hydropsalis cayennensis* 20–23cm (8–9in); male 30–40g, female 25–46g. **BEHAVIOR** Nocturnal. **ADULT MALE** Reddish-brown collar; distinct white eye-line; white outertail feathers; white bar on outer primaries. **ADULT FEMALE** Duller; lacks collar; white outertail feathers and outer primaries. **VOICE** High whistle. **STATUS AND RANGE** Very rare and local permanent resident on Martinique in south and Caravelle Peninsula. Threatened in West Indies. **HABITAT** Grassy fields.

**P PUERTO RICAN NIGHTJAR** *Antrostomus noctitherus* 22cm (8.5in); 36g. **BEHAVIOR** Nocturnal. **DESCRIPTION** Small nightjar, mottled gray, brown, and black. Black throat edged with pale band. **MALE** White throat band and portion of outertail feathers. **FEMALE** Pale gray throat band and tips of outertail feathers. Identical to but smaller than Eastern Whip-poor-will. **VOICE** Emphatic, repeated whistle, *whip, whip, whip* … Also emphatic clucking. **STATUS AND RANGE** Endemic to Puerto Rico; locally common on southwest coast eastward locally to Guayama. Endangered. **HABITAT** Dry semi-deciduous forests with open understory and dense leaf-litter.

**RUFOUS NIGHTJAR** *Antrostomus rufus* 28cm (11in); 87–98g. **BEHAVIOR** Nocturnal. **DESCRIPTION** Medium-sized nightjar. Mottled reddish-brown with white throat band; short, rounded wings. Nearly identical to Chuck-will's-widow. **VOICE** Loud rendition of local name *Jacques-pas-papa-pouw*, emphasis on last syllable. Calls mostly at dusk and only during breeding season. **STATUS AND RANGE** Locally common permanent resident in northeastern St Lucia. Endangered in West Indies. **HABITAT** Relatively undisturbed dry scrub forests.

**CHUCK-WILL'S-WIDOW** *Antrostomus carolinensis* 31cm (12in); 120g. **BEHAVIOR** Nocturnal; sometimes perches on roads. **DESCRIPTION** Large nightjar, mottled reddish-brown; breast primarily blackish; white throat band. **MALE** White inner webs on outertail feathers. **FEMALE** Outertail feathers tipped pale gray, blend to dark. **VOICE** Whistles name. Seldom calls in West Indies. **STATUS AND RANGE** Rare breeding resident in Bahamas. Migrants and non-breeding residents occur September–May where common in Hispaniola; uncommon in Bahamas, Cuba, Jamaica, and Saba; rare in Puerto Rico, Virgin and Cayman Islands. **HABITAT** Woodlands from coast to mid-elevations; also cave entrances.

**C CUBAN NIGHTJAR (GREATER ANTILLEAN NIGHTJAR)** *Antrostomus cubanensis* 25–29cm (10–11.5in); male 68–80g, female 50–70g. **BEHAVIOR** Nocturnal. Flutters from ground to catch insects. **DESCRIPTION** Mottled dark grayish-brown overall; breast spotted white. Throat dark with pale tan bar at base. Tail and wings rounded. **MALE** Outertail feathers tipped white. **FEMALE** Outertail feathers tipped pale gray. **VOICE** Plaintive, repeated *tuk, tu-wurrrr*, the *tuk* hardly audible. Calls mainly at dawn and dusk. **STATUS AND RANGE** Endemic to Cuba. Fairly common through most of Cuba. Some consider this and Hispaniolan Nighjar one species: the Greater Antillean Nightjar. **HABITAT** Moderately dense forests, particularly bordering wooded swamps.

**H HISPANIOLAN NIGHTJAR (GREATER ANTILLEAN NIGHTJAR)** *Antrostomus ekmani* 26–30cm (10–12in). **BEHAVIOR** Nocturnal. Often perches on road edges. Flutters from ground to capture insects. **DESCRIPTION** Identical to Cuban Nightjar but with larger white (male) or pale gray (female) tail patches. **VOICE** A plaintive, frequently repeated *pi-tan-guaaaa*, reflecting its local name. Calls mainly at dawn and dusk. **STATUS AND RANGE** Endemic to Hispaniola, where fairly common in western Dominican Republic at mid-elevations from 300 to 750m (1000 to 2500ft). Status in Haiti unknown but likely rare and local due to limited habitat. **HABITAT** Forests and wooded areas.

WHITE-TAILED NIGHTJAR

PUERTO-RICAN NIGHTJAR

RUFOUS NIGHTJAR/CHUCK-WILL'S-WIDOW

CUBAN NIGHTJAR/HISPANIOLAN NIGHTJAR

**NORTHERN POTOO** *Nyctibius jamaicensis* 43–46cm (17–18in); 210–280g. **BEHAVIOR** Nocturnal, arboreal, perches upright on stumps or posts, sallies to catch insects. **DESCRIPTION** Large, with long tail. Eye yellow, but appears reddish in light. **VOICE** Guttural *kwah, waugh, waugh, waugh, kwaah*. Also hoarse *waark-cucu*. **STATUS AND RANGE** Fairly common permanent resident in Jamaica, where widespread primarily below 1000m (3300ft). Generally locally uncommon to rare in Hispaniola. A few records from eastern Cuba. **HABITAT** Arid and humid forests and scrublands adjacent to open areas. Also palm groves, pastures, and cattle corrals. In Jamaica, also on golf courses.

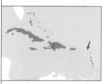

**ANTILLEAN NIGHTHAWK** *Chordeiles gundlachii* 20–25cm (8–10in); 50g. **BEHAVIOR** Flocks, active dusk and dawn. **DESCRIPTION** Dark, hawk-like, with slender, pointed wings and conspicuous white wing patch. Nearly identical to Common Nighthawk; distinguished with certainty only by call. All other species of similar appearance, lack white wing patches. **FLIGHT** Erratic and darting. **VOICE** Loud, raspy *que-re-be-bé*. **STATUS AND RANGE** Common breeding resident in Bahamas, Cuba, Cayman Islands, Jamaica, and Hispaniola primarily April–August. Locally common breeding bird in Puerto Rico, Virgin Islands, and Guadeloupe during same months. Generally rare migrant through Lesser Antilles. **HABITAT** Open fields, pastures, pine barrens, savannas, and coastal fringes.

**COMMON NIGHTHAWK** *Chordeiles minor* 20–25cm (8–10in); 55–95g. **BEHAVIOR** Flocks, active dusk and dawn. **DESCRIPTION** Virtually identical to Antillean Nighthawk, which has tan, rather than blackish, wing linings and is sometimes tanner below and paler above, but these are not consistent field marks. Identified with certainty only by call. **FLIGHT** Erratic and darting. **VOICE** Distinctive, nasal *neet*. Rarely calls during migration. **STATUS AND RANGE** Migrant throughout West Indies September–October and April–May. Abundance uncertain, but likely uncommon. **HABITAT** Open areas such as pastures and savannas, including human settlements.

## NIGHTJAR TAILS

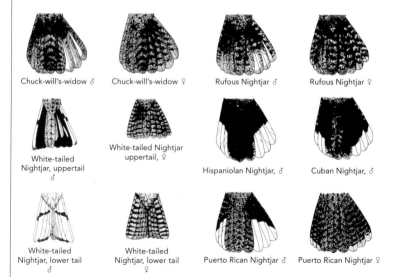

Chuck-will's-widow ♂    Chuck-will's-widow ♀    Rufous Nightjar ♂    Rufous Nightjar ♀

White-tailed Nightjar, uppertail ♂    White-tailed Nightjar uppertail, ♀    Hispaniolan Nightjar, ♂    Cuban Nightjar, ♂

White-tailed Nightjar, lower tail ♂    White-tailed Nightjar, lower tail ♀    Puerto Rican Nightjar ♂    Puerto Rican Nightjar ♀

NORTHERN POTOO

ANTILLEAN NIGHTHAWK/
COMMON NIGHTHAWK

**Swifts:** The most aerial land birds, pursuing flying insects all day without landing to rest. Flight is fast and erratic, with shallow, rapid flapping of stiff, bow-shaped wings.

**WHITE-COLLARED SWIFT** *Streptoprocne zonaris* 20–22cm (8–8.5in); 100g. Aerial, flocks. Large swift, black with distinctive white collar. VOICE High-pitched *screee-screee* or rapid *chip-chip-chip-chip*. STATUS AND RANGE Common permanent resident in Jamaica and Hispaniola. Declining in Haiti. Uncommon permanent resident locally in Cuba. Rare but regular visitor to Grenada. Vagrant elsewhere. HABITAT Primarily over foothills, mountain valleys, and forests, including open areas. Less regular over lowlands.

**BLACK SWIFT** *Cypseloides niger* 15–18cm (5.75–7in); 50g. Aerial, flocks. Fairly large, black swift, with slightly forked tail. Most similar swifts smaller, with shorter tails, more darting flight, and quicker wingbeats. STATUS AND RANGE Widespread in West Indies. Locally common permanent resident in Jamaica and Hispaniola (some depart after breeding); rare and local in Cuba. Common breeding resident April–September in Guadeloupe, Dominica, and Martinique; uncommon in Puerto Rico, St Lucia, St Vincent, and Barbados; rare in Monserrat. Infrequent migrant in Virgin Islands and other Lesser Antilles. HABITAT Mountains; less frequently lowlands.

**CHIMNEY SWIFT** *Chaetura pelagica* 12–14cm (4.75–5.5in); 25g. Aerial, flocks. Medium-sized; dark; pale brown chin and throat. Short, rounded tail barely visible in flight. (Black Swift larger; more conspicuous, slightly forked tail.) VOICE Loud, rapid twittering. STATUS AND RANGE Irregular, generally an uncommon migrant in Cayman Islands, decidedly uncommon and local in Bahamas, rare in Cuba, and very rare in Jamaica, Hispaniola, Puerto Rico, and Virgin Islands (St Croix). Vagrant elsewhere. Occurs August–October and April–May. HABITAT Cities and towns. Also open fields and woodlands.

**SHORT-TAILED SWIFT** *Chaetura brachyura* 10cm (4in); 16–22g. Aerial, flocks. Small. Pale gray rump and undertail-coverts contrast with blackish plumage. Tail very short. (Other small Lesser Antillean swifts are more uniform in color and have longer tails.) STATUS AND RANGE Common breeding resident in St Vincent and St Lucia March–September; most depart after breeding. Vagrant elsewhere. HABITAT Towns, open areas, and forests in lowlands and hills.

**GRAY-RUMPED SWIFT** *Chaetura cinereiventris* 11cm (4.25in); 14–20g. Aerial, flocks. Small, with black upperparts and triangular gray rump patch. Black, longish tail gives slender appearance; gray underparts. STATUS AND RANGE Common permanent resident in Grenada. Primarily in mountains. Vagrant elsewhere. HABITAT Typically over forests.

Ⓜ **LESSER ANTILLEAN SWIFT** *Chaetura martinica* 11cm (4.25in); 13g. Aerial, flocks. Small swift with dull brownish-gray upperparts, gray rump, dark gray underparts, and short gray tail. (Gray-rumped Swift nearly identical, but does not overlap range.) STATUS AND RANGE Fairly common permanent resident in Dominica, Martinique, St Lucia, and St Vincent. Uncommon in Guadeloupe. These islands comprise entire range. HABITAT Primarily over mountain forests, also lowland forests and open areas.

Ⓜ **ANTILLEAN PALM-SWIFT** *Tachornis phoenicobia* 10–11cm (4–4.25in); 9g. Aerial, flocks. Small, with white rump, black breast band. (Bank Swallow lacks white rump.) STATUS AND RANGE Common permanent resident in Cuba, Jamaica, and locally so in Hispaniola. Decidedly rare visitor in Puerto Rico, particularly Mona Island. Vagrant elsewhere. HABITAT Open cultivated areas, sugarcane plantations, edges of palm savannas, and urban zones.

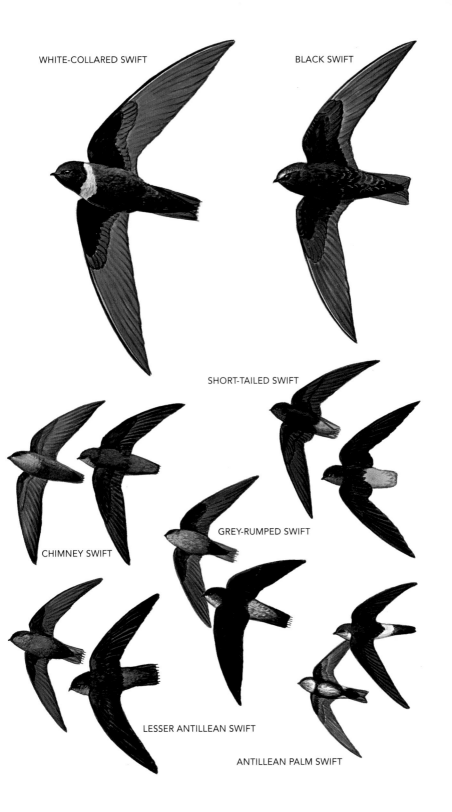

WHITE-COLLARED SWIFT

BLACK SWIFT

SHORT-TAILED SWIFT

CHIMNEY SWIFT

GREY-RUMPED SWIFT

LESSER ANTILLEAN SWIFT

ANTILLEAN PALM SWIFT

**Martins and Swallows:** These birds dart erratically on the wing pursuing flying insects. Their wings are noticeably pointed. Highly gregarious, they are often seen perched on wires.

**PURPLE MARTIN** *Progne subis* 20–22cm (8–8.5in); 50g. **BEHAVIOR** Flocks. **ADULT MALE** Entirely bluish-purple. Indistinguishable from Cuban Martin. **ADULT FEMALE AND IMMATURE** Scaled pattern on grayish-brown breast; light gray patches on sides of neck; indistinct border between darker breast and whitish belly. (Female Caribbean Martin has brown wash on breast, rather than scaled pattern.) **VOICE** Gurgling, including high *twick-twick*. Also high, melodious warble. **STATUS AND RANGE** Irregular but generally fairly common migrant in northern Bahamas, Cuba, and Cayman Islands; uncommon in southern Bahamas. Occurs primarily mid-August through mid-October, rare in March and April, less frequent in other months. Very rare or vagrant elsewhere in West Indies. May occur in numbers during migration. **HABITAT** Towns and open areas.

**CUBAN MARTIN** *Progne cryptoleuca* 20–22cm (8–8.5in). **BEHAVIOR** Flocks. **MALE** Bluish-purple overall. Indistinguishable from Purple Martin. **FEMALE** White belly and abdomen contrast sharply with brown breast, sides, throat, and chin. (Female Purple Martin paler brown on breast; throat and chin blend gradually into whitish belly. Both sexes of Caribbean Martin similar to female Cuban Martin in pattern of underparts, but white below restricted to lower belly and abdomen. Also, female Caribbean Martin has less contrast between white and dark of underparts.) **VOICE** Gurgling, including high-pitched *twick-twick*, like a vibrating wire. Also strong, melodious warble. **STATUS AND RANGE** Common breeding resident in Cuba February–October. Breeds nowhere else. Very rare migrant in Puerto Rico. Vagrant to Bahamas and Guadeloupe. **HABITAT** Cities and towns. Also swamp borders and open areas, particularly in lowlands.

**CARIBBEAN MARTIN** *Progne dominicensis* 20cm (8in); 40g. **BEHAVIOR** Flocks. **DESCRIPTION** Bicolored martin. **MALE** Upperparts, head, and throat blue; belly and abdomen white. **FEMALE AND IMMATURE** Blue of underparts replaced by brownish wash that blends into white of belly. **VOICE** Gurgling, including high *twick-twick*. Also melodious warble and gritty churr. **STATUS AND RANGE** Fairly common breeding resident in much of West Indies January–September. Rare migrant in Cayman Islands primarily March–May. Vagrant to Bahamas and Cuba. **HABITAT** Towns, open areas, freshwater bodies, and coastal rock promontories.

**NORTHERN ROUGH-WINGED SWALLOW** *Stelgidopteryx serripennis* 12.5–14cm (5–5.5in); 16g. **BEHAVIOR** Flocks. **DESCRIPTION** Brown above, with white underparts blending to pale brown on throat. **STATUS AND RANGE** Irregular, ranging from fairly common to decidedly uncommon migrant and less frequent non-breeding resident in Cuba. Generally uncommon to rare in Bahamas, Jamaica, Hispaniola, and Cayman Islands. Rare in Puerto Rico and Virgin Islands. Very rare in Guadeloupe. Vagrant to other Lesser Antilles. Occurs August–April with peak in March–April. Sometimes occurs in numbers. **HABITAT** Open fields and wetlands.

**BANK SWALLOW** *Riparia riparia* 12.5–14cm (5–5.5in); 15g. **BEHAVIOR** Flocks. **DESCRIPTION** Dark breast band; dark brown upperparts. (Antillean Palm Swift has white rump; longer, narrower wings; more rapid, darting flight.) **STATUS AND RANGE** Irregular, ranging from locally common to uncommon in Cayman Islands, but through most of West Indies a decidedly uncommon to rare migrant primarily September–December and April–May. Very rare in southern Lesser Antilles and smaller islands of chain. **HABITAT** Primarily open coastal areas.

PURPLE MARTIN/
CUBAN MARTIN
adult ♂

CUBAN MARTIN

adult ♀

CARIBBEAN MARTIN

NORTHERN ROUGH-WINGED SWALLOW

BANK SWALLOW

**TREE SWALLOW** *Tachycineta bicolor* 12.5–15cm (5–5.75in); 20g. **BEHAVIOR** Flocks. **ADULT** Blue-green above, with entirely white underparts and slightly notched tail. Wing linings pale gray. (Bahama Swallow has deeply forked tail and white wing linings.) **IMMATURE** Brown upperparts. **VOICE** Mostly silent in West Indies. **STATUS AND RANGE** Irregular but generally common migrant and non-breeding resident in Cuba primarily November–May, but occurring September–June. Locally common to uncommon migrant in Cayman Islands primarily April–May. Generally uncommon migrant in northern Bahamas and Jamaica; rare in southern Bahamas, Hispaniola, Puerto Rico, Virgin Islands (St Croix), and Guadeloupe; and very rare or vagrant elsewhere. **HABITAT** Open areas, swamps, marshes, rice fields, and other wetlands.

**S BAHAMA SWALLOW** *Tachycineta cyaneoviridis* 15.5cm (6in); 18g. **BEHAVIOR** Flocks. **ADULT** Dark greenish above, with blue wings, white underparts including wing linings, and deeply forked tail. (Tree Swallow has slightly notched tail and pale gray wing linings.) **FEMALE** Slightly duller. **IMMATURE** Brownish upperparts; tail less forked. **VOICE** Metallic *chep* or *chi-chep*. **STATUS AND RANGE** Virtual Bahamas endemic. Common on Abaco; uncommon on Andros and Grand Bahama; rare on New Providence. These islands comprise entire breeding range. Rare migrant or visitor to other islands of Bahamas and to Cuba (primarily Cayo Coco) January–March. **HABITAT** Pine forests, towns, clearings, and near cliffs.

**H GOLDEN SWALLOW** *Tachycineta euchrysea* 12.5cm (5in). **BEHAVIOR** Flocks. **DESCRIPTION** Small swallow. **ADULT** Iridescent bluish-green upperparts with golden sheen; white underparts; moderately forked tail. (Tree Swallow has shallower tail notch, relatively shorter wings, and no golden sheen on upperparts.) **FEMALE** Duller, grayish on breast. **IMMATURE** Duller above; gray breast band. **VOICE** Soft twittering. **STATUS AND RANGE** Endemic to Hispaniola, where uncommon, local, and declining. Formerly in Jamaica but now extirpated. Endangered. **HABITAT** Relatively open country and pine forests of high mountains, also over rain forests.

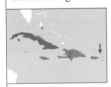

**CAVE SWALLOW** *Petrochelidon fulva* 12.5–14cm (5–5.5in); 20g. Flocks. Dark reddish-brown rump and forehead; pale reddish-brown ear-patch, throat, breast, and sides; slightly notched tail. (Cliff Swallow has dark reddish-brown throat and ear-patch and lighter forehead.) **VOICE** Chattering or twittering. Also musical *twit*. **STATUS AND RANGE** Common breeding resident in Greater Antilles. Present year-round in Jamaica, Hispaniola, and Puerto Rico; in Cuba most depart September–February. Rare breeding resident on South Andros (Bahamas). Rare migrant in Cayman Islands, Virgin Islands, and Guadeloupe. Vagrant elsewhere. **HABITAT** Fields, wetlands, cliffs, and towns.

**BARN SWALLOW** *Hirundo rustica* 15–19cm (5.75–7.5in); 16g. **BEHAVIOR** Flocks. **ADULT** Primarily tan underparts; dark reddish-brown throat; deeply forked tail with white spots. **IMMATURE** Throat and upper breast tan; remainder of underparts white; tail less deeply forked. **VOICE** Thin, unmusical *chit*. **STATUS AND RANGE** Generally common migrant throughout West Indies primarily September–October and April–May. Some remain as non-breeding residents November–March, and fewer occur June–August. **HABITAT** Open areas over fields and swamps, primarily along coast.

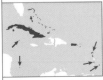

**CLIFF SWALLOW** *Petrochelidon pyrrhonota* 12.5–15cm (5–5.75in); 22g. **BEHAVIOR** Flocks. **DESCRIPTION** Dark reddish-brown chin, throat, and ear-patch; pale tan forehead and rump; slightly notched tail. (Cave Swallow has darker forehead and much paler ear-patch and throat.) **VOICE** Short, melodious, repeated note. **STATUS AND RANGE** Uncommon migrant in Cayman Islands, Guadeloupe, Barbados, and San Andrés; rare in Bahamas, Cuba, Puerto Rico, Virgin Islands, Dominica, and St Lucia; very rare or vagrant elsewhere in West Indies. Occurs late August–early December and late March–early May. **HABITAT** Primarily along coast.

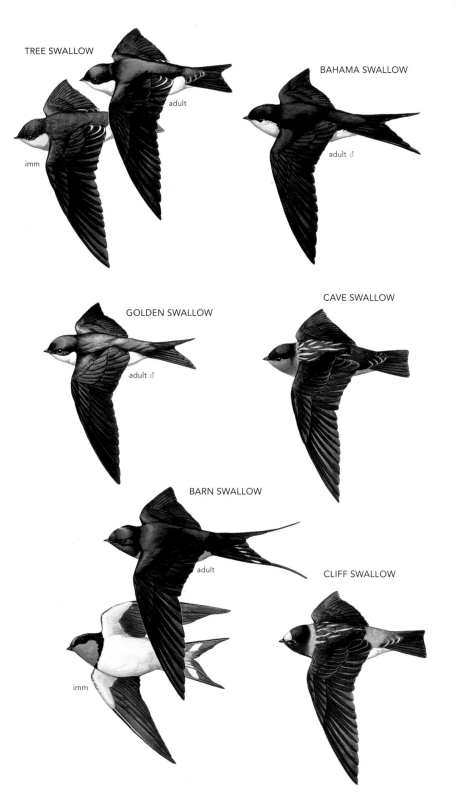

TREE SWALLOW

imm

adult

BAHAMA SWALLOW

adult ♂

GOLDEN SWALLOW

adult ♂

CAVE SWALLOW

BARN SWALLOW

adult

imm

CLIFF SWALLOW

**RUFOUS-VENTED CHACHALACA** *Ortalis ruficauda* 55cm (22in); male 650g, female 550g. **BEHAVIOR** Primarily terrestrial. **DESCRIPTION** Large, long-tailed, chicken-like bird. Olive-brown upperparts; gray head and hindneck; bronze-colored tail tipped with reddish-brown; gray underparts; reddish-brown flanks and undertail-coverts and bare red throat. **VOICE** Repeated *cocrico, cocrico* … **STATUS AND RANGE** Uncommon permanent resident in Grenadines, where occurs in northern Bequia and western portion of Union Island. **HABITAT** Scrub and woodlands.

**RING-NECKED PHEASANT** *Phasianus colchicus* Male 76–92cm (30–36in), female 50–63cm (20–25in); male 1.2kg, female 900g. **BEHAVIOR** Terrestrial. **DESCRIPTION** Large, chicken-like bird with long, pointed tail. **MALE** Iridescent green head with crest; red face wattle; very long tail; incomplete white neck band. **FEMALE** Mottled brown; tail shorter. **STATUS AND RANGE** Introduced widely in West Indies, but failed to survive on most islands. Locally common in Cuba on Isle of Youth (near Los Indios). Rare on Eleuthera in Bahamas, very rare and local in Dominican Republic (La Romana Province), and a few birds on Barbados. **HABITAT** Brush and hedgerows.

**HELMETED GUINEAFOWL** *Numida meleagris* 53cm (21in); 1.3kg. **BEHAVIOR** Terrestrial and flocks. **DESCRIPTION** Unusual body shape; dark gray feathering with white spots; nearly naked head and neck. **VOICE** Wild cackles. **STATUS AND RANGE** Introduced in West Indies, where widespread domestically in farmyards, but locally feral. In feral state, uncommon locally in Dominican Republic and Barbuda; rare in Cuba, Puerto Rico, Virgin Islands, St Martin (Isle Pinel), and Grenadines (Baliceaux). **HABITAT** Primarily dry scrubland.

**RED JUNGLEFOWL** *Gallus gallus* Male 71cm (28in), female 43cm (17in); weight variable. **BEHAVIOR** Terrestrial. **MALE (ROOSTER)** Resplendently plumaged; red comb head wattle; long, bushy tail. **FEMALE (HEN)** Smaller comb and wattle; brownish plumage. **VOICE** Universally recognized *cock-a-doodle-doo*. **STATUS AND RANGE** Well known, introduced; feral fairly widely in Bahamas and very locally in Dominican Republic, Puerto Rico (particularly Mona Island), Virgin Islands, and Grenadines (Diamond Islands and Canouan). Domesticated birds common on farms throughout West Indies. **HABITAT** Dry and moist forests.

**NORTHERN BOBWHITE** *Colinus virginianus* 25cm (10in); 180g. **BEHAVIOR** Terrestrial, flocks, does not fly until underfoot. **DESCRIPTION** Small, resembling small chicken. **MALE** White throat and eyebrow stripe. **FEMALE** Tan throat and eyebrow stripe. **VOICE** Clear, whistled *bob, bob-white*, rising at end, repeated. **STATUS AND RANGE** Common permanent resident in Cuba. Introduced and now locally common in northern Bahamas; uncommon and local in Hispaniola. Introductions on other islands unsuccessful. **HABITAT** Scrubland and pasture with dense cover.

**INDIAN PEAFOWL** *Pavo cristatus* Male 2.5m (8.3ft), female 1m (4.3ft); 4–6kg. **BEHAVIOR** Terrestrial. **MALE (PEACOCK)** Primarily blue; magnificent, huge tail raises to broad fan. **FEMALE (PEAHEN)** Grayish-brown; white belly and face; greenish neck and breast; distinctive crest. **VOICE** Loud scream, *My arm!* **STATUS AND RANGE** Widely introduced in West Indies to farmyards and gardens. Feral and fairly common on Little Exuma in Bahamas. **HABITAT** Thick broadleaf coppice.

RUFOUS-VENTED CHACHALACA

RING-NECKED PHEASANT

RED JUNGLEFOWL

HELMETED GUINEAFOWL

NORTHERN BONWHITE

INDIAN PEAFOWL
(not to scale)

**Pigeons and Doves:** A cosmopolitan family of plump, stocky birds. Most are gregarious in habit, though some, such as the quail-doves in the West Indies, are solitary. A clapping or whirring of the wings is often conspicuous as they take flight and most species are strong fliers. Doves are generally smaller and longer-tailed than pigeons.

**J** **CRESTED QUAIL-DOVE** *Geotrygon versicolor* 31cm (12in); 225g. Difficult to detect. **BEHAVIOR** Terrestrial. Pumps head and bobs tail while walking. **DESCRIPTION** Plump, with short but distinct crest, primarily gray head and underparts, bronze-colored hindneck and reddish-brown upper back and much of wings. **VOICE** Mournful two- to three-syllable *woof-woo-wooo*, first note sharp with following notes softer and lower in pitch. **STATUS AND RANGE** Endemic to Jamaica. Fairly common locally, particularly Blue Mountains and Cockpit Country. **HABITAT** Wet forest undergrowth of mountains and limestone hills.

**G** **BLUE-HEADED QUAIL-DOVE (BLUE-HEADED PARTRIDGE-DOVE)** *Starnoenas cyanocephala* 30–33cm (12–13in); 250g. Difficult to detect. **BEHAVIOR** Terrestrial. **DESCRIPTION** The largest Cuban quail-dove. Conspicuous light blue head; white facial stripe; mark on throat. **VOICE** Two similar notes: *uuuu-up, uuuu-up*, the last syllable rising and stopping quickly. **STATUS AND RANGE** Endemic to Cuba. Fairly rare and very local. Principal areas include Guanahacabibes Peninsula, Pinares de La Güira, and Zapata Peninsula. Endangered. Genus and subfamily also endemic to Cuba. **HABITAT** Deciduous forests with a dense canopy, open understory, and stony forest floor, particularly with ample leaf-litter.

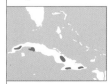

**C** **GRAY-FRONTED QUAIL-DOVE (GRAY-HEADED QUAIL-DOVE)** *Geotrygon caniceps* 28cm (11in); 170g. Difficult to detect. **BEHAVIOR** Terrestrial. Displays peculiar neck and tail movements. **DESCRIPTION** Pigeon-like, with metallic purplish-blue sheen on back and a completely gray crown. **VOICE** Continuous, low *uup-uup-uup-uup* without pauses. **STATUS AND RANGE** Endemic to Cuba, where rare and very local, mainly in Zapata Peninsula and Sierra del Rosario. Threatened. **HABITAT** Low-elevation wet forests bordering swamps and middle altitudes in dense, moist woods.

**H** **WHITE-FRONTED QUAIL-DOVE (GRAY-FRONTED QUAIL-DOVE)** *Geotrygon leucometopia* 28cm (11in); 170g. Difficult to detect. **BEHAVIOR** Terrestrial. Displays peculiar neck and tail movements. **DESCRIPTION** Pigeon-like, with metallic purplish-blue sheen on back and a white forehead. **VOICE** Prolonged *coo-o-o*. **STATUS AND RANGE** Endemic to the Dominican Republic, where uncommon and very local. Endangered. Formerly considered a subspecies of Gray-fronted Quail-Dove. **HABITAT** Primarily dense mountain forests and shade coffee plantations, sometimes near sea level.

CRESTED QUAIL-DOVE

BLUE-HEADED QUAIL-DOVE

GRAY-FRONTED QUAIL-DOVE

WHITE-FRONTED QUAIL-DOVE

**RUDDY QUAIL-DOVE** *Geotrygon montana* 25cm (10in); 110g. Difficult to detect. **BEHAVIOR** Terrestrial. **DESCRIPTION** Plump, predominantly reddish-brown with whitish stripe beneath eye. **VOICE** Mournful *coo* gradually fading in strength and sometimes pitch, like blowing across mouth of bottle. Very ventriloquial. **STATUS AND RANGE** Fairly common permanent resident in Puerto Rico; locally common in Cuba, Jamaica, and Hispaniola; uncommon on large, forested islands of Lesser Antilles. Very rare in Virgin Islands (St John and St Croix). **HABITAT** Primarily dense forests and plantations of shade coffee in hills and mountains, also locally on the coast.

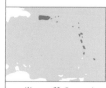

**M BRIDLED QUAIL-DOVE** *Geotrygon mystacea* 30cm (12in); 230g. Difficult to detect. **BEHAVIOR** Terrestrial. **DESCRIPTION** White streak below eye; brown upperparts (except for crown and neck); reddish-brown limited to patch on wing. Underparts grayish-brown. **VOICE** Mournful *who-whooo*, on one pitch or descending toward the end, loudest in middle of second syllable and then trailing off. Sometimes first syllable omitted. Similar to Key West Quail-Dove. **STATUS AND RANGE** Locally common permanent resident in larger forested Virgin Islands; generally uncommon to rare permanent resident in Lesser Antilles. Extremely rare and local in Puerto Rico. These islands comprise entire range. **HABITAT** Dense mountain forests with thick undergrowth; sometimes coastal forests.

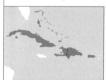

**M KEY WEST QUAIL-DOVE** *Geotrygon chrysia* 28–30cm (11–12in); 170g. Difficult to detect. **BEHAVIOR** Terrestrial. **DESCRIPTION** White line under eye; reddish-brown back and wings, primarily white underparts. (Bridled Quail-Dove has browner upperparts and is much darker below. Ruddy Quail-Dove has more reddish-brown underparts and a duller streak below eye.) **VOICE** Moan on one pitch, gradually increasing in volume and then fading rapidly. Very ventriloquial. Similar to call of Bridled Quail-Dove. **STATUS AND RANGE** Fairly common permanent resident locally in northern Bahamas, Cuba, Hispaniola, and Puerto Rico; uncommon in southern Bahamas (Caicos Islands). These islands comprise entire range. **HABITAT** Dense woods and scrubby thickets with ample leaf-litter, primarily arid and semi-arid zones, but also in moist and wet mountain forests with undisturbed understory.

RUDDY QUAIL-DOVE

♀

♂

BRIDLED QUAIL-DOVE

KEY WEST QUAIL-DOVE

**▯ RING-TAILED PIGEON** *Patagioenas caribaea* 41cm (16in); 250g. **BEHAVIOR** Arboreal. **DESCRIPTION** Large, with black band across uppertail; lacks white in wings. **VOICE** Throaty *cru-cru-crooooo*, last note lower. Also mournful, soft *uhu-cooo*, repeated, last syllable louder and more emphatic. **STATUS AND RANGE** Endemic to Jamaica, where fairly common locally, particularly Cockpit Country, Blue and John Crow Mountains. Threatened. **HABITAT** Forested inland hills and mountains. Descends to lower elevations in cooler months.

**Ⓜ PLAIN PIGEON** *Patagioenas inornata* 38–40cm (15–16in); 250g. **BEHAVIOR** Arboreal and gregarious. **DESCRIPTION** Paler than other large pigeons; white edge to wing-coverts, reddish-brown on wings and back. **FLIGHT** Thin white band across wing. **VOICE** Deep, deliberate *whoo, wo-oo* or *who, oo-oo*. **STATUS AND RANGE** Uncommon and local permanent resident in Hispaniola, particularly Dominican Republic; rare and local in Cuba, Jamaica, and Puerto Rico. Endangered. These islands comprise entire range. **HABITAT** Savannas, open woodlands, coastal scrub, dry limestone forests, and forest edges in lowlands, also to moderate elevations.

**Ⓜ SCALY-NAPED PIGEON** *Patagioenas squamosa* 36–40cm (14–16in); 250g. Arboreal and gregarious. **DESCRIPTION** Slate-gray. **VOICE** *Who are you!* **STATUS AND RANGE** Permanent resident through much of West Indies. Common in Puerto Rico, Virgin Islands, and much of Lesser Antilles; fairly common only locally in Hispaniola. In Cuba, uncommon and local. Extremely rare in Jamaica. These islands comprise virtually entire range. **HABITAT** Typically mountain forests; sometimes well-wooded lowlands; on St Christopher and Barbados occurs in towns and villages.

**Ⓜ WHITE-CROWNED PIGEON** *Patagioenas leucocephala* 33–36cm (13–14in); 250g. **BEHAVIOR** Arboreal; flocks. **DESCRIPTION** Dark gray with white crown. **VOICE** *Who took two?* (Faster and less deliberate than Scaly-naped Pigeon.) Second syllable rises. **STATUS AND RANGE** Widespread in West Indies, where common breeding resident generally year-round in Bahamas, Cuba, Jamaica, and Antigua; locally common in Hispaniola, Puerto Rico, San Andrés, and Providencia. Uncommon in Virgin Islands, Anguilla, and St Bartholomew; rare in St Martin and Guadeloupe. Common breeding resident April–September in Cayman Islands, but most depart November–January. Very rare in southern Lesser Antilles. These islands comprise nearly entire range. Threatened. **HABITAT** Coastal woodlands and mangroves when breeding, sometimes mountains when not breeding.

**CARIBBEAN DOVE** *Leptotila jamaicensis* 30–33cm (12–13in); 120–190g. Terrestrial; flocks. Plump, with white face and underparts; long red legs; cinnamon-colored underwings; gray crown; white-tipped outertail feathers. Other ground-dwelling woodland doves have darker underparts. **VOICE** High-pitched, plaintive *cu-cu-cu-oooo*, *Who cooks for you?* or *What's that to you-oo?* Last note drawn out, accented, descending, and broken into two syllables. **STATUS AND RANGE** Locally common permanent resident in Jamaica; uncommon permanent resident on Grand Cayman (Cayman Islands); fairly common on San Andrés; introduced on New Providence (Bahamas), where common. **HABITAT** Primarily undergrowth in drier forests with dense cover in lowlands and foothills. Sometimes open areas, gardens, and dense secondary forests.

**Ⓢ GRENADA DOVE** *Leptotila wellsi* 31cm (12in). Primarily terrestrial. **ADULT** Unmarked gray-brown upperparts; white forehead to crown; cinnamon-colored breast; white belly; no markings on wings; outertail feathers tipped with white. **FLIGHT** Cinnamon-colored underwings. **VOICE** Distinctive, descending *hoooo*, repeated like clockwork. **STATUS AND RANGE** Endemic to Grenada; uncommon and extremely local. Occurs at remarkably high density in small amount of remaining habitat. Found in southwestern peninsula around Mount Hartman Bay Estate and on west coast at Halifax Harbor. Critically endangered. **HABITAT** Lowlands and hillsides with mature dry scrub forest. Favors mixture of closed canopy, dense scrub, and large areas of bare ground.

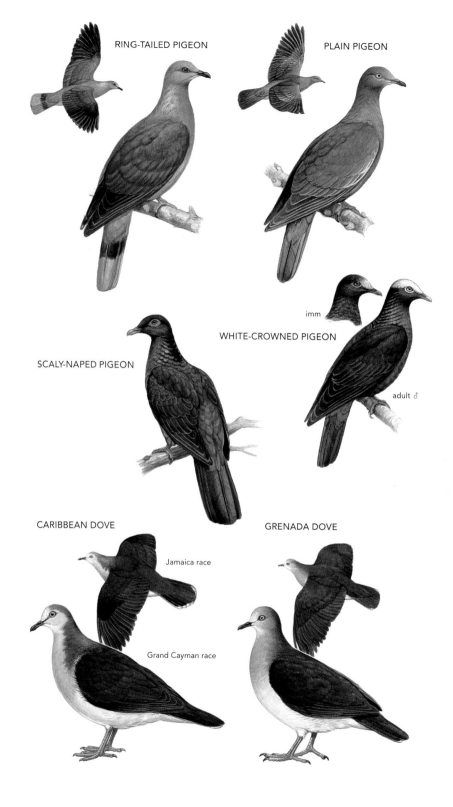

RING-TAILED PIGEON

PLAIN PIGEON

SCALY-NAPED PIGEON

WHITE-CROWNED PIGEON

imm

adult ♂

CARIBBEAN DOVE

GRENADA DOVE

Jamaica race

Grand Cayman race

**COMMON GROUND DOVE** *Columbina passerina* 15–18cm (5.75–7in); 30g. **BEHAVIOR** Primarily terrestrial. **DESCRIPTION** The only tiny dove in West Indies. Plumage varies among islands. **MALE** Bluish-gray crown and hindneck. **FEMALE** More uniformly gray. **FLIGHT** Flashes reddish-brown wing patch. **VOICE** Monotonous, often repeated call of either single or double notes, *coo, coo, coo, coo* … or *co-coo, co-coo, co-coo* … or *hoop, hoop, hoop* … in staccato fashion. **STATUS AND RANGE** Very common permanent resident throughout West Indies. **HABITAT** Most lowland habitats except heavily wooded areas.

**WHITE-WINGED DOVE** *Zenaida asiatica* 28–30cm (11–12in); 150g. **BEHAVIOR** Usually gregarious. **DESCRIPTION** Large, white central wing patch. Tail tip white. **VOICE** Single pitch, like *two bits for two*. Also yodel-like cooing between two notes. **STATUS AND RANGE** Occurs throughout West Indies, where common permanent resident in southern Bahamas, Greater Antilles, Cayman Islands, San Andrés, and Providencia. Uncommon in northern Bahamas, Virgin Islands, and Guadeloupe; rare in Lesser Antilles. Increasing abundance in West Indies. **HABITAT** Scrubland, mangroves, open woodlands, and urban gardens. Primarily coastal.

**EARED DOVE** *Zenaida auriculata* 22–25cm (8.5–10in); 110g. **BEHAVIOR** Terrestrial, often flocks. **DESCRIPTION** Grayish-brown above with few small black spots on scapulars. Underparts brown to undertail-coverts, and reddish-brown tips on outer feathers of short tail. Lacks white in wings or tail. **VOICE** Like Zenaida Dove but shorter. **STATUS AND RANGE** Fairly common permanent resident on St Lucia and common on Barbados, St Vincent, Grenadines, and Grenada. Uncommon on Martinique, and very rare on Guadeloupe. Gradually expanding range in West Indies. **HABITAT** Semi-arid brushlands, primarily in lowlands.

**ZENAIDA DOVE** *Zenaida aurita* 25–28cm (10–11in); 160g. White band on trailing edge of secondaries; white-tipped, rounded tail. (Mourning Dove lacks white in wing and has longer, pointed tail.) **VOICE** Gentle cooing, almost identical to Mourning Dove, *coo-oo, coo, coo, coo*, second syllable rising sharply. Rendered as *Mar-y boil brown rice*. **STATUS AND RANGE** Generally a common permanent resident throughout West Indies. Slightly less abundant in Cayman Islands, and in southern Lesser Antilles, where Eared Dove is more common. These islands comprise most of Zenaida Dove's range. Absent from San Andrés and Providencia. **HABITAT** Open areas, gardens, and hotel grounds. Also open woodlands, scrub thickets, and pine woods with dense understory. Primarily coastal.

**MOURNING DOVE** *Zenaida macroura* 28–33cm (11–13in); 120g. **BEHAVIOR** Often flocks. **DESCRIPTION** Long, wedge-shaped tail fringed with white. Lacks white in wing. (Zenaida and White-winged Doves have white wing markings.) **VOICE** Mournful cooing almost identical to Zenaida Dove, *coo-oo, coo, coo, coo*, second syllable rising sharply. **STATUS AND RANGE** Common permanent resident in Cuba and Hispaniola; locally common in Bahamas, Jamaica, and Puerto Rico. Rare migrant in Cayman and Virgin Islands. Expanding range in West Indies. **HABITAT** Primarily lowland open country, dry coastal forests, and agricultural lands, often near fresh water. Also agricultural areas in mountains.

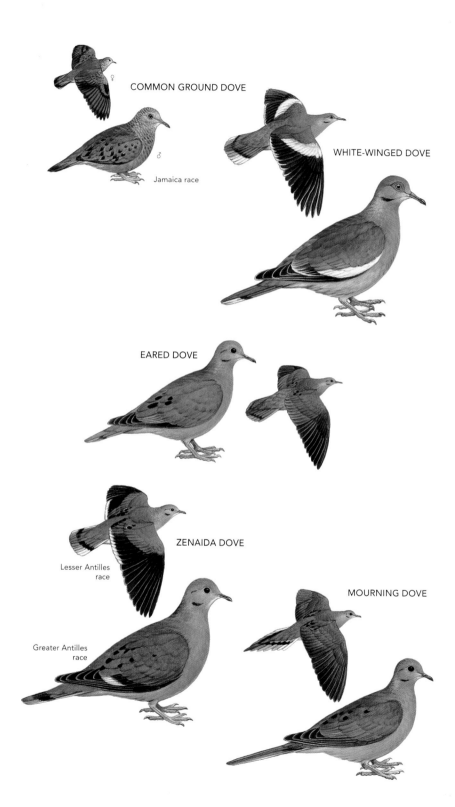

COMMON GROUND DOVE

♀

♂

Jamaica race

WHITE-WINGED DOVE

EARED DOVE

ZENAIDA DOVE

Lesser Antilles
race

Greater Antilles
race

MOURNING DOVE

**ROCK PIGEON (ROCK DOVE)** *Columba livia* 33–36cm (13–14in); 350g. **BEHAVIOR** Flocks. **DESCRIPTION** Very variable. Often gray with black tail band and white rump. **VOICE** Gentle cooing. **STATUS AND RANGE** Introduced. Common and feral through much of West Indies. **HABITAT** Tame resident of city streets.

**EURASIAN COLLARED-DOVE** *Streptopelia decaocto* 28–30cm (11–12in); male 150–260g, female 112–196g. Medium-sized dove, gray with dark primaries and black band on hindneck. Larger and browner than domestic Ringed Turtle-Dove with gray rather than whitish undertail-coverts, and much darker primaries. **VOICE** Repeated three-syllable *kuk-koooooó-kook*, with brief pauses between phrases. Harsh, nasal *mew* in flight or upon landing. (Domestic Ringed Turtle-Dove has two-syllable, throaty call.) **STATUS AND RANGE** Introduced. Common permanent resident in Bahamas, Cuba, Hispaniola, Puerto Rico, Virgin Islands, Cayman Islands (Grand Cayman), and Lesser Antilles. Uncommon in Jamaica. Absent from San Andrés and Providencia. Increasing throughout West Indies. **HABITAT** Urban areas.

**RINGED TURTLE-DOVE (BARBARY DOVE)** *Streptopelia risoria* 25–28cm (10–11in); 130–160g. Medium-sized dove, light tan above and white below, with black collar around hindneck. Tail long and rounded. (Eurasian Collared-Dove darker, with gray rather than whitish undertail-coverts and much darker primaries.) **VOICE** Variable soft cooing. **STATUS AND RANGE** A domesticated form of the African Collared-Dove (*S. roseogrisea*); numerous individuals have escaped from captivity. Occurs in semi-domesticated state in rural Puerto Rico and St Croix (Virgin Islands), where breeds in wild. Suspected to breed on Cayman Islands. Will likely interbreed with Eurasian Collared-Dove. **HABITAT** Around rural habitations, mangroves, swamps, and woodlands.

**PIED IMPERIAL-PIGEON** *Ducula bicolor* 35–42cm (14–17in); 365–510g. A large white pigeon with black flight feathers and tail. **VOICE** Variable, including a loud, low-pitched moaning *coo-hoo*, or *moo-oop*. **STATUS AND RANGE** Introduced to New Providence (Bahamas), where established, particularly in eastern part of island. **HABITAT** Wooded areas including mangroves.

ROCK PIGEON

EURASIAN COLLARED-DOVE

RINGED TURTLE-DOVE

PIED IMPERIAL PIGEON

**Cuckoos:** Slender birds with long tails and long, thin, down-turned bills. Their movements are slow and deliberate, and their flight is direct.

**H HISPANIOLAN LIZARD-CUCKOO** *Coccyzus longirostris* 41–46cm (16–18in); 110g. Large, with pale gray breast, long tail, and straight, slender bill. Reddish-brown wing patch. **VOICE** Throaty *ka-ka-ka-ka-ka-ka-ka-ka-kau-kau-ko-ko*, descending. **STATUS AND RANGE** Endemic to Hispaniola, where generally common and widespread at all elevations. **HABITAT** Forests and shade coffee plantations.

**P PUERTO RICAN LIZARD-CUCKOO** *Coccyzus vieilloti* 40–48cm (16–19in); male 75–83g, female 88–110g. Large, with long tail and two-toned underparts. **VOICE** Emphatic *ka-ka-ka-ka* ... accelerating, becoming louder. **STATUS AND RANGE** Endemic to Puerto Rico; fairly common at all elevations. **HABITAT** Dense forests and shade coffee plantations.

**J JAMAICAN LIZARD-CUCKOO** *Coccyzus vetula* 38cm (15in); 86–104g. Fairly large, with long tail and long, straight bill. Lower underparts pale reddish-brown. Reddish-brown wing patch, red eye-ring. **VOICE** Rapid, low, trailing *cak-cak-cak-ka-ka-ka-k-k*. **STATUS AND RANGE** Endemic to Jamaica; common and widespread. **HABITAT** Moist or wet mid-elevation forests, dry and secondary forests, woodlands, and wooded ravines.

**J CHESTNUT-BELLIED CUCKOO** *Coccyzus pluvialis* 48–56cm (19–22in); 130–190g. Large, with long tail and down-curved bill. Primarily reddish underparts; pale gray throat and upper breast. **VOICE** Throaty, accelerating *quawk-quawk-ak-ak-ak-ak-ak*. **STATUS AND RANGE** Endemic to Jamaica, where common and widespread. **HABITAT** Open, wet forests at mid-elevations. Also open woodlands, dense second-growth forests, and gardens.

**M GREAT LIZARD-CUCKOO** *Coccyzus merlini* 44–55cm (17–22in); male 125–175g, female 165–255g. Large, with long tail and bill. **VOICE** Long, increasingly loud *ka-ka-ka* ... **STATUS AND RANGE** Common and widespread in Cuba. In Bahamas, uncommon and limited to Andros and Eleuthera. These islands comprise entire range. **HABITAT** Dense woods.

**H BAY-BREASTED CUCKOO** *Coccyzus rufigularis* 43–51cm (17–20in); 130g. **BEHAVIOR** Shy and secretive. **DESCRIPTION** Large, with dark reddish-brown throat and breast; thick, curved bill. Reddish-brown wing patch; long tail. **VOICE** Strong *cua*, followed by guttural, accelerating *u-ak-u-ak-ak-ak-ak-ak-ak-ak*. **STATUS AND RANGE** Endemic to Hispaniola, where rare and local in Dominican Republic. Status in Haiti unknown, but likely very rare and local if not absent. Endangered. **HABITAT** Primarily transition zone between dry forest and moist broadleaf forest at low to moderate elevations. Also mixed pine and broadleaf forests.

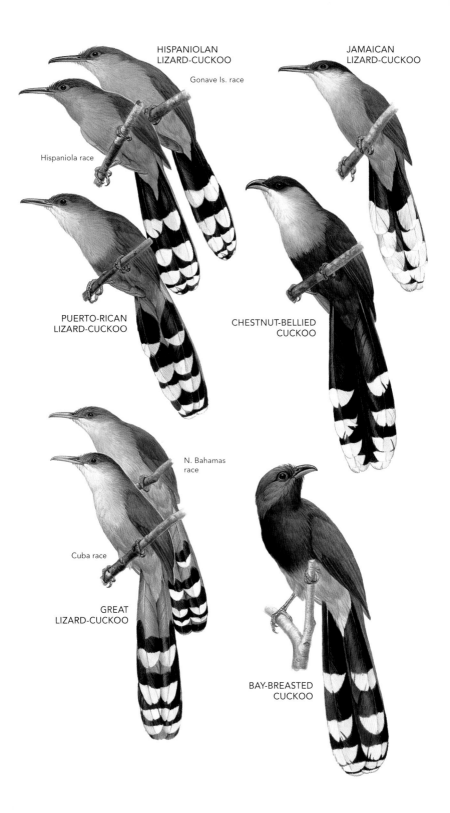

HISPANIOLAN
LIZARD-CUCKOO

Gonave Is. race

Hispaniola race

JAMAICAN
LIZARD-CUCKOO

PUERTO-RICAN
LIZARD-CUCKOO

CHESTNUT-BELLIED
CUCKOO

N. Bahamas
race

Cuba race

GREAT
LIZARD-CUCKOO

BAY-BREASTED
CUCKOO

**YELLOW-BILLED CUCKOO** *Coccyzus americanus* 28–32cm (11–12.5in); 60g. White underparts; long tail; down-curved bill, yellow at base. Reddish-brown wing patch. **VOICE** Throaty *ka-ka-ka-ka-ka-ka-ka-ka-ka-kow, kow, kow, kow*; volume increases and slows at end. **STATUS AND RANGE** Occurs through West Indies, where residents augmented by migrants. Uncommon breeding resident May–August in Cuba, Hispaniola, and Puerto Rico; rarely in Grand Bahama (Bahamas), Jamaica, and Virgin Islands. Migrants occur primarily September–October but also March–April. Highly variable abundance annually. As migrant, generally common in Bahamas, Cuba, Hispaniola, and Puerto Rico; uncommon in Cayman Islands and Jamaica; rare in Virgin Islands; generally uncommon to very rare in Lesser Antilles, San Andrés, and Providencia. **HABITAT** Lowland scrub and dry forests.

**BLACK-BILLED CUCKOO** *Coccyzus erythropthalmus* 30cm (12in); 50g. White underparts; long tail; dark, down-curved bill; reddish eye-ring. (Yellow-billed Cuckoo lacks a truly red eye-ring and has reddish-brown in primaries and more conspicuous white marking under tail.) **VOICE** *Cu-cu-cu-cu.* **STATUS AND RANGE** Very rare migrant in northern Bahamas, Cuba, Hispaniola, and Guadeloupe. Vagrant elsewhere. Occurs September–November and April–May. **HABITAT** Scrublands, lowland forests.

**MANGROVE CUCKOO** *Coccyzus minor* 28–30cm (11–12in); 60g. Black ear-patch and tan abdomen. Slender; long tail; long, down-curved bill, yellow at base. (All other cuckoos lack black ear-patch.) **VOICE** Slower, more nasal than Yellow-billed Cuckoo. **STATUS AND RANGE** Fairly common permanent resident throughout West Indies. **HABITAT** Dry scrub, mangroves, thickets.

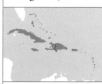

**SMOOTH-BILLED ANI** *Crotophaga ani* 30–33cm (12–13in); 100g. **BEHAVIOR** Small flocks. **DESCRIPTION** Large, with black, parrot-like bill and long tail. **VOICE** A noisy bird. Loud, squawky whistle, *a-leep.* **FLIGHT** Straight, with rapid shallow wing strokes followed by short glides. **STATUS AND RANGE** Widespread in West Indies, where common permanent resident in Bahamas, Greater Antilles, Virgin and Cayman Islands, Montserrat, Guadeloupe, Dominica, St Vincent, Grenada, San Andrés, and Providencia. Rare in Martinique and St Lucia. Absent from northern Lesser Antilles and Barbados. **HABITAT** Scattered trees and bushes in open lowlands.

**ⒸZAPATA WREN** *Ferminia cerverai* 16cm (6.25in). Sparrowsized. Brown striped with black except for grayish underparts. Tail, bill, and legs long. Wings short and round. Highly secretive. (House Wren smaller, less heavily barred, does not occur in sawgrass marshes.) **VOICE** High, strong, and very musical. Starts with low guttural note, transforming to canary-like warble. Usually repeats song three times. Also harsh notes and sharp *chip*s of various tones. **STATUS AND RANGE** Endemic to Cuba, where limited to Zapata Swamp. Endangered. Genus also endemic to Cuba. **HABITAT** Sawgrass marshes.

**HOUSE WREN** *Troglodytes aedon* 11.5–13cm (4.5–5in); 10g. **BEHAVIOR** Cocks tail above back. **DESCRIPTION** Small, active brown bird with relatively large head. **ADULT** Reddish-gray above; pale eyebrow stripe; variably dark brown to whitish below. Bill all dark or with lower mandible yellow; wings and tail heavily barred black. **VOICE** Bursting, gurgling warble. Also sharp chatter. **STATUS AND RANGE** Common permanent resident in Dominica, Grenada, and St Vincent. Rare and local in St Lucia, where confined to northeastern dry coastal scrub. St Lucia race threatened. Very rare migrant in northern Bahamas. Some consider Lesser Antillean forms distinct species. **HABITAT** Moist upland forests to arid coastal scrub and human settlements.

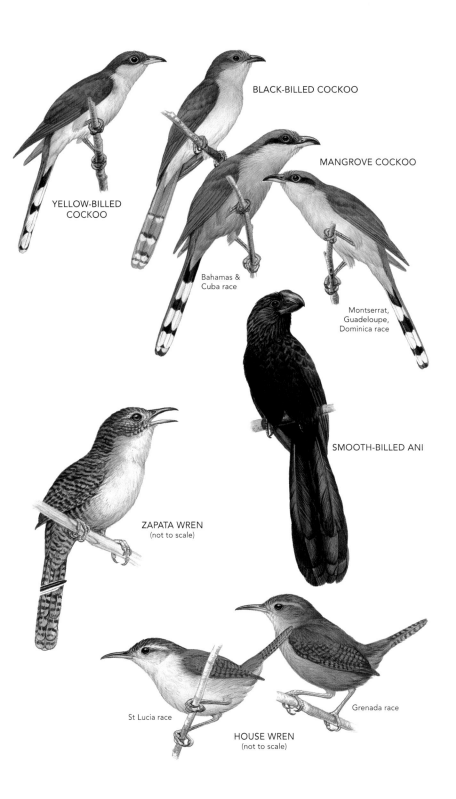

YELLOW-BILLED
COCKOO

BLACK-BILLED COCKOO

MANGROVE COCKOO

Bahamas &
Cuba race

Montserrat,
Guadeloupe,
Dominica race

SMOOTH-BILLED ANI

ZAPATA WREN
(not to scale)

St Lucia race

Grenada race

HOUSE WREN
(not to scale)

**Hummingbirds:** Tiny birds with extremely rapid wingbeats and the ability to hover in front of blossoms to feed. They can also fly backward. Most are brilliantly iridescent but appear black in poor light. They have long, pointed bills for probing into flowers. Hummers can be very aggressive around their feeding territories.

**C** **BEE HUMMINGBIRD** *Mellisuga helenae* 5.5–6cm (2.2–2.4in); 1.9–2.6g. The world's smallest bird. Short, white-tipped tail. MALE Iridescent red throat plumes. FEMALE Inconspicuous white spot behind eye; black spot on lores. VOICE Twitter, long and quite high. Also low warbling notes. STATUS AND RANGE Endemic to Cuba, where rare and local. Threatened. Genus endemic to West Indies. HABITAT Primarily coastal forests and forest edges, also mountain valleys, forests of interior, swamplands, and gardens.

**M** **VERVAIN HUMMINGBIRD** *Mellisuga minima* 6cm (2.5in); 2.4g. BEHAVIOR Often hovers with tail cocked up. DESCRIPTION Tiny hummer with straight black bill. Chin and throat sometimes flecked; sides and flanks dull green. MALE Tail deeply notched. FEMALE Tail rounded, tipped white. VOICE Loud, rhythmic, high-pitched, metallic squeaks. Also throaty buzz. STATUS AND RANGE Unique to Jamaica and Hispaniola, common and widespread on both islands. These islands comprise entire range. Nested on Mona Island (Puerto Rico). Genus endemic to West Indies. HABITAT All open areas with small flowers, open woodlands, and shade coffee.

**P** **PUERTO RICAN EMERALD** *Chlorostilbon maugaeus* Male 8.5–9.5 cm (3.3–3.7in), female 7.5–8.5 cm (3–3.3in); 3.4–3.8g. Small hummer with forked tail and no crest. MALE Green above and below, with black tail and pinkish base on lower mandible. FEMALE Underparts white, bill entirely black, outertail feathers tipped white. Tail may be forked, notched, or even-edged. (Antillean Crested Hummingbird has crest and rounded tail.) VOICE Series of *tic*s and a trill with buzz at the end. STATUS AND RANGE Endemic to Puerto Rico. Common in mountains, irregular on coast, particularly drier south coast. HABITAT Forests and edges, including shade coffee, also lowland wooded areas.

**M** **CUBAN EMERALD** *Chlorostilbon ricordii* Male 10.5–11.5cm (4–4.5in), female 9.5–10.5cm (3.7–4.1in); 2.5–5g. Medium-sized hummer with long, forked tail and long, thin bill, pinkish below. VOICE Short, squeaking twitter. STATUS AND RANGE Common, widespread permanent resident in Cuba. In Bahamas, common on Grand Bahama, Abaco, and Andros; absent elsewhere. These islands comprise entire range. HABITAT All habitats from coast to mid-elevations.

**H** **HISPANIOLAN EMERALD** *Chlorostilbon swainsonii* 10.5cm (4.1in); 4.9g. Tiny hummer with straight bill. MALE Green overall, dull black breast spot, deeply forked tail, lower mandible pinkish. FEMALE Dull grayish below, metallic green sides, whitish outertail tips. (Female Antillean Mango larger, bill darker.) VOICE Sharp, metallic *tic*s. STATUS AND RANGE Endemic to Hispaniola, where generally common, though threatened in Haiti. HABITAT Moist forests and shade coffee plantations in mountains, hills, and karst. Also clearings.

**M** **ANTILLEAN CRESTED HUMMINGBIRD** *Orthorhyncus cristatus* 8.5–9.5cm (3.3–3.7in); 3.5g. Tiny, adults possess a crest. ADULT MALE Pointed crest; underparts blackish. ADULT FEMALE Crest less evident; underparts pale gray. IMMATURE Lacks crest. VOICE Emphatic notes. STATUS AND RANGE Common permanent resident throughout Lesser Antilles, Virgin Islands, and on Puerto Rico's eastern coastal plain. These islands comprise entire range. Genus also endemic to West Indies. HABITAT Primarily lowland openings, gardens, forest edges, and arid habitats; also mountain forests on some islands.

BEE HUMMINGBIRD

VERVAIN HUMMINGBIRD
Hispaniola race

CUBAN EMERALD

PUERTO RICAN EMERALD

Southern
Lesser Antilles
race

ANTILLEAN CRESTED
HUMMINGBIRD

HISPANIOLAN EMERALD

Northern
Lesser Antilles
race

**M**ANTILLEAN MANGO *Anthracothorax dominicus* 11–12.5cm (4.3–5in); 4–8g. Large hummer with down-curved black bill. ADULT MALE Primarily black below; throat green. FEMALE Whitish below and on tail tips. IMMATURE MALE Black stripe down center of whitish underparts. VOICE Unmusical, thin trill, quite loud. Also sharp chipping notes. STATUS AND RANGE Common resident at all elevations in Hispaniola. Common on southern coast and northern haystack hills of Puerto Rico. Nearly absent from east coast. Increasingly rare in Virgin Islands. These islands comprise entire range. HABITAT Clearings and scrub. Also gardens and shade coffee plantations.

**P** GREEN MANGO *Anthracothorax viridis* 11.5cm (4.5in); 6.6–7.2g. Large hummer with entirely emerald-green underparts, black, down-curved bill, and rounded tail. VOICE Trill-like twitter; loud, harsh rattling or chattering notes; a hard *tic*. STATUS AND RANGE Endemic to Puerto Rico; common in central and western mountains; decidedly uncommon in eastern mountains and on coast. HABITAT Mountain forests and coffee plantations.

**J** JAMAICAN MANGO *Anthracothorax mango* 13cm (5in); 8.5–9.1g. Large hummer with black underparts; reddish-purple cheeks and sides of neck. ADULT MALE Underparts velvet-black. ADULT FEMALE Duller. VOICE Sharp, raspy *tic*s. STATUS AND RANGE Endemic to Jamaica; widespread and common. HABITAT Forest edges, banana plantations, gardens, open woodlands near coast, and sea-level forests. Sometimes lowland dry limestone forest edges.

**GREEN-BREASTED MANGO** *Anthracothorax prevostii* 12.5cm (5in); 7g. ADULT MALE Blended black, green, and violet-blue underparts. ADULT FEMALE Slightly paler. IMMATURE Underparts with black median stripe. STATUS AND RANGE Common permanent resident on Providencia and San Andrés. HABITAT Primarily open coastal areas with scattered trees and bushes.

**M** PURPLE-THROATED CARIB *Eulampis jugularis* 11.5cm (4.5in); 10g. Large hummer with purplish-red throat and breast, emerald-green wings, and down-curved bill. FEMALE Longer, more sharply down-curved bill than male. VOICE Sharp *chewp*, repeated rapidly when agitated. STATUS AND RANGE Limited to Lesser Antilles. Fairly common permanent resident on St Bartholomew, Saba, Guadeloupe, Dominica, Martinique, St Lucia, and St Vincent; uncommon on St Eustatius, St Christopher, Nevis, Antigua, and Montserrat. Vagrant elsewhere in West Indies. These islands comprise entire range. Genus also endemic to West Indies. HABITAT Mountain forests and banana plantations; occasionally sea level.

**M** GREEN-THROATED CARIB *Eulampis holosericeus* 11.5–12cm (4.5–4.7in); 5–8g. Large hummer with green breast and slightly down-curved bill. Blue breast mark visible in good light. VOICE Sharp *chewp* and loud wing rattle. STATUS AND RANGE Common permanent resident throughout Lesser Antilles, Virgin Islands, and eastern Puerto Rico. These islands comprise entire range. Genus also endemic to West Indies. HABITAT Gardens and rain forests at all elevations in Lesser Antilles. In Puerto Rico, primarily coastal.

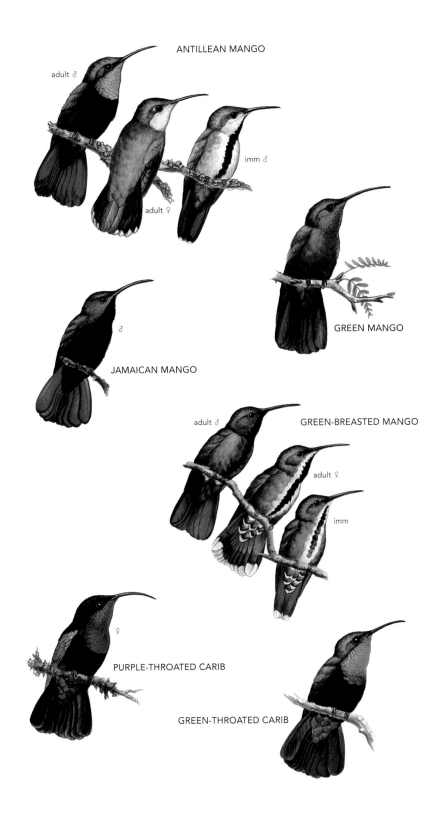

ANTILLEAN MANGO

adult ♂

adult ♀

imm ♂

GREEN MANGO

JAMAICAN MANGO

♂

GREEN-BREASTED MANGO

adult ♂

adult ♀

imm

PURPLE-THROATED CARIB

♀

GREEN-THROATED CARIB

**RUBY-THROATED HUMMINGBIRD** *Archilochus colubris* 8–9.5cm (3–3.7in); 3.2g. **MALE** Red throat; moderately forked tail. **FEMALE** Grayish sides; dark bill; rounded, white-tipped tail. Often has white spot behind eye. (Female Cuban and Hispaniolan Emeralds have paler bill, more conspicuous white stripe behind eye, and greenish sides.) **VOICE** Peculiar twitter, similar to mouse. **STATUS AND RANGE** Rare migrant to northern Bahamas and Cuba March–April, very rare non-breeding resident November–February. Decidedly rare migrant and non-breeding resident in Cayman Islands March–April. Vagrant elsewhere in West Indies. **HABITAT** Gardens, wood edges, and clusters of trees.

Ⓜ**BLUE-HEADED HUMMINGBIRD** *Cyanophaia bicolor* 9.5cm (3.7in); 4.6g. **MALE** Head, throat, upper breast, and tail violet-blue. **FEMALE** Shiny green above with bronze sheen on mantle; grayish-white below with flecks of green on sides; blackish ear-patch. **VOICE** Shrill, metallic notes, rapidly descending. **STATUS AND RANGE** Common permanent resident of Dominica and Martinique. Usually mid-elevations. These islands comprise entire range. Genus endemic to West Indies. **HABITAT** Moist open areas in mountain forests, along mountain streams, and in wooded edges of fields.

**RUFOUS-BREASTED HERMIT** *Glaucis hirsutus* 12.5cm (5in); 7g. Long, down-curved bill, yellow lower mandible; white-tipped, rounded tail. **MALE** Upperparts dull green. **FEMALE** Upperparts more reddish. **VOICE** High *sweep*, sometimes repeated. Less frequently *sweep, swee-swee.* **STATUS AND RANGE** Fairly common permanent resident in Grenada in mountains above 450m (1500ft). **HABITAT** Mountain forests, forest edges, and banana, cocoa, and nutmeg plantations.

Ⓙ**STREAMERTAIL** *Trochilus polytmus* Male (with tail plumes) 22–25cm (8.5–10in), female 10.5cm (4.1in); 5g. **ADULT MALE** Two extremely long tail feathers, green underparts, black hood. **ADULT FEMALE** White underparts. Subspecies in extreme eastern Jamaica has entirely black rather than primarily red bill. **VOICE** Loud, metallic *ting* or *teet* and prolonged *twink-twink-twink* … dropping in pitch. In flight, male's streamers hum. **STATUS AND RANGE** Endemic to Jamaica, where widespread. Red-billed and black-billed subspecies considered distinct species by some. Genus endemic to Jamaica. **HABITAT** Sea-level to elfin forest and all human-made habitats; forages mainly throughout mid-strata and at forest edge.

Ⓢ**BAHAMA WOODSTAR** *Nesophlox evelynae* 9–9.5cm (3.5–3.7in); 3g. **ADULT MALE** Deeply forked tail with reddish-brown inner feathers. Reddish-violet throat, reddish-brown lower underparts. **ADULT FEMALE** White throat and breast; rounded, reddish-brown tail and lower underparts. **VOICE** Sharp *tit, titit, tit, tit, titit*, often speeding to rapid rattle. **STATUS AND RANGE** Endemic to Bahamas and Turks and Caicos, where common, but absent from Great and Little Inagua. Genus also endemic to Bahamas. **HABITAT** Gardens, scrub, woodlands, forest edges, clearings, and mixed pine forests.

Ⓢ**INAGUA WOODSTAR (BAHAMA WOODSTAR)** *Nesophlox lyrura* 9–9.5cm (3.5–3.7in); 3g. Similar to Bahama Woodstar, but male has more strongly forked tail, longer outertail feathers, and fully iridescent forehead. **VOICE** Similar to Bahama Woodstar, but song shorter, simpler, and softer. **STATUS AND RANGE** Endemic to Great and Little Inagua (Bahamas) where common. Genus also endemic to Bahamas. **HABITAT** Gardens, scrub, and thickets.

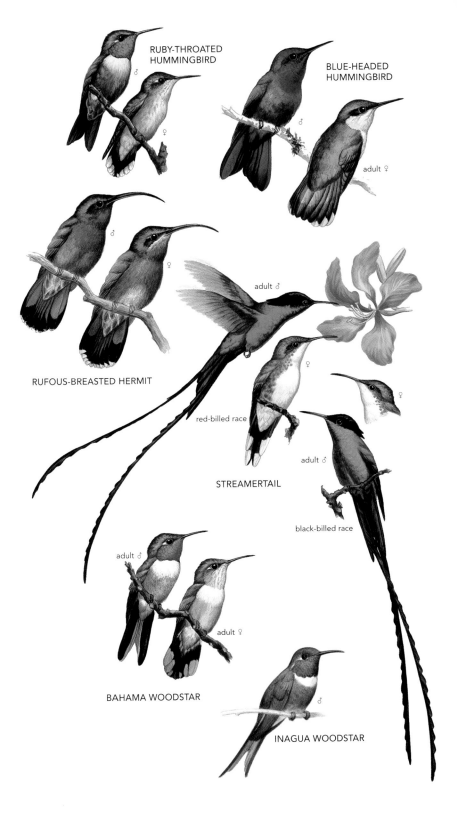

RUBY-THROATED
HUMMINGBIRD
♂
♀

BLUE-HEADED
HUMMINGBIRD
♂
adult ♀

RUFOUS-BREASTED HERMIT
♂
♀

adult ♂

red-billed race
♀

adult ♂

STREAMERTAIL

black-billed race

adult ♂
adult ♀

BAHAMA WOODSTAR

♂

INAGUA WOODSTAR

**Todies:** Small, chunky birds with green upperparts, a red throat, and a long, broad bill. Todies sally short distances to snatch insects. Family is endemic to the West Indies.
**Trogons:** Brightly colored and long-tailed, trogons typically perch motionless until darting to snatch insects in undulating flight or hovering to take small fruits from a stem.

**P** **PUERTO RICAN TODY** *Todus mexicanus* 11cm (4.3in); 6g. Tiny, chunky; bright green above; red throat; long, broad, reddish bill. **VOICE** Loud, nasal *beep* or *bee-beep*. Wing rattles in flight. **STATUS AND RANGE** Endemic to Puerto Rico, where common and widespread from coast to mountains. **HABITAT** Forested areas from wet to dry, including dense thickets.

**J** **JAMAICAN TODY** *Todus todus* 9cm (3.5in); 6.5g. Tiny, chunky; bright green above; red throat; long, broad, reddish bill. Flanks pink; abdomen and sides of breast pale yellow. **VOICE** Almost silent during non-breeding season. Calls include a loud *beep* and a rapid, guttural "throat-rattling" given during territorial displays while perched. **STATUS AND RANGE** Endemic to Jamaica, where widespread and common from coast to mountains. **HABITAT** Wet, moist, and dry forest; most abundant in wooded hills and mountains.

**C** **CUBAN TODY** *Todus multicolor* 11cm (4.3in); 6g. Small, stubby; primarily green; with big head, no neck, large flat bill, and red throat. Flanks pink; sides of throat blue; undertail-coverts yellow. **FLIGHT** Characteristic wing rattle. **VOICE** Typically a soft *pprreeee-pprreeee*. Sometimes a peculiar short *tot-tot-tot-tot*. **STATUS AND RANGE** Endemic to Cuba, where common and widespread. **HABITAT** Wooded and semi-wooded areas, forests, stream edges, and areas with earthen embankments at all elevations.

**H** **BROAD-BILLED TODY** *Todus subulatus* 11–12cm (4.3–4.5in); 9g. Bright green above; grayish-white tinted yellow below; pink sides; red throat. Lower mandible entirely reddish. (Narrow-billed Tody is whiter below and usually has black-tipped bill. Best distinguished by voice.) **VOICE** Monotonous, often repeated whistle, *terp, terp, terp*, uttered in complaining tone. Single-note call of same tone contrasts with Narrow-billed Tody's two-note call. **STATUS AND RANGE** Endemic to Hispaniola; common in lowlands. **HABITAT** Semi-arid areas from lowlands to 1700m (5600ft) in forests, including pine; also scrub, shade coffee plantations, and some mangroves. Frequents ravines.

**H** **NARROW-BILLED TODY** *Todus angustirostris* 11cm (4.3in); 7g. Tiny, chunky; brilliant green upperparts; red throat; whitish underparts tinted yellow; pinkish sides. Lower mandible reddish, usually with black tip. (Broad-billed Tody grayish-white below with entirely red lower mandible. Since Narrow-billed Tody sometimes lacks black tip on lower mandible, best distinguished by voice.) **VOICE** Frequently repeated, two-part *chip-chee*, accented on the second syllable. Also chattering, trilly *chippy-chippy-chippy-chip*, dropping in pitch, but not in tone. **STATUS AND RANGE** Endemic to Hispaniola, where common primarily at higher elevations. Threatened in Haiti. **HABITAT** Dense, wet forests, including pine. Frequents ravines and earthen embankments.

**C** **CUBAN TROGON** *Priotelus temnurus* 25–28cm (10–11in); 65g. Red belly, green back, blue crown; short, broad bill; long, peculiar tail with much white on underside. **VOICE** Very varied. Most commonly a repeated *toco-toco-tocoro-tocoro* … Also a low, short, mournful call, difficult to locate. **STATUS AND RANGE** Endemic to Cuba, where widely distributed and common. Genus endemic to West Indies. **HABITAT** Wet and dry forests at all altitudes. Primarily shady areas.

**H** **HISPANIOLAN TROGON** *Priotelus roseigaster* 27–30cm (10.5–12in); 75g. Green upperparts, red belly, yellow bill, gray throat and breast. Long tail marked with white below. **MALE** Wings with fine black-and-white barring. **FEMALE** Lacks wing barring. **VOICE** *Toca-loro; coc, ca-rao;* or *cock-craow*, repeated. Also cooing and puppy-like whimpering. **STATUS AND RANGE** Endemic to Hispaniola. In Dominican Republic still locally common in undisturbed habitat, but declining. During non-breeding season, descends to lower elevations. Locally abundant in Haiti (Massif de la Hotte), but declining. Threatened. Genus endemic to West Indies. **HABITAT** Mountain forests, including mature pine and broadleaf forests. Local in mangroves.

adult

PUERTO RICAN TODY

JAMAICAN TODY

imm

CUBAN TODY

BROAD-BILLED
TODY

NARROW-BILLED
TODY

CUBAN TROGON

♂

♀

HISPANIOLAN TROGON

**Kingfishers:** This is a distinctive group with large heads, crests, and long, pointed bills. The two West Indian species hover well above the water and then dive to capture fish.
**Woodpeckers:** Use their chisel-like bills to bore into trees for insects and to excavate nest cavities. Males of most species have red head markings; flight undulating.

**RINGED KINGFISHER** *Megaceryle torquata* 38–41cm (15–16in); 250–325g. Large, with crest and large bill; primarily reddish-brown underparts. **FEMALE** Blue breast band. **FLIGHT** Reddish underwing-coverts. (Belted Kingfisher smaller, with white lower belly and underwing-coverts.) **VOICE** Loud, harsh rattle. **STATUS AND RANGE** Fairly common permanent resident in Dominica, uncommon and local in Guadeloupe. **HABITAT** Large streams, lakes, and reservoirs.

**BELTED KINGFISHER** *Megaceryle alcyon* 28–36cm (11–14in); 150g. **DESCRIPTION** Large bill; crest. **MALE** Blue breast band. **FEMALE** One blue and one orange breast band. (Ringed Kingfisher is larger and heavier-billed, has more extensive reddish-brown underparts and reddish underwing-coverts.) **VOICE** Loud, harsh rattle. **STATUS AND RANGE** Generally fairly common migrant and non-breeding resident throughout West Indies September–April; records from every month. **HABITAT** Calm bodies of water, both saline and fresh.

Ⓜ **WEST INDIAN WOODPECKER** *Melanerpes superciliaris* 27–32cm (10.5–12.5in); 65–125g. Upperparts and wings barred black and white, underparts pale cinnamon to brownish-gray, abdomen red. **ADULT MALE** Crown to hindneck red. **ADULT FEMALE** Top of head black or tan; only back of crown and hindneck red. **VOICE** Distinctive loud, high-pitched *krruuu-krruu-kruu* … , frequently repeated. **STATUS AND RANGE** Known only from Bahamas, Cuba, and Cayman Islands. Common and widespread in Cuba. In Bahamas, common on Abaco, uncommon on San Salvador (northern fringe), nearly extirpated from Grand Bahama. In Cayman Islands, only on Grand Cayman, where fairly common. Grand Bahama race endangered. **HABITAT** Primarily dry forests, scrub, coastal forests, and palm groves. On Abaco, settlements.

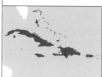

**YELLOW-BELLIED SAPSUCKER** *Sphyrapicus varius* 20–23cm (8–9in); 50g. White wing patch. **ADULT** Red forehead and crown, rarely black. Black-and-white facial pattern, black breast band. **ADULT MALE** Red throat. **ADULT FEMALE** White throat. **IMMATURE** Pale brown plumage, lightly spotted. Faint facial stripes. **STATUS AND RANGE** Migrant and non-breeding resident in West Indies, primarily October–April. Common in Bahamas and Cuba; uncommon in Jamaica, Cayman Islands, and San Andrés. Decidedly uncommon to rare in Hispaniola and rare in Puerto Rico and Virgin Islands. **HABITAT** Forests, forest edges, woodlands, and gardens, from coast to mountains.

**NORTHERN FLICKER** *Colaptes auratus* 30–32cm (12–12.5in); 90g. **BEHAVIOR** Sometimes on ground. **DESCRIPTION** Fairly large, with conspicuous black bar across breast. Yellow underwings and undertail; beige underparts with black spots; large white rump patch spotted with black; red patch on hindneck. **ADULT MALE** Black mustache stripe. **ADULT FEMALE** Lacks mustache stripe. **VOICE** Long cackle, *pic-pic-pic-pic-pic-pic-pic.* (Can be confused with Fernandina's Flicker.) Also softer and lower *fli-quer, fli-quer.* **STATUS AND RANGE** Fairly common permanent resident in Grand Cayman (Cayman Islands) and locally in Cuba. **HABITAT** All areas with trees, from forests to gardens.

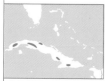

Ⓒ **FERNANDINA'S FLICKER** *Colaptes fernandinae* 30–34cm (12–14in). **BEHAVIOR** Often on ground. **DESCRIPTION** Large. Almost entirely yellowish-tan with fine black barring. No red on head. Underwings yellow. **MALE** Black mustache stripe. **FEMALE** Lacks mustache stripe. **VOICE** Loud *pic-pic-pic-pic-pic-pic,* slightly slower and deeper than Northern Flicker. Also loud, short *ch-ch-ch,* with nasal resonance. **STATUS AND RANGE** Endemic to Cuba, where rare and local. Endangered. **HABITAT** Savanna edges and open forests with scattered trees and dense leaf-litter.

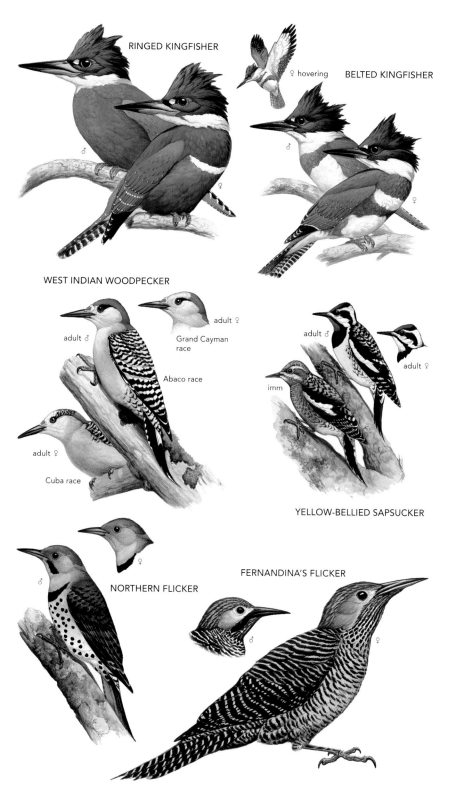

RINGED KINGFISHER

♀ hovering

BELTED KINGFISHER

♂

♀

♂

♀

WEST INDIAN WOODPECKER

adult ♂

adult ♀
Grand Cayman race

Abaco race

adult ♂

imm

adult ♀

adult ♀

Cuba race

YELLOW-BELLIED SAPSUCKER

♂

♀

NORTHERN FLICKER

FERNANDINA'S FLICKER

♂

♀

**C CUBAN GREEN WOODPECKER** *Xiphidiopicus percussus* 21–25cm (8–10in); 45–95g (male 20% heavier). Small, with noticeable crest. Green on upperparts, yellowish underparts; white face with black stripe behind eye; red patch on breast. **MALE** Red crown. **FEMALE** Black crown. **VOICE** Short, low and harsh *jorr-jorr-jorr* ... Also higher-pitched, shorter *eh-eh-eh*. **STATUS AND RANGE** Endemic to Cuba, where common and widespread. Genus endemic to Cuba. **HABITAT** Many forest types including wet and dry, open and dense, mountains and lowlands; also mangroves.

**H ANTILLEAN PICULET** *Nesoctites micromegas* 13–16cm (5–6.25in); 33g. **BEHAVIOR** Criss-crosses along twigs and vines. **DESCRIPTION** Tiny, chunky, atypical woodpecker. **ADULT** Olive above, pale yellowish with heavy dark spots below. Yellow on crown. **ADULT MALE** Red patch in center of crown. **VOICE** Staccato *kuk-ki-ki-ki-ke-ku-kuk*, surprisingly loud. **STATUS AND RANGE** Endemic to Hispaniola, where locally common in Dominican Republic. Occurs from lowlands to mountains, not usually at highest elevations. Less common and more local in Haiti, where threatened. Genus endemic to Hispaniola. **HABITAT** Dry and humid forests, including pines mixed with broadleaf trees, thorn forests, dense second growth, semi-arid areas, and mangroves.

**H HISPANIOLAN WOODPECKER** *Melanerpes striatus* 22–25cm (8.5–10in); 65g. Medium-sized, with white and black patches on hindneck; red hindcrown and uppertail-coverts; whitish to yellow eye. **MALE** Larger and longer-billed. **VOICE** Strong, variable, including loud, rolling call interrupted with throaty noises. Call notes *wup* and *ta-a*. Short *bdddt* with three to five distinct notes. **STATUS AND RANGE** Endemic to Hispaniola; common and widespread. **HABITAT** Primarily in hilly, partly cultivated and partly wooded areas, and in palms scattered among cultivated fields. From coast to humid mountain forests.

**J JAMAICAN WOODPECKER** *Melanerpes radiolatus* 24–26cm (9.5–10.5in); 95–130g. Red hindcrown and hindneck; whitish face; black upperparts; wings finely streaked with white. **MALE** Red crown. **FEMALE** Brownish-olive crown. **VOICE** Loud, rollicking *chee-ee-urp* cry, similar to Olive-throated Parakeet. Call variable: single note or rapid series of three or more *churp-chur-churp* notes. **STATUS AND RANGE** Endemic to Jamaica, where common and widespread. The only woodpecker in Jamaica, except for the uncommon Yellow-bellied Sapsucker. **HABITAT** Coastal coconut groves to forested mountain summits, including both dry and wet forests, forest edges, woodlands, shade coffee plantations, and gardens.

**P PUERTO RICAN WOODPECKER** *Melanerpes portoricensis* 23–27cm (9–10.5in); 45–70g. Red throat and breast; white rump and forehead; blackish upperparts. **ADULT MALE** Underparts primarily red with grayish-brown sides. **ADULT FEMALE AND IMMATURE** Less red on underparts. **VOICE** Wide variety of calls, most commonly *wek, wek, wek-wek-wek-wek-wek* ... becoming louder and faster. **STATUS AND RANGE** Endemic to Puerto Rico; common and widespread. **HABITAT** Coastal plantations to mountain forests, but primarily hills and lower mountains, including shade coffee.

**S GUADELOUPE WOODPECKER** *Melanerpes herminieri* 24–29cm (9.5–11.5in); male 90g, female 75g. **ADULT** Black overall with reddish wash on throat and belly, most noticeable in breeding season. **MALE** Bill about 20% longer than female's. **FLIGHT** Direct, unlike most other woodpeckers. **VOICE** *Wa-uh* or *wa-ah*, and staccato *cht-cht-cht-cht-cht-cht-cht-cht*. **STATUS AND RANGE** Endemic to Guadeloupe, where common and widespread. **HABITAT** Sea level to tree line at 1000m (3300ft) in every forest type including semi-deciduous and evergreen forests, coconut palms, and swamp forests.

**HAIRY WOODPECKER** *Dryobates villosus* 18cm (7in); 40g. Upperparts mostly black with white on back; underparts mostly white. Black eye-line and mustache stripe on otherwise white face; white outertail feathers. **MALE** Red patch on back of head. **FEMALE** Lacks red head patch. **VOICE** Loud *keek*. **STATUS AND RANGE** Fairly common permanent resident in northern Bahamas (Grand Bahama, Abaco, Andros, and New Providence). **HABITAT** Primarily pine woods.

ANTILLEAN
PICULET

CUBAN GREEN
WOODPECKER

HISPANIOLAN
WOODPECKER

JAMAICAN
WOODPECKER

GUADELOUPE
WOODPECKER

PUERTO RICAN
WOODPECKER

HAIRY
WOODPECKER

**Parrots:** A distinctive family easily recognized by their raucous calls, large heads, and extremely heavy bills, which they often use to assist their movements among tree branches. All are gregarious, and all native species in the region are green. Flight is direct, with rapid, shallow wingbeats.

**J YELLOW-BILLED PARROT** *Amazona collaria* 28–31cm (11–12in); 260g. **BEHAVIOR** Flocks. **DESCRIPTION** Yellow bill; white forehead and eye-ring; bluish forecrown and ear-coverts; maroon throat and base of tail; blue primaries and secondaries. **VOICE** Perched— High-pitched *tah-tah-eeeeep.* Flight—Bugling *tuk-tuk-tuk-taaah,* lower pitched and last syllable more drawn out than in Black-billed Parrot. **STATUS AND RANGE** Endemic to Jamaica, where locally common and more widespread than Black-billed Parrot. Threatened. **HABITAT** Primarily mid-elevation wet forests of hills and mountains.

**S ST LUCIA PARROT** *Amazona versicolor* 42–46cm (16.5–18in); 700–800g. **BEHAVIOR** Flocks. **DESCRIPTION** Large, with violet-blue forehead, cheeks, and forecrown; red band across throat extending down center of breast; wings green with violet-blue primaries and a red patch. **VOICE** Raucous squawks. **STATUS AND RANGE** Endemic to St Lucia, where uncommon and local. Numbers slowly increasing. Endangered. **HABITAT** Primarily moist mountain forests. Also secondary forests and cultivated areas.

**J BLACK-BILLED PARROT** *Amazona agilis* 26cm (10in). **BEHAVIOR** Flocks. **DESCRIPTION** Blackish bill and eye-ring. Flight feathers primarily blue. Some have red patch in wing visible in flight. Base of tail red. **VOICE** Perched—*rrak* and *muh-weep.* Flight—*tuh-tuk.* Also a sharp screech. Calls are higher-pitched than Yellow-billed Parrot's. **STATUS AND RANGE** Endemic to Jamaica, where fairly common, particularly on Mount Diablo and in Cockpit Country. Threatened. **HABITAT** Mid-level moist forests of hills and mountains.

**S ST VINCENT PARROT** *Amazona guildingii* 41–46cm (16–18in); 660–700g. **BEHAVIOR** Flocks. **DESCRIPTION** Large and dramatically patterned, with variable coloration. Two major color phases—one predominantly green, the other golden-brown. Intermediates occur. Creamy white forehead shades to orange-yellow on hindcrown; violet-blue cheeks; black wings with yellow-orange patches conspicuous in flight. Tail orange at base, with wide central band of violet and broad yellow tip. **VOICE** Loud, unparrot-like *gua, gua, gua …* in flight. **STATUS AND RANGE** Endemic to St Vincent, where uncommon and critically endangered. Occurs primarily in upper reaches of Buccament, Cumberland, and Wallilibou valleys. **HABITAT** Mature moist mountain forests.

**S IMPERIAL PARROT** *Amazona imperialis* 46–51cm (18–20in); male 900g, female 650g. **BEHAVIOR** Flocks. **DESCRIPTION** Large, with dark maroon-purple head. Dark violet band on hindneck appears black in low light. Wings green with red speculum, primaries dull violet-blue. Underparts purple-violet from breast to abdomen. **VOICE** Flight— Distinctive, trumpeting, metallic *eeeee-er* that descends at end. Perched—Shrieks, squawks, whistles, and bubbly trills. More shrill and metallic than Red-necked Parrot. **STATUS AND RANGE** Endemic to Dominica, where formerly uncommon and local on Morne Diablotin in Northern Forest Reserve. Hurricane Maria (2017) reduced population. Critically endangered. **HABITAT** Mid- to high-elevation wet forests.

**S RED-NECKED PARROT** *Amazona arausiaca* 33–36cm (13–14in); 620g. **BEHAVIOR** Flocks. **DESCRIPTION** Blue crown, face, and chin; bright red spot on throat; red wing patch. Smaller of the two parrots on Dominica. **VOICE** Two-syllable *rrr-eee,* like a drawn-out hiccup. **STATUS AND RANGE** Endemic to Dominica, where local and rare. Formerly locally common in Northern Forest Reserve prior to 2017 hurricane, but now reduced. Endangered. **HABITAT** Moist primary rain forests, generally at mid-elevations.

YELLOW-BILLED
PARROT

ST LUCIA
PARROT

BLACK-BILLED
PARROT

ST VINCENT
PARROT

IMPERIAL
PARROT

RED-NECKED
PARROT

**■ HISPANIOLAN PARROT** *Amazona ventralis* 28–31cm (11–12in); 250–300g. **BEHAVIOR** Flocks. **DESCRIPTION** White forehead, dark ear-spot, and maroon belly. Bright blue primaries and secondaries. **VOICE** Flight—Loud bugling. Perched—Loud squawks and screeches. **STATUS AND RANGE** Endemic to Hispaniola, where locally common only in major forest reserves. Uncommon and local elsewhere. Numbers declining. Threatened. **HABITAT** All elevations in forests, woodlands, and scrub.

**■ PUERTO RICAN PARROT** *Amazona vittata* 30cm (12in); 320g. **BEHAVIOR** Flocks. **DESCRIPTION** White eye-ring, red forehead, and two-toned blue primaries. **VOICE** Raucous squawks including distinct bugling flight call. **STATUS AND RANGE** Endemic to Puerto Rico, where rare and very local. Reintroduced population around Río Abajo was expanding, but hurricanes of 2017 reduced their numbers and nearly extirpated original population in Luquillo Mountains. Critically endangered. **HABITAT** Mid-elevation wet forests and northwestern limestone hills.

**RED-CROWNED PARROT** *Amazona viridigenalis* 30–33cm (12–13in); 295–345g. **BEHAVIOR** Flocks. **DESCRIPTION** Red forecrown and light green cheeks. **FLIGHT** Orange-red wing patch and blue primaries. (Puerto Rican Parrot has red only on forehead and lacks orange-red wing patch.) **VOICE** Distinctive, not as raspy and raucous as most parrots: *keet, kau-kau-kau-kau*. **STATUS AND RANGE** Introduced. Rare and very local primarily on southern coast of Puerto Rico. **HABITAT** Lowland moist forests and scrub.

**■ ROSE-THROATED PARROT (CUBAN PARROT)** *Amazona leucocephala* 28–33cm (11–13in); 240–260g. **BEHAVIOR** Flocks. **DESCRIPTION** Chin, throat, and lower face pale red. Forehead and eye-ring white, primaries blue. Variable among islands. **VOICE** Noisy squawks. In flight, harsh *squawk-squawk*. Calls vary among populations. **STATUS AND RANGE** Entire range confined to Bahamas, Cuba, and Cayman Islands. In Bahamas, only on Abaco and Great Inagua, where fairly common. Locally common in Cuba. In Cayman Islands, common on Grand Cayman and uncommon on Cayman Brac. Threatened. **HABITAT** Forests at all elevations and palm savannas.

**ORANGE-WINGED PARROT** *Amazona amazonica* 32cm (12.5in); 300–470g. **BEHAVIOR** Flocks. **DESCRIPTION** Yellow cheeks and crown; blue lores and eyebrow stripe. **FLIGHT** Orange-red wing patch and blue primaries. **VOICE** Call *kweet, kweet, kweet, kweet* is higher-pitched, weaker, and less raucous than most other parrots in West Indies. **STATUS AND RANGE** Introduced. Uncommon very locally in Puerto Rico. Moderately widespread in center of Martinique. Uncommon and local around Bridgeport in Barbados. Uncommon but widespread in Grenada. **HABITAT** Lowland second-growth forests and urban areas with ornamental trees.

**YELLOW-CROWNED PARROT** *Amazona ochrocephala* 36cm (14in); 380–500g. **BEHAVIOR** Flocks. **DESCRIPTION** Large, with yellow crown. **VOICE** Raucous squawks. **STATUS AND RANGE** Introduced. Very local around George Town in Grand Cayman (Cayman Islands), and in Barbados around Belleville. Not well established. **HABITAT** Woodlands and areas with fruiting trees.

HISPANIOLAN
PARROT

PUERTO RICAN
PARROT

RED-CROWNED
PARROT

Cayman
Islands
race

ROSE-THROATED
PARROT

Bahamas
race

Cuba
race

ORANGE-WINGED
PARROT

YELLOW-CROWNED
PARROT

**H** **HISPANIOLAN PARAKEET** *Psittacara chloropterus* 30–33cm (12–13in); 150g.
**BEHAVIOR** Flocks. **DESCRIPTION** Large parakeet with long, pointed tail, white eye-ring,
red edge along bend of wing. **FLIGHT** Red underwing-coverts. **VOICE** Screeches. **STATUS
AND RANGE** Endemic to Hispaniola, where locally common, but rapidly declining. In
Dominican Republic, primarily in Sierra de Bahoruco and Sierra de Neiba. In Haiti,
common in Massif de la Selle and the Citadelle area in Massif du Nord. Uncommon
elsewhere in Haiti. Threatened. **HABITAT** Forests and woodlands at all elevations.

**C** **CUBAN PARAKEET** *Psittacara euops* 24–27cm (9.5–10.5in); 90g. **BEHAVIOR** Flocks.
**DESCRIPTION** Long, pointed tail; scattered red feathers on head, sides of neck, and bend
of wing. **FLIGHT** Red underwing-coverts. **VOICE** Loud, characteristic *crick-crick-crick.*
**STATUS AND RANGE** Endemic to Cuba, where uncommon and local in Zapata Peninsula,
Trinidad Mountains, Sierra de Najasa, and eastern mountain ranges. Endangered.
**HABITAT** Woodlands, forest edges, riverine forests, savannas, and tree stumps near swamps.

**OLIVE-THROATED PARAKEET** *Eupsittula nana* 30.5cm (12in);
80g. **BEHAVIOR** Flocks. **DESCRIPTION** Small, with long, pointed tail.
Dark brownish-olive underparts; pale eye-ring and bill. (Hispaniolan
Parakeet has red on bend of wing.) **VOICE** Screeches. **STATUS AND
RANGE** Common and widespread permanent resident in Jamaica.
Introduced to Dominican Republic, where locally common at
lower elevations of Sierra de Bahoruco and increasing. **HABITAT** Scrub, woodlands, forests,
croplands, and gardens from coast to lower mountains.

**ORANGE-FRONTED PARAKEET** *Eupsittula canicularis* 23–24cm (9–9.5in); 70g.
**BEHAVIOR** Flocks. **DESCRIPTION** Medium-sized, with orange forehead, white eye-ring,
long, pointed tail, and blue primaries. **VOICE** Raspy squawks. **STATUS AND RANGE** Introduced.
Uncommon and local in Puerto Rico, particularly in northeast. **HABITAT** Wooded pastures
and urban areas with ornamental trees.

**BROWN-THROATED PARAKEET** *Eupsittula pertinax* 23–
28cm (9–11in); 80–100g. **BEHAVIOR** Flocks. **DESCRIPTION** Fairly
large, with yellowish-orange face and forehead. Long, pointed tail;
throat and breast dull yellowish-brown; primaries blue. **VOICE**
Raucous squawks. **STATUS AND RANGE** Introduced. In Virgin
Islands, fairly common permanent resident on St Thomas,
particularly eastern end. Small numbers on St John and reports from Tortola and Jost Van
Dyke. Uncommon on Saba. Rare on San Andrés. **HABITAT** On St Thomas, wooded
thickets in hills.

**MONK PARAKEET** *Myiopsitta monachus* 28cm (11in); 130g.
**BEHAVIOR** Flocks. **DESCRIPTION** Fairly large, with gray crown,
throat, and breast. Long, pointed tail; flight feathers blue. **VOICE**
Raucous squawks. **STATUS AND RANGE** Introduced. Common in
Puerto Rico, particularly on coast. Common on Grand Bahama in
Bahamas. Small population on Grand Cayman in Cayman Islands.
**HABITAT** Coastal palm groves, urban gardens.

**WHITE-WINGED PARAKEET (CANARY-WINGED PARAKEET)** *Brotogeris
versicolurus* 23cm (9in); 70g. **BEHAVIOR** Flocks. **DESCRIPTION** Small, but larger than
Budgerigar. Ivory-colored bill; yellow band bordering wing. Tail long and pointed.
**FLIGHT** Wings flash large whitish-yellow triangular patches. **VOICE** High-pitched squawks.
**STATUS AND RANGE** Introduced. Locally common in Puerto Rico. **HABITAT** Woodlands
from coast to foothills. Also towns and urban areas.

HISPANIOLAN
PARAKEET

CUBAN PARAKEET

imm

OLIVE-THROATED
PARAKEET

ORANGE-
FRONTED
PARAKEET

adult

BROWN-
THROATED
PARAKEET

MONK
PARAKEET

WHITE-WINGED
PARAKEET

**ROSE-RINGED PARAKEET** *Psittacula krameri* 42cm (17in); 120–140g. **BEHAVIOR** Flocks. **DESCRIPTION** Very large parakeet. Green with long tail, red bill; male has black neck ring (absent in female). **VOICE** Squawks. **STATUS AND RANGE** Introduced. Well established in Jamaica in suburbs of St Andrew Parish; in northern portion of Martinique; and widely in Barbados, particularly around major towns, along southern end, and on west coast. In Grand Cayman (Cayman Islands), a small population breeds in George Town. A few birds in Cuba, Puerto Rico, and Guadeloupe. Reports from other islands. **HABITAT** Gardens and trees in urban areas.

**RED-MASKED PARAKEET** *Psittacara erythrogenys* 33cm (13in); 165–200g. **BEHAVIOR** Flocks. **DESCRIPTION** Large parakeet with long, pointed tail, primarily red head, and white eye-ring. **FLIGHT** Red under leading edge of wing. **VOICE** Squawks. **STATUS AND RANGE** Introduced in Puerto Rico, where uncommon and local. Occurs along north coast, particularly Caño Tiburones, but decimated by 2017 hurricane. **VOICE** Squawks. **HABITAT** Lowlands, often around treed urban areas.

**ROSY-FACED LOVEBIRD** *Agapornis roseicollis* 17–18cm (7–7.5in); 45–60g. A very small, green parrot with a pinkish-red face, throat, and upper breast. Rump is blue. **VOICE** Various squeaky calls. **STATUS AND RANGE** Introduced to Puerto Rico, where local around coastal plain and foothills, particularly Guaynabo, Bayamón, and San Juan, where increasing. **HABITAT** Open fields and urban areas.

**GREEN-RUMPED PARROTLET** *Forpus passerinus* 13cm (5in); 25g. **BEHAVIOR** Flocks. **DESCRIPTION** Very small, with short tail and pale bill. **MALE** Greenish-blue rump and wings. **FEMALE** Lacks blue in wings. Yellower breast. **VOICE** Shrill, squeaky chattering. **STATUS AND RANGE** Introduced. Common and widespread in Jamaica. **HABITAT** Primarily open country, particularly drier lowlands and hills.

**BUDGERIGAR** *Melopsittacus undulatus* 18cm (7in); 22–32g. **BEHAVIOR** Flocks. **DESCRIPTION** The typical pet shop parakeet or "budgie." Natural coloration green below, yellow head, and back heavily barred with black. Blue, white, and other color variations. **VOICE** Sharp screech. **STATUS AND RANGE** Introduced. Regularly escapes or is released throughout West Indies, but not known to be established. Rare in Puerto Rico (primarily San Juan), in Tortola (Virgin Islands), and very rare in Barbados. **HABITAT** Open areas with short grass, urban areas, golf courses.

imm

ROSE-RINGED PARAKEET

RED-MASKED PARAKEET

♂

ROSY-FACED LOVEBIRD

GREEN-RUMPED
PARROTLET

BUDGERIGAR

**COCKATIEL** *Nymphicus hollandicus* 30–33cm (12–13in); 80–100g. A crested parrot, primarily gray with a large white wing mark and an orange circle behind the eye. Tail long and pointed. **MALE** Head yellow or white. **FEMALE** Head pale gray. **VOICE** Various whistles and screeches. **STATUS AND RANGE** Introduced on a number of islands. Occurs locally in small numbers on Puerto Rico, Virgin Islands (Tortola and Virgin Gorda), and Barbados. Not known with certainty to be established. **HABITAT** Urban areas and human settlements.

**SCARLET MACAW** *Ara macao* 88–95cm (35–38in); 1kg. **BEHAVIOR** Flocks. **DESCRIPTION** Very large red parrot with blue wings, lower back, and undertail-coverts; wing-coverts yellow. **VOICE** Loud squawks. **STATUS AND RANGE** Introduced to Cuba, where occurs inland along north coast of Holguin Province. **HABITAT** Forests, open areas with palms, and sometimes among human habitations.

**RED-AND-GREEN MACAW** *Ara chloropterus* 88–95cm (35–38in); 1–1.3kg. **BEHAVIOR** Flocks. **DESCRIPTION** Very large red parrot with blue wings, lower back, and undertail-coverts; wing-coverts green. (Scarlet Macaw very similar except wing-coverts are yellow.) **VOICE** Loud squawks. **STATUS AND RANGE** Introduced to Cuba, where occurs inland along north coast of Holguin Province. **HABITAT** Forests, open areas with palms, and sometimes among human habitations.

**BLUE-AND-YELLOW MACAW** *Ara ararauna* 80–85cm (32–34in); 1–1.2kg. **BEHAVIOR** Flocks. **DESCRIPTION** Very large parrot, primarily blue above and yellow below. **VOICE** Loud squawks. **STATUS AND RANGE** Introduced to Cuba, where occurs inland along north coast of Holguin Province; and Puerto Rico, where locally uncommon in Guaynabo, Bayamón, and Río Piedras. **HABITAT** Forests, open areas with palms, and among human habitations.

**WHITE COCKATOO (UMBRELLA COCKATOO)** *Cacatua alba* 46–61cm (18–24in); 550g. **BEHAVIOR** Flocks. **DESCRIPTION** Medium-sized, entirely white cockatoo with a usually flattened but noticeable crest, which makes head seem very large. Crest can be fanned. Bill black. **FEMALE** Smaller body, head, and bill; reddish-brown iris (male's iris dark brown or black). **FLIGHT** Pale yellow underwings and undertail. **VOICE** Nasal *keh* or *keeh-ah* calls. **STATUS AND RANGE** Introduced in Puerto Rico, where very local between Bayamón and Guaynabo. **HABITAT** Forests, woodlands, clearings, areas with fruiting trees.

**CHANNEL-BILLED TOUCAN** *Ramphastos vitellinus* 48–51cm (19–20in); 300–430g. Black overall with an enormous black bill; yellow breast edged with white; blue bare facial patch and base of bill (red in some races); red lower breast, rump, and undertail-coverts. Male slightly larger. Much more often heard than seen, particularly early morning and late evening. **FLIGHT** Swoops and glides. **VOICE** A high-pitched *pyok*, often repeated. **STATUS AND RANGE** Introduced in 1989 to Grenada, where now uncommon and local. **HABITAT** Mid-elevation semi-deciduous forest and agricultural areas.

COCKATIEL

♂

SCARLET MACAW

RED-AND-GREEN MACAW

BLUE-AND-YELLOW MACAW

♀

WHITE COCKATOO

CHANNEL-BILLED TOUCAN

♂ displaying

♂

**J** SAD FLYCATCHER *Myiarchus barbirostris* 16.5cm (6.5in); 14g. **BEHAVIOR** Sallies for insects. **ADULT** Relatively small, with dark crown and yellow underparts, except for chin and throat. Faint wing bars. **VOICE** Emphatic *pip, pip-pip*. Sometimes *pip-pip-pireee*, rising at end. **STATUS AND RANGE** Endemic to Jamaica, where widespread and common. **HABITAT** Primarily forests and woodlands from lowlands to mid-elevations. Less frequent in semi-arid lowlands and in fairly open forests at higher elevations.

**M** STOLID FLYCATCHER *Myiarchus stolidus* 20cm (8in); 20–26g. **BEHAVIOR** Sallies for insects. **DESCRIPTION** Medium-sized, with two pale white wing bars. Primaries heavily fringed white. Throat and breast whitish; abdomen and belly pale yellow; bill black, moderately heavy. **VOICE** Rolling *whee-ee-ee, swee-ip, bzzrt*. Also plaintive *jui* in Hispaniola. **STATUS AND RANGE** Common permanent resident throughout Jamaica and Hispaniola. These islands comprise entire range. **HABITAT** Lowland forests and edges, including arid woodlands, scrub, and mangroves. Less frequent in wet mid-elevation forests. In Hispaniola, also pine woods.

**M** LA SAGRA'S FLYCATCHER *Myiarchus sagrae* 19–22cm (7.5–8.5in); 20–29g. **BEHAVIOR** Sallies for insects. **DESCRIPTION** Medium-sized, with unusual leaning posture and flat-headed appearance. Long, usually all-black bill, two inconspicuous white wing bars. **VOICE** Two-syllable whistle, *tra-hee*. Also short, plaintive whistle, *huit*. **STATUS AND RANGE** Common permanent resident in northern Bahamas and Great Inagua in southern Bahamas, Cuba, and Grand Cayman (Cayman Islands). These islands comprise entire range. **HABITAT** Pine woods, mixed woodlands, dense thickets, mangroves, and forests, at all elevations.

**P** PUERTO RICAN FLYCATCHER *Myiarchus antillarum* 18.5–20cm (7.25–8in); 22–25g. Medium-sized, with faint wing bars. Light brownish-gray underparts, lighter toward tail; lacks yellow wash. Best identified by call. **VOICE** Plaintive whistle, *whee*. Also *whee-a-wit-whee*. **STATUS AND RANGE** Common permanent resident in Puerto Rico. In Virgin Islands, uncommon on St John, Anegada, and Beef Island; rare on St Thomas and Virgin Gorda. These islands comprise entire range. **HABITAT** Wooded areas, including mangrove borders, arid scrub, coffee plantations, haystack hills, and mountain forests, except higher slopes.

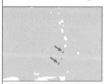

**M** GRENADA FLYCATCHER *Myiarchus nugator* 20cm (8in); 37g. **BEHAVIOR** Sallies from exposed perch for insects. Flicks tail. **DESCRIPTION** Slightly erectile crest; black bill with pinkish lower mandible; two pale brown wing bars; primaries with reddish edges; long tail with reddish edges. **VOICE** Loud *quip* or harsh *queuk*. **STATUS AND RANGE** Common permanent resident known only from St Vincent, Grenadines, and Grenada at all elevations. **HABITAT** Open areas around settlements and lowland scrub, especially near palms.

**M** LESSER ANTILLEAN FLYCATCHER *Myiarchus oberi* 19–22cm (7.5–8.5in); 22–37g. Mostly yellow underparts from upper belly to undertail-coverts. Tail feathers with reddish inner webs. **VOICE** Loud, plaintive whistle, *peeu-wheeet*. Also short whistles, *oo-ee, oo-ee*, or *e-oo-ee*. **STATUS AND RANGE** Common permanent resident on Barbuda, St Christopher, Nevis, Dominica, Martinique, and St Lucia. Rare on Guadeloupe. These islands comprise its entire range. **HABITAT** Primarily edges of dense woodlands, forests, and tree plantations at or above 100m (330ft). Infrequently lower-altitude second growth or scrub.

SAD FLYCATCHER

STOLID FLYCATCHER

LA SAGRA'S FLYCATCHER

PUERTO RICAN FLYCATCHER

GRENADA FLYCATCHER

LESSER ANTILLEAN FLYCATCHER

**□ RUFOUS-TAILED FLYCATCHER** *Myiarchus validus* 24cm (9.5in); 39–43g. **BEHAVIOR** Sallies from dense cover for insects. **DESCRIPTION** Large, with rusty tail and primaries. Belly and abdomen yellow. **VOICE** Fast, rolling, descending *pree-ee-ee-ee-ee*, like horse's neigh. Also *chi-chi-chiup*. **STATUS AND RANGE** Endemic to Jamaica, where fairly common, primarily mid-elevations. **HABITAT** Primarily moist, mid-elevation forests, but also dry limestone and lowland forests, as well as montane forests.

**GREAT CRESTED FLYCATCHER** *Myiarchus crinitus* 18–20.5cm (7–8in); 28–39g. **BEHAVIOR** Sallies for insects. **ADULT** Wings and tail with reddish-brown; whitish wing bars; throat and breast gray; belly bright yellow. **VOICE** Loud, harsh *wheeep* with rising inflection. **STATUS AND RANGE** Decidedly rare migrant and non-breeding resident in Cuba September–April. Very rare in northern Bahamas. Vagrant elsewhere in West Indies. **HABITAT** Forests.

**WESTERN KINGBIRD** *Tyrannus verticalis* 21–24cm (8–9.5in); 40g. **ADULT** Head and hindneck pale, with dark gray line through eye; pale gray upper breast; yellow belly; conspicuous white edges to outertail feathers. **STATUS AND RANGE** Generally a decidedly rare migrant in northern Bahamas south to Eleuthera primarily October and November. A vagrant elsewhere in West Indies. **HABITAT** Open country.

**☐ GIANT KINGBIRD** *Tyrannus cubensis* 23cm (9in). **BEHAVIOR** Sallies from exposed perch for insects. **DESCRIPTION** Very large bill. Upperparts dark, especially crown, which is flat with no sign of crest; underparts white. Crown patch rarely visible. (Loggerhead Kingbird smaller, with smaller bill and darker crown with distinctive crest-like bulge toward back of head. Also, more distinctive white terminal band on squarer tail.) **VOICE** Loud, coarsely whistled *tooweup, tawe-tawe-tawoo*, or a similar version. Male and female sometimes duet. **STATUS AND RANGE** Endemic to Cuba, where rare and local. Most abundant around Moa. Endangered. **HABITAT** Primarily forest edges, often bordering rivers, swamps, or savannas, but also open forests with tall trees in mountains. Sometimes woodlands, pine forests, and semi-open woodlands with tall trees. Frequents exposed perches.

RUFOUS-TAILED FLYCATCHER

GREAT CRESTED FLYCATCHER

WESTERN KINGBIRD

GIANT KINGBIRD

**EASTERN KINGBIRD** *Tyrannus tyrannus* 22–23cm (8.5–9in); 40g. ADULT Upperparts dark gray; head and tail black. White underparts; two indistinct wing bars; tail with terminal white band. Crown patch usually concealed. (Loggerhead Kingbird has heavier bill, brownish-gray back washed with olive, yellow wash on lower bill, and much less white on tail tip.) STATUS AND RANGE Irregular, ranging from locally common to very uncommon migrant in western Cuba and Grand Cayman (Cayman Islands). Rare in northern Bahamas, eastern Cuba, Jamaica, and San Andrés. Occurs most regularly September and October, less frequently April and early May. HABITAT Semi-open woodlands, including gardens in urban areas. Often perches in tall trees.

**GRAY KINGBIRD** *Tyrannus dominicensis* 22–25cm (8.5–10in); 45g. BEHAVIOR Sallies from exposed perch for insects. DESCRIPTION Gray above, pale gray-white below, with distinct dark mask extending under eye; slightly notched tail. Crown patch rarely visible. VOICE Emphatic *pi-tirr-ri*. STATUS AND RANGE Conspicuous and common throughout West Indies. Permanent resident from Hispaniola east through Lesser Antilles. Most breeding birds from Bahamas, Cuba, Jamaica, and Cayman Islands migrate off-island November–March. Some leave Lesser Antilles as well. HABITAT Mountains and lowlands, in open areas with scattered trees.

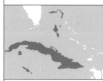

**M LOGGERHEAD KINGBIRD** *Tyrannus caudifasciatus* 24–26cm (9.5–10in); 45g. BEHAVIOR Sallies from exposed perch for insects. DESCRIPTION Distinctively two-toned: dark above and white below. Crown blackish, with rarely seen orange-yellow patch. Square tail with white trailing edge. Bill large. Gray Kingbird paler above, particularly on head. Similar Eastern Kingbird smaller, bill smaller, back blacker, tail whiter tipped. VOICE Variable; usually loud, mallet-like chattering with *bzze-beep* or *bee-beep* elements. Song bubbling, repeated. STATUS AND RANGE Common and widespread permanent resident through northern Bahamas, Cuba, Jamaica, and Cayman Islands. These islands comprise entire range. HABITAT Woodlands, pine and broadleaf forests, shade coffee, mangrove swamps, and open areas with scattered trees from lowlands to mid-elevations.

**H HISPANIOLAN KINGBIRD (LOGGERHEAD KINGBIRD)** *Tyrannus gabbii* 24–26cm (9.5–10in); 45g. BEHAVIOR Sallies from perch low to ground for insects. DESCRIPTION Distinctively two-toned: dark above and white below. Crown brownish-black, with rarely seen yellow patch. Square tail lacks white trailing edge. Bill large. VOICE Similar to Loggerhead Kingbird but song longer. Usually a long, rolling trill, often ending with several explosive notes. STATUS AND RANGE Endemic to Hispaniola, where decidedly uncommon and local. Numbers have declined precipitously. Some consider this a subspecies of Loggerhead Kingbird. HABITAT Primarily densely forested areas from middle to upper elevations. Sometimes broadleaf and pine forests, and coffee plantations. Infrequent in lowlands.

**P PUERTO RICAN KINGBIRD (LOGGERHEAD KINGBIRD)** *Tyrannus taylori* 24–26cm (9.5–10in); 45g. BEHAVIOR Sallies from exposed perch for insects. DESCRIPTION Distinctively two-toned: dark above and white below. Crown blackish, with rarely seen yellow patch. Slightly notched tail lacks white trailing edge. Bill large. VOICE Similar to Loggerhead Kingbird but song shorter. Also a melodious laugh like an unenthusiastic Puerto Rican Woodpecker call. STATUS AND RANGE Endemic to Puerto Rico, where common and fairly widespread though uncommon in Luquillo Mountains. Some consider this a subspecies of Loggerhead Kingbird. HABITAT Only forested areas, particularly coffee plantations. Also haystack hills and some mangrove swamps.

EASTERN KINGBIRD

GRAY KINGBIRD

LOGGERHEAD KINGBIRD

HISPANIOLAN KINGBIRD

PUERTO RICAN
KINGBIRD

**FORK-TAILED FLYCATCHER** *Tyrannus savana* Male 37–40cm (14.5–16in) with tail, female 28–30cm (11–12in) with tail; 30g. **BEHAVIOR** Flocks. **ADULT MALE** Black head; pale gray back; blackish-brown wings; white underparts. Tail in breeding plumage very long, with white-edged streamers; shorter during molt. **ADULT FEMALE AND IMMATURE** Duller; tail shorter. **STATUS AND RANGE** Uncommon and irregular migrant in Grenada primarily July and August, and generally rare in most other Lesser Antilles from Guadeloupe southward. Vagrant elsewhere in West Indies. Sometimes occurs in numbers. **HABITAT** Open areas, savannas, pastures, airports, and mangroves.

**SCISSOR-TAILED FLYCATCHER** *Tyrannus forficatus* Male with tail 58cm (23in), female 36cm (14in); 40g. Pale, with conspicuously long tail. Wings and tail blackish. (Fork-tailed Flycatcher has black cap and is white below, rather than pinkish-orange.) **STATUS AND RANGE** Very rare in western Cuba and northern Bahamas primarily late October–December. Vagrant to other islands, particularly Cayman Islands. **HABITAT** Open and semi-open country.

**J** **JAMAICAN ELAENIA** *Myiopagis cotta* 12.5cm (5in); 12g. **BEHAVIOR** Sallies from exposed perches. **DESCRIPTION** Small, with whitish eyebrow stripe, small black bill, and yellowish primary edges. Lacks wing bars. Crown patch sometimes exposed. **VOICE** Rapid, high-pitched *ti-si-si-sip* or *si-sip*, last note lower. **STATUS AND RANGE** Endemic to Jamaica, where uncommon but widespread. **HABITAT** Primarily wet forests at moderate elevations. Also open woodlands, scrublands, shade coffee, and dry lowland forests.

**EASTERN PHOEBE** *Sayornis phoebe* 16.5–18cm (6.5–7in); 18g. **BEHAVIOR** Flicks tail. Sallies for insects. **DESCRIPTION** Dark head; no eye-ring; blackish wings; no wing bars. Underparts whitish with pale yellow wash, especially during September and October. **STATUS AND RANGE** Generally a rare migrant and non-breeding resident in northern Bahamas and western Cuba mid-September–February. Decidedly rare in eastern Cuba. More abundant in some years. **HABITAT** Woodland edges, fence lines, and hedgerows. Often near freshwater.

**WILLOW FLYCATCHER** *Empidonax traillii* 15cm (5.75in); 15g. Underparts grayish-white with almost no yellow; chin white. Lacks noticeable eye-ring; has whitish wing bars. (Eastern Wood-Pewee has heavier, whitish wing bars. Acadian Flycatcher slightly yellower below, with more conspicuous eye-ring and greener back. Nearly indistinguishable from Least Flycatcher except by call.) **VOICE** *Fi-bi-o*, cross between whistle and buzz. Also harsh *fitz*. **STATUS AND RANGE** Very rare migrant in Cuba mid-September through mid-October. Vagrant elsewhere in West Indies. **HABITAT** Wetland edges, woodlands, tree clumps, and gardens.

**ACADIAN FLYCATCHER** *Empidonax virescens* 12cm (4.75in); 13g. Yellowish eye-ring; two grayish or whitish wing bars; lower mandible yellowish; throat and belly white. (Yellow-bellied Flycatcher yellower below. Willow Flycatcher less yellow below, with less conspicuous eye-ring. Differences minimal.) **VOICE** Usually silent during migration, but may give emphatic *see-ya*! **STATUS AND RANGE** Rare migrant in Cuba and northern Bahamas September–October and February–April. Likely very rare in Grand Cayman (Cayman Islands). Vagrant elsewhere in West Indies. **HABITAT** Open woodlands, forest edges, tree clumps, and gardens.

**YELLOW-BELLIED FLYCATCHER** *Empidonax flaviventris* 15cm (5.75in); 15g. Yellowish underparts including throat. Eye-ring broad and yellowish, two whitish or yellowish wing bars, lower mandible pale orange. (Acadian Flycatcher less yellow below; throat white.) **VOICE** Usually silent during migration but sometimes gives a rising whistle, *churee*, or a harsher, more emphatic *chu-weet*! rising at end. **STATUS AND RANGE** Very rare and irregular migrant in Cuba and San Andrés in September–October and April. **HABITAT** Forests, woodlands, tree clumps, wetland edges, and gardens.

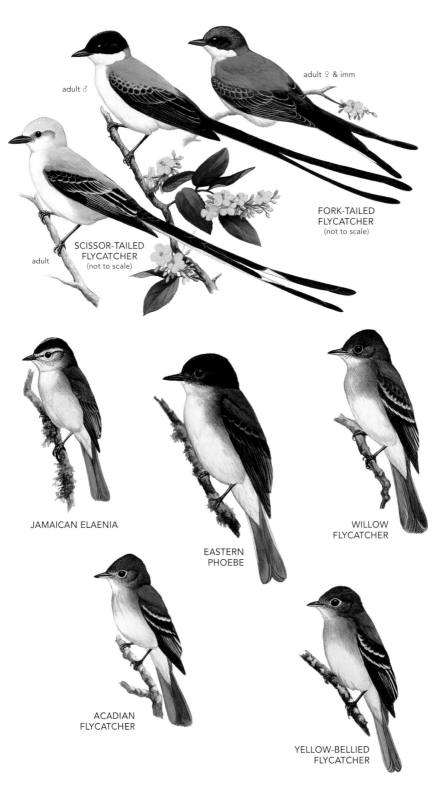

adult ♂

adult ♀ & imm

FORK-TAILED
FLYCATCHER
(not to scale)

SCISSOR-TAILED
FLYCATCHER
(not to scale)

adult

JAMAICAN ELAENIA

EASTERN
PHOEBE

WILLOW
FLYCATCHER

ACADIAN
FLYCATCHER

YELLOW-BELLIED
FLYCATCHER

**CARIBBEAN ELAENIA** *Elaenia martinica* 15.5–18cm (6–7in); 22g. Throat and lower belly whitish with light yellowish wash; breast pale gray; lower mandible pinkish; two whitish wing bars. Slight crest; displays crown patch when agitated. **VOICE** Repetitious *jui-up, wit-churr*, last syllable softest. Song drawn-out *pee-wee-reereeree*. Calls well into day. **STATUS AND RANGE** Generally common and widespread permanent resident in Cayman and Virgin Islands, Puerto Rico, and Lesser Antilles. Rare on Providencia and San Andrés. **HABITAT** Woodlands, scrub, and forests. Primarily dry lowlands, but sometimes in mountains.

**YELLOW-BELLIED ELAENIA** *Elaenia flavogaster* 16.5cm (6.5in); 25g. Bill whitish-pink below; two white wing bars. Often raises crest slightly. (Caribbean Elaenia smaller, less prominent crest, less yellow on belly.) **VOICE** Harsh, drawn-out *creup* or *creup-wi-creup*. Members of pair often sing together. **STATUS AND RANGE** Common permanent resident in St Vincent, Grenadines, and Grenada. **HABITAT** Primarily lowland forest edges, open woodlands, scrub, and gardens.

**J LARGE JAMAICAN ELAENIA (GREATER ANTILLEAN ELAENIA)** *Elaenia fallax* 15cm (5.75in). A small, nondescript flycatcher. Faint dark eye-line, pale eye-ring; two distinct wing bars; small bill with pinkish base; breast yellowish-gray; pale yellowish-white belly. Neck and breast faintly streaked. Head appears slightly crested. Whitish crown patch usually not seen. (Jamaican Elaenia has distinctive eyebrow stripe and yellowing primary edges.) **VOICE** Harsh *pwee-chi-chi-chiup, see-ere, chewit-chewit*. Also a trill. **STATUS AND RANGE** Endemic to Jamaica, where generally uncommon throughout island. Some consider this and Hispaniolan Elaenia a single species: the Greater Antillean Elaenia. **HABITAT** Forest edges, particularly in mountains.

**H HISPANIOLAN ELAENIA (GREATER ANTILLEAN ELAENIA)** *Elaenia cherriei* 15cm (5.75in); 14g. A small, nondescript flycatcher. Faint dark eye-line; two distinct wing bars; small black bill; pale gray breast; white belly. Head appears slightly crested. **VOICE** Harsh *pwee-chi-chi-chiup, see-ere, chewit-chewit*. Also a trill sung at dawn. **STATUS AND RANGE** Endemic to Hispaniola, where locally common. Some consider this and Large Jamaican Elaenia a single species: the Greater Antillean Elaenia. **HABITAT** Primarily pine forests, but also wet broadleaf forests and open country with scattered trees.

**J JAMAICAN BECARD** *Pachyramphus niger* 18cm (7in); 40g. Heavyset; large head; stubby bill; short tail; behaves like flycatcher. **ADULT MALE** Black, shows white mark at base of wing in flight. **ADULT FEMALE AND IMMATURE** Reddish-brown above, pale gray below, cheeks and throat cinnamon-colored. **VOICE** Two hoarse *queeck*s followed by musical *co-ome and tell me what you hee-ear*; gradually rises, then falls. **STATUS AND RANGE** Endemic to Jamaica; widespread and fairly common locally. **HABITAT** Tall open forests and edges in hills and lower mountains, infrequently lowlands. Also closed forests, woodlands, pastures with large trees, and gardens.

CARIBBEAN ELAENIA

YELLOW-BELLIED
ELAENIA

LARGE
JAMAICAN
ELAENIA

HISPANIOLAN
ELAENIA

adult ♂

adult ♀ & imm

JAMAICAN
BECARD

**OLIVE-SIDED FLYCATCHER** *Contopus cooperi* 19cm (7.5 in); 32–37g. **BEHAVIOR** Sallies. Moderate size, distinctive white band down center of underparts, white patches on sides of rump (not always visible), sides and flanks gray to faintly striped. Tail short. **STATUS AND RANGE** Very rare on San Andrés and vagrant on Providencia. **HABITAT** Dead tree snags, often at clearing edges.

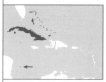

**EASTERN WOOD-PEWEE** *Contopus virens* 16cm (6.25in); 14g. **BEHAVIOR** Sallies. **ADULT** Two whitish wing bars; whitish underparts washed dark gray on sides and breast; sometimes complete breast bar. Generally lacks eye-ring. Dull orange lower mandible; undertail-coverts sometimes yellowish. **VOICE** Plaintive whistle, *pee-a-wee*, slurring down, then up. **STATUS AND RANGE** Irregular, ranging from locally fairly common to uncommon migrant in Cuba and Cayman Islands; uncommon to rare in northern Bahamas, Providencia, and San Andrés. Very rare or vagrant elsewhere in West Indies. Most frequent September and October, less so March and April. Few November to January records. **HABITAT** Mixed and coastal woodlands, forests, forest edges, scrub, open areas, and gardens.

**WESTERN WOOD-PEWEE** *Contopus sordidulus* 15–17cm (5.75–6.75in); 13g. **BEHAVIOR** Sallies. Accurately distinguished from Eastern Wood-Pewee only by voice. **VOICE** Nasal, descending *peeyee* or *peeer*. **STATUS AND RANGE** Very rare migrant in Cuba and San Andrés September–October, less so March–April. Vagrant elsewhere. **HABITAT** Woodlands and river groves.

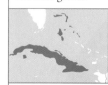

**CRESCENT-EYED PEWEE (CUBAN PEWEE)** *Contopus caribaeus* 15–16.5cm (5.75–6.5in); 10g. **BEHAVIOR** Sallies from exposed perch for insects; flicks tail upon landing. **DESCRIPTION** Often erect crest. White crescent behind eye. Lacks wing bars. **VOICE** Prolonged, thin whistle. Sometimes feeble *vi-vi.* **STATUS AND RANGE** Common in northern Bahamas and Cuba, its entire range. **HABITAT** Pine forests, woods, forest edges, scrub, swamp edges, and mangroves.

**HISPANIOLAN PEWEE** *Contopus hispaniolensis* 15–16cm (5.75–6.25in); 11g. **BEHAVIOR** Sallies from exposed perch for insects; flicks tail upon landing. **DESCRIPTION** Underparts gray with olive, yellow, or brown wash; wing bars inconspicuous or absent. Lower mandible pale at base. **VOICE** Strong, mournful *purr, pip-pip-pip-pip.* Dawn song loud, rapid-fire volley with paired syllables rising in pitch. **STATUS AND RANGE** Endemic to Hispaniola, where common and widespread. **HABITAT** Pine and broadleaf forests, forest edges, shade coffee, and orchards, at all elevations.

**JAMAICAN PEWEE** *Contopus pallidus* 15cm (5.75in); 10g. **BEHAVIOR** Sallies for insects, flicks tail upon landing. **DESCRIPTION** Small flycatcher with dark olive-gray upperparts, darker on head. Underparts grayish-brown. Lower mandible orangish; wing bars absent or indistinct. Tail slightly notched. **VOICE** Plaintive *pee.* Also, rising then falling *oéeoh.* Dawn song two alternating phrases, *paleet, weeleeah.* **STATUS AND RANGE** Endemic to Jamaica, where common and widespread. **HABITAT** All forest types, forest edges, and coffee plantations from 300m (1000ft) to highest mountains.

**LESSER ANTILLEAN PEWEE** *Contopus latirostris* 15cm (5.75in); 10g. **BEHAVIOR** Sallies from exposed perch for insects. **DESCRIPTION** Small flycatcher with brownish-olive upperparts. Underparts vary among islands from cinnamon-colored (Puerto Rico) to reddish-brown (St Lucia); nearly black wings and tail. Lower mandible pale at base. Some consider Puerto Rico and St Lucia forms distinct species. **VOICE** Emphatic rising *pree-e-e* and high-pitched, repeated *peet-peet-peet.* **STATUS AND RANGE** Fairly common but local permanent resident known only from Puerto Rico, Guadeloupe, Dominica, Martinique, and St Lucia. Sporadic reports from St Christopher. **HABITAT** Moist mid-elevation mountain forests and woods, sparingly in lower and drier forests, mangroves, and scrub near sea level.

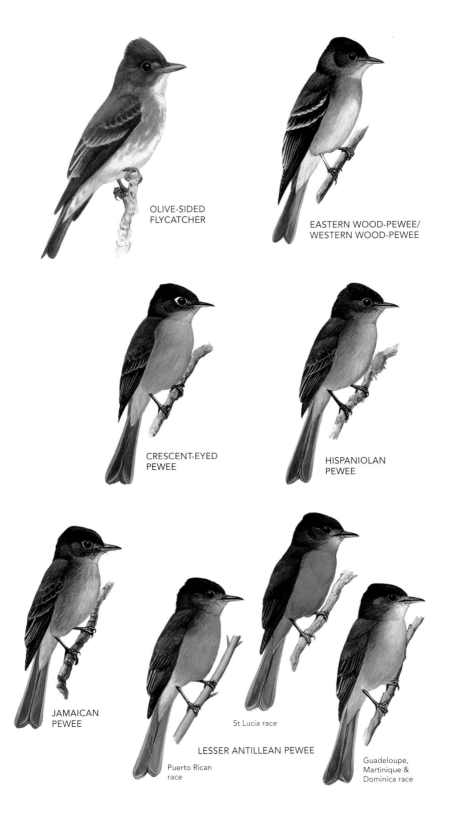

OLIVE-SIDED
FLYCATCHER

EASTERN WOOD-PEWEE/
WESTERN WOOD-PEWEE

CRESCENT-EYED
PEWEE

HISPANIOLAN
PEWEE

JAMAICAN
PEWEE

St Lucia race

LESSER ANTILLEAN PEWEE

Puerto Rican
race

Guadeloupe,
Martinique &
Dominica race

**PALMCHAT** *Dulus dominicus* 20cm (8in); 40g. **BEHAVIOR** Arboreal; forms flocks. **DESCRIPTION** Dark brown above; underparts whitish and heavily streaked with brown. **VOICE** Noisy, particularly around nest, producing array of strange slurring, whistled notes. **STATUS AND RANGE** Endemic to Hispaniola, where common, conspicuous, and widespread in lowlands to mid-elevations. Family also endemic to Hispaniola. **HABITAT** Primarily royal palm savannas, also other open areas with scattered trees.

**CEDAR WAXWING** *Bombycilla cedrorum* 18–18.5cm (7–7.25in); 30g. **BEHAVIOR** Flocks. **DESCRIPTION** Crest; yellow-tipped tail. **VOICE** Clear, short, high-pitched trill. Also unmusical *che-che-check*. **STATUS AND RANGE** Highly irregular, varying from uncommon to locally abundant in Grand Cayman (Cayman Islands) primarily January–May. Generally uncommon migrant and non-breeding resident in Cuba October–April, though numbers vary greatly year to year. Some years fairly common. Generally rare in northern Bahamas, Jamaica, and Hispaniola primarily December–March; very rare or vagrant elsewhere in West Indies. Often occurs in numbers. **HABITAT** Mountain rain forests to lowland cultivated edges and urban gardens.

**CUBAN GNATCATCHER** *Polioptila lembeyei* 10.5cm (4.1in); 5g. **BEHAVIOR** Cocks tail; active. **DESCRIPTION** Small and slender. Gray above, grayish-white below. Long black tail with white outer feathers. White eye-ring; black crescent from eye to behind ear. (Blue-gray Gnatcatcher lacks black facial crescent.) **FEMALE** Paler. **VOICE** Loud and melodious. Song begins with four whistles, followed by trill and thin varied whisper, *pss-pss-pss-pss-tttiizzzt-zzzz-ttizzz-tzi-tzi-tzi*. **STATUS AND RANGE** Endemic to Cuba; common locally on east and south-central coast. Absent in west. **HABITAT** Fairly dense coastal thorn scrub, sometimes inland in similar vegetation.

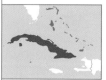

**BLUE-GRAY GNATCATCHER** *Polioptila caerulea* 11cm (4.25in); 6g. **BEHAVIOR** Cocks tail; active. **DESCRIPTION** Small and slender. Grayish above, white below; white eye-ring. Long black tail with white outer feathers. **MALE** Bluish tint to upperparts and fine black eyebrow stripe during breeding. **FEMALE** Paler; lacks eyebrow stripe. **VOICE** Mew-like call, similar to Gray Catbird, usually two syllables, *zpee-zpee*. Also soft whisper-like song. **STATUS AND RANGE** Common permanent resident on larger islands of Bahamas, augmented by migrants September–November. Common migrant and non-breeding resident in Cuba September–April, and decidedly uncommon migrant and rare non-breeding resident in Cayman Islands. Vagrant elsewhere. **HABITAT** Scrubland and pine forests in Bahamas. In Cayman Islands, also mangroves. In Cuba, all lowland and mid-elevation habitats from forests to gardens.

**BROWN-HEADED NUTHATCH** *Sitta pusilla* 9.5–11cm (3.75–4.25in); 10g. **BEHAVIOR** Forages up and down tree trunks, often upside down. **DESCRIPTION** Bluish-gray upperparts; brown crown; dark brown line through eye; white hindneck patch. **VOICE** Weak, fast, squeaky, high-pitched chatter; also a unique warble. **STATUS AND RANGE** Very rare and local permanent resident on Grand Bahama in Bahamas. West Indies race endangered. **HABITAT** Limited to pine forest.

CEDAR WAXWING

imm

adult

PALMCHAT

CUBAN GNATCATCHER
(not to scale)

♂

BLUE-GRAY GNATCATCHER
(not to scale)

♀

br ♀

adult

BROWN-HEADED NUTHATCH

**SAN ANDRÉS VIREO** *Vireo caribaeus* 12.5cm (5in); 9g. Pale yellow stripe above bill to eye; grayish-brown eye; whitish to pale yellow underparts; two white wing bars. (Thick-billed Vireo has blackish lores, yellower underparts, and darker eye.) **VOICE** Repetitive chatter on single syllable; two-syllable *se-wi*, repeated; also a variable three-syllable call. **STATUS AND RANGE** Endemic to San Andrés, where fairly common. Appears recently established on Providencia, where rare. **HABITAT** Mangroves, forests, bushes, scrubby pastures.

**THICK-BILLED VIREO** *Vireo crassirostris* 13.5cm (5.25in); 13g. Variable. Blackish lores; dark eye; two white wing bars; bright yellow spectacles sometimes broken around eye. Underparts in southern Bahamas yellow; in northern Bahamas, Cuba, and Cayman Islands grayish with yellow tint. **IMMATURE** Lacks blackish lores. **VOICE** Bubbly, variable *chik-didle-wer-chip*, like White-eyed Vireo, but slower and less emphatic. **STATUS AND RANGE** Common permanent resident in Bahamas, Cayo Paredón Grande off north-central Cuba, Île Tortue off Hispaniola, Cayman Islands (absent from Little Cayman), and perhaps Providencia. Reports from Providencia and San Andrés likely pertain to Mangrove Vireo. These islands comprise nearly entire range. **HABITAT** Undergrowth, woodland edges, scrublands, and bushes.

**MANGROVE VIREO (PROVIDENCIA VIREO)** *Vireo pallens* 11.5cm (4.5in); 9–13g. Dull yellow eyebrow stripe and underparts; two white wing bars. (Thick-billed Vireo has grayish-green crown and hindneck that contrast with brownish-green upperparts.) **VOICE** A chattering, rapid repetition of two to ten identical notes. **STATUS AND RANGE** Fairly common on Providencia and very rare on San Andrés. Reports of Thick-billed Vireo from Providencia and San Andrés likely pertain to Mangrove Vireo. Some consider this a distinct species. **HABITAT** Dry scrub typically at higher elevations, infrequently in mangroves.

**FLAT-BILLED VIREO** *Vireo nanus* 12–13cm (4.75–5in); 11g. Light gray below, washed pale yellow. Outertail feathers have white tips; two white wing bars; white eye. **VOICE** Chattering, high-pitched *weet-weet-weet* ... , often repeated. **STATUS AND RANGE** Endemic to Hispaniola; uncommon and local. **HABITAT** Primarily lowlands in semi-arid scrub and undergrowth. Also moist hills.

**CUBAN VIREO** *Vireo gundlachii* 13cm (5in); 11–15g. Chunkier than warbler, with larger bill. Bulging eyes bordered by smudgy yellowish eye-ring. Yellowish underparts; faint wing bars. **VOICE** High, oft-repeated *wi-chiví, wi-chiví, wi-chiví* ... **STATUS AND RANGE** Endemic to Cuba, where common and widespread. **HABITAT** Brushland, forest edges, and dense scrub and thickets primarily in lowlands, but also in hills and mountains.

THICK-BILLED VIREO

Bahamas race

Île Tortue race

SAN ANDRÉS VIREO

MANGROVE VIREO

FLAT-BILLED VIREO

CUBAN VIREO

**JAMAICAN VIREO** *Vireo modestus* 12.5cm (5in); 10g. **BEHAVIOR** Flicks tail upward. **DESCRIPTION** Two whitish wing bars; pinkish lower mandible; whitish eye. **IMMATURE** Dark eye; yellow of underparts confined to central stripe. **VOICE** Repeats phrase several minutes, then changes. Phrases rapid and high-pitched, often *sewi-sewi*, also scolding *chi-chi-chi* ... **STATUS AND RANGE** Endemic to Jamaica; widespread and common. **HABITAT** Most forests, forest edges, thickets, particularly arid lowlands.

**YELLOW-THROATED VIREO** *Vireo flavifrons* 12.5cm (5.5in); 18g. Yellow spectacles; two white wing bars; dark eye. Chin, throat, and breast yellow. **VOICE** Wheezy *chee-wee, chee-woo, u-wee, chee-wee* ... , also scolding *chi-chi-chur-chur-chur-chur-chur*. **STATUS AND RANGE** Irregular, ranging from locally fairly common to very uncommon migrant and non-breeding resident in Bahamas, Cuba, Puerto Rico, and Virgin and Cayman Islands September–April. Rare in Hispaniola, Guadeloupe, and Barbados; very rare elsewhere in West Indies. **HABITAT** Widespread in many forest types and scrub.

**WHITE-EYED VIREO** *Vireo griseus* 12.5cm (5in); 11g. Whitish below; yellow sides and spectacles; two white wing bars. **ADULT** White eye. **IMMATURE** Duller; dark eye. **VOICE** Loud, slurred, three to seven syllables, such as *chip-a-tee-weeo-chip*, repeated with variations. More rapid and less emphatic than Thick-billed Vireo. Also churring note. **STATUS AND RANGE** Generally a common migrant and non-breeding resident in western Cuba; uncommon in Bahamas, eastern Cuba, Puerto Rico, and Cayman Islands; rare in Jamaica and Guadeloupe; very rare in Hispaniola and Virgin Islands. Vagrant to Lesser Antilles other than Guadeloupe. Occurs primarily October–March. Likely more frequent than records indicate. **HABITAT** Undergrowth, scrub, coastal thickets, and brushy woodlands.

**BLUE-HEADED VIREO** *Vireo solitarius* 12.5–15cm (5–5.75in); 14–19g. Blue-gray head with white spectacles; two white wing bars. **VOICE** Short, garbled two- to three-syllable phrases. **STATUS AND RANGE** Very rare migrant and non-breeding resident in northern Bahamas and western Cuba September–April. Vagrant elsewhere in West Indies. **HABITAT** Low, dense shrubs.

JAMAICAN VIREO

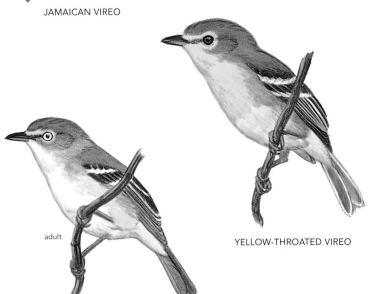

adult

WHITE-EYED VIREO

YELLOW-THROATED VIREO

BLUE-HEADED VIREO

**P** **PUERTO RICAN VIREO** *Vireo latimeri* 12.5cm (5in); 10–15g. Two-toned underparts: throat and breast pale gray, belly and abdomen pale yellow. Incomplete white eye-ring and brown eye. **VOICE** Melodious whistle, usually three to four syllables repeated for several minutes, then changed; also a chattering *chur-chur-churr-rrr*. **STATUS AND RANGE** Endemic to Puerto Rico, where common. Most common in haystack hills of north coast and forested valleys of south coast, where declining. Uncommon in higher elevations of Cordillera Central, Cayey Mountains, and Luquillo Mountains. **HABITAT** Forests of all types and all elevations, including mangroves, dry coastal scrub, moist limestone hills, and wet mountain forests.

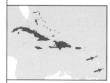

**RED-EYED VIREO** *Vireo olivaceus* 15cm (5.75in); 17g. Gray cap; white eyebrow stripe bordered by black eye-line; and crown stripe. Lacks black "whisker." (Black-whiskered Vireo has black whisker stripe, tanner underparts, duller green on back, and paler gray on crown.) **ADULT** Red eye. **VOICE** Calls primarily in April. Nasal, high *chway*. Also abrupt phrases, often repeated. (Black-whiskered Vireo has longer phrases.) **STATUS AND RANGE** Irregular, ranging from locally fairly common to very uncommon migrant in Bahamas, Cuba, Jamaica, Puerto Rico, Virgin Islands, Cayman Islands, Guadeloupe, and Barbados primarily September–October and less frequent in November and April. Decidedly rare in Hispaniola, but likely more frequent than records indicate. Very rare or vagrant elsewhere in West Indies. **HABITAT** Dry and wet forests, open woodlands, scrub, and gardens, from coast to mountains.

**BLACK-WHISKERED VIREO** *Vireo altiloquus* 15–16.5cm (5.75–6.5in); 18g. Whitish eyebrow stripe; dark eye-line; black mustache stripe; no wing bars. **ADULT** Red iris. **VOICE** Monotonous, throughout day. Short, melodious two- to three-syllable phrases, each different, separated by pauses. Also a complaining *shway*. **STATUS AND RANGE** Common breeding resident nearly throughout West Indies February–August. Some birds present year-round in Hispaniola, Puerto Rico, Lesser Antilles, San Andrés and Providencia. Absent November–January in Bahamas, Cuba, Jamaica, and Cayman Islands. **HABITAT** All forest types at all elevations.

**YELLOW-GREEN VIREO** *Vireo flavoviridis* 14cm (5.5in); 16–21g. Similar to the widespread Black-whiskered Vireo, but lacks mustache stripe and has distinctive yellow sides. **VOICE** Similar to Black-whiskered Vireo. **STATUS AND RANGE** A rare migrant on San Andrés primarily in October, very rare on Providencia. **HABITAT** Woodlands and scrub.

PUERTO RICAN VIREO

RED-EYED VIREO

adult

BLACK-WHISKERED VIREO

adult

YELLOW-GREEN VIREO

**◻ BLUE MOUNTAIN VIREO** *Vireo osburni* 12.5–15cm (4.75–5.75in); 21g. Robust gray vireo; large, with dark bill. Lacks facial markings and wing bars. **VOICE** Trilling or bubbling whistle, descending slightly in tone. Also harsh *burr*, descending at end. **STATUS AND RANGE** Endemic to Jamaica, where uncommon. **HABITAT** Mainly humid and moist mountain forests, also upland woods and shade coffee.

**YUCATAN VIREO** *Vireo magister* 15cm (5.75in); 17–24g. Olive-gray crown and back; whitish or pale tan eyebrow stripe; dark gray eye-line; white underparts with yellowish abdomen; brown eye; no wing bars. **VOICE** Two-note whistle, *whoi whu*, and three-syllable *sweet, brid-get*, very similar to Black-whiskered Vireo. **STATUS AND RANGE** Common permanent resident on Grand Cayman (Cayman Islands) east of Savannah. **HABITAT** Relatively dense vegetation in low-elevation woodlands and mangroves.

**WARBLING VIREO** *Vireo gilvus* 12.5–15cm (5–5.75in); 11–18g. Pale gray upperparts; slightly lighter crown and hindneck; whitish eyebrow stripe. Throat to belly whitish, often with wash of pale or greenish-yellow. (Orange-crowned Warbler lacks gray crown and has faint greenish-yellow eyebrow stripe.) **VOICE** A complaining *shway* similar to Black-whiskered, Red-eyed, and Philadelphia Vireos. **STATUS AND RANGE** Rare migrant to northern Bahamas September–October and April. Very rare or vagrant to Greater Antilles. **HABITAT** Forests and gardens.

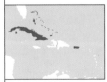

**PHILADELPHIA VIREO** *Vireo philadelphicus* 11.5–13cm (4.5–5in); 10–16g. Gray crown; gray-olive upperparts; variable yellow below. Dark lores; whitish eyebrow stripe; brown eye; no wing bars. (Warbling Vireo has whiter breast and lacks dark lores. Tennessee Warbler has slenderer bill; in non-breeding plumage, has yellowish eyebrow stripe and greenish crown. In breeding plumage, much whiter below.) **VOICE** A complaining *shway*. **STATUS AND RANGE** A decidedly rare migrant in Bahamas, Cuba, Jamaica, Puerto Rico, and Cayman Islands primarily in October, but also April–May. Vagrant elsewhere in West Indies. **HABITAT** Forests, woodlands, and gardens.

BLUE MOUNTAIN VIREO

YUCATAN VIREO

imm

adult

WARBLING VIREO

imm

PHILADELPHIA VIREO

adult

**ELFIN-WOODS WARBLER** *Setophaga angelae* 12.5–13.5cm (5–5.25in); 7.5–8.5g. ADULT Thin white eyebrow stripe; white patches on ear-coverts and neck; incomplete eye-ring; black crown. IMMATURE Black replaced by greenish (*see* Plate 91). VOICE Series of short, rapid, unmusical notes on one pitch, swelling and terminating with short double syllables slightly lower. Also short, metallic *chip*. STATUS AND RANGE Endemic to Puerto Rico, where uncommon and local. Limited to forests in and around Luquillo and Maricao forests. Threatened. HABITAT Dense vines of canopy in humid mountain forests; sometimes at lower elevations.

**BLACKPOLL WARBLER** *Setophaga striata* 12.5–14cm (5–5.5in); 13g. BREEDING MALE Black cap, white cheek. BREEDING FEMALE Grayish above, whitish below; lightly streaked sides; white wing bars and undertail-coverts. NON-BREEDING ADULT AND IMMATURE *See* Plate 90. VOICE Thin, high-pitched *zeet-zeet-zeet-zeet* … ; also, distinctive *zheet*. STATUS AND RANGE Throughout West Indies, where fairly common migrant in Bahamas, Cuba, Hispaniola, Puerto Rico, and Guadeloupe; uncommon to rare on most other islands. Occurs primarily October–November and in May. HABITAT Mangroves, brush, scrub forests, open areas with trees, and mixed woodlands.

**ARROWHEAD WARBLER** *Setophaga pharetra* 13cm (5in); 10g. BEHAVIOR Flicks tail down. ADULT MALE Streaked black and white; two white wing bars. ADULT FEMALE Dark gray streaks. IMMATURE Yellowish-olive above, pale yellowish below with fine grayish streaks; wing bars; yellowish eye-ring; some white in tail (*see* plate 91). (Jamaican Vireo similar to immature, but lacks eye-ring, dark eye-line, and white in tail. Flicks tail up.) VOICE Soft, generally two series of rising *tswee* notes followed by jumble of notes. Also, watery *chip*. STATUS AND RANGE Endemic to Jamaica, where locally common. HABITAT Moist and humid forests at all elevations. Infrequently, wet lowland forests.

**BLACK-AND-WHITE WARBLER** *Mniotilta varia* 12.5–14cm (5–5.5in); 11g. BEHAVIOR Forages up and down tree trunks, often upside down. DESCRIPTION Black-and-white striped crown. MALE Black cheek patch. FEMALE Whiter, particularly on cheek, throat, and sides. VOICE Thin *tee-zee, tee-zee, tee-zee, tee-zee*, varying in length. Also, buzzy *chit*. STATUS AND RANGE Through West Indies, where migrant and non-breeding resident primarily August–April. Common in Bahamas, Greater Antilles, Cayman and Virgin Islands, San Andrés, Providencia, and Lesser Antilles south to Martinique; rare in Barbados; very rare in St Lucia. HABITAT Forests and wooded areas at all elevations.

**CERULEAN WARBLER** *Setophaga cerulea* 10–13cm (4–5in); 9g. Two white wing bars. ADULT MALE Light blue head and upper-parts; dark band across breast. ADULT FEMALE AND IMMATURE MALE Upperparts grayish-blue, underparts dull white with yellow-ish tinge on throat and upper breast and faint streaks on sides. IMMATURE FEMALE *See* Plate 91. VOICE A thin *chip*. STATUS AND RANGE Very rare migrant in Bahamas, Cuba, Jamaica, Grand Cayman (Cayman Islands), and San Andrés, primarily September and October, less frequent in April. Vagrant else-where in West Indies. HABITAT Forest canopy, also low bushes and small trees.

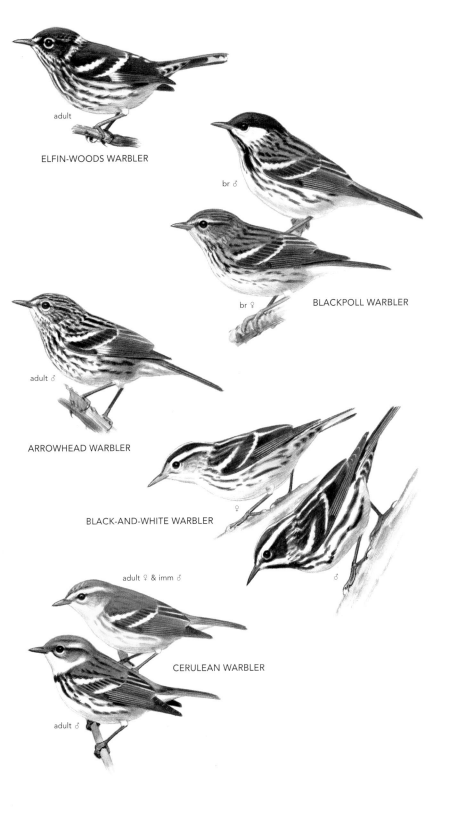

ELFIN-WOODS WARBLER

adult

br ♂

BLACKPOLL WARBLER

br ♀

ARROWHEAD WARBLER

adult ♂

BLACK-AND-WHITE WARBLER

♀

adult ♀ & imm ♂

♂

CERULEAN WARBLER

adult ♂

**NORTHERN WATERTHRUSH** *Parkesia noveboracensis* 12.5–15cm (5–5.75in); 18g. **BEHAVIOR** Bobs and teeters; terrestrial. **DESCRIPTION** Pale tan below with dark brown streaks. Prominent pale tan eyebrow stripe that narrows behind eye, and fine blackish-brown streaks on throat. (*See* Louisiana Waterthrush.) **VOICE** Sharp, emphatic *tchip*. **STATUS AND RANGE** Throughout West Indies, where common migrant and non-breeding resident in Bahamas, Greater Antilles, Virgin and Cayman Islands, St Bartholomew, Antigua, Guadeloupe, San Andrés, and Providencia primarily September–April. Uncommon in remaining Lesser Antilles. **HABITAT** Borders of standing water, primarily saline and brackish, in or near mangroves and coastal scrub forests.

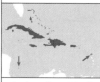

**LOUISIANA WATERTHRUSH** *Parkesia motacilla* 14.5–16cm (5.5–6.25in); 20g. **BEHAVIOR** Bobs and teeters; terrestrial. **DESCRIPTION** White below, with dark brown streaks. White eyebrow stripe, broader behind eye; lacks streaks on throat. (Northern Waterthrush has fine streaks on throat, and pale tan eyebrow stripe does not broaden behind eye.) **VOICE** Sharp *chink*, higher and more ringing than Northern Waterthrush. **STATUS AND RANGE** Through much of West Indies, where migrant and non-breeding resident August–March. Common in Cuba, Jamaica, and Puerto Rico; uncommon in northern Bahamas, and Hispaniola; rare in southern Bahamas, Virgin Islands, Cayman Islands, Guadeloupe, San Andrés, and Providencia; generally vagrant to Lesser Antilles south to St Vincent. **HABITAT** Edges of flowing fresh water, often at higher elevations. Also sinkhole lakes and standing pools.

**OVENBIRD** *Seiurus aurocapilla* 14–16.5cm (5.5–6.5in); 19g. **BEHAVIOR** Bobs and tilts tail up; terrestrial. **DESCRIPTION** Orange crown bordered with blackish stripes; bold white eye-ring; white underparts heavily marked with large dark streaks. **FEMALE** Slightly duller. **VOICE** A loud, sharp *chek*. **STATUS AND RANGE** Nearly throughout West Indies, where common migrant and non-breeding resident in Bahamas, Greater Antilles, and San Andrés August–May; uncommon in Virgin and Cayman Islands, Guadeloupe, and Providencia; generally rare in Lesser Antilles south to St Vincent. **HABITAT** Principally woodlands, shade coffee, and primary forest floors, often near streams or pools.

**RUBY-CROWNED KINGLET** *Regulus calendula* 11.5cm (4.5in); 6g. Tiny, with olive-colored upperparts, bold white eye-ring, and two whitish wing bars. **MALE** Usually concealed red crest. **FEMALE** *See* Plate 92. **VOICE** A fast, sharp *ji-dit*. **STATUS AND RANGE** Very rare migrant and non-breeding resident in northern Bahamas and western tip of Cuba (Guanahacabibes) October–March. Vagrant elsewhere in West Indies. **HABITAT** Generally low, scrubby vegetation.

**BLACK-THROATED BLUE WARBLER** *Setophaga caerulescens* 12–14cm (4.75–5.5in); 10g. **MALE** Blue above; black face and band along sides; white wing spot. **FEMALE** *See* Plate 93. **VOICE** A dull *chip*. **STATUS AND RANGE** Throughout West Indies, where common migrant and non-breeding resident in Bahamas, Greater Antilles, and Cayman Islands September–May; decidedly uncommon in Virgin Islands, San Andrés, and Providencia; rare in Guadeloupe, decidedly so in other Lesser Antilles. **HABITAT** Forests, forest edges, shade coffee, and woodlands, primarily in mountains. Also moist to wet lowlands. Infrequently dry forests.

**⑤ WHISTLING WARBLER** *Catharopeza bishopi* 14.5cm (5.75in); 14–19g. **BEHAVIOR** Cocks tail. **ADULT** Blackish hood, upperparts, and broad breast band; broad white eye-ring, chin, and mark by bill. **IMMATURE** Brownish-gray hood, upperparts, and breast band; white eye-ring and mark by bill. **VOICE** Clear, rapid whistles, increasingly loud and becoming slurred, ending with two to three emphatic notes. **STATUS AND RANGE** Endemic to St Vincent, where rare in humid hill and mountain forests from 300m (1000ft) upward. Threatened. Genus also endemic to St Vincent. **HABITAT** Prefers ravines, gorges, and valleys with primary or secondary forest. Most frequently near ground in low undergrowth, sometimes ranging to underside of forest canopy, but usually below 4m (13ft).

NORTHERN WATERTHRUSH

LOUISIANA WATERTHRUSH

OVENBIRD

RUBY-CROWNED KINGLET

BLACK-THROATED BLUE WARBLER

WHISTLING WARBLER

imm

adult

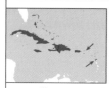

**PRAIRIE WARBLER** *Setophaga discolor* 12cm (4.75in); 8g. **BEHAVIOR** Bobs tail. **DESCRIPTION** Yellow underparts; black side streaks. **IMMATURE FEMALE** *See* Plate 91. **STATUS AND RANGE** Through much of West Indies as migrant and non-breeding resident late August–April. Common in Bahamas, Greater Antilles, and Cayman Islands; uncommon in Virgin Islands, Anguilla, and Guadeloupe; generally rare in northern Lesser Antilles. Uncommon in San Andrés and rare in Providencia primarily in October. Very rare or vagrant from Dominica south. **VOICE** A dry, husky *chip*. **HABITAT** Dry coastal forests, thickets, pastures with scattered trees, mangroves, pine forests, and gardens, at all elevations.

**YELLOW-THROATED WARBLER** *Setophaga dominica* 13cm (5in); 9g. Yellow throat and upper breast; white eyebrow stripe, neck patch, belly, and abdomen; sides streaked. (*See* Bahama Warbler.) Does not bob tail like Kirtland's Warbler. **VOICE** A series of *sweet* notes descending in pitch toward end. Also high-pitched, slightly metallic *tsip*. **STATUS AND RANGE** Generally common migrant and non-breeding resident in Bahamas, Greater Antilles, and Cayman Islands; rare in Virgin Islands, San Andrés, and Providencia; vagrant in Lesser Antilles. Occurs primarily August–March. **HABITAT** Pine forests, gardens, developed areas, Australian pine (*Casuarina*), lowland forests, and coconut palms. Often forages in tree crowns and sometimes picks insects off human structures.

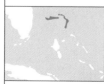

**⑤ BAHAMA WARBLER** *Setophaga flavescens* 13–14cm (5–5.5in); 10g. **BEHAVIOR** Often climbs tree trunks. **DESCRIPTION** White eyebrow stripe and neck patch. Yellow underparts extend to abdomen and to stripes on sides. (Yellow-throated Warbler has more extensive white on side of neck; less extensive yellow on underparts, which is limited to throat and upper breast and does not extend to belly or onto striped sides; bill smaller; song descends.) **VOICE** A series of *sweet* notes ascending in pitch toward end. Also high-pitched, slightly metallic *tsip*. **STATUS AND RANGE** Endemic to Bahamas, where common on Grand Bahama, Little Abaco, and Great Abaco. These islands encompass entire range. **HABITAT** Restricted to pine forest.

**YELLOW-RUMPED WARBLER** *Setophaga coronata* 14cm (5.5in); 12g. Yellow rump and patch on side of breast; white throat. (A yellow-throated form could occur as a vagrant.) **IMMATURE** *See* Plate 90. **VOICE** Hard, characteristic *check*. **STATUS AND RANGE** Migrant and non-breeding resident throughout West Indies primarily November–April. Generally fairly common in Bahamas, Cuba, Jamaica, Cayman Islands, and San Andrés; uncommon in Hispaniola, Puerto Rico, Virgin Islands, Guadeloupe, and Providencia. Rare or very rare in most Lesser Antilles. Very irregular occurrence year to year. **HABITAT** Gardens, woodlands, thickets, areas with scattered vegetation. Also mangroves and swamp edges. Especially where fruits present.

**CANADA WARBLER** *Cardellina canadensis* 12.5–15.5cm (5–5.75in); 10g. **ADULT MALE** Bluish-gray upperparts; bold yellow spectacles; yellow underparts with black stripes forming a necklace. (Oriente Warbler has yellow cheeks and lacks stripes on breast.) **ADULT FEMALE** *See* Plate 90. **IMMATURE** Olive-brown wash on upperparts; virtually no necklace. **VOICE** A low *tchup*. **STATUS AND RANGE** Rare migrant in Cayman Islands; very rare in northern Bahamas, Cuba, Puerto Rico, San Andrés, and Providencia. Vagrant elsewhere in West Indies. Occurs primarily September and October. **HABITAT** Primarily lowlands in moderately open vegetation among scattered trees, usually near swamps or other standing water.

PRAIRIE WARBLER

adult

YELLOW-THROATED WARBLER

br

BAHAMA WARBLER

br

YELLOW-RUMPED WARBLER

adult ♀ &
non-br ♂

br ♂

adult ♂

CANADA WARBLER

**MAGNOLIA WARBLER** *Setophaga magnolia* 11.5–12.5cm (4.5–5in); 10g. White tail markings; white eyebrow stripe and wing bars; yellow throat and rump. (Yellow-rumped Warbler has some white in tail and has white, not yellow, throat.) NON-BREEDING ADULT AND IMMATURE *See* Plate 90. VOICE Hard, sonorous *tseek*. STATUS AND RANGE Generally fairly common migrant in Bahamas, Cuba, Jamaica, Puerto Rico, and San Andrés; uncommon in Hispaniola, Virgin Islands, Cayman Islands, Guadeloupe, and Providencia; very rare to vagrant in other Lesser Antilles. Occurs September–May, but less frequent as a non-breeding resident November–March. HABITAT Open woodlands in lowlands, swamp edges, and bushes. Sometimes gardens.

**CAPE MAY WARBLER** *Setophaga tigrina* 12.5–14cm (5–5.5in); 11g. Heavy striping on breast; yellowish rump. Usually a yellow neck patch. (Magnolia Warbler lacks yellow neck patch.) IMMATURE *See* Plate 90. VOICE A very thin, short *tsit*. STATUS AND RANGE Migrant and non-breeding resident throughout West Indies primarily October–April. Common in Bahamas, Greater Antilles, Virgin Islands, Cayman Islands, San Andrés, and Providencia; uncommon in Guadeloupe; generally very rare in other Lesser Antilles. HABITAT Mountain forests to coastal thickets, mangroves, and gardens. Almost anywhere plants are flowering.

**BLACK-THROATED GREEN WARBLER** *Setophaga virens* 12.5cm (5in); 9g. Yellowish-gray cheeks surrounded by characteristic yellow band. ADULT MALE Black chin, throat, upper breast, and side streaks. ADULT FEMALE AND IMMATURE MALE Duller; chin yellowish. IMMATURE FEMALE *See* Plate 91. VOICE Short, crisp *tsip*. STATUS AND RANGE Migrant and non-breeding resident throughout West Indies September–May. Common in western Cuba; uncommon and generally local in Bahamas, eastern Cuba, Jamaica, Hispaniola, Puerto Rico, Cayman Islands, and San Andrés; rare in Virgin Islands and Guadeloupe; very rare in other Lesser Antilles. HABITAT Primarily mid-elevation broadleaf and pine forests as well as shade coffee. May occur at all elevations. Sometimes woodlands and gardens.

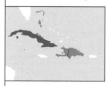

**PINE WARBLER** *Setophaga pinus* 12.5–14.5cm (5–5.75in); 12g. ADULT MALE Olive upperparts; unstreaked back; two white wing bars; faint yellow eyebrow stripe; variable yellow on chin and throat; faint gray to blackish streaks on breast and upper flanks. (Bay-breasted Warbler has streaked back.) ADULT FEMALE Duller. IMMATURE *See* Plate 91. VOICE Musical trill usually on one pitch. Also strong *tzip*. STATUS AND RANGE Common permanent resident in northern Bahamas and Dominican Republic. Threatened in Haiti. Very rare migrant to western Cuba and Cayman Islands October and November. Vagrant elsewhere in West Indies. HABITAT Mature pine forests or barrens.

**KIRTLAND'S WARBLER** *Setophaga kirtlandii* 14–15cm (5–5.75in); 12–16g. BEHAVIOR Bobs tail and often feeds on ground. BREEDING MALE Bluish-gray above; black streaks on back; two inconspicuous whitish wing bars; broken white eye-ring; bright yellow throat and belly; black streaks on sides. Forehead and lores black; more contrast. IMMATURE FEMALE Brownish-gray above with eye-ring and flank streaks fainter. ADULT FEMALE AND NON-BREEDING MALE *See* Plate 91. Similar Yellow-throated Warbler does not bob tail. VOICE A moderately harsh *chip*. STATUS AND RANGE Uncommon to rare migrant and non-breeding resident principally in central Bahamas October–April. Endangered. HABITAT Primarily low broadleaf scrub and early-succession shrublands, especially where berries are present.

**BLACKBURNIAN WARBLER** *Setophaga fusca* 13cm (5in); 10g. ADULT FEMALE, NON-BREEDING MALE, AND IMMATURE MALE Bright orange-yellow throat, breast, eyebrow stripe, and sides of neck. White back stripes and wing bars; dark side stripes. BREEDING MALE Orange throat and facial markings. IMMATURE FEMALE *See* Plate 91. VOICE Fine, weak *tsseek, tsseek*. STATUS AND RANGE Decidedly uncommon migrant in Cayman Islands (Grand Cayman) and San Andrés; rare in Bahamas, Cuba, Jamaica, and Providencia; very rare in Hispaniola, Puerto Rico, Virgin Islands (St John, Guana Island), and Guadeloupe; vagrant to other Lesser Antilles. Occurs primarily September–October and April–May. HABITAT Conifers, tall trees, and botanical gardens.

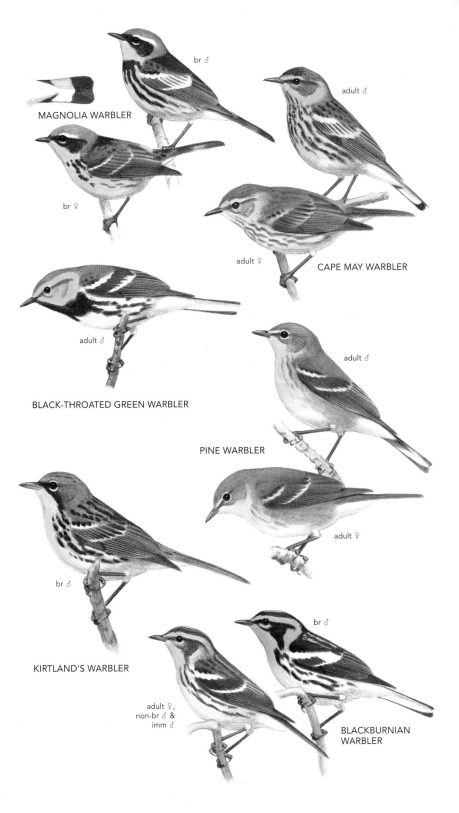

MAGNOLIA WARBLER

br ♂

br ♀

adult ♂

adult ♀

CAPE MAY WARBLER

BLACK-THROATED GREEN WARBLER

adult ♂

PINE WARBLER

adult ♂

adult ♀

KIRTLAND'S WARBLER

br ♂

br ♂

adult ♀,
non-br ♂ &
imm ♂

BLACKBURNIAN
WARBLER

**NASHVILLE WARBLER** *Leiothlypis ruficapilla* 11.5–12.5cm (4.5–5in); 7–14g. Conspicuous white eye-ring in all plumages; grayish head contrasts with yellowish-green upperparts. **ADULT** Pale bluish-gray head, yellow underparts except for white belly. **IMMATURE** *See* Plate 92. **VOICE** A dull *jeet*. **STATUS AND RANGE** Rare migrant and non-breeding resident in northern and central Bahamas, western Cuba, and cays off north-central coast, and also Cayman Islands mid-September through mid-April. Very rare or vagrant elsewhere in West Indies. **HABITAT** Woodlands.

**ⓒ ORIENTE WARBLER** *Teretistris fornsi* 13cm (5in); 8–13g. Gray upperparts; yellow underparts. No wing bars or white in plumage. Yellow eye-ring; long, slightly down-curved bill. (Female Prothonotary Warbler has less distinctive separation between yellowish-olive crown and yellow of face; also has white in tail.) **VOICE** Shrill *tsi-tsi-tsi* … , repeated several times, practically indistinguishable from Yellow-headed Warbler. **STATUS AND RANGE** Endemic to Cuba; locally common in eastern part of island. Particularly common in southern provinces of Granma, Santiago de Cuba, and Guantánamo. Bird family also endemic to Cuba. **HABITAT** Forests, scrub, and borders of swamps from coast to highest mountains.

**WILSON'S WARBLER** *Cardellina pusilla* 11–12.5cm (4.25–5in); 8g. **ADULT MALE** Distinct black cap; bright yellow forehead and eyebrow stripe. **ADULT FEMALE AND IMMATURE MALE** Duller; hint of black cap. **IMMATURE FEMALE** *See* Plate 92. **VOICE** A husky *chuck*. **STATUS AND RANGE** Rare migrant and even rarer non-breeding resident September–April in Cayman Islands; very rare in northern Bahamas and western and central Cuba. Vagrant elsewhere in West Indies. **HABITAT** Dense vegetation at all altitudes, but primarily in lowlands.

**KENTUCKY WARBLER** *Geothlypis formosa* 12.5–14.5cm (5–5.75in); 14g. **ADULT MALE** Yellow spectacles; black facial mark and crown; yellow underparts. **ADULT FEMALE AND IMMATURE MALE** Less black on face and crown. **IMMATURE FEMALE** *See* Plate 93. **VOICE** A sharp *check*. **STATUS AND RANGE** Rare migrant and decidedly rare non-breeding resident in Bahamas, Cuba, Hispaniola, Puerto Rico, Virgin and Cayman Islands, Guadeloupe, and Providencia late August–April. Very rare or vagrant elsewhere in West Indies. **HABITAT** Dense undergrowth and thickets in moist mature broadleaf forest understory.

**HOODED WARBLER** *Setophaga citrina* 12.5–14.5cm (5–5.75in); 10g. **BEHAVIOR** Flicks and fans tail, showing white outertail feathers. **MALE** Distinctive black hood. **ADULT FEMALE** Variable hood, from almost complete to black markings only on crown. (*See also* Plate 93.) **IMMATURE FEMALE** Lacks hood; yellow face sharply demarcated. (Adult female and immature Wilson's Warblers smaller, with yellow eyebrow stripe and no white in tail.) **VOICE** A metallic *chink*. **STATUS AND RANGE** Uncommon migrant and non-breeding resident in Bahamas, Greater Antilles, Cayman Islands, and Providencia September–April. Rare in Virgin Islands and Guadeloupe. Common on San Andrés. Very rare or vagrant in most of Lesser Antilles. **HABITAT** Moist mature broadleaf forest undergrowth and mangroves.

NASHVILLE WARBLER

adult

ORIENTE WARBLER

WILSON'S WARBLER

adult ♂

KENTUCKY WARBLER

adult ♂

adult ♀

HOODED WARBLER

♂

**⑤ BAHAMA YELLOWTHROAT** *Geothlypis rostrata* 15cm (5.75in); 16g. Relatively large, slow-moving, with relatively heavy bill. **MALE** Black mask; gray cap; yellow throat, breast, and upper belly. Mask edging varies from whitish to yellow. **FEMALE** Lacks mask. Yellow throat, breast, and belly; gray crown; whitish eye-ring and eyebrow stripe. Similar to Common Yellowthroat. (*See also* Plate 93.) **VOICE** Loud, clear *witchity, witchity, witchit*, very similar to Common Yellowthroat. Also deep, sharp *tchit*, less gravelly than Common Yellowthroat. **STATUS AND RANGE** Endemic to northern Bahamas: common on Grand Bahama, Abaco, Eleuthera, Cat Island; uncommon on Andros; rare on New Providence. **HABITAT** Scrub, coppice edges, and pine woods with thatch palm understory. Prefers woodier habitat than Common Yellowthroat.

**COMMON YELLOWTHROAT** *Geothlypis trichas* 11.5–14cm (4.5–5.5in); 10g. **ADULT MALE** Conspicuous black facial mask, edged above by whitish; yellow throat and breast. **ADULT FEMALE** Lacks facial mask; bright yellow throat and breast contrast with whitish belly; narrow whitish eye-ring; usually pale, whitish eyebrow stripe. (*See also* Plate 93.) **IMMATURE** Duller and browner than adult female. (Bahama Yellowthroat larger; less active; heavier bill; yellow of underparts extends to belly; crown gray.) **VOICE** A sharp, gravelly *tchit*. The clear song *witchity, witchity, witchity, witch* is heard rarely before northward migration. **STATUS AND RANGE** Common migrant and non-breeding resident in Bahamas, Greater Antilles, Cayman Islands, and San Andrés; uncommon to rare in Virgin Islands, Guadeloupe, and Providencia; vagrant to other Lesser Antilles. Occurs primarily October–early May. **HABITAT** Wet grass and brush, overgrown fields and abandoned pastures, savannas, marshes, usually at freshwater edges.

**CONNECTICUT WARBLER** *Oporornis agilis* 13.5–15cm (5.25–5.75in); 15g. Difficult to detect. **BEHAVIOR** Usually terrestrial; bobs up and down. **DESCRIPTION** Large, stocky, with distinctive hood and white eye-ring. Dull yellow from belly to undertail-coverts, which extend nearly to end of tail. (Mourning Warbler sometimes has eye-ring, but this is thin and broken in front; undertail-coverts shorter.) **ADULT MALE** Hood bluish-gray. **ADULT FEMALE AND IMMATURE** Hood pale gray-brown; whitish throat. (*See also* Plate 93.) **VOICE** A nasal, raspy *witch*. **STATUS AND RANGE** Rare migrant in Hispaniola and very rare in Bahamas, Puerto Rico, Virgin Islands, Cayman Islands, and Guadeloupe. Likely very rare in Cuba, but few records. Occurs primarily September and October. **HABITAT** Moist woodland understory, usually near water.

**MOURNING WARBLER** *Geothlypis philadelphia* 13–14.5cm (5–5.75in); 10–18g. Difficult to detect. **BEHAVIOR** Primarily terrestrial. **ADULT MALE** Bluish-gray hood; black breast patch; no eye-ring. **ADULT FEMALE** Hood pale gray or brownish; incomplete eye-ring; whitish throat; no black on breast. **IMMATURE** *See* Plate 93. (Connecticut Warbler has bold white, complete eye-ring and longer undertail-coverts.) **VOICE** A distinctive, metallic *jink*. **STATUS AND RANGE** Very rare southbound migrant in West Indies primarily September and October, but a few remain as non-breeding residents. Vagrant to any particular island, with records from Bahamas, Cuba, Jamaica, Hispaniola, Puerto Rico, Virgin Islands, Cayman Islands, and San Andrés. **HABITAT** Wet thickets, second growth, and swamp edges.

♀

♂

BAHAMA
YELLOWTHROAT

adult ♀

adult ♂

COMMON
YELLOWTHROAT

adult ♂

adult ♀
and imm

CONNECTICUT
WARBLER

adult ♀

adult ♂

MOURNING
WARBLER

**PALM WARBLER** *Setophaga palmarum* 12.5–14cm (5–5.5in); 10g. **BEHAVIOR** Bobs tail, often on ground. **BREEDING** Dark reddish-brown crown. **NON-BREEDING** *See* Plate 90. **VOICE** A distinctive *tsick*. **STATUS AND RANGE** Common in Bahamas, Cuba, Jamaica, Hispaniola, and Cayman Islands; uncommon in Puerto Rico, Virgin Islands, San Andrés, and Providencia; rare in Guadeloupe and vagrant elsewhere in Lesser Antilles. Migrant and non-breeding resident in West Indies primarily October–April. **HABITAT** Generally brush and bushes near coast, including mangroves. Also open areas with sparse brush, plantation edges, and gardens.

**S** **VITELLINE WARBLER** *Setophaga vitellina* 13cm (5in); 7g. **BEHAVIOR** Bobs tail. **ADULT MALE** Olive-green above, entirely yellow below, with faint side stripes and distinct facial pattern. **ADULT FEMALE** *See* Plate 91. **IMMATURE** Crown gray, throat pale gray; facial markings whitish. (Prairie Warbler has more conspicuous side stripes, whitish undertail-coverts, more contrast in facial markings.) **VOICE** Slightly harsh four- to five-syllable *szwee-szwee-szwee-zee*. Also shorter, deeper call. **STATUS AND RANGE** Endemic to Cayman and Swan Islands; locally common on Grand Cayman, and very common on Little Cayman and Cayman Brac. **HABITAT** Dry scrub and woodlands, particularly inland. Also disturbed urban areas and gardens.

**YELLOW WARBLER** *Setophaga petechia* 11.5–13.5cm (4.5–5.25in); 13g. **ADULT MALE** Yellow overall including outertail feathers; reddish streaks on breast and sides. Head varies from yellow (Bahamas and Cuba) to entirely reddish-brown (Martinique). **ADULT FEMALE AND IMMATURE** *See* Plates 90 and 92. **VOICE** Variable; typically loud, clear, and rapid *sweet-sweet-sweet-ti-ti-ti-weet*. Also thin *zeet* and hard *chip*. **STATUS AND RANGE** Common permanent resident widely in West Indies, and migrants augment local numbers September–April. Uncommon in northern Bahamas; rare and non-breeding in Grenada, St Vincent, and Providencia; vagrant on Saba. **HABITAT** Primarily mangroves, coastal scrub on some islands. In Martinique, ranges up into mountain forests.

**NORTHERN PARULA** *Setophaga americana* 10.5–12cm (4–4.75in); 9g. Grayish-blue above with greenish-yellow back; yellow throat and breast; white wing bars; incomplete white eye-ring. **NON-BREEDING ADULT AND IMMATURE** May have faint black and reddish band across breast. **BREEDING MALE** Breast band conspicuous. **VOICE** Ascending insect-like buzz with sharp end note; heard March–May. **STATUS AND RANGE** Widespread migrant and non-breeding resident August–May in West Indies. Common in Bahamas, Greater Antilles, Virgin and Cayman Islands, and San Andrés. Generally uncommon in northern Lesser Antilles and Guadeloupe, while rare to vagrant farther south. **HABITAT** Primarily dry forests and scrub of lowlands; also moist mountain forests and gardens with large trees.

**BLUE-WINGED WARBLER** *Vermivora cyanoptera* 12cm (4.75in); 8g. Overall bright yellow with bluish wings, white wing bars, and black eye-line. (Prothonotary Warbler lacks white wing bars and black eye-line.) **VOICE** A sharp, loud *jeet*. **STATUS AND RANGE** Generally rare migrant and non-breeding resident in Bahamas, Cuba, Hispaniola, Puerto Rico, larger Virgin Islands, Cayman Islands, and Guadeloupe primarily October–March. Very rare in Jamaica. Vagrant elsewhere in West Indies. **HABITAT** Moist forests, trees near Australian pine (*Casuarina*), and sometimes thickets and bushes.

**PROTHONOTARY WARBLER** *Protonotaria citrea* 13.5cm (5.25in); 15g. **MALE** Golden-yellow overall except blue-gray wings and tail. **FEMALE** *See* Plate 93. **VOICE** A metallic *tink*, similar to waterthrushes. **STATUS AND RANGE** Throughout West Indies, where numbers vary year to year, but generally uncommon migrant in Bahamas, Greater Antilles, Cayman Islands, Guadeloupe, San Andrés, and Providencia primarily August–October and March–early April. Rare in Virgin Islands and remaining Lesser Antilles. **HABITAT** In or near mangrove swamps. In Cuba, also gardens and tree clumps.

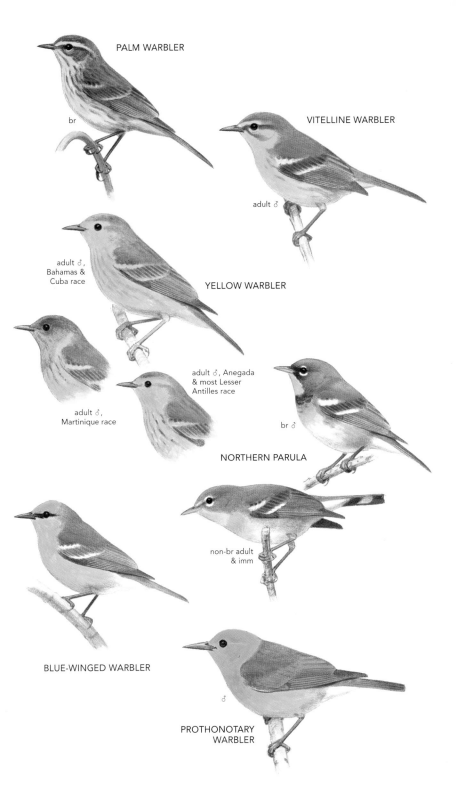

PALM WARBLER

br

VITELLINE WARBLER

adult ♂

adult ♂,
Bahamas &
Cuba race

YELLOW WARBLER

adult ♂,
Martinique race

adult ♂, Anegada
& most Lesser
Antilles race

NORTHERN PARULA

br ♂

non-br adult
& imm

BLUE-WINGED WARBLER

♂

PROTHONOTARY
WARBLER

**⬛YELLOW-HEADED WARBLER** *Teretistris fernandinae* 13cm (5in); 6–18g. Gray overall, paler below; yellowish head and neck; long, slightly down-curved bill; no wing bars. (Prothonotary Warbler primarily yellow below.) **VOICE** Peculiar, shrill *tsi-tsi-tsi* … , repeated several times. Nearly identical to call of Oriente Warbler. **STATUS AND RANGE** Endemic to Cuba, where common in western and central parts of island. Bird family also endemic to Cuba. **HABITAT** Sea level to mid-elevations. Primarily shrubs with much tangled vegetation and vines. Also open forests.

**ORANGE-CROWNED WARBLER** *Leiothlypis celata* 11.5–14cm (4.5–5.5in); 8–11g. Unmarked, dull olive-green upperparts; faint greenish-yellow eyebrow stripe; thin, broken yellow eye-ring; greenish-yellow underparts faintly streaked pale gray; yellow undertail-coverts. (*See also* Plate 91.) (Tennessee Warbler unstreaked below and has white undertail-coverts. Philadelphia and Warbling Vireos have white eyebrow stripe and gray cap.) **VOICE** A sharp *chip*. **STATUS AND RANGE** Rare migrant and non-breeding resident in northern Bahamas primarily October–February. Vagrant elsewhere in West Indies. **HABITAT** Scrubby areas.

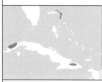

**⬛OLIVE-CAPPED WARBLER** *Setophaga pityophila* 12.5cm (5in); 8g. Greenish-yellow crown; yellow throat and breast bordered by black spots; two whitish wing bars. (Yellow-throated Warbler has white eyebrow stripe and white patch on side of neck.) **VOICE** High, melodious, whistle-like song, generally eight quick notes, *wisi-wisi-wisi* … dropping, then rising on last note. Also characteristic *tsip*. **STATUS AND RANGE** Endemic to Cuba and Bahamas; common but extremely local. In Cuba, confined to Pinar del Río and eastern region of Oriente. In Bahamas, only on Grand Bahama and Abaco. **HABITAT** Pine forests, sometimes nearby mixed pine-hardwood forests.

**⬛ST LUCIA WARBLER** *Setophaga delicata* 12.5cm (5in); 6–8g. Bluish-gray upperparts; yellow throat and breast; yellow eyebrow stripe; crescent below eye edged black. **FEMALE** Similar, but black edging to crown stripe less pronounced; less white in tail. **VOICE** Loud trill variable in pitch and speed. Also medium-strength *chick*. **STATUS AND RANGE** Endemic to St Lucia, where common and widespread. **HABITAT** Principally mid- and high-elevation forests.

**⬛ADELAIDE'S WARBLER** *Setophaga adelaidae* 12.5cm (5in); 6–10g. Bluish-gray upperparts; yellow throat and breast; yellow and white eyebrow stripe and crescent below eye. **FEMALE** Similar, but duller facial markings; less white in tail. **VOICE** Loud trill variable in pitch and speed. Also medium-strength *chick*. **STATUS AND RANGE** Endemic to Puerto Rico; common and widespread, but absent in Luquillo Mountains. Also common on Vieques and Culebra. Recent range expansion to Virgin Islands (St Thomas, St John). **HABITAT** Primarily dry coastal scrubland and thickets and moist limestone forests of haystack hills.

**⬛BARBUDA WARBLER** *Setophaga subita* 12.5cm (5in); 6–8g. Bluish-gray upperparts; yellow throat and breast. Conspicuous eyebrow stripe and crescent below eye. **FEMALE** Similar, but duller facial markings; less white in tail. **VOICE** Loud trill variable in pitch and speed. Also medium-strength *chick*. **STATUS AND RANGE** Endemic to Barbuda, where common. **HABITAT** Thickets near wetlands and inland canals.

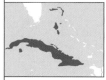

**YELLOW-BREASTED CHAT** *Icteria virens* 19cm (7.5in); 25g. Difficult to detect. Upperparts, wings, and long tail olive-green. Black, thick bill; white lores and eye-ring. Throat, breast, and upper belly yellow; lower belly and undertail-coverts white. **VOICE** A variety of call notes including a sharp *kik*. **STATUS AND RANGE** Very rare migrant and less frequent non-breeding resident in northern Bahamas and Cuba late August–early May. Vagrant elsewhere in West Indies. **HABITAT** Low, dense vegetation.

YELLOW-HEADED WARBLER

ORANGE-CROWNED WARBLER

OLIVE-CAPPED WARBLER

ST LUCIA WARBLER

ADELAIDE'S WARBLER

BARBUDA WARBLER

YELLOW-BREASTED CHAT

**AMERICAN REDSTART** *Setophaga ruticilla* 11–13.5cm (4.25–5.25in); 8g. BEHAVIOR Flicks and spreads tail. ADULT MALE Black upperparts, throat, and breast; large orange patches in wings and tail. ADULT FEMALE Head gray; upperparts greenish-gray; large yellow patches in wings and tail. IMMATURE Head greenish-gray; yellow patches reduced. VOICE Song variable but most often a series of increasingly loud notes, sometimes slurred or accented at end. Call note a loud *tschip*, also *srelee*. STATUS AND RANGE Throughout West Indies, where common migrant and non-breeding resident in Bahamas, Greater Antilles, Cayman and Virgin Islands, San Andrés, Providencia, and northern Lesser Antilles south to Guadeloupe. Uncommon in Dominica, Martinique, and Barbados; rare in St Lucia, St Vincent, and Grenada. Occurs primarily late August–early May. HABITAT Usually forests and woodlands from coast to mountains. Also gardens and shrubby areas.

**GOLDEN-WINGED WARBLER** *Vermivora chrysoptera* 12.5cm (5in); 9g. Yellow wing patch; gray or black throat; cheek patch. Forehead yellow; underparts whitish. ADULT MALE Throat and cheek patch black. FEMALE AND IMMATURE Paler and more subdued. Throat and cheek patch gray. VOICE A rather strong *chip*. STATUS AND RANGE Decidedly rare migrant and non-breeding resident in Hispaniola, Puerto Rico, Virgin Islands, and Cayman Islands (only as migrant); very rare in Bahamas, Cuba, and Jamaica primarily September–April. Vagrant elsewhere in West Indies. HABITAT Gardens and woodlands in Cuba; high mountain forests in Puerto Rico. Prefers tree canopies.

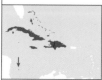

**TENNESSEE WARBLER** *Leiothlypis peregrina* 11.5–12.5cm (4.5–5in); 7–18g. NON-BREEDING ADULT Olive-green above, yellowish below; yellowish eyebrow stripe, noticeable eye-line. BREEDING MALE Bright olive-green above, white below; gray crown; white eyebrow stripe, pale gray line through eye. BREEDING FEMALE Crown duller and greenish; breast with yellowish wash. IMMATURE *See* Plate 92. (Orange-crowned Warbler has faint breast streaks and yellow undertail-coverts.) VOICE Short, fine *tseet-tseet-tseet* … repeated frequently. STATUS AND RANGE Uncommon migrant and less frequent non-breeding resident in northern Bahamas, western Cuba, Cayman Islands, San Andrés, and Providencia September–May, but most regularly October–November; rare in eastern Cuba, Hispaniola, and Providencia. Vagrant elsewhere in West Indies. Sometimes occurs in numbers. HABITAT Woodlands, gardens, and scrub.

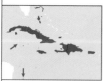

**BAY-BREASTED WARBLER** *Setophaga castanea* 12.5–15cm (5–5.75in); 13g. BEHAVIOR Slow-moving canopy dweller. BREEDING MALE Reddish-brown cap and band on chin, throat, and sides; pale tan neck patch. BREEDING FEMALE Duller. NON-BREEDING ADULT AND IMMATURE *See* Plate 90. VOICE Weak *tsee-tsee-tsee*. Also a sharp *jeet*. STATUS AND RANGE Irregular but generally uncommon migrant in Cayman Islands, San Andrés, and Providencia primarily October–November and April–May. More frequent northbound in Cayman Islands and southbound in others. Rare migrant in northern Bahamas, western Cuba, Jamaica, San Andrés, and Providencia. Decidedly rare in eastern Cuba, Hispaniola, and Puerto Rico. Vagrant elsewhere in West Indies. HABITAT Forest edges, woodlands, gardens, and open areas with scattered trees.

**CHESTNUT-SIDED WARBLER** *Setophaga pensylvanica* 11.5–13.5cm (4.5–5.25in); 9g. BEHAVIOR Cocks tail. BREEDING MALE Yellow cap; reddish band along sides; white underparts. BREEDING FEMALE Duller. NON-BREEDING ADULT AND IMMATURE *See* Plate 92. VOICE A harsh *tschip*. STATUS AND RANGE Irregular, but generally decidedly uncommon migrant and non-breeding resident in northern Bahamas, western Cuba, Jamaica, Puerto Rico, Virgin Islands, Cayman Islands, and San Andrés; rare in southern Bahamas, eastern Cuba, Hispaniola, Guadeloupe, and Providencia September–May. Vagrant to other Lesser Antilles. HABITAT Open woodlands, gardens with trees.

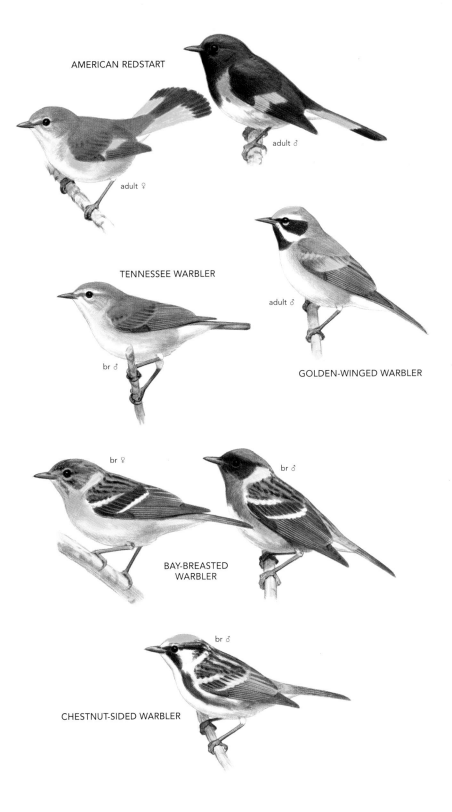

AMERICAN REDSTART

adult ♂

adult ♀

TENNESSEE WARBLER

br ♂

adult ♂

GOLDEN-WINGED WARBLER

br ♀

br ♂

BAY-BREASTED WARBLER

br ♂

CHESTNUT-SIDED WARBLER

**SWAINSON'S WARBLER** *Limnothlypis swainsonii* 14cm (5.5in); 19g. Very difficult to detect. **BEHAVIOR** Primarily terrestrial. **DESCRIPTION** Head brownish-gray with brown crown, whitish eyebrow stripe, and blackish line through eye. Back, wings, and tail unmarked olive grayish-brown. Underparts whitish, grayer on sides. **VOICE** Sharp, metallic *chip*. **STATUS AND RANGE** Uncommon migrant and non-breeding resident in Bahamas, Cuba, and Jamaica; rare in Hispaniola, Puerto Rico, and Cayman Islands. Occurs September–April. **HABITAT** Heavy leaf-litter in canebrakes, thickets, dense woodland understory, and wet limestone forests.

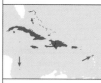

**WORM-EATING WARBLER** *Helmitheros vermivorum* 14cm (5.5in); 13g. Plain greenish-gray upperparts, wings, and tail; tan head with black stripes on crown and through eye; underparts pale tan, whiter on throat and belly. **VOICE** Rarely heard song is a rapid, thin trill, somewhat insect-like. Call note a thin, slightly musical *thip* or *thip-thip*. **STATUS AND RANGE** Generally fairly common migrant and non-breeding resident in Bahamas, Cuba, Jamaica, Cayman Islands, and San Andrés September–April; uncommon in Hispaniola, Puerto Rico, and Providencia; rare in Virgin Islands and Guadeloupe. Vagrant elsewhere in West Indies. **HABITAT** Dense forests at all elevations.

Ⓜ**PLUMBEOUS WARBLER** *Setophaga plumbea* 12–14cm (4.75–5.5in); 9–11g. **BEHAVIOR** Flicks tail. **ADULT** Plain gray upperparts; white eyebrow stripe, especially in front of eye; two white wing bars; underparts mostly pale gray with some white through center of breast. **IMMATURE** *See* Plate 92. **VOICE** Musical three-syllable *pa-pi-a*. Also loud rattle. **STATUS AND RANGE** Common permanent resident in Guadeloupe and Dominica. These islands encompass entire range. **HABITAT** Moist mountain forests, sometimes drier scrub forests and mangroves.

Ⓗ**HISPANIOLAN HIGHLAND-TANAGER (WHITE-WINGED WARBLER)** *Xenoligea montana* 13.5–14cm (5.25–5.5in); 12g. Bold white wing patch; white outertail feathers; white line above eye to forehead. **VOICE** Low chattering *suit ... suit ... suit ... chir ... suit ... suit ... suit ... suit ... chir ... chi ...* Also thin *tseep*. **STATUS AND RANGE** Endemic to Hispaniola, where common very locally in Dominican Republic in Cordillera Central, Sierra de Bahoruco, and Sierra de Neiba. In Haiti, very rare in Massif de la Hotte and Massif de la Selle. Endangered. Family also endemic to Hispaniola. **HABITAT** Primarily mature broadleaf forest undergrowth, low trees, and thickets and wet shrubs in higher mountains. Favored fruit is Florida trema (*Trema micrantha*).

Ⓗ**GREEN-TAILED GROUND-TANAGER (GREEN-TAILED WARBLER)** *Microligea palustris* 12–14cm (4.75–5.5in); 10–15g. **BEHAVIOR** Usually low to ground. **DESCRIPTION** Slender, with long tail. **ADULT** Incomplete white eye-ring; red eye; greenish lower back, rump, wings, and tail. **IMMATURE** Greener above and olive-tinted below; brown iris. **VOICE** *Sip-sip-sip*; also rasping notes. **STATUS AND RANGE** Endemic to Hispaniola, where locally common, but declining. In Haiti, high elevations in Massif de la Selle and near sea level in far northwest. In Dominican Republic, local from sea level to high mountains. Family also endemic to Hispaniola. **HABITAT** Dense thickets or disturbed patches of wet broadleaf forests, primarily in mountains. Also moist forest, scrub, and semi-arid areas.

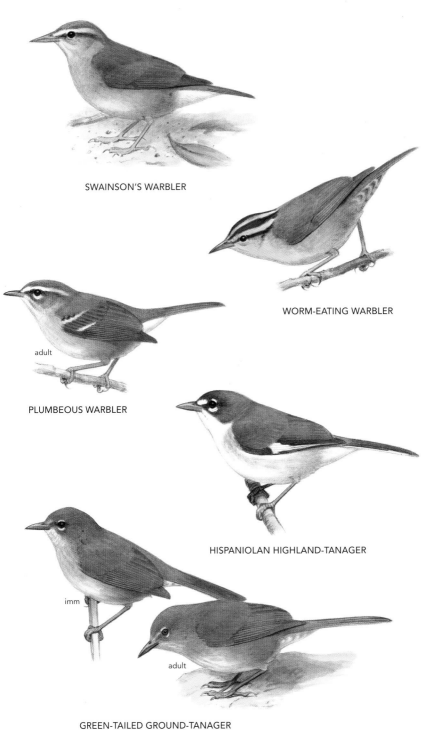

SWAINSON'S WARBLER

WORM-EATING WARBLER

adult

PLUMBEOUS WARBLER

HISPANIOLAN HIGHLAND-TANAGER

imm

adult

GREEN-TAILED GROUND-TANAGER

**CANADA WARBLER** *Cardellina canadensis* 12.5–15.5cm (5–5.75in); 10g. ADULT FEMALE Gray streaks on breast; yellow spectacles. ADULT MALE *See* Plate 82.

**PALM WARBLER** *Setophaga palmarum* 12.5–14cm (5–5.5in); 10g. Bobs tail. NON-BREEDING Yellowish undertail-coverts; olive-colored rump; faint eyebrow stripe; brownish back. BREEDING *See* Plate 86.

**YELLOW WARBLER** *Setophaga petechia* 11.5–13.5cm (4.5–5.25in); 13g. ADULT FEMALE Yellow overall. Faintly streaked or unstreaked below; no reddish-brown on head. (*See also* Plate 92.) IMMATURE Upperparts olive-gray; underparts grayish-white; yellow in wings. ADULT MALE *See* Plate 86.

**CAPE MAY WARBLER** *Setophaga tigrina* 12.5–14cm (5–5.5in); 11g. IMMATURE Striped breast; yellowish rump; tan patch behind cheek. ADULT *See* Plate 83.

**MAGNOLIA WARBLER** *Setophaga magnolia* 11.5–12.5cm (4.5–5in); 10g. NON-BREEDING ADULT AND IMMATURE Pale eyebrow stripe; white eye-ring; gray head. Yellow underparts, tan band nearly across breast. BREEDING ADULT *See* Plate 83.

**BLACKPOLL WARBLER** *Setophaga striata* 12.5–14cm (5–5.5in); 13g. NON-BREEDING ADULT AND IMMATURE Difficult to identify. White wing bars and undertail-coverts; faint side streaks; pale legs. (Non-breeding adult and immature Bay-breasted Warbler unstreaked below; pale tan undertail-coverts; black legs.) BREEDING ADULT *See* Plate 80.

**YELLOW-RUMPED WARBLER** *Setophaga coronata* 14cm (5.5in); 12g. Yellow rump and patch on side of breast; white throat. IMMATURE Duller. ADULT AND NON-BREEDING MALE *See* Plate 82.

**BAY-BREASTED WARBLER** *Setophaga castanea* 12.5–15cm (5–5.75in); 13g. NON-BREEDING ADULT AND IMMATURE Back greenish-gray; unstreaked tannish below, including undertail-coverts; tannish flanks; white wing bars; usually blackish legs. (Non-breeding adult and immature Blackpoll Warbler finely streaked below, pale legs, white undertail-coverts. Pine Warbler has unstreaked back.) BREEDING ADULT *See* Plate 88.

CANADA
WARBLER

adult ♀

non-br

PALM WARBLER

imm

YELLOW
WARBLER

adult ♀

imm

CAPE MAY WARBLER

non-br adult
& imm

MAGNOLIA WARBLER

imm

YELLOW-RUMPED WARBLER

non-br adult
& imm

BLACKPOLL
WARBLER

BAY-BREASTED
WARBLER

non-br adult
& imm

**P** **ELFIN-WOODS WARBLER** *Setophaga angelae* 12.5–13.5cm (5–5.25in); 7.5–8.5g. IMMATURE Overall greenish-gray with thin white eyebrow stripe; white patches on ear-coverts and neck; incomplete eye-ring; streaks below. ADULT *See* Plate 80.

**J** **ARROWHEAD WARBLER** *Setophaga pharetra* 13cm (5in); 10g. BEHAVIOR Flicks tail down. IMMATURE Yellowish-olive above, pale yellowish below with fine grayish streaks; wing bars; yellowish eye-ring; some white in tail. (Jamaican Vireo lacks eye-ring, dark eye-line, and white in tail. Flicks tail up). ADULT MALE *See* Plate 80.

**CERULEAN WARBLER** *Setophaga cerulea* 10–13cm (4–5in); 9g. IMMATURE FEMALE Olive-green above, yellower below; two white wing bars. ADULTS AND IMMATURE MALE *See* Plate 80.

**PRAIRIE WARBLER** *Setophaga discolor* 12cm (4.75in); 8g. BEHAVIOR Bobs tail. IMMATURE FEMALE Yellow underparts; blackish streaks on sides; whitish facial markings. ADULT *See* Plate 82.

**BLACK-THROATED GREEN WARBLER** *Setophaga virens* 12.5cm (5in); 9g. IMMATURE FEMALE Yellowish-gray cheek; faint side streaks. ADULT MALE *See* Plate 83.

**ORANGE-CROWNED WARBLER** *Leiothlypis celata* 11.5–14cm (4.5–5.5in); 8–11g. Upperparts unmarked olive-green; underparts greenish-yellow, streaked pale gray; yellow undertail-coverts; greenish-yellow eyebrow stripe; thin broken yellow eye-ring. (*See also* Plate 87.)

**BLACKBURNIAN WARBLER** *Setophaga fusca* 13cm (5in); 10g. IMMATURE FEMALE Yellowish throat, breast, eyebrow stripe, and sides of neck; white back stripes and wing bars. OTHER PLUMAGES *See* Plate 83.

**PINE WARBLER** *Setophaga pinus* 12.5–14.5cm (5–5.75in); 12g. IMMATURE Grayish-brown above; grayish-tan below; two white wing bars; whitish eyebrow stripe. ADULTS *See* Plate 83.

**KIRTLAND'S WARBLER** *Setophaga kirtlandii* 14–15cm (5–5.75in); 12–16g. ADULT FEMALE AND NON-BREEDING MALE Upperparts bluish-gray; black streaks on back; throat and belly yellow; black side streaks; broken eye-ring; forehead and lores dark gray. Bobs tail. BREEDING MALE *See* Plate 83.

**S** **VITELLINE WARBLER** *Setophaga vitellina* 13cm (5in); 7g. BEHAVIOR Bobs tail. ADULT FEMALE Upperparts olive-green; underparts entirely yellow, usually with faint side stripes; facial pattern faint. ADULT AND IMMATURE MALE *See* Plate 86.

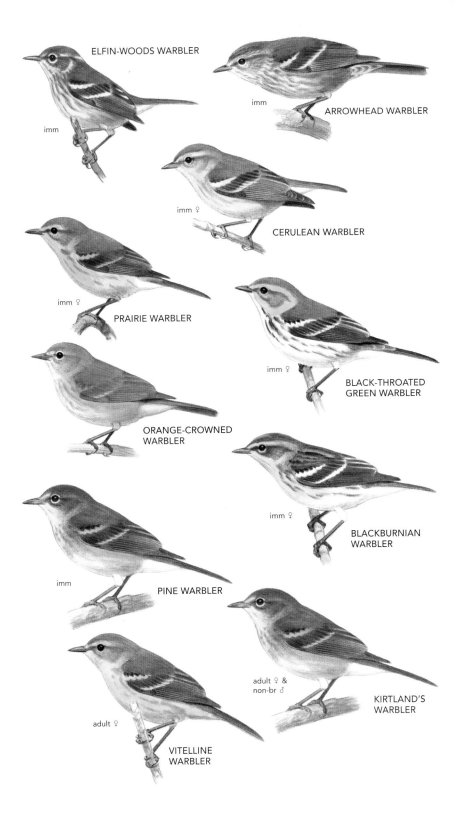

ELFIN-WOODS WARBLER

imm

ARROWHEAD WARBLER

imm

imm ♀

CERULEAN WARBLER

imm ♀

PRAIRIE WARBLER

imm ♀

BLACK-THROATED
GREEN WARBLER

ORANGE-CROWNED
WARBLER

imm ♀

BLACKBURNIAN
WARBLER

imm

PINE WARBLER

adult ♀ &
non-br ♂

KIRTLAND'S
WARBLER

adult ♀

VITELLINE
WARBLER

**CHESTNUT-SIDED WARBLER** *Setophaga pensylvanica* 11.5–13.5cm (4.5–5.25in); 9g. **NON-BREEDING ADULT AND IMMATURE** Yellowish-green above; white eye-ring; pale gray underparts; two yellowish wing bars. **BREEDING MALE** *See* Plate 88.

**WILSON'S WARBLER** *Cardellina pusilla* 11–12.5cm (4.25–5in); 8g. **IMMATURE FEMALE** Lacks black on cap. Yellow forehead, eyebrow stripe, lores, and underparts. **ADULT MALE** *See* Plate 84.

**YELLOW WARBLER** *Setophaga petechia* 11.5–13.5cm (4.5–5.25in); 10g. **ADULT FEMALE** Yellow overall. Faintly streaked or unstreaked below; no reddish-brown on head. (*See also* Plate 90.) **NON-BREEDING FEMALE** Underparts with some pale tan. **IMMATURE** *See* Plate 90. **ADULT MALE** *See* Plate 86.

**RUBY-CROWNED KINGLET** *Regulus calendula* 11.5cm (4.5in); 6g. Tiny, with olive-colored upperparts, bold white eye-ring, and two whitish wing bars. **FEMALE** Lacks red crest. **MALE** *See* Plate 81.

**TENNESSEE WARBLER** *Leiothlypis peregrina* 11.5–12.5cm (4.5–5in); 10g. **IMMATURE** Olive-green above; yellowish-green below except for white undertail-coverts. **BREEDING MALE** *See* Plate 88.

Ⓜ **PLUMBEOUS WARBLER** *Setophaga plumbea* 12–14cm (4.75–5.5in); 9–11g. Flicks tail. **IMMATURE** Greenish-gray upperparts; eyebrow stripe either white or whitish; underparts pale tan on sides and flanks. **ADULT** *See* Plate 89.

**NASHVILLE WARBLER** *Leiothlypis ruficapilla* 11.5–12.5cm (4.5–5in); 7–14g. **IMMATURE** White eye-ring; brownish-gray head contrasts with yellowish-green upperparts; underparts paler yellow with whitish throat and tan sides. **ADULT** *See* Plate 84.

CHESTNUT-SIDED WARBLER

non-br adult
& imm

WILSON'S WARBLER

imm ♀

adult ♀

YELLOW WARBLER

non-br ♀

RUBY-CROWNED KINGLET

♀

TENNESSEE WARBLER

imm

PLUMBEOUS WARBLER

imm

imm

NASHVILLE WARBLER

**COMMON YELLOWTHROAT** *Geothlypis trichas* 11.5–14cm (4.5–5.5in); 10g. ADULT FEMALE Lacks facial mask; bright yellow throat and breast contrast with whitish belly; narrow, whitish eye-ring; usually pale tan eyebrow stripe. (*See also* Plate 85.) IMMATURE Duller and browner than adult female. ADULT MALE AND FEMALE *See* Plate 85.

**HOODED WARBLER** *Setophaga citrina* 12.5–14.5cm (5–5.75in); 10g. Flicks and fans tail, showing white outertail feathers. ADULT FEMALE Variable hood, from almost complete to black markings only on crown. MALE AND ADULT FEMALE *See* Plate 84.

**BLACK-THROATED BLUE WARBLER** *Setophaga caerulescens* 12–14cm (4.75–5.5in); 10g. FEMALE Narrow whitish eyebrow stripe; white wing spot, sometimes absent in young females. MALE *See* Plate 81.

**PROTHONOTARY WARBLER** *Protonotaria citrea* 13.5cm (5.25in); 15g. FEMALE Golden-yellow face, throat, and breast; blue-gray wings and tail. MALE *See* Plate 86.

**KENTUCKY WARBLER** *Geothlypis formosa* 12.5–14.5cm (5–5.75in); 14g. IMMATURE FEMALE Black on face absent, replaced by gray on lores. ADULT MALE *See* Plate 84.

**MOURNING WARBLER** *Geothlypis philadelphia* 13–14.5cm (5–5.75in); 10–18g. BEHAVIOR Primarily terrestrial. IMMATURE Hood pale gray or brownish; incomplete whitish eye-ring; throat yellowish. ADULTS *See* Plate 85.

**S** **BAHAMA YELLOWTHROAT** *Geothlypis rostrata* 15cm (5.75in); 16g. Relatively large, slow- moving, with relatively heavy bill. FEMALE Lacks mask. Yellow throat, breast, and belly; gray crown; whitish eye-ring and eyebrow stripe. MALE AND FEMALE *See* Plate 85.

**CONNECTICUT WARBLER** *Oporornis agilis* 13.5–15cm (5.25–5.75in); 15g. BEHAVIOR Primarily terrestrial. DESCRIPTION Large, stocky. ADULT FEMALE AND IMMATURE Pale gray-brown hood; whitish throat; white eye-ring; undertail-coverts extend nearly to end of tail. OTHER PLUMAGES *See* Plate 85.

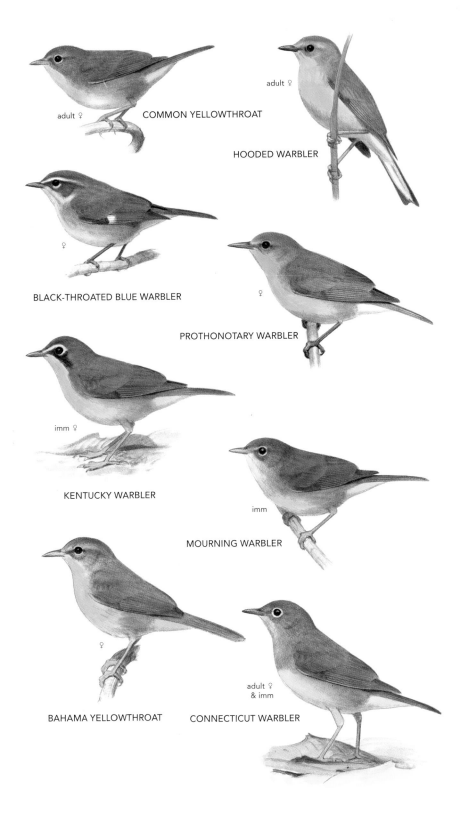

COMMON YELLOWTHROAT

adult ♀

HOODED WARBLER

adult ♀

BLACK-THROATED BLUE WARBLER

♀

PROTHONOTARY WARBLER

♀

KENTUCKY WARBLER

imm ♀

MOURNING WARBLER

imm

BAHAMA YELLOWTHROAT

♀

CONNECTICUT WARBLER

adult ♀ & imm

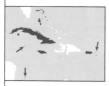

**SWAINSON'S THRUSH** *Catharus ustulatus* 17.5cm (7in); 35g. Difficult to detect. **BEHAVIOR** Moderately terrestrial. **DESCRIPTION** Grayish-brown above; whitish below, with brownish spots on breast. Whitish eye-ring and lores give spectacled appearance. **STATUS AND RANGE** Generally a decidedly uncommon to rare migrant in northern Bahamas, Cuba (primarily western), Jamaica, Cayman Islands (sometimes locally common), and San Andrés. Very rare in Puerto Rico. Occurs regularly and at times in numbers in Guana Island (British Virgin Islands). Vagrant elsewhere in West Indies. Occurs primarily in October, but found September–November and March–May. Abundance fluctuates year to year. **HABITAT** Open woods and tree clumps with much leaf-litter and little undergrowth. Also gardens.

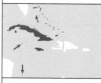

**VEERY** *Catharus fuscescens* 16–18cm (6.25–7in); 25–43g. Difficult to detect. **BEHAVIOR** Primarily terrestrial. **DESCRIPTION** Upperparts reddish-brown, rarely olive-brown. Underparts whitish with faint spots on pale tan breast. Inconspicuous grayish eye-ring. More reddish-brown above and more lightly spotted below than other migrant thrushes. **STATUS AND RANGE** Rare migrant in northern Bahamas, Cuba, Jamaica, Cayman Islands, and San Andrés; very rare in southern Bahamas. Vagrant elsewhere in West Indies. Sometimes occurs in numbers. Occurs primarily September–October and April–May, but some overwinter. **HABITAT** Open forests, woodlands with substantial undergrowth, scrub, and gardens.

**HERMIT THRUSH** *Catharus guttatus* 16–19cm (6.25–7.5in); 20–37g. Difficult to detect. **BEHAVIOR** Highly terrestrial. **DESCRIPTION** Olive-brown upperparts, reddish-brown tail, and whitish underparts with tan wash. Large spots on breast form streaks from sides of throat to flanks. Narrow whitish eye-ring. (Swainson's, Bicknell's, and Gray-cheeked Thrushes, and Veery, similar but lack contrasting dark back and reddish-brown tail.) **STATUS AND RANGE** Very rare migrant and non-breeding resident in northern Bahamas October–April. Vagrant elsewhere in West Indies. **HABITAT** Forest thickets.

**GRAY-CHEEKED THRUSH** *Catharus minimus* 17–19cm (6.7–7.5in); 26–50g. Difficult to detect and identify. **BEHAVIOR** Highly terrestrial in dense thickets. **DESCRIPTION** Grayish-brown above, whitish below; spots on breast and throat. Gray cheeks; no conspicuous eye-ring; no reddish-brown coloration. Extremely similar to Bicknell's Thrush. (Swainson's Thrush has distinct whitish eye-ring.) **STATUS AND RANGE** Rare migrant in northern Bahamas, Cuba (primarily western), Cayman Islands, and San Andrés September–November and March–May. Apparently very rare or vagrant elsewhere in West Indies. Status unclear due to similarity to Bicknell's Thrush and stealthy behavior. **HABITAT** Open forests and woodlands.

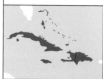

**BICKNELL'S THRUSH** *Catharus bicknelli* 16–19cm (6.25–7.5in); 26–33g. Difficult to detect and identify. **BEHAVIOR** Highly terrestrial in dense vegetation. **DESCRIPTION** Brownish upperparts; white underparts and sides of throat; breast tan, boldly spotted black. Grayish cheeks and lores; dark reddish-brown tail. (Gray-cheeked Thrush slightly larger, grayer above with darker lores, whiter breast, and pinkish rather than yellow on lower mandible, but characters overlap. Too similar to separate accurately.) **VOICE** Generally silent in West Indies. **STATUS AND RANGE** Decidedly uncommon and local migrant and non-breeding resident in Hispaniola and Puerto Rico late September–early May. Likely rare migrant in Bahamas, particularly southernmost islands, eastern Cuba, and Jamaica September–November and March–May. Perhaps rare also as non-breeding resident on latter two islands December–February. Probably very rare in western Cuba. Likely more frequent than records indicate. Threatened. **HABITAT** Broadleaf forests, generally at higher elevations. Also woods or gardens with large trees.

SWAINSON'S THRUSH

VEERY

HERMIT THRUSH

GRAY-CHEEKED THRUSH/BICKNELL'S THRUSH

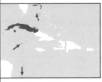

**WOOD THRUSH** *Hylocichla mustelina* 18–21cm (7–8.25in); 40–70g. Difficult to detect. **BEHAVIOR** Highly terrestrial. **DESCRIPTION** Cinnamon-colored crown, conspicuous white eye-ring, and white underparts with heavy dark spots. (Ovenbird smaller, with cinnamon-colored crown bordered by black stripes.) **VOICE** Short *pit-pit-pit* notes. **STATUS AND RANGE** Decidedly rare migrant in northern Bahamas, western Cuba, and Cayman Islands; very rare in San Andrés. Vagrant elsewhere. Occurs primarily mid-September to November and March–April (absent from San Andrés during latter months). A few may remain in Cuba and San Andrés December–February. **HABITAT** Mature semi-deciduous forests, tree plantations, and large gardens.

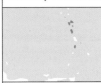

**M FOREST THRUSH** *Turdus lherminieri* 25–30cm (10–12in); 100g. Upperparts grayish-brown; underparts brown with white spots on breast, flanks, and upper belly, giving scaled effect. Legs, bill, and skin around eye yellow. Scaled underparts distinguish it from Spectacled Thrush. **VOICE** Soft, musical, clear notes. **STATUS AND RANGE** Common permanent resident in Guadeloupe, fairly common in Montserrat, uncommon in Dominica, very rare in St Lucia and declining. These islands comprise entire range. Threatened. Genus also endemic to West Indies. **HABITAT** Moist and wet mountain forests. Also swamp forests in Guadeloupe.

**COCOA THRUSH** *Turdus fumigatus* 22–24cm (8.5–9.5in); 55–80g. **BEHAVIOR** Primarily terrestrial. **ADULT** Upperparts rich brown; underparts paler. Whitish throat patch with brown streaks; dark bill. **VOICE** Loud musical phrases, each short and differing from one another, with brief pause between each. Sometimes plaintive, four-note call, first two notes higher. Also *weeo, weeo, weeo.* **STATUS AND RANGE** Common permanent resident in St Vincent and Grenada. **HABITAT** Forests, cacao plantations, and croplands with scattered trees. More frequent at higher elevations.

**SPECTACLED THRUSH (BARE-EYED ROBIN)** *Turdus nudigenis* 23–24cm (9–9.5in); 50–75g. **ADULT** Plain olive-gray upperparts, paler underparts; white throat with brown streaks. Broad, pale yellow eye-ring; yellowish bill and feet. (Forest Thrush has scaled underparts.) **VOICE** Loud, liquid, variable *cheerily cheer-up cheerio,* especially at dawn. Also squeaky *miter-ee.* **STATUS AND RANGE** Fairly common permanent resident in Martinique, St Lucia, St Vincent, Grenadines, and Grenada. Uncommon in Guadeloupe. Expanding range northward through Lesser Antilles. **HABITAT** Primarily lowlands in drier and moderately moist open woodlands, plantations, second growth, and forest borders.

**M RED-LEGGED THRUSH** *Turdus plumbeus* 25–28cm (10–11in); 66–86g. Gray upperparts; reddish legs and bill; red eye-ring; large white tail tips. Underparts very variable (see illustrations). **VOICE** Low *wéecha*; rapid, high-pitched *chu-wéek, chu-wéek, chu-wéek*; and loud *wheet-wheet.* Song melodious but monotonous one- to three-syllable phrases similar to Pearly-eyed Thrasher. **STATUS AND RANGE** Common and widespread permanent resident in northern and central Bahamas, Cuba, Hispaniola, Puerto Rico, and Dominica. Fairly common in Cayman Brac (Cayman Islands). These islands comprise entire range. **HABITAT** Woodlands and forests at all elevations, scrub, thick undergrowth, gardens, and shade coffee plantations.

**J WHITE-CHINNED THRUSH** *Turdus aurantius* 24–26cm (9.5–10in); 82g. **BEHAVIOR** Cocks tail upward; highly terrestrial. **ADULT** Dark gray above, paler below; conspicuous white diagonal bar on wing; white chin; orange bill and legs. **VOICE** Variable. Musical song, a shrill whistle, *p'lice, p'lice,* and repeated chicken-like clucking. **STATUS AND RANGE** Endemic to Jamaica, where common and widespread. **HABITAT** Primarily forests, woodlands, road edges, cultivated areas, and gardens, in mountains at middle and high elevations. Less frequent in lowlands.

WOOD THRUSH

FOREST THRUSH

Dominica race

Montserrat race

SPECTACLED THRUSH
(BARE-EYED ROBIN)

adult

COCOA THRUSH

RED-LEGGED THRUSH

Hispaniola & Puerto Rico
race

WHITE-CHINNED THRUSH

Cuba race

adult

**NORTHERN WHEATEAR** *Oenanthe oenanthe* 15cm (6in); 18–33g. **BEHAVIOR** Active, flicks and fans tail, terrestrial. **DESCRIPTION** White rump and tail patches. **FEMALE AND NON-BREEDING MALE** Pale reddish-brown below, grayish-brown above; white eyebrow stripe. **BREEDING MALE** Gray upperparts, black ear-patch. **STATUS AND RANGE** Very rare in West Indies though vagrant on any particular island. Recorded from Bahamas, Cuba, Puerto Rico, Guadeloupe, Barbados, and Dominica. **HABITAT** Open ground such as lots, fields, and meadows.

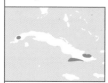

**C CUBAN SOLITAIRE** *Myadestes elisabeth* 19–20cm (7.5–7.75in); 22–33g. **BEHAVIOR** Sallies for insects like flycatchers. **DESCRIPTION** Plain-colored; white eye-ring; dark mustache stripe; white outertail feathers; small bill. **VOICE** Very high-pitched flute-like song. Melodious and varied. Similar to rubbing wet finger against fine glass. **STATUS AND RANGE** Endemic to Cuba, where common, but quite local in mountain ranges. In western Cuba, only in Sierra de los Órganos, Sierra del Rosario, and Sierra de la Güira. In east, more widely distributed. Threatened. **HABITAT** Dense, humid forests of hills and mountains.

**M RUFOUS-THROATED SOLITAIRE** *Myadestes genibarbis* 19–20cm (7.5–7.75in); 24–30g. Reddish-brown throat, foreneck, and undertail-coverts; light gray breast; white outer feathers visible in flight. On St Vincent, black above with olive uppertail-coverts. **VOICE** Hauntingly beautiful minor-key whistle, most often at dawn. **STATUS AND RANGE** Fairly common permanent resident in Jamaica, Hispaniola, Dominica, Martinique, St Lucia, and St Vincent. These islands comprise entire range. **HABITAT** Dense, moist mountain forests.

**AMERICAN ROBIN** *Turdus migratorius* 23–28cm (9–11in); 60–90g. Primarily dull red underparts. **MALE** Blackish head and tail. **FEMALE** Paler. **STATUS AND RANGE** Rare migrant and non-breeding resident October–April in northern Bahamas and very rare in western Cuba. Numbers vary year to year. Vagrant elsewhere. **HABITAT** Open woodlands, gardens, parks, and open scrub.

**J WHITE-EYED THRUSH** *Turdus jamaicensis* 23–24cm (9–9.5in); 60g. **ADULT** Dark gray above, paler below. Reddish-brown head, conspicuous whitish eye, white breast bar. **IMMATURE** Breast boldly streaked; throat unstreaked. **VOICE** Repeated phrases like Northern Mockingbird, but louder and less variable. Whistled *hee-haw* often included. Also other high-pitched, harsh call notes. **STATUS AND RANGE** Endemic to Jamaica; fairly common in mountains. **HABITAT** Wet forests from hills to mountain summits. Also shade coffee plantations and other wooded areas at moderate elevations.

**H LA SELLE THRUSH** *Turdus swalesi* 26cm (10in); 100g. **BEHAVIOR** Primarily terrestrial. **DESCRIPTION** Grayish-black head and upperparts; a few white streaks on throat. Red lower breast and sides; broad white streak on belly. (American Robin has less extensive white on belly.) **VOICE** Series of deliberate *tu-re-oo* and *cho-ho-cho* calls continued indefinitely. Also loud *wheury-wheury-wheury* and gurgling notes. **STATUS AND RANGE** Endemic to Hispaniola, where uncommon and very local in Haiti in Massif de la Selle; rare and local in Dominican Republic in Sierra de Bahoruco, Sierra de Neiba, and Cordillera Central. Endangered. **HABITAT** Low, dense vegetation and wet forests, including pines in high mountains.

NORTHERN WHEATEAR

br ♂

♀ & non-br ♂

CUBAN SOLITAIRE

St Vincent race

imm

Jamaica race

RUFOUS-THROATED SOLITAIRE

AMERICAN ROBIN

♂

adult

WHITE-EYED THRUSH

LA SELLE THRUSH

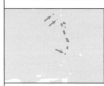

Ⓜ**BROWN TREMBLER** *Cinclocerthia ruficauda* 23–26cm (9–10in); 45–70g. BEHAVIOR Droops wings and trembles, cocks tail over back. DESCRIPTION Dark reddish-olive upperparts; grayish-brown underparts; long bill, slightly down-curved near tip; yellow eye. (Gray Trembler grayer above, whiter below.) VOICE Semimelodic phrases; harsh alarm notes. STATUS AND RANGE Fairly common permanent resident in Saba, Guadeloupe, and Dominica; locally common in St Vincent; uncommon in St Christopher, Nevis, Montserrat, and St Lucia; rare in Antigua and Martinique. These islands comprise entire range. Genus also endemic to West Indies. HABITAT Wet forests, especially edges around clearings in upland valleys and in palm brakes; also secondary forests and drier woodlands. In St Lucia, only dry forests and scrub.

Ⓜ**GRAY TREMBLER** *Cinclocerthia gutturalis* 23–26cm (9–10in); 65–75g. BEHAVIOR Droops wings and trembles; cocks tail over back. DESCRIPTION Upperparts dark olive-gray, underparts grayish-white (Martinique) or bright white (St Lucia), but best distinguished by voice. Bill very long and slightly down-curved near tip; eye white. VOICE Wavering, whistled phrases; also harsh alarm notes. STATUS AND RANGE Fairly common permanent resident in Martinique and St Lucia, which account for entire range. Genus also endemic to West Indies. HABITAT Mature moist forests, usually at higher elevations. Less often in second growth, dry scrub, and open woodlands at lower elevations.

**NORTHERN MOCKINGBIRD** *Mimus polyglottos* 23–28cm (9–11in); 50g. BEHAVIOR Cocks tail. DESCRIPTION Gray above, grayish-white below. Wings and tail conspicuously marked with white; long tail. (Bahama Mockingbird larger; lacks white in wings.) VOICE Clear, melodious phrases, each repeated several times. Also loud *tchack*. STATUS AND RANGE Common permanent resident throughout Bahamas, Greater Antilles, Virgin and Cayman Islands. Introduced to New Providence. HABITAT Open country with scattered bushes or trees, including semiarid scrub, open mangrove forests, gardens, parks, and settled areas. Primarily lowlands.

**TROPICAL MOCKINGBIRD** *Mimus gilvus* 23–24cm (9–9.5in); 45g. Gray upperparts and head; broad, blackish eye-line; white eyebrow stripe; wings darker than back; two wing bars. Tail long, conspicuously tipped with white. VOICE Repeated couplets of musical whistles and phrases lasting several seconds. Also harsh *chuck*. STATUS AND RANGE Common permanent resident on Guadeloupe (primarily Grande-Terre), Dominica, Martinique, St Lucia, St Vincent, Grenadines, Grenada, and San Andrés. Expanding range northward. HABITAT Open areas around human dwellings, dry lowland scrub, and agricultural areas.

Ⓜ**BAHAMA MOCKINGBIRD** *Mimus gundlachii* 28cm (11in); 60–85g. Large; upperparts brownish-gray with fine streaks; underparts whitish with dark streaks on sides. Long, broad tail, almost fan-shaped in flight, tipped with white; two white wing bars not conspicuous in flight. (Pearly-eyed Thrasher has darker upperparts, pale bill, and white eye.) VOICE Series of phrases, each repeated several times. STATUS AND RANGE Generally common permanent resident in Bahamas and southern Jamaica (Hellshire Hills). Uncommon in cays off northern Cuba. These islands comprise entire range. Vagrant elsewhere. HABITAT Semi-arid scrub, woodlands. Infrequently around human habitation.

Guadeloupe race

Dominica race

BROWN TREMBLER

Martinique race

GRAY TREMBLER

adult

imm

adult

NORTHERN MOCKINGBIRD

Southern Lesser
Antilles race

San Andrés race

TROPICAL MOCKINGBIRD

BAHAMA MOCKINGBIRD

**GRAY CATBIRD** *Dumetella carolinensis* 23cm (9in); 40g. Difficult to detect. Entirely gray with black cap, reddish-brown undertail-coverts, and long tail often cocked slightly upward. **VOICE** Distinctive soft, cat-like *mew*. Also *pert-pert-pert*. Song disconnected phrases including mews, imitations, and pauses. **STATUS AND RANGE** Common migrant and non-breeding resident in Bahamas, Cuba (central and western), Cayman Islands, San Andrés, and Providencia; uncommon in Jamaica and eastern Cuba; rare in Hispaniola and Puerto Rico; very rare elsewhere in West Indies. Occurs primarily October–May. **HABITAT** Thickets, dense undergrowth, urban gardens, particularly areas with abundant fruit.

**Ⓜ WHITE-BREASTED THRASHER** *Ramphocinclus brachyurus* Martinique 20–21cm (7.75–8.25in); St Lucia 23–25cm (9–10in); 48–60g. **BEHAVIOR** Often droops wings; may twitch or flick wings when excited or curious. Primarily terrestrial. **ADULT** Dark brown upperparts, clear white underparts; red eye; long, slightly down-curved bill. **STATUS AND RANGE** Local, rare, permanent resident in Martinique and St Lucia. In Martinique, found at Presqu'ile de la Caravelle. In St Lucia, restricted to two areas: one in the north between Petite Anse and the Fond d'Or River and the second in the Mandelé Range in the east. These islands comprise entire range. Critically endangered. Genus also endemic to West Indies. **HABITAT** Dense thickets of semi-arid wooded stream valleys and ravines.

**BROWN THRASHER** *Toxostoma rufum* 29cm (11.5in); 24–30g. Upperparts reddish-brown; long tail; pale white wing bars; pale tan underparts boldly streaked dark brown; dark brown mustache streak; yellow-orange eye; long dark bill. **STATUS AND RANGE** Decidedly rare migrant and non-breeding resident in northern Bahamas. Vagrant elsewhere in West Indies. Occurs primarily in October and November, but some birds remain through winter. **HABITAT** Dense undergrowth.

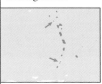

**Ⓜ SCALY-BREASTED THRASHER** *Allenia fusca* 23cm (9in); 55–95g. White underparts heavily scaled with grayish-brown from throat to belly; one whitish wing bar; black bill; yellow-brown eye; tail tipped white. (Pearly-eyed Thrasher larger, with large yellowish bill; no wing bars.) **VOICE** Repeats phrases similar to Tropical Mockingbird, but with less vigor. **STATUS AND RANGE** Generally fairly common permanent resident from Saba and St Bartholomew south to St Vincent. Extirpated on St Eustatius, Barbuda, Barbados, and Grenada. These islands comprise entire range. Genus also endemic to West Indies. **HABITAT** Moist and semi-arid forests and woodlands.

**Ⓜ PEARLY-EYED THRASHER** *Margarops fuscatus* 28–30cm (11–12in); 75g. Upperparts brown; underparts white, streaked with brown. White eye; large yellowish bill; large white patches on tail tip. (Scaly-breasted Thrasher smaller; bill black; one whitish wing bar.) **VOICE** Series of one- to three-syllable phrases with lengthy pauses between. Also many raucous call notes. **STATUS AND RANGE** Common permanent resident in southern Bahamas, spreading northward. Common in Puerto Rico, Virgin Islands, and Lesser Antilles south to St Lucia, except Martinique, where uncommon. On Hispaniola, only in northeast corner, Punta Cana, and Beata Island. Outside West Indies occurs on Bonaire. Genus nearly endemic to West Indies. **HABITAT** Thickets, woodlands, and forests at all elevations from mangroves and coastal palm groves to mountaintops. Also urban areas.

GREY CATBIRD

WHITE-BREASTED THRASHER

BROWN THRASHER

SCALY-BREASTED THRASHER

PEARLY-EYED THRASHER

**RED-LEGGED HONEYCREEPER** *Cyanerpes cyaneus* 13cm (5in); 15g. Small, with long, slender, down-curved bill. **BREEDING MALE** Purplish-blue; light blue crown; red legs. Underwing mostly yellow. **ADULT FEMALE** Dull olive-green, paler below with faint whitish streaks. **NON-BREEDING ADULT MALE** Similar to female, but wings and tail black. **IMMATURE** Similar to adult female, but more lightly streaked. **VOICE** Short, harsh *chrik-chrik*. **STATUS AND RANGE** Rather rare and local permanent resident in Cuba. **HABITAT** Forests and forest edges, particularly favors bottlebrush (*Callistemon citrinus*) trees.

**■ ORANGEQUIT** *Euneornis campestris* 14cm (5.5in); 14–19g. Small, with slightly down-curved black bill. **ADULT MALE** Gray-blue overall with orangish-red throat. **FEMALE AND IMMATURE** Crown and hindneck olive-gray; grayish-white below with faint streaks. **VOICE** Thin, high-pitched *tseet* or *swee*. **STATUS AND RANGE** Endemic to Jamaica, where locally common. Genus also endemic to Jamaica. **HABITAT** Humid forests and woodlands at all altitudes, most frequently mid-elevations. Also shade coffee plantations.

**BANANAQUIT** *Coereba flaveola* 10–12.5cm (4–5in); 9g. Highly variable. **ADULT** In most, curved bill; white eyebrow stripe and wing spot; yellow breast, belly, and rump. Black color phase in Grenada and St Vincent has slight greenish-yellow wash on breast and lacks white eyebrow stripe and wing spot. **IMMATURE** Duller. **VOICE** Variable. Generally thin, high-pitched ticks, clicks, and insect-like buzzes. Call note unmusical *tsip*. **STATUS AND RANGE** Very common permanent resident throughout West Indies except Cuba, where rare but may be resident in cays on north-central coast (Ciego de Ávila). **HABITAT** All habitats except highest peaks and driest lowlands.

**SCARLET TANAGER** *Piranga olivacea* 18cm (7in); 29g. **FEMALE** Overall yellowish-green plumage; distinctive bill shape; white wing linings in flight. **NON-BREEDING MALE** Similar to female, but wings black. (Female Baltimore Oriole more yellowish, with more pointed bill and whitish wing bars.) **BREEDING MALE** Red with black wings and tail. **STATUS AND RANGE** Irregular, but generally locally common to uncommon migrant primarily September–October, less frequent March–May in Cayman Islands; rare in northern Bahamas, Cuba, Jamaica, Puerto Rico, San Andrés, and Providencia. Very rare in southern Bahamas, Virgin Islands, and northern Lesser Antilles south to Antigua and Guadeloupe. Generally vagrant to Hispaniola and southern Lesser Antilles except Barbados, where decidedly rare but regular northbound migrant primarily April–May. **HABITAT** Open woods, forest edges, and gardens with trees.

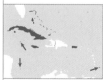

**SUMMER TANAGER** *Piranga rubra* 18–19.5cm (7–7.5in); 30g. Large-billed tanager. **ADULT MALE** Entirely red, brighter below; wings slightly darker. **FEMALE** Yellowish olive-green above; yellowish-orange below. **IMMATURE MALE** Similar to female, but with reddish tinge. (Female Scarlet Tanager yellow-green below; lacks orange tinge; has whitish rather than yellow wing linings.) **STATUS AND RANGE** Irregular but generally uncommon migrant and rare non-breeding resident in Bahamas, western Cuba, Jamaica, and Cayman Islands September–May. Rare in eastern Cuba, Puerto Rico; very rare in Barbados, San Andrés, and Providencia; vagrant elsewhere in West Indies. **HABITAT** Woodlands, forest edges, and gardens, primarily at mid-elevations.

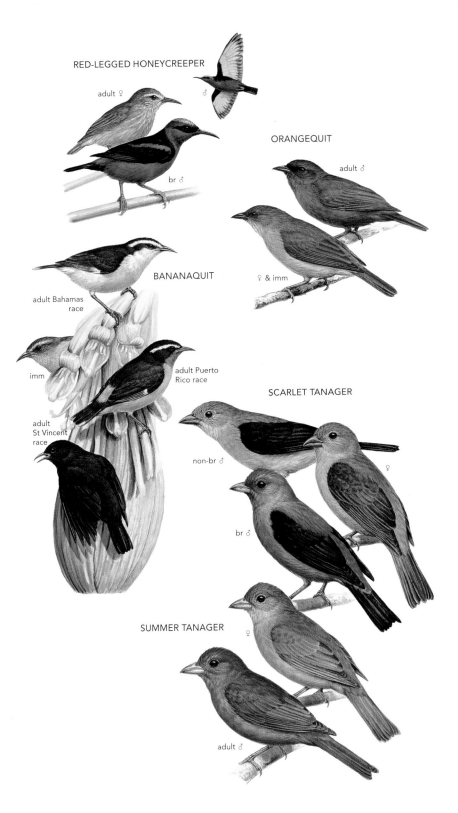

RED-LEGGED HONEYCREEPER

adult ♀

♂

br ♂

ORANGEQUIT

adult ♂

♀ & imm

BANANAQUIT

adult Bahamas race

imm

adult Puerto Rico race

adult St Vincent race

SCARLET TANAGER

non-br ♂

br ♂

♀

SUMMER TANAGER

♀

adult ♂

**M ANTILLEAN EUPHONIA** *Euphonia musica* 12cm (4.75in); 13g. Small and compact, with sky-blue crown and hindneck. **MALE** Variable, from greenish like female (Lesser Antilles) to primarily dark above and rich yellow below, on rump, and on forehead (Puerto Rico). **FEMALE** Duller. Greenish above, yellowish-green below; yellowish rump and forehead. **VOICE** Rapid, subdued, almost tinkling *ti-tit*; hard, metallic *chi-chink*; plaintive *whee*; jumbled, tinkling song mixed with explosive notes. **STATUS AND RANGE** Locally common in Hispaniola and Puerto Rico. Threatened in Haiti. Uncommon in Lesser Antilles, including Barbuda, Antigua, Guadeloupe, Dominica, Martinique, St Lucia, St Vincent, and Grenadines. Appears extirpated from Grenada. **HABITAT** Dense forests from dry lowlands to wet mountaintops. Favors mistletoe berries.

**J JAMAICAN EUPHONIA** *Euphonia jamaica* 11.5cm (4.5in); 17g. Small, compact, and drab, with stubby dark bill. Arboreal. **ADULT MALE** Grayish-blue overall; yellow belly. **FEMALE AND IMMATURE** Two-toned: head and underparts bluish-gray; back, wings, and flanks olive- green. **VOICE** Staccato churring, like motor starting. Also pleasant, squeaky whistle. **STATUS AND RANGE** Endemic to Jamaica, where common and widespread. **HABITAT** Primarily open secondary forests of lowland hills, but at all elevations in open areas with trees, woodlands, forest edges, shrubbery, and gardens.

**P PUERTO RICAN SPINDALIS** *Spindalis portoricensis* 16.5cm (6.5in); 23–41g. **MALE** Black head striped white. Underparts primarily yellow; reddish-orange wash on breast and hindneck. **FEMALE** Underparts dull whitish; gray streaks on sides and flanks; whitish mustache stripe; inconspicuous white eyebrow stripe. **VOICE** Variable thin, high-pitched whistle, *zeé-tit-zeé-tittit-zeé*. Also soft *teweep*. **STATUS AND RANGE** Endemic to Puerto Rico, where common and widespread. Family also endemic to West Indies. **HABITAT** Woodlands, forests, and gardens at all elevations.

**H HISPANIOLAN SPINDALIS** *Spindalis dominicensis* 16.5cm (6.5in); 25–33g. **MALE** Black head striped white. Underparts yellow; reddish-brown wash on breast. **FEMALE** Underparts whitish with fine stripes; whitish mustache stripe. **VOICE** Weak, high-pitched *thseep*. Also thin, high-pitched whistle. **STATUS AND RANGE** Endemic to Hispaniola, where locally common in mountains, less so on coast. Family also endemic to West Indies. **HABITAT** Forests.

**M WESTERN SPINDALIS** *Spindalis zena* 15cm (5.75in); 18–30g. **MALE** Black head striped white. **FEMALE** Two whitish facial stripes. **VOICE** Variable, generally very high-pitched, thin, ventriloquial whistle. **STATUS AND RANGE** Common permanent resident throughout Cuba and Bahamas. Fairly common permanent resident on Grand Cayman (Cayman Islands). Family also endemic to West Indies. **HABITAT** In Bahamas, native and Australian pines, coppice. In Cayman Islands, open woods and brush. In Cuba, all elevations in open woods, brush, and mangroves.

**J JAMAICAN SPINDALIS** *Spindalis nigricephala* 18cm (7in); 38–64g. Primarily orangish-yellow underparts. **MALE** Black head striped white; considerable white on wings. **FEMALE** Gray throat and upper breast. **VOICE** Soft *seep* and high, thin whistles. **STATUS AND RANGE** Endemic to Jamaica, where common and widespread, particularly hills and mountains. Family also endemic to West Indies. **HABITAT** Forests, woodlands, and brushy areas.

ANTILLEAN EUPHONIA

♀

♂ Hispaniola race

♂ Puerto Rico race

JAMAICAN EUPHONIA

adult ♂

♀ & imm

HISPANIOLAN SPINDALIS

♂

♀

♂

PUERTO RICAN SPINDALIS

♀

♂ Cuba race

JAMAICAN SPINDALIS

♂

♂ Bahamas race

WESTERN SPINDALIS

♀

♂

**M LESSER ANTILLEAN TANAGER** *Stilpnia cucullata* 14–15cm (5.5–5.75in); 26–30g. **MALE** Iridescent orangish-yellow above, sometimes with greenish cast; dark reddish-brown cap; bluish-green wings and tail. **FEMALE** Duller, with greenish upperparts. **VOICE** Weak, high-pitched series of single notes followed by twitter. **STATUS AND RANGE** Common permanent resident in St Vincent and Grenada. These islands comprise entire range. **HABITAT** Forests, gardens, and second growth at all elevations.

**H BLACK-CROWNED PALM-TANAGER** *Phaenicophilus palmarum* 18cm (7in); 30g. **ADULT** Black crown; white throat blends to gray breast. **VOICE** Nasal *pi-au*, pleasant dawn song, and low *chep*. **STATUS AND RANGE** Endemic to Hispaniola, where common in lowlands, less frequently high elevations. In Haiti, generally common, but rare west of Port-au-Prince. Family also endemic to Hispaniola. **HABITAT** Primarily semi-arid and humid thickets, but wherever there are trees, from towns to dense forests.

**H GRAY-CROWNED PALM-TANAGER** *Phaenicophilus polio-cephalus* 18cm (7in); 27g. **ADULT** Black mask; gray crown; sharp contrast between white throat and gray breast. **VOICE** *Peee-u*. **STATUS AND RANGE** Endemic to Hispaniola, where common, but local on southern peninsula of Haiti and islands of Île-à-Vache, Grande Cayemite, and Gonâve. In Dominican Republic, rare in Sierra de Bahoruco and southern part of Loma del Toro and Hoyo de Pelempito. Threatened. Family also endemic to Hispaniola. **HABITAT** Forests at all elevations. Also open areas and gardens.

**P PUERTO RICAN TANAGER** *Nesospingus speculiferus* 18–20cm (7–8in); 29–40g. **ADULT** Olive-brown above, white below; pale brownish stripes on breast; white wing spot. **IMMATURE** Lacks wing spot. **VOICE** Noisy. Harsh *chuck* or *chewp* frequently runs into chatter. **STATUS AND RANGE** Endemic to Puerto Rico, where common in higher mountains, but regular locally at moderate altitudes. Family also endemic to Puerto Rico. **HABITAT** Undisturbed mountain forests, also second growth.

**H WESTERN CHAT-TANAGER** *Calyptophilus tertius* 20cm (8in); 50g. **BEHAVIOR** Primarily terrestrial. **DESCRIPTION** Mockingbird-shaped, with long, rounded tail. Dark brown above; white throat and breast; yellow lores; fringe on bend of wing. Lacks eye-ring. **VOICE** Emphatic, clear, whistling *chip-chip-swerp-swerp-swerp*, a buzzy *wee-chee-chee-chee-chee* or *chirri-chirri-chirri-chip-chip-chip*, repeated. Also sharp *chick*. **STATUS AND RANGE** Endemic to Hispaniola. Uncommon and local in higher mountains in Haiti and in Sierra de Bahoruco in Dominican Republic. Critically endangered. Family also endemic to Hispaniola. **HABITAT** Wet broadleaf forests.

**H EASTERN CHAT-TANAGER** *Calyptophilus frugivorus* 17cm (6.75in); 32g. **BEHAVIOR** Primarily terrestrial. **DESCRIPTION** Similar to Western Chat-tanager but smaller, with yellow eye-ring. **VOICE** Similar to Western Chat-Tanager. **STATUS AND RANGE** Endemic to Hispaniola. Uncommon and local in Cordillera Central and Sierra de Neiba in Dominican Republic. Unrecorded for decades from Samaná Peninsula and Gonâve Island. Critically endangered. Family also endemic to Hispaniola. **HABITAT** Primarily dense undergrowth along streams in deciduous forests.

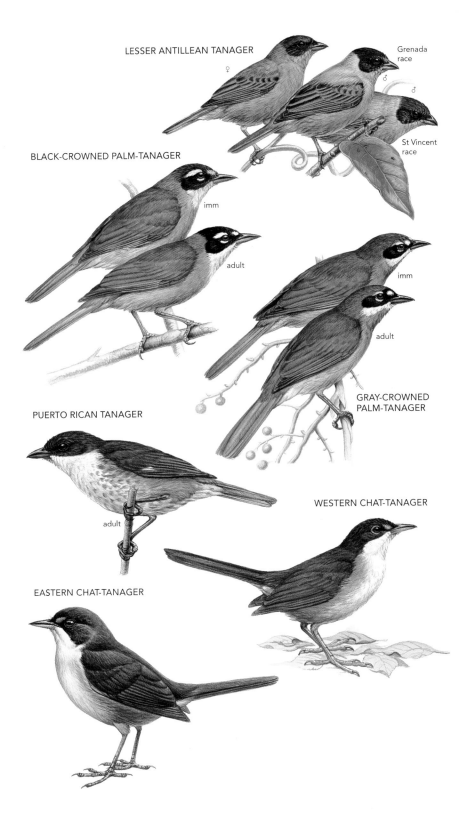

LESSER ANTILLEAN TANAGER

♀

Grenada race

♂

♂

St Vincent race

BLACK-CROWNED PALM-TANAGER

imm

adult

imm

adult

GRAY-CROWNED PALM-TANAGER

PUERTO RICAN TANAGER

adult

WESTERN CHAT-TANAGER

EASTERN CHAT-TANAGER

**EASTERN MEADOWLARK** *Sturnella magna* 23cm (9in); male 100g, female 80g.
**BEHAVIOR** Often perches on fence posts or wires and feeds on ground. Flicks tail when on ground. **DESCRIPTION** Medium-sized, with yellow underparts and conspicuous black "V" on breast. Outertail feathers white; crown and upperparts striped. **VOICE** Distinctive, high whistle on two or three tones, *tsee-ya, tsee-ya-ir*. Also peculiar harsh, loud alarm note. **STATUS AND RANGE** Common permanent resident in Cuba, where widespread. **HABITAT** Open grasslands, savannas, marshes, and pastures with only scattered trees or bushes primarily in lowlands.

**ORCHARD ORIOLE** *Icterus spurius* 16.5–18cm (6.5–7in); 20g. **ADULT MALE** Reddish-brown breast, belly, lower back, and bend of wing. **FEMALE** Grayish olive-green above; brighter on head and rump; dull yellow below; two white wing bars; bright olive-green tail. **IMMATURE MALE** Similar to female, but with black chin and throat. **STATUS AND RANGE** Very rare migrant in Cuba (primarily western) and Puerto Rico in October and April–May. Less frequent as non-breeding resident November–March. Vagrant elsewhere in West Indies. **HABITAT** Woodlands and gardens.

**BALTIMORE ORIOLE** *Icterus galbula* 18–20cm (7–8in); 35g. **ADULT MALE** Orange and black plumage; white wing bar; orange tail patches. **ADULT FEMALE AND IMMATURE** Brownish above, orange-yellow below with two whitish wing bars. **STATUS AND RANGE** Uncommon migrant and rare non-breeding resident in Bahamas, Cuba, and Jamaica September–May. Decidedly uncommon to rare in Hispaniola, Puerto Rico, larger Virgin Islands, Cayman Islands, and Guadeloupe. Vagrant to other Lesser Antilles and San Andrés. **HABITAT** All elevations in gardens with trees, semi-arid scrubland, open woodlands, swamps, and forest edges.

**Ⓜ JAMAICAN ORIOLE** *Icterus leucopteryx* 21cm (8in); 34–42g. Bright yellow to dull greenish-yellow with black mask and "bib" and large white wing patch. **IMMATURE** Two bars. **VOICE** Whistled *you cheat* or *cheat-you*. **STATUS AND RANGE** Common permanent resident in Jamaica and San Andrés. These islands comprise entire range. **HABITAT** In Jamaica, nearly all forests, woodlands, and areas with trees except mangroves. Also gardens.

**VENEZUELAN TROUPIAL** *Icterus icterus* 23–27cm (9–10.5in); 59–67g. Large size, orange-yellow and black, extensive white wing patches. **VOICE** Clear whistles, *troup, troup* ... or *troup-ial, troup-ial* ... **STATUS AND RANGE** Probably introduced. Common in Puerto Rico throughout lowlands, but also occurs in mid-elevations of central mountains. In Virgin Islands, occurs on south and east coasts of St Thomas, on Water Island, and on St John. **HABITAT** Principally arid scrublands, but also human habitations.

non-br adult

br adult

EASTERN
MEADOWLARK

ORCHARD ORIOLE

imm ♂

adult ♂

♀

BALTIMORE ORIOLE

adult ♂

♀ & imm

adult

JAMAICAN ORIOLE

imm

Jamaica race

VENEZUELAN TROUPIAL

**S** **MARTINIQUE ORIOLE** *Icterus bonana* 18–21cm (7–8in); 29g. **ADULT** Reddish-brown hood and reddish-orange shoulder, rump, lower belly, and abdomen. **VOICE** Clear whistles and harsh, scolding call. **STATUS AND RANGE** Endemic to Martinique, where uncommon. Most frequent in south and north center of island. Threatened. **HABITAT** Nearly all forests from dry coast to humid mountains. Also plantations and gardens with trees.

**S** **MONTSERRAT ORIOLE** *Icterus oberi* 20–22cm (8–8.5in); male 37.5g, female 34g. **ADULT MALE** Yellowish lower back, rump, shoulder, lower breast, belly, and abdomen. **ADULT FEMALE** Mainly yellowish-green above; underparts bright yellow. **IMMATURE** Duller. **VOICE** Loud whistles; also harsh, scolding *chuur*. **STATUS AND RANGE** Endemic to Montserrat, where rare. Found only in Soufrière Hills and Centre Hills. Endangered. **HABITAT** Mid-elevation forests.

**S** **ST LUCIA ORIOLE** *Icterus laudabilis* 20–22cm (8–8.5in); male 40g, female 35g. **ADULT MALE** Primarily black; lower back, rump, shoulder, and lower belly orange or orange-yellow. **ADULT FEMALE** Duller. **IMMATURE** Mostly greenish, with blackish throat. **VOICE** Drawn-out melodic whistles. **STATUS AND RANGE** Endemic to St Lucia, where uncommon and declining. Threatened. **HABITAT** Woodlands, including moderately dry and moist forests from near sea level to about 700m (2300ft); often associated with palms.

**H** **HISPANIOLAN ORIOLE** *Icterus dominicensis* 20–22cm (8–8.5in); 33–40g. **BEHAVIOR** Sometimes flocks. **ADULT** Yellow shoulders, rump, belly, and undertail-coverts. **IMMATURE** Upperparts brownish-gray with olive rump, underparts olive with tawny breast, yellowish abdomen, and sometimes blackish throat. **VOICE** Short series of weak, high-pitched whistles, also sharp *check*. **STATUS AND RANGE** Endemic to Hispaniola, where common and widespread, primarily in lowlands, but occurs to mid-elevations. **HABITAT** Particularly palms, also forest edges (not pines), shade coffee.

**S** **BAHAMA ORIOLE (BLACK-COWLED ORIOLE)** *Icterus northropi* 20–22cm (8–8.5in). **ADULT** Yellow shoulders, rump, and much of underparts from lower breast to undertail-coverts. **IMMATURE** Upperparts brownish with yellowish-green rump, underparts dull yellowish, wings black, throat black or reddish-brown. **VOICE** Rising whistle followed by two quick notes, repeated and ending with whistle, *poor Willy, poor Willy, poor*, also sharp *keek* or *check* note. **STATUS AND RANGE** Endemic to Bahamas, occurring only on Andros, where common on its three major islands of North Andros, Mangrove Cay, and South Andros. Formerly on Abaco, where likely extirpated. Critically endangered. **HABITAT** Particularly coconut palms, also gardens, pine forests, forest edges, and woodlands.

**C** **CUBAN ORIOLE (BLACK-COWLED ORIOLE)** *Icterus melanopsis* 20–22cm (8–8.5in); male 38g, female 34g. Yellow shoulders, rump, belly, and undertail-coverts. **IMMATURE** Upperparts mainly olive-green with yellow rump, underparts olive with variably blackish throat. **VOICE** Whistled songs of varying length slurred downward, also harsh *tick*. **STATUS AND RANGE** Endemic to Cuba, where common and widespread. **HABITAT** Forests, forest edges, woodlands, and gardens from coast to mid-elevations, particularly near palms.

**P** **PUERTO RICAN ORIOLE (BLACK-COWLED ORIOLE)** *Icterus portoricensis* 20–22cm (8–8.5in); male 41g, female 37g. Yellow shoulders, rump, abdomen, and undertail-coverts. **IMMATURE** Upperparts brownish-gray with olive-yellow rump, underparts tawny brown with yellowish-brown throat. **VOICE** High-pitched whistles; some exclamatory, others scratchy; rarely heard. Also sharp *keek* or *check*. **STATUS AND RANGE** Endemic to Puerto Rico, where fairly common. **HABITAT** Forests, forest edges, woodlands, and gardens from coast to mid-elevations, particularly near palms.

MONTSERRAT ORIOLE

adult ♂

adult ♀

MARTINIQUE ORIOLE

adult

ST LUCIA ORIOLE

adult ♂

imm

HISPANIOLAN ORIOLE

adult

BAHAMA ORIOLE

adult

adult

imm

PUERTO RICAN
ORIOLE

adult

CUBAN ORIOLE

imm

**CUBAN BLACKBIRD** *Ptiloxena atroviolacea* 25–28cm (10–11in); male 90g, female 76g. **BEHAVIOR** Flocks. **DESCRIPTION** Grackle-sized black bird with glossy purplish iridescence, dark eye, and square tail. (Female Red-shouldered Blackbird smaller. Male Shiny Cowbird smaller, with more conspicuous sheen.) **VOICE** Vast variety of calls; most typical is loud, repetitive *ti-o*, with metallic tone. **STATUS AND RANGE** Endemic to Cuba, where common and widespread. Genus also endemic to Cuba. **HABITAT** Primarily gardens in urban and rural areas, also woodlands from lowlands to mid-elevations.

**SHINY COWBIRD** *Molothrus bonariensis* 18–20cm (7–8in); male 40g, female 30g. **BEHAVIOR** Flocks. **DESCRIPTION** Medium-sized dark bird with conical bill. **ADULT MALE** Glossy black with purplish sheen. (Female Red-shouldered Blackbird has finer bill and lacks purplish sheen.) **ADULT FEMALE** Drab grayish-brown upperparts; lighter brown underparts; faint eyebrow stripe. **IMMATURE** Resembles adult female, but underparts finely streaked. **VOICE** Whistles followed by melodious trill. Variety of short call notes. **STATUS AND RANGE** Common permanent resident through much of West Indies, but rare and local in Virgin Islands; infrequent small flocks during migration to Cayman Islands; very rare in southern Bahamas and northern Lesser Antilles. Absent from San Andrés and Providencia. **HABITAT** Primarily open country and edges in lowlands. Favors dairies.

**BROWN-HEADED COWBIRD** *Molothrus ater* Male 19cm (7.5in), female 17cm (6.75in); male 50g, female 37g. **BEHAVIOR** Flocks. **MALE** Black with metallic greenish sheen; head brown. **FEMALE** Brownish-gray. Grayer than Shiny Cowbird, with whitish throat and no eyebrow stripe. **VOICE** Distinctive harsh rattle and creaky whistles. **STATUS AND RANGE** Rare non-breeding resident in northern Bahamas primarily October–February. Records from southern Bahamas and Cuba. Expanding range. **HABITAT** Farms, gardens, and rural areas.

**JAMAICAN BLACKBIRD** *Nesopsar nigerrimus* 18cm (7in); 39g. Medium-sized, entirely black, with slender, pointed bill and short tail. Arboreal. (Shiny Cowbird has more conical bill; not strictly arboreal. Male Jamaican Becard stockier, with stubbier bill.) **VOICE** Loud, wheezy *zwheezoo-whezoo whe*. Also *check*. **STATUS AND RANGE** Endemic to Jamaica, where uncommon but widely distributed. Occurs mostly at higher elevations. Threatened. Genus also endemic to Jamaica. **HABITAT** Wet mountain forests with bromeliads and mosses. Occasionally lower elevations.

**YELLOW-HEADED BLACKBIRD** *Xanthocephalus xanthocephalus* Male 26.5cm (10.5in), female 22cm (8.5in); male 100g, female 60g. **ADULT MALE** Black overall with orange-yellow hood and white wing patch. **ADULT FEMALE** Grayish-brown above; yellowish-orange eyebrow stripe, throat, breast, and line below cheek. **STATUS AND RANGE** Very rare in Cayman Islands. Vagrant elsewhere in West Indies. **HABITAT** Swamps and marshes.

CUBAN BLACKBIRD

adult ♀

SHINY COWBIRD

adult ♂

BROWN-HEADED COWBIRD

♀

♂

JAMAICAN BLACKBIRD

non-br adult ♂

non-br adult ♀

YELLOW-HEADED BLACKBIRD

### 🅜 GREATER ANTILLEAN GRACKLE *Quiscalus niger* 25–30cm (10–12in); male 85g, female 60g. BEHAVIOR Flocks. DESCRIPTION Fairly large, with dark plumage, long tail, and conical, pointed bill. ADULT MALE Glossy metallic-blue to violet-black plumage; yellow eye; deeply V-shaped tail. ADULT FEMALE Duller; tail with smaller "V." IMMATURE Dull brownish-black; tail flat; eye

pale brown. VOICE Highly variable, including high *cling, cling, cling*. STATUS AND RANGE Common permanent resident in Cuba, Jamaica, Hispaniola, Puerto Rico, and Cayman Islands. These islands comprise entire range. HABITAT Primarily open areas in lowlands, gardens, and mangroves.

### CARIB GRACKLE *Quiscalus lugubris* Male 26cm (10in), female 22cm (8.5in); male 73g, female 54g. BEHAVIOR Flocks. ADULT MALE Black with violet, green, or steel-blue sheen; yellowish-white eye; tail long and V-shaped. ADULT FEMALE Smaller; varies from relatively dark to quite pale; tail shorter, less V-shaped. IMMATURE Brownish-black. VOICE Three to seven syllables with rising

inflection. Also whistles and chucks. STATUS AND RANGE Common permanent resident on most Lesser Antilles from Anguilla to Grenada. Possibly introduced to Lesser Antilles north of Montserrat. HABITAT Primarily open areas in lowlands.

### BOAT-TAILED GRACKLE *Quiscalus major* Male 40cm (16in), female 27cm (10.5in); male 200g, female 115g. Large grackle; long tail and pointed bill. BEHAVIOR Flocks. ADULT MALE Glossy purplish-blue overall, eye usually brownish; long, deeply V-shaped tail. ADULT FEMALE Brown overall, paler below, eye usually dark. (Great-tailed Grackle larger; eye yellow; head flatter; voice more melodious.) VOICE Very vocal; series of harsh *jeeb* notes and chucks, gurgles, rattles, and squeaks. STATUS AND RANGE Established in Bahamas; small population on New Providence around Nassau and Paradise Island. A few birds on Grand Bahama. Probably arrived via tour boat. HABITAT Areas near lakes and ponds, including golf courses.

### GREAT-TAILED GRACKLE *Quiscalus mexicanus* Male 43cm (17in), female 33cm (13in); male 230g, female 125g. Largest grackle; long tail and pointed bill. BEHAVIOR Flocks. ADULT MALE Black with glossy purple sheen on head, back, and underparts; yellow eye; very long, deeply V-shaped tail. ADULT FEMALE Brown overall, yellow eye. IMMATURE Like adult female but dark eye, facial

markings more distinct, dark barring on belly and abdomen. (Boat-tailed Grackle smaller; eye dull yellow or brownish; head more rounded; voice less melodious.) VOICE Very vocal; wide variety of clear whistles such as an ascending *kriiik*; also rattles and snapping sounds. STATUS AND RANGE Common resident in San Andrés and rare in Providencia. Recently established in Jamaica, where common locally in suburbs of Portmore near Kingston, spreading toward center of island. Breeding locally in Hispaniola (Dominican Republic). Reported from several locations in Puerto Rico. Range expanding. HABITAT Urban areas.

GREATER ANTILLEAN GRACKLE

adult ♂

CARIB GRACKLE

adult ♀

adult ♂

BOAT-TAILED GRACKLE

adult ♀

adult ♂

GREAT-TAILED GRACKLE

adult ♀

adult ♂

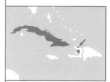

**🅜 TAWNY-SHOULDERED BLACKBIRD** *Agelaius humeralis* 19–22cm (7.5–8.5in); male 37g, female 29g. **BEHAVIOR** Flocks. **DESCRIPTION** Medium-sized, black, with tawny shoulder patch, most conspicuous in flight. **IMMATURE** Shoulder patch much smaller, sometimes not visible, giving appearance of female Red-shouldered Blackbird. **VOICE** Strong, short *chic-chic* resembles *chip* of Northern Yellowthroat. Sometimes harsh call similar to Red-shouldered Blackbird, but softer, shorter, and less shrill. **STATUS AND RANGE** Native only to Cuba, where common, and Haiti, where uncommon and local. In Haiti near Port-de-Paix, lower Artibonite River delta, and near Saint-Marc. Threatened in Haiti. Vagrant elsewhere. These islands comprise entire range. **HABITAT** Coastal marshes, scrub, woodlands, gardens, farms, swamp edges, pastures, rice fields, only in lowlands.

**🅟 YELLOW-SHOULDERED BLACKBIRD** *Agelaius xanthomus* 20–23cm (8–9in); male 41g, female 35g. **BEHAVIOR** Flocks. **ADULT** Entirely glossy black with yellow shoulder patches. (Puerto Rican Oriole more extensively yellow.) **IMMATURE** Duller; abdomen brown. **VOICE** Raspy *tnaaa*; whistled *tsuu*, descending scale; melodious *eh-up*, second syllable lower and accented; *chuck*. **STATUS AND RANGE** Endemic to Puerto Rico, where local along southwestern coast and on Mona Island. Decidedly uncommon elsewhere. Critically endangered. **HABITAT** Primarily mangroves and arid scrublands.

**RED-WINGED BLACKBIRD** *Agelaius phoeniceus* Male 23cm (9in), female 19cm (7.5in); male 64g, female 42g. **BEHAVIOR** Sometimes in large flocks. **DESCRIPTION** Medium-sized, black. **ADULT MALE** Scarlet shoulder patch edged yellowish. Identical to male Red-shouldered Blackbird. **FEMALE** Brown above; grayish-white below, heavily streaked dark brown; pale tannish eyebrow stripe. **IMMATURE MALE** Dark mottled brown; faint pale eyebrow stripe; small reddish-brown shoulder patch. **VOICE** Bubbling, shrill *ok-a-lee*, repeated often. Also sharp *chek*. **STATUS AND RANGE** Common permanent resident very locally in northern Bahamas south to Andros and Eleuthera. **HABITAT** Swamps and marshes.

**🅒 RED-SHOULDERED BLACKBIRD** *Agelaius assimilis* Male 22cm (8.5in), female 20cm (8in); male 50g, female 40g. **BEHAVIOR** Sometimes in large flocks. **DESCRIPTION** Medium-sized, black. **ADULT MALE** Scarlet shoulder patch edged yellowish. **FEMALE** Entirely black. **IMMATURE MALE** Shoulder patch reddish-brown. (Male Shiny Cowbird has purplish sheen and heavier bill. Cuban Blackbird is larger; no shoulder patch. Red-winged Blackbird does not overlap in range.) **VOICE** Harsh creaking and rather shrill, non-melodious *o-wi-hiii*, repeated often. Also, short *cheap, chek-chek-chek*, or single *chek*. **STATUS AND RANGE** Endemic to Cuba, where locally common in western and central part of island. **HABITAT** Swamps and marshes.

**BOBOLINK** *Dolichonyx oryzivorus* 18.5cm (7.25in); male 47g, female 37g. **BEHAVIOR** Flocks. **NON-BREEDING ADULT** Central pale tan crown stripe; unmarked pale tan underparts; streaked sides; pointed tail. **BREEDING MALE** Black below, grayish-tan hindneck, white patches on wings and lower back. **BREEDING FEMALE** Similar, but with whitish throat. **VOICE** Distinctive *pink*. **STATUS AND RANGE** Irregular through much of West Indies primarily as migrant August–November and March–May. Generally common in Bahamas; uncommon in Cayman Islands; uncommon and local in Cuba, Jamaica, Puerto Rico, Virgin Islands, Guadeloupe, and Barbados; rare in Hispaniola, St Bartholomew, Antigua, and Dominica; very rare or vagrant among other Lesser Antilles and San Andrés. Sometimes occurs in numbers. Declining. **HABITAT** Rice fields, pastures, and grassy areas.

YELLOW-SHOULDERED
BLACKBIRD

adult

adult

TAWNY-SHOULDERED
BLACKBIRD

imm

RED-WINGED
BLACKBIRD

RED-SHOULDERED BLACKBIRD

♀

♀

♂

BOBOLINK

br ♂

RED-WINGED/RED-SHOULDERED
BLACKBIRD

non-br adult

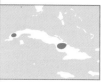

**G CUBAN PALM CROW (PALM CROW)** *Corvus minutus* 43cm (17in); 265–315g. **BEHAVIOR** Sometimes forms small flocks, flicks tail upward on alighting. **DESCRIPTION** Large, completely black, with faint violet sheen fading to dull brown-black in worn plumage. Nostrils covered by bristles. Slightly smaller than Cuban Crow; neck appears shorter in flight. Identify by voice. Identical to Hispaniolan Palm Crow, but ranges do not overlap. **VOICE** Harsh, nasal *craaao*; pitch initially rises abruptly, levels off, falls slightly at end. **STATUS AND RANGE** Endemic to Cuba, where rare and very local. Confined to northwestern part of Sierra de Los Órganos in Pinar del Río Province and to central Camagüey Province. Endangered. Some consider this and Hispaniolan Palm Crow a single species. **HABITAT** Forests, scrub, and palm savannas.

**H HISPANIOLAN PALM CROW (PALM CROW)** *Corvus palmarum* 43cm (17in); 290g. **BEHAVIOR** Sometimes flocks. Flicks tail downward. **DESCRIPTION** Large, completely black, with purplish and bluish sheen fading to dull brown-black in worn plumage. Considerably smaller and less robust than White-necked Crow. Identify by voice. **FLIGHT** Wings appear shorter than White-necked Crow's, and wing flapping is steadier. **VOICE** Harsh, nasal *aaar* (vowel sound as in "fast"), often with a complaining quality; also *cao-cao* in pairs or series. **STATUS AND RANGE** Endemic to Hispaniola, where locally common. Some consider this and Cuban Palm Crow a single species. **HABITAT** Primarily mountain pine forests, irregular at lower elevations.

**M CUBAN CROW** *Corvus nasicus* 45–48cm (17.5–19in); 330–510g. **BEHAVIOR** Usually flocks. **DESCRIPTION** Large, noisy black crow with purple sheen and conspicuous nostrils. **VOICE** Much louder and noisier than parrots, especially in large flocks. Characteristic high-pitched call with nasal quality, *caah-caaah*. Also turkey-like gobbling, and diverse guttural phrases similar to parrots. **STATUS AND RANGE** Common permanent resident in Cuba. In Bahamas, common on North Caicos, Middle Caicos, and Providenciales. Rare or absent on other islands of Turks and Caicos. These islands comprise entire range. **HABITAT** Primarily thin forests, but also palm plantations, treed borders of swamps, croplands, and garbage dumps.

**H WHITE-NECKED CROW** *Corvus leucognaphalus* 48–51cm (19–20in). **BEHAVIOR** Flocks. **DESCRIPTION** Large, entirely black, with large bill. Upperparts have violet sheen; white at base of neck not seen except in display. Distinguished from smaller Hispaniolan Palm Crow by voice. **VOICE** Wide variety, including *caw*, clucking, gurgling, bubbling, and laugh-like calls and squawks. **STATUS AND RANGE** Endemic and locally common in Hispaniola, but declining. Threatened. **HABITAT** Primarily moist uplands, but occurs from semi-arid scrublands and open lowlands with scattered trees to mountain pine forests.

**J JAMAICAN CROW** *Corvus jamaicensis* 38cm (15in); 340g. **BEHAVIOR** Sometimes small flocks. **DESCRIPTION** Large, entirely dull black, with large bill. **FLIGHT** Slow and labored. **VOICE** Loud *craa-craa*, also semi-musical jabbering. **STATUS AND RANGE** Endemic to Jamaica, where locally common. Most frequent in Cockpit Country and John Crow Mountains. **HABITAT** Primarily mid-elevations in undisturbed wet limestone forests. Less frequent in disturbed wooded areas, plantations, and park-like country at mid-elevations.

**EUROPEAN STARLING** *Sturnus vulgaris* 22cm (8.5in); 75g. **BEHAVIOR** Flocks. **DESCRIPTION** Glossy black, with short tail. **BREEDING ADULT** Bill yellow. **NON-BREEDING ADULT** Underparts heavily flecked with white spots; dark bill. **FLIGHT** Straight, unlike other black birds in region. Wings distinctively swept back. **VOICE** Wide variety of whistles, squeaks, and raspy notes. **STATUS AND RANGE** Introduced. Fairly common year-round resident in Jamaica, and on Grand Bahama, Abaco, New Providence, and Biminis in Bahamas. Rare and local elsewhere in Bahamas; vagrant elsewhere in West Indies. **HABITAT** Primarily open lowlands, including pastures and gardens.

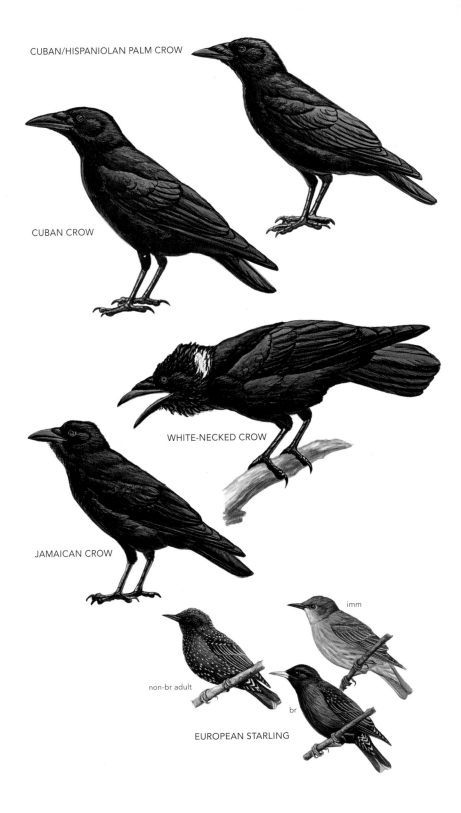

CUBAN/HISPANIOLAN PALM CROW

CUBAN CROW

WHITE-NECKED CROW

JAMAICAN CROW

imm

non-br adult

br

EUROPEAN STARLING

**C** **CUBAN BULLFINCH** *Melopyrrha nigra* 14–15cm (5.5–5.75in); 9–18g. **BEHAVIOR** Flocks. **DESCRIPTION** Small, dark, with thick, curved bill, and white band on edge of wing. **MALE** Shiny black. **FEMALE** Duller grayish-black, smaller wing band. **IMMATURE** Brownish wings and tail, less white on wing, bill pale. **FLIGHT** White underwings. **VOICE** Call note staccato *chi-dip*, and thin *tsee*. Song a thin melodious warble, descending, then ascending, *ti, ti, ti, ti-si-sssiiittt-sssiii*. **STATUS AND RANGE** Endemic to Cuba, where common and widespread. Occurs at low to mid-elevations. Genus endemic to West Indies. **HABITAT** Thickets, brushy pastures, and forests including mangroves.

**S** **CAYMAN BULLFINCH (CUBAN BULLFINCH)** *Melopyrrha taylori* 14–15cm (5.5–5.75in); 9–18g. **BEHAVIOR** Small flocks. **DESCRIPTION** Small, dark, with thick, curved bill, and white band on edge of wing. **MALE** Black. **FEMALE** Grayish-black on head and upperparts, with olive-gray lower abdomen and flanks. **IMMATURE** Like adult female, but white reduced or absent from wing, bill pale. **FLIGHT** White underwings. **VOICE** Call note buzzing, insect-like *chi-p*, and *zee-zee*, first note higher pitched. Song a trill, *zee-zee-zee*, then falls and rises over series of 8–30 *tssi* notes. **STATUS AND RANGE** Endemic to Grand Cayman in Cayman Islands. Most abundant at North Side, North Sound Estates, and South Sound Swamp. Some consider this a subspecies of Cuban Bullfinch. Genus endemic to West Indies. **HABITAT** Dry scrub, dry forest, woodlands, gardens, and pastures.

**M** **GREATER ANTILLEAN BULLFINCH** *Melopyrrha violacea* 14–18cm (5.5–7in); 18–32g. Chunky, with thick bill, reddish-brown eyebrow stripe, throat, and undertail-coverts. **ADULT MALE** Black overall. **ADULT FEMALE** Duller black. **IMMATURE** Olive-brown. (Puerto Rican Bullfinch has reddish-brown crown and does not overlap in range.) **VOICE** Shrill, insect-like *t'zeet, t'seet, t'seet, tseet, seet, seet, seet, seet, seet*. Also thin *spit*. **STATUS AND RANGE** Common permanent resident on most larger islands of Bahamas, Hispaniola, and Jamaica. These islands comprise entire range. Genus endemic to West Indies. **HABITAT** Dense thickets and undergrowth at all elevations from dry coastal scrub to wet mountain forests, including gardens with dense cover.

**P** **PUERTO RICAN BULLFINCH** *Melopyrrha portoricensis* 16.5–19cm (6.5–7.5in); 23–45g. **ADULT** Black, with reddish-brown throat, undertail-coverts, and crown band. (Greater Antillean Bullfinch has less reddish-brown in crown. Lesser Antillean Bullfinch nearly lacks this color in crown. Ranges do not overlap.) **IMMATURE** Dark olive-green; only undertail-coverts reddish-brown. **VOICE** Two to ten distinctive rising whistles followed by buzz. Also whistled *coochi, coochi, coochi*, and medium-strength *check*. **STATUS AND RANGE** Endemic to Puerto Rico, where common and widespread. Genus endemic to West Indies. **HABITAT** Forests and dense thickets of all types and at all elevations.

CUBAN BULLFINCH

♂

CAYMAN BULLFINCH

♂

♀

imm    GREATER ANTILLEAN BULLFINCH

adult ♂

PUERTO RICAN BULLFINCH

imm

adult

**🅜LESSER ANTILLEAN BULLFINCH** *Loxigilla noctis* 14–15.5cm (5.5–6in); 13–23g. MALE All black with reddish-brown chin, throat, and over eye. Some have red undertail-coverts. FEMALE AND IMMATURE Brownish-olive above, gray below; orangish undertail-coverts. (St Lucia Black Finch has pink legs and larger bill; bobs tail; female has gray crown.) VOICE Short, crisp trill; harsh *chuk*; thin, wiry *tseep, tseep*; and a lengthy twitter. STATUS AND RANGE Common permanent resident through Lesser Antilles, but absent from Barbados and very rare in Grenadines. Locally common in Virgin Islands, where spreading. These islands comprise entire range. Genus endemic to West Indies. HABITAT Shrubbery, gardens, thickets, and forest understory at all elevations.

**🅢BARBADOS BULLFINCH** *Loxigilla barbadensis* 14–15.5cm (5.5–6in); 13–18g. BEHAVIOR Often on ground. DESCRIPTION Brownish-olive above, gray below; orangish undertail-coverts. VOICE An unmusical *swee-swee-swee-swee-swee* … STATUS AND RANGE Endemic to Barbados, where common and widespread. Genus endemic to West Indies. HABITAT Forests, woodlands, shrubbery, open areas, gardens, and human habitation.

**🅢ST LUCIA BLACK FINCH** *Melanospiza richardsoni* 13–14cm (5–5.5in); 18–23g. BEHAVIOR Bobs tail; primarily terrestrial. DESCRIPTION Heavy bill, pink legs. ADULT MALE Entirely black. FEMALE Gray crown contrasts with brown back; brownish-gray below. (Lesser Antillean Bullfinch has smaller bill; lacks pink legs; does not bob tail; female has grayish underparts and lacks gray crown.) VOICE Burry *tick-zwee-swisiwis-you* with accents on second and last notes; similar to Bananaquit. STATUS AND RANGE Endemic to St Lucia, where uncommon and fairly local. Endangered. Genus endemic to West Indies. HABITAT Moist and semi-arid forests to 700m (2300ft).

**BLUE-BLACK GRASSQUIT** *Volatinia jacarina* 11cm (4.25in); 8–12g. BEHAVIOR Frequently hops off perch into air, typically while singing. ADULT MALE Entirely glossy blue-black; wingpits sometimes white. ADULT FEMALE Olive-brown above and yellowish-tan below, heavily streaked with gray on breast and sides. IMMATURE Similar, but grayer above and more darkly streaked below. VOICE Emphatic *eee-slick*. STATUS AND RANGE Common breeding resident in Grenada June–September. Most abundant in dry southwest. Believed to migrate to South America outside breeding season. HABITAT Shrubby fields, roadsides, low scrubby second growth, farms, primarily at low elevations.

LESSER ANTILLEAN BULLFINCH

Guadeloupe-Domenica race

♂

St Lucia race

♂

♀ & imm

BARBADOS BULLFINCH

♀ & imm

adult ♂

ST LUCIA BLACK FINCH

adult ♀

adult ♂

BLUE-BLACK GRASSQUIT

**YELLOW-SHOULDERED GRASSQUIT** *Loxipasser anoxanthus* 10.5–11.5cm (4.1–4.5in); 10.5–12.5g. ADULT MALE Two-toned: black head and underparts, yellowish wings and back; undertail-coverts reddish-brown. ADULT FEMALE Gray below, yellowish-green above; yellow patch on bend of wing. Undertail-coverts pale reddish-brown. Yellowish in wing and rusty undertail-coverts distinguish it from Black-faced Grassquit. VOICE Five notes, descending with echo-like quality. STATUS AND RANGE Endemic to Jamaica, where fairly common and widespread. Genus also endemic to Jamaica. HABITAT Forest edges from wet to dry and all elevations. Also woodlands and gardens near wooded areas.

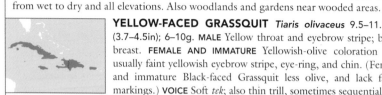

**YELLOW-FACED GRASSQUIT** *Tiaris olivaceus* 9.5–11.5cm (3.7–4.5in); 6–10g. MALE Yellow throat and eyebrow stripe; black breast. FEMALE AND IMMATURE Yellowish-olive coloration and usually faint yellowish eyebrow stripe, eye-ring, and chin. (Female and immature Black-faced Grassquit less olive, and lack facial markings.) VOICE Soft *tek*; also thin trill, sometimes sequentially at different pitches. STATUS AND RANGE Common permanent resident in Cuba, Jamaica, Hispaniola, Puerto Rico, and Cayman Islands. HABITAT Primarily open grassy areas from lowlands to moderate elevations, sometimes high mountains.

**BLACK-FACED GRASSQUIT** *Melanospiza bicolor* 10–11.5cm (4–4.5in); 7–13g. MALE Black head and underparts. FEMALE AND IMMATURE Drab brownish-olive overall. Drabber than Yellow-faced Grassquit and lack faint facial markings. (Male Yellow-shouldered Grassquit has yellowish back and wings; female a yellow wing patch.) VOICE Emphatic buzz often followed by second, louder effort. Also soft musical *tsip*. STATUS AND RANGE Generally common permanent resident through West Indies, though virtually absent from Cuba, occurring very rarely on a few cays off north-central island. Absent from Cayman Islands. Genus endemic to West Indies. HABITAT Open areas with grasses and shrubs, forest clearings, road edges, sugarcane plantations, and gardens.

**YELLOW-BELLIED SEEDEATER** *Sporophila nigricollis* 8.5–10cm (3.3–4in); 8.5–11g. ADULT MALE Black hood; pale blue-gray bill; yellowish-white underparts. FEMALE AND IMMATURE Olive-brown above, yellowish-white below; dark bill. VOICE Brief melodious, warbling song frequently followed by buzzy notes. STATUS AND RANGE Common breeding resident in Grenada; uncommon and local in Grenadines (Carriacou and Union Island). Occurs March–November, then migrates to South America. HABITAT Shrubby fields and thickets, field edges, and roadsides.

**RED SISKIN** *Spinus cucullatus* 10cm (4in). BEHAVIOR Flocks. MALE Primarily orange-red with black hood. FEMALE Orange rump, wing markings, and wash on breast. VOICE High-pitched twitter and *chi-tit* similar to Indian Silverbill. STATUS AND RANGE Introduced to Puerto Rico, where very local in dry foothills of southeast. Few recent reports. Perhaps extirpated. HABITAT Thick scrub, often in dry ravines.

**ANTILLEAN SISKIN** *Spinus dominicensis* 11cm (4.25in); 9g. BEHAVIOR Flocks. DESCRIPTION Small, chunky bird with light yellow bill. MALE Black head and yellowish body; tail black with two yellow patches. FEMALE Olive-green above, yellowish-white below, with faint pale gray streaks; two yellow wing bars; pale yellowish rump. VOICE Soft *chut-chut* and higher-pitched *swee-ee*. Also low, bubbling trill. STATUS AND RANGE Endemic to Hispaniola, where locally common in western Dominican Republic in interior hills and mountains. Wanders to lower elevations. In Haiti, uncommon and local primarily in Massif de la Selle, but also Massif de la Hotte and a few other locations. HABITAT Pine forests and associated grassy clearings and forest edges.

YELLOW-SHOULDERED GRASSQUIT

adult ♂

adult ♀

YELLOW-FACED GRASSQUIT

♂

Puerto Rico race

♀ & imm

BLACK-FACED GRASSQUIT

♂

♀ & imm

YELLOW-BELLIED SEEDEATER

adult ♂

♀ & imm

RED SISKIN

♀

♂

ANTILLEAN SISKIN

♀

♂

**C CUBAN GRASSQUIT** *Phonipara canora* 11.5cm (4.5in); 6–9.5g. **BEHAVIOR** Flocks. **DESCRIPTION** Small, with olive upperparts. Conspicuous yellow crescent divides face and breast. **MALE** Black face and breast. **FEMALE** Yellow less marked; face dark reddish-brown. **VOICE** Shrill, raspy *chiri-wichi-wichi*, *chibiri-wichi-wichi*, resembling Bee Hummingbird. Also *chip*. **STATUS AND RANGE** Endemic to Cuba, where common and widespread. Introduced to New Providence (Bahamas), where fairly common throughout island. Genus endemic to Cuba. **HABITAT** Primarily semi-arid country; also pine undergrowth, edges of woods, bushy areas, shade coffee and citrus plantations, farms with much shrubbery, from coast to mid-elevations.

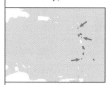

**GRASSLAND YELLOW-FINCH** *Sicalis luteola* 10–12.5cm (4–5in); 14.5–18g. **BEHAVIOR** Loose flocks. **ADULT MALE** Upperparts pale yellow, heavily streaked with blackish; underparts and rump yellow. **ADULT FEMALE** Similar, but duller. **IMMATURE** Like female, but with blackish streaks on breast. **VOICE** Distinctive buzzy trill. **STATUS AND RANGE** Probably introduced to Barbados and spread to other islands. Uncommon and local permanent resident in Antigua, Guadeloupe, Martinique, St Lucia, and Barbados. Very rare and local in Grenada. **HABITAT** Open grassy fields, pastures, and runway edges.

**SAFFRON FINCH** *Sicalis flaveola* 14–15cm (5.5–5.75in); 12–23g. **BEHAVIOR** Loose flocks. **ADULT** Medium-sized; entirely yellow with an orange crown. **MALE** Crown bright orange. **FEMALE** Crown yellowish-orange. **IMMATURE** Generally gray, paler below, with yellow undertail-coverts and, with age, a yellow breast band. (Yellow and Prothonotary Warblers smaller; with finer bill; not in grassy habitats.) **VOICE** Soft or loud, sharp *pink*; a whistled *wheat* on one pitch; a fairly loud, melodious, but slightly harsh *chit, chit, chit, chi-chit*, of differing duration. **STATUS AND RANGE** Introduced. Widespread and common in Jamaica. Fairly common in Puerto Rico, but local in and around Santurce. Uncommon from Guaynabo to Arecibo and ascending to mountain towns. Also Mayagüez. **HABITAT** Cultivated lawns. Also roadsides and farmlands with seeding grasses.

**VILLAGE WEAVER** *Ploceus cucullatus* 17cm (6.75in); male 40g, female 33g. **BEHAVIOR** Flocks. **DESCRIPTION** Chunky, with heavy bill. **MALE** Distinctive orange-yellow overall, with black hood and red eye. (Adult male Baltimore Oriole also black and orange-yellow but slimmer, with longer bill and tail.) **FEMALE** Yellowish-green on face and breast, with yellow wing bars. (Female Antillean Siskin smaller, with paler and less massive bill, and no eyebrow stripe.) **VOICE** Steady high-pitched chatter with musical whistling calls. **STATUS AND RANGE** Introduced. Common and widespread in Hispaniola. A small local population primarily along northwest coast of Martinique, but range expanding. Reports from Guadeloupe. **HABITAT** Mostly lowlands in rice fields, vegetation near water, and open woodlands and scrub. Also gardens.

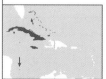

**DICKCISSEL** *Spiza americana* 15–18cm (5.75–7in); male 29g, female 25g. **BEHAVIOR** Flocks. **DESCRIPTION** Yellowish wash on breast; dull yellow eyebrow stripe; thick bill; reddish-brown bend of wing. **NON-BREEDING MALE** Pale but noticeable black throat patch. **FEMALE** Black on throat confined to few streaks. **BREEDING MALE** Dark black throat patch; yellow below more extensive. **STATUS AND RANGE** Irregular, but generally rare migrant September–November and March–April in Bahamas, Cayman Islands (Grand Cayman), San Andrés, and Providencia (most frequent in April on latter three islands); very rare in Cuba and Jamaica; vagrant elsewhere in West Indies. Sometimes occurs in numbers. **HABITAT** Open grasslands with scattered trees.

CUBAN GRASSQUIT

GRASSLAND YELLOW-FINCH

adult ♂

imm

SAFFRON FINCH

VILLAGE WEAVER

imm

DICKISSEL

br ♂

**PIN-TAILED WHYDAH** *Vidua macroura* Breeding male 30–33cm (12–13in), female and non-breeding male 11.5cm (4.5in); 12–19g. **BEHAVIOR** Flocks. **BREEDING MALE** Black and white, with long tail plumes and red bill. **FEMALE AND NON-BREEDING MALE** Mottled reddish-brown above; red bill; black-and-white facial stripes. **IMMATURE** More grayish-brown; whitish eyebrow stripe. Bill blackish, pinkish-red at base. **VOICE** Twittering, sometimes with loud chattering and whistles. Also emphatic *sweet*. **STATUS AND RANGE** Introduced. Uncommon and local on coast of Puerto Rico, less frequent in mountains. Hurricanes of 2017 decimated northern and eastern populations. A few records from Hispaniola (Dominican Republic). **HABITAT** Lawns and fields with short grass.

**YELLOW-CROWNED BISHOP** *Euplectes afer* 11.5–12.5cm (4.5–5in); 11–20g. **BEHAVIOR** Flocks. **BREEDING MALE** Yellow rump and crown; entirely black underparts. **FEMALE AND NON-BREEDING MALE** Mottled brown above and pale tan below. Yellowish eyebrow stripe contrasts sharply with dark brown eye-line. Breast and crown finely striped. (Female and non-breeding male Northern Red Bishops have paler cheek patch; pale, rather than dark brown, eye-line; no yellow in eyebrow stripe. Grasshopper Sparrow has whitish central crown stripe.) **VOICE** Series of *sweet* and *chuck* notes similar to Northern Red Bishop. **STATUS AND RANGE** Introduced. Uncommon and very local in Puerto Rico and Jamaica. May be extirpated from Puerto Rico due to hurricanes in 2017. **HABITAT** High grass and reeds near fresh water.

**NORTHERN RED BISHOP (ORANGE BISHOP)** *Euplectes franciscanus* 12.5cm (5in); 12–22g. **BEHAVIOR** Flocks. **BREEDING MALE** Orange-red plumage with black belly and crown. **FEMALE AND NON-BREEDING MALE** Mottled brown above and pale tan below with pale tan eyebrow stripe. Breast and crown finely striped. (*See also* Plate 116.) **IMMATURE** Like female, but more tannish. (Grasshopper Sparrow has golden spot near bill and single, central whitish crown stripe.) **VOICE** Breeding males sing sputtering song. **STATUS AND RANGE** Introduced. Common in lowlands of southwest Puerto Rico. Prior to hurricanes of 2017 occurred around entire coast; likely to recolonize. Uncommon and very local in lowlands of southeast Jamaica (declining), St Croix (Virgin Islands), Guadeloupe (Grande-Terre); reports from Martinique. **HABITAT** Primarily sugarcane fields bordered by grassy edges, sometimes open areas.

**JAVA SPARROW** *Lonchura oryzivora* 15–16.5cm (5.75–6.5in); 23–28g. **BEHAVIOR** Flocks. **ADULT** Primarily gray above and below; broad, pinkish-red bill; white cheek patch; black crown. **IMMATURE** Similar but duller bill, tannish-white cheeks, and brownish body. **VOICE** Hard, metallic *chink*. **STATUS AND RANGE** Introduced. Uncommon and declining in Puerto Rico in San Juan area. Nearly extirpated by hurricanes of 2017. Recent reports from Jamaica. **HABITAT** Primarily urban areas with short grass, such as athletic fields and large lawns.

**ROSE-BREASTED GROSBEAK** *Pheucticus ludovicianus* 19–20cm (7.5–8in); 45g. **BEHAVIOR** Often flocks. **MALE** Pinkish-red breast; black head and back; white wing bars; pink wing linings in flight. **FEMALE** Large, with heavy bill, white crown stripes, and white wing bars. Streaked underparts; yellow wing linings in flight. **STATUS AND RANGE** Occurs through West Indies, where irregular, but at times locally common migrant in Cayman Islands, San Andrés, and Providencia primarily September–October and March–April. In Cayman Islands less frequent as non-breeding resident November–February. Uncommon primarily as migrant in Bahamas, Cuba, and Hispaniola; rare in Jamaica, Puerto Rico, Virgin Islands, and Guadeloupe; very rare among other larger Lesser Antilles. **HABITAT** Scrub, woodlands, forest edges. Also gardens.

PIN-TAILED
WHYDAH

br ♂

♀ & non-br ♂

YELLOW-CROWNED BISHOP

br ♂

♀ & non-br ♂

NORTHERN RED BISHOP

br ♂

♀ & non-br ♂

ROSE-BREASTED
GROSBEAK

♀

♂

imm

adult

JAVA SPARROW

**C ZAPATA SPARROW** *Torreornis inexpectata* 16.5cm (6.5in); 20–29g. Plump; yellow belly and abdomen; white throat; dark mustache stripe; dark reddish-brown crown; olive-gray upperparts. **VOICE** Four distinct calls. Most typical is short, somewhat metallic trill, repeated at intervals. It is high-pitched and penetrating, *tziii-tzziii-tzzi-ii* ... **STATUS AND RANGE** Endemic to Cuba, where very local. Common on Cayo Coco; uncommon in Zapata Swamp north of Santo Tomás; rarer in coastal areas east of Guantánamo Bay. Endangered. **HABITAT** Sawgrass country with scattered bushes; dry vegetation, semi-deciduous woods, and swampy areas.

**M LESSER ANTILLEAN SALTATOR** *Saltator albicollis* 22cm (8.5in); 37–51g. Upperparts dull green. **ADULT** Whitish eyebrow stripe; black bill with orange-white tip; underparts streaked with olive-green; black mustache stripe. **IMMATURE** Duller facial markings and breast streaks. **VOICE** Series of harsh, loud notes that rise and fall. **STATUS AND RANGE** Common permanent resident in Guadeloupe, Dominica, Martinique, and St Lucia. These islands comprise entire range. **HABITAT** Thickets, second growth, dry scrub, and forest edge undergrowth.

**H HISPANIOLAN CROSSBILL** *Loxia megaplaga* 15cm (5.75in); 28g. Flocks. Crossed bill tips; two white wing bars on black wings. **ADULT MALE** Pale red overall. **ADULT FEMALE** Yellowish rump and finely streaked breast. **IMMATURE** Browner and more heavily streaked. **VOICE** High-pitched, emphatic, repeated *chu-chu-chu-chu*. **STATUS AND RANGE** Endemic to Hispaniola, where uncommon and local in highest mountains. Declining. Endangered. **HABITAT** Pine forests.

**INDIGO BUNTING** *Passerina cyanea* 12.5cm (5in); 14g. **BEHAVIOR** Flocks. **NON-BREEDING MALE** Brown overall; traces of blue in wings and tail. **FEMALE** Dull brown; very pale breast stripes and wing bars; no conspicuous markings. Female's faint breast stripes and wing bars distinguish it from immature mannikins. **BREEDING MALE** Entirely blue. **VOICE** Emphatic *twit*. Sometimes thin song of paired phrases. **STATUS AND RANGE** Migrant and non-breeding resident in West Indies October–early May. Common in Bahamas, Cuba, larger Virgin Islands, Cayman Islands (particularly April–May), and San Andrés; uncommon in Jamaica, Hispaniola, and Puerto Rico; rare in Guadeloupe and Providencia. Generally very rare elsewhere in West Indies. Sometimes occurs in numbers. **HABITAT** Rice fields, grassy areas bounded by heavy thickets, rows of trees or woodlands, pasture edges and scrub.

**BLUE GROSBEAK** *Passerina caerulea* 16.5–19cm (6.5–7.5in); 28g. **BEHAVIOR** Flicks tail. **MALE** Entirely blue with reddish-brown wing bars. **FEMALE** Brown overall; large with heavy bill; reddish-brown wing bars. Hints of blue sometimes on wings and rump. **STATUS AND RANGE** Throughout West Indies, where varying year to year, but generally common migrant (September–October, April) and rare non-breeding resident (November–March) in Cuba; uncommon in Bahamas and Cayman Islands; rare in Hispaniola and Puerto Rico; very rare in Jamaica, Virgin Islands, Lesser Antilles, San Andrés, and Providencia. **HABITAT** Forest edges, Australian pine (*Casuarina*) groves, rice fields, seeding grass, and gardens.

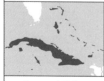

**PAINTED BUNTING** *Passerina ciris* 13cm (5in); 13–19g. **ADULT MALE** Blue head, red underparts, and green back. **ADULT FEMALE AND YOUNG MALE** Green above, yellowish-green below. Brighter green than vireos, and bill much heavier. **IMMATURE** Much duller, but may show hints of green. **VOICE** Loud *chip*. **STATUS AND RANGE** Fairly common migrant November and March in northern and central Bahamas and western and central Cuba. Uncommon on these islands as non-breeding resident December–February as well as in southern Bahamas and eastern Cuba. Rare in Cayman Islands and vagrant elsewhere in West Indies. **HABITAT** Thickets, brush, and grassy areas, particularly semi-arid areas, often near water.

ZAPATA SPARROW

LESSER ANTILLEAN SALTATOR

adult

adult ♀

INDIGO BUNTING

adult ♂

HISPANIOLAN CROSSBILL

♀

br ♂

adult ♀ &
young ♂

BLUE GROSBEAK

♀

adult ♂

♂

PAINTED BUNTING

**RED AVADAVAT (STRAWBERRY FINCH)** *Amandava amandava* 10cm (4in); 9g. **BEHAVIOR** Flocks. **BREEDING MALE** Primarily deep red with white spots on wings, flanks, and sides. **ADULT FEMALE AND NON-BREEDING MALE** Brown above, paler below. Red uppertail-coverts and bill; white spots on wing; dark eye-line. **IMMATURE** Similar, but lacks red; wing spots tannish. **VOICE** Musical *sweet* and *sweet-eet*. Also melodious whistles and warbles. **STATUS AND RANGE** Introduced. Common in Guadeloupe, mainly on Grande-Terre. Rare in Martinique. Appears extirpated in Hispaniola and Puerto Rico. **HABITAT** Grassy edges, often by freshwater swamps and canals, also sugarcane borders.

**BLACK-RUMPED WAXBILL** *Estrilda troglodytes* 10cm (4in) 8g. **BEHAVIOR** Flocks. **ADULT** Red eye-line; red bill; black tail and uppertail-coverts. (Common Waxbill is darker below with barring on sides; tail brown.) **IMMATURE** Lacks red eye-line; bill pale pink. **VOICE** Call notes include *pit, cheww* or *chit-cheww*, like bullet ricocheting off rock. **STATUS AND RANGE** Introduced in Guadeloupe, where locally common, and Martinique, where uncommon and local. Extirpated from Puerto Rico. **HABITAT** High grass near sugarcane and agricultural fields.

**COMMON WAXBILL** *Estrilda astrild* 10cm (4in); 6–11g. **BEHAVIOR** Flocks. **ADULT** Red eye-line and bill; sides faintly barred; reddish wash on belly; tail and uppertail-coverts brown. (Black-rumped Waxbill is paler below with no barring on sides; tail black). **IMMATURE** Bill black, other markings paler. **VOICE** Variety of twittering and buzzing calls. **STATUS AND RANGE** Introduced in Martinique, where locally common and well established. **HABITAT** Grassy areas including edges of sugarcane and other agricultural areas. Also thickets.

**ORANGE-CHEEKED WAXBILL** *Estrilda melpoda* 10cm (4in); 7–10g. **BEHAVIOR** Flocks. **ADULT** Orange cheek patch; reddish bill and uppertail-coverts. **IMMATURE** Lacks orange cheek; bill pale pink. **VOICE** Clear *pee*, singly or in series. Flocks have characteristic twitter. **STATUS AND RANGE** Introduced. Common on coastal plain of Puerto Rico (sparse in Central Mountains and eastern portion of island), and Guadeloupe. Rare in Martinique. **HABITAT** Tall seeding grass in agricultural areas, sugarcane borders, and road edges.

**INDIAN SILVERBILL** *Euodice malabarica* 11.5cm (4.5 in); 10–14g. **BEHAVIOR** Flocks. **DESCRIPTION** Overall light brown upperparts, white underparts and rump, and dark tail. Heavy bill is bluish. **VOICE** Usually quick, two-syllable *chit-tit*. Rarely a loud, musical song. **STATUS AND RANGE** Introduced. Common on southwestern coast of Puerto Rico. Rare and local in metropolitan San Juan. Recent records from St Croix (Virgin Islands). **HABITAT** Arid scrub, pastures, and gardens where grass is in seed.

RED AVADAVAT

br ♂

imm

adult ♀ & non-br ♂

BLACK-RUMPED WAXBILL

adult

imm

COMMON WAXBILL

adult

imm

adult

imm

ORANGE-CHEEKED WAXBILL

INDIAN SILVERBILL

## SCALY-BREASTED MUNIA (NUTMEG MANNIKIN)

*Lonchura punctulata* 11.5cm (4.5in); 14g. BEHAVIOR Flocks. ADULT Cinnamon-colored hood and scalloped underparts are diagnostic. IMMATURE Cinnamon-colored above; paler below. VOICE Soft, plaintive, whistled *peet* dropping in pitch and fading at end. STATUS AND RANGE Introduced. Locally common and spreading in Cuba (primarily Havana and west), Hispaniola, Jamaica, Puerto Rico (particularly lowlands, but increasing islandwide), and Guadeloupe. Fairly common locally in Grand Cayman (Cayman Islands), and in St Christopher primarily around Basseterre. Formerly fairly common in Dominica prior to 2017 hurricane, but still present. HABITAT Lowland open areas such as sugarcane borders, road edges, and urban parks.

## BRONZE MANNIKIN *Spermestes cucullata* 10 cm (4 in); 8–12g. BEHAVIOR Flocks.

ADULT Black hood, dark grayish-brown back, and white belly with scalloped pattern on sides and flanks. IMMATURE Hood and scalloped markings faint or lacking. VOICE Coarse *crrit*. STATUS AND RANGE Introduced. Common around coast of Puerto Rico. Eastern population reduced by hurricanes of 2017. HABITAT Fields, lawns, and wherever grass is in seed.

## CHESTNUT MUNIA (CHESTNUT MANNIKIN) *Lonchura*

*atricapilla* 11.5cm (4.5in); 10–16g. BEHAVIOR Flocks. ADULT Black hood; cinnamon-colored back. Underparts pale brown with black belly patch. IMMATURE Cinnamon-brown above and pale tan below. VOICE Thin, nasal *honk*. STATUS AND RANGE Introduced. Uncommon and local in Jamaica, but increasing. Uncommon and local in Martinique. HABITAT High grass bordering dense vegetation, primarily in lowlands.

## TRICOLORED MUNIA (TRICOLORED MANNIKIN) *Lonchura malacca* 11.5cm (4.5in); 10–14g. BEHAVIOR Flocks. ADULT Black hood; cinnamon-colored back. Underparts white with black belly patch. IMMATURE Cinnamon-brown above and pale tan below. VOICE Thin, nasal *honk*. STATUS AND RANGE Introduced. Locally common in Cuba and Hispaniola; uncommon and very local in Jamaica; rare and local in Puerto Rico, where decimated by hurricanes of 2017. HABITAT High grass bordering dense vegetation.

## WHITE-HEADED MUNIA *Lonchura maja* 11cm (4.25in); 11–14g. BEHAVIOR Flocks.

ADULT Head, throat, and neck white; rest of body deep brown; bill bluish. IMMATURE Brown, paler on head and underparts. VOICE High-pitched *pee*. STATUS AND RANGE Introduced to Martinique, where locally common. HABITAT Brush, scrub, and grassy edges of sugarcane and other agricultural areas.

## CHESTNUT-BELLIED SEED-FINCH *Sporophila angolensis* 11cm (4.25in); 8g.

Extremely heavy bill. MALE Primarily black with reddish-brown lower breast, belly, and abdomen. Also white wing mark and underwing linings. FEMALE Brown overall, paler below. White underwing linings. VOICE Long series of musical whistles, speeding up and changing to a warble or twitter. STATUS AND RANGE Uncommon and local on Martinique. Introduced and established by 1984. HABITAT Grassy clearings and edges of sugarcane and other agricultural areas. Also shrubby edges.

SCALY-BREASTED MUNIA

adult

imm

BRONZE MANNIKIN

adult

imm

CHESTNUT MUNIA

adult

imm

TRICOLORED MUNIA

adult

imm

WHITE-HEADED MUNIA

adult

imm

♂

♀

CHESTNUT-BELLIED
SEEDFINCH

**WHITE-CROWNED SPARROW** Zonotrichia leucophrys 14–17cm (5.5–6.75in); 21–38g. ADULT Conspicuously black-and-white striped crown; gray underparts. IMMATURE Crown stripes brown and pale tan. STATUS AND RANGE Irregular, generally rare migrant October–November and rarer still non-breeding resident December–April in northern Bahamas and central and western Cuba. Rare as migrant in Cayman Islands primarily in October. Very rare or vagrant elsewhere in West Indies. HABITAT Open woodlands, gardens with trees, forest edges, and brushy fields.

**RUFOUS-COLLARED SPARROW** Zonotrichia capensis 15–16.5cm (5.75–6.5in); 17–31g. ADULT Black neck band; reddish-brown hindneck; gray crown with black stripes. Often displays slight crest. IMMATURE Duller and spotted below. Lacks black or reddish-brown markings. VOICE Accelerating trill, *whis-whis-whis-whis-whiswhisu-whiswhis*. STATUS AND RANGE Locally common permanent resident in Hispaniola. HABITAT Mountains, in forest edges and streamside thickets. Also undergrowth of pine forests.

**CHIPPING SPARROW** Spizella passerina 12.5–14.5cm (5–5.75in); 11–15g. NON-BREEDING ADULT AND IMMATURE Crown brown (immature) or reddish-brown (adult) with black streaks, dark eye-line, and grayish-tan or brown cheeks. Underparts gray in adult and tannish-gray in immature. BREEDING ADULT Reddish-brown crown; gray cheeks; white eyebrow stripe; black line through eye. (Grasshopper Sparrow has golden spot in front of eye. *See also* Clay-colored Sparrow.) STATUS AND RANGE Very rare migrant and non-breeding resident in northern Bahamas and central and western Cuba October–April. Vagrant to southern Bahamas. HABITAT Pastures, open areas, grassy fields, bushy thickets, and croplands.

**NORTHERN RED BISHOP** Euplectes franciscanus 12.5cm (5in); 12–22g. FEMALE AND NON-BREEDING MALE Mottled brown; pale tan eyebrow stripe; underparts, crown, and breast finely striped. (*See also* Plate 112.)

**GRASSHOPPER SPARROW** Ammodramus savannarum 12.5cm (5in); 17g. ADULT Golden mark forward of eyebrow stripe; whitish central crown stripe. (Brown-plumaged Yellow-crowned and Northern Red Bishops lack single central crown stripe.) IMMATURE Paler mark by bill; fine streaks on breast and flanks. VOICE Long, thin, insect-like *buzz*, then hiccup. Very thin, high-pitched twitter. Gritty, insect-like *kr-r-it*. STATUS AND RANGE Common but local permanent resident in Jamaica, Hispaniola, and Puerto Rico. Migrant and non-breeding resident October–April in Cuba, where uncommon, and in Bahamas and Cayman Islands, where rare. HABITAT Weedy fields, pastures with tall grass, rice plantations.

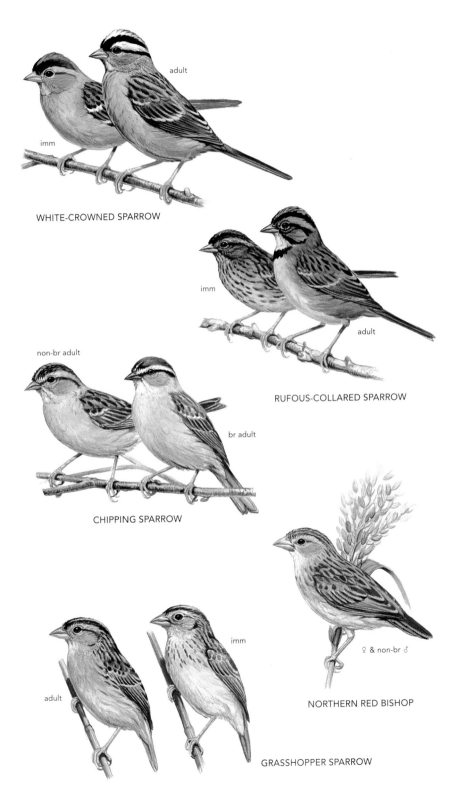

WHITE-CROWNED SPARROW

adult

imm

RUFOUS-COLLARED SPARROW

imm

adult

non-br adult

CHIPPING SPARROW

br adult

NORTHERN RED BISHOP

♀ & non-br ♂

GRASSHOPPER SPARROW

adult

imm

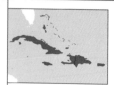

**LINCOLN'S SPARROW** *Melospiza lincolnii* 13.5–15cm (5.25–5.75in); 18g. Difficult to detect. **ADULT** Central crown stripe, eyebrow stripe, ear-patch, and sides of neck pale gray. Breast pale tan, finely streaked black. **IMMATURE** Similar, but eyebrow stripe tannish-white. **STATUS AND RANGE** Decidedly rare migrant and less frequent non-breeding resident in Bahamas, Cuba, and Jamaica. Very rare in Hispaniola and Puerto Rico. Occurs October–April. Vagrant elsewhere in West Indies. **HABITAT** Moist highland forest thickets, especially around clearings. Also coastal thickets and borders of dense forests.

**SAVANNAH SPARROW** *Passerculus sandwichensis* 15–19cm (5.75–7.5in); 20g. Slender; underparts heavily streaked brown; eyebrow stripe usually yellowish, conspicuous, sometimes pale tan; pale central crown stripe; dark mustache stripe. (Immature Grasshopper Sparrow has finer, paler streaks below.) **VOICE** High-pitched, melodious call of three *chip*s, then two wispy notes, the last shorter and lower, *chip-chip-chip-tisisiiii-tisi*. **STATUS AND RANGE** Generally uncommon migrant and non-breeding resident in northern Bahamas and Cuba. Rare in Cayman Islands (Grand Cayman). Occurs October–April. Vagrant elsewhere. **HABITAT** Open fields, pastures, bushy savannas, and sparse thickets near coast.

**CLAY-COLORED SPARROW** *Spizella pallida* 12–13.5cm (4.75–5.25in); 12g. **ADULT** Pale brownish above; bold black streaks on back; brownish or grayish rump; white median stripe on crown; wide whitish eyebrow and mustache stripes; brown cheek patch outlined by thin dark lines; pale lores; gray hindneck contrasting with back. **IMMATURE** Similar, but fine streaks on breast; head pattern less well defined. **STATUS AND RANGE** Generally, rare migrant in Cayman Islands in October and very rare migrant and non-breeding resident in northern Bahamas and Cuba October–February. Irregular occurrence. Vagrant elsewhere in West Indies. **HABITAT** Coastal thickets, borders of salt ponds, and bushy areas.

**HOUSE SPARROW** *Passer domesticus* 15cm (5.75in); 28g. **BEHAVIOR** Flocks. **MALE** Black bib, gray crown, and pale cheek. **FEMALE AND IMMATURE** Pale tan eyebrow stripe and underparts; brown upperparts streaked with black. **VOICE** Distinctive *chirp*. **STATUS AND RANGE** Introduced. Common and widespread in northern Bahamas, Cuba, Hispaniola, Puerto Rico, Virgin Islands, and northern Lesser Antilles south to Guadeloupe. Uncommon and local in southern Bahamas (Great Inagua, Turks and Caicos), Cayman Islands (George Town), St Vincent, and Grenadines. Rare and local in Jamaica. Range expanding. **HABITAT** Urban areas.

**AMERICAN PIPIT** *Anthus rubescens* 16.5cm (6.5in); 20g. **BEHAVIOR** Flocks, primarily terrestrial. Regularly bobs tail. **DESCRIPTION** Thin bill; long tail. Conspicuous white outertail feathers in flight. **NON-BREEDING ADULT** Tannish-white eyebrow stripe, two faint wing bars; pale pinkish-tan underparts (October, November) or pale gray underparts (January–March), with blackish stripes concentrated on breast. **STATUS AND RANGE** Generally very rare migrant and non-breeding resident in Bahamas south to San Salvador October–March. Sometimes occurs in numbers. Vagrant elsewhere in West Indies. **HABITAT** Sandy areas.

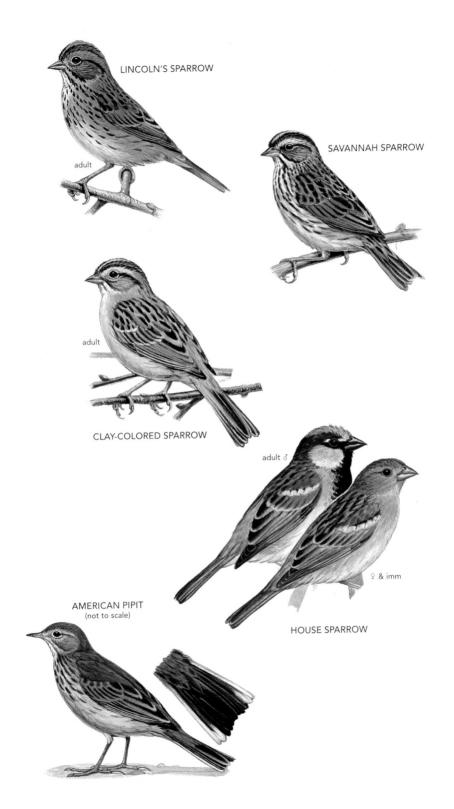

LINCOLN'S SPARROW

adult

SAVANNAH SPARROW

adult

CLAY-COLORED SPARROW

adult ♂

♀ & imm

HOUSE SPARROW

AMERICAN PIPIT
(not to scale)

**TRINDADE PETREL** *Pterodroma arminjoniana* 35–39cm (14–15in); wingspan 88–100cm (3–3.3ft); 270–475g. Medium-sized. Wings long and narrow, beat faster than shearwaters. Coloration variable, with dark, light, and intermediate morphs. Dark morph—Similar to Sooty Shearwater, but tail longer, bill heavier, and less white on underwings. Light morph—Underparts white, but with dark patch nearly surrounding neck. Underwings darker than similar shearwaters in region with white underparts. Intermediate morph—Variable coloration between the dark and light morphs. **STATUS AND RANGE** Vagrant to West Indies. Frequents Gulf Stream. **HABITAT** At sea.

**BLACK-BROWED ALBATROSS** *Thalassarche melanophris* 80–95cm (31–37in); wingspan 2–2.4m (7–8ft); 3–4.5kg. A very large, primarily white seabird with stiff, long wings. Note dark eye mark, yellow bill tipped with orange, and white underwings edged with black. **STATUS AND RANGE** Vagrant to the West Indies, where it could occur off any island. **HABITAT** At sea.

**BULWER'S PETREL** *Bulweria bulwerii* 25–29cm (10–11.5in); wingspan 63–73cm (2–2.5ft); 75–140g. Larger than other storm-petrels of region and with a long, pointed tail. Entirely sooty-brown with no white markings. In flight note pale diagonal bars traversing upper side of wings. **FLIGHT** Buoyant and erratic low over the water, with short wingbeats followed by glides. Does not follow boats. **STATUS AND RANGE** Vagrant to West Indies, where recorded primarily off Guadeloupe and Dominica, but could occur off any island. **HABITAT** At sea.

**DOVEKIE** *Alle alle* 17–20cm (6.75–8in); 140–190g. Small, stout seabird with short, thick neck, large head, and short, stubby black bill. **NON-BREEDING ADULT** Black above; white below extending well around neck. **BREEDING ADULT** Head and breast entirely black. **FLIGHT** Wingbeats blurringly rapid. **STATUS AND RANGE** Vagrant to West Indies October–December where most likely seen in Bahamas and Cuba. **HABITAT** At sea.

**BLACK NODDY** *Anous minutus* 35–39cm (14–16in); wingspan 76cm (2.5ft); 100–145g. Entirely blackish-brown with white crown. Very similar to Brown Noddy, but with longer, thinner bill; white of crown extending farther down hindneck; neck noticeably more slender; underwings darker. Best distinguished by voice. **VOICE** Sharp, dry nasal cackles, chatters, and squeaky notes. Also plaintive, piping, whistled *wheeeaeee*, with rising inflection. **STATUS AND RANGE** Vagrant to West Indies. **HABITAT** Well offshore and around rocky islets.

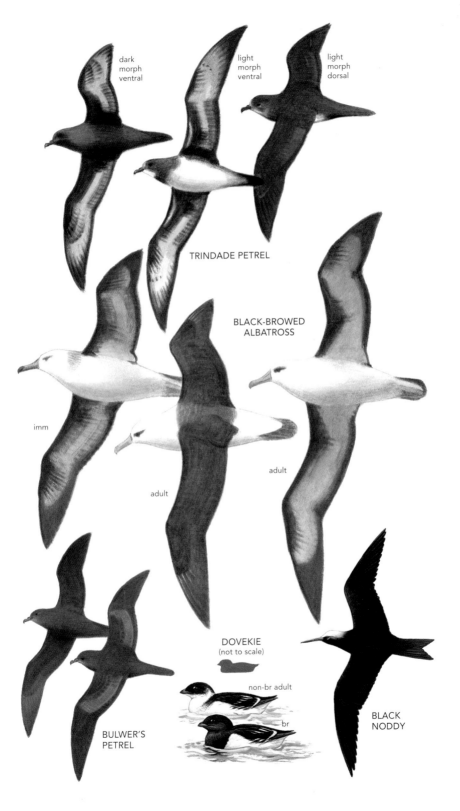

dark morph ventral

light morph ventral

light morph dorsal

TRINDADE PETREL

BLACK-BROWED ALBATROSS

imm

adult

adult

BULWER'S PETREL

DOVEKIE
(not to scale)

non-br adult

br

BLACK NODDY

**FRANKLIN'S GULL** *Leucophaeus pipixcan* 37cm (14.5in); wingspan 90cm (3ft); 280g. FIRST YEAR Narrow black tail band; white breast and underparts; gray back; partial blackish hood, and white forehead. NON-BREEDING ADULT Similar, but only partial black hood; whitish forehead. BREEDING ADULT Black head; fairly dark gray mantle and wingtips with black bar bordered with white on both sides. First year and non-breeding adults have more distinctive partial black hood and white forehead. (Laughing Gull is larger, with heavier, more curved bill; darker undersides of primaries; and longer legs noticeable when standing.) STATUS AND RANGE Vagrant to West Indies. HABITAT Bays and estuaries.

**SABINE'S GULL** *Xema sabini* 27–33cm (11–13in); wingspan 84cm (33in); 85g. A small gull. In all plumages the tricolored wing pattern in flight, particularly the large triangular wing patch, is diagnostic. Tail slightly forked. STATUS AND RANGE Vagrant to West Indies. Could occur on any island. HABITAT Generally at sea.

**WHISKERED TERN** *Chlidonias hybrida* 23–29cm (9–12in); wingspan 64–70cm (25–28in); 60–100g. Small, with slightly notched tail. NON-BREEDING ADULT Primarily pale gray above with ample black in primaries. Rear of crown black, extends to eye; legs red. BREEDING ADULT Black crown and dark gray underparts highlight white cheek. (Non-breeding Black Tern is darker above and has dark patch on side of neck. Non-breeding White-winged Tern's whitish rump contrasts with darker back.) STATUS AND RANGE Vagrant to West Indies, particularly Barbados. HABITAT Inland freshwater bodies, also calm coastal waters.

**WHITE-WINGED TERN** *Chlidonias leucopterus* 22–27cm (9–10.5in); wingspan 58–67cm (23–26in); 42–79g. Small, with slightly notched tail. NON-BREEDING ADULT Black ear-spot and rear of crown; white rump; lacks dark neck mark. BREEDING ADULT Black except for white tail and rear of body. Wings pale gray with black underwing linings; legs red. (Non-breeding Black Tern has gray rump, dark mark on side of neck, dark legs, and darker wings, especially upper forewing.) STATUS AND RANGE Vagrant in West Indies, particularly Barbados. HABITAT Inland freshwater bodies.

**COLLARED PRATINCOLE** *Glareola pratincola* 24–28cm (9.5–11in); wingspan 60–70cm (24–28in); 60–100g. BEHAVIOR Hawks for insects. DESCRIPTION Primarily brown with pale tan throat edged in black; base of bill orange-red. FLIGHT Long, pointed wings reddish-brown below; tail long and forked; rump white. STATUS AND RANGE Vagrant to West Indies, where recorded from Lesser Antilles (Barbados and Guadeloupe). Could occur on any island. HABITAT Open country, usually near water.

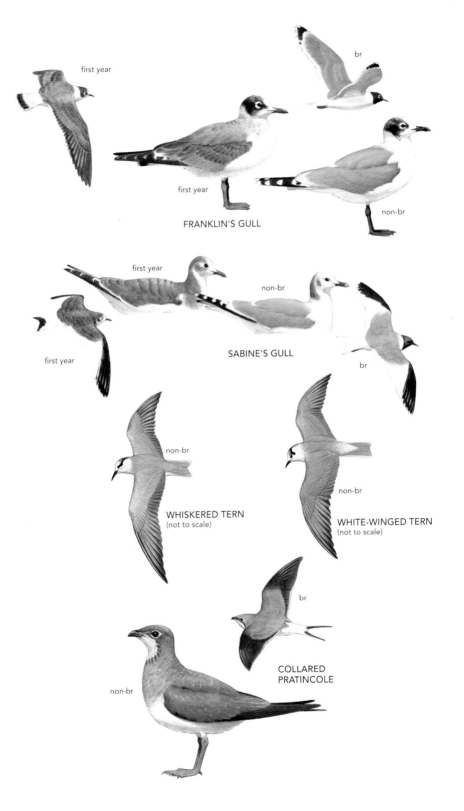

first year

br

first year

non-br

FRANKLIN'S GULL

first year

non-br

first year

SABINE'S GULL

br

non-br

WHISKERED TERN
(not to scale)

non-br

WHITE-WINGED TERN
(not to scale)

br

COLLARED
PRATINCOLE

non-br

**STRIATED HERON** *Butorides striata* 40–48cm (16–19in); 160g. Small, with short neck, greenish-yellow to orangish legs. Pale gray cheek and sides of neck differentiate it from Green Heron. The unusual brown morph is very similar to the Green Heron but is paler with grayish to reddish-brown on sides of its neck rather than the chestnut color of Green Heron. Also, its belly is usually grayer. **IMMATURE** Heavily streaked below. **VOICE** *Kek*, *kak*, or *que* notes; piercing *skyow* when disturbed. **STATUS AND RANGE** Vagrant to West Indies, where most frequent in Lesser Antilles and Puerto Rico. **HABITAT** All water bodies.

**WESTERN REEF-HERON** *Egretta gularis* 55–65cm (22–25.5in); wingspan 1.1m (3.6ft); 400g. Stout bill. Two color phases and intermediates. **BREEDING ADULT** Dark phase—Dark gray; chin and throat white, lower breast and belly tinged brown, legs black, bill brownish-black; feet yellowish-green. White phase—White; two long head plumes, legs dark olive-green, feet yellow, lores greenish-yellow or green, bill yellowish-brown, with paler lower mandible. **IMMATURE** White; variably brown; bill dull brown. (Snowy and Little Egrets have less bulky bodies, longer legs, and shorter and thicker necks, and lack slight droop to bill.) Only dark phase has been recorded to date in West Indies. **STATUS AND RANGE** Vagrant in Barbados. Occurred regularly from 1990s to 2006, but no recent records. **HABITAT** Ponds and lagoons.

**EURASIAN SPOONBILL** *Platalea leucorodia* 80–90cm (32–36in); wingspan 1.1–1.4m (3.7–4.5ft); 1–2kg. Large water bird. White, with long, spatula-like bill. **STATUS AND RANGE** Vagrant to Lesser Antilles, particularly Barbados. **HABITAT** Shallow saltwater lagoons and other water edges.

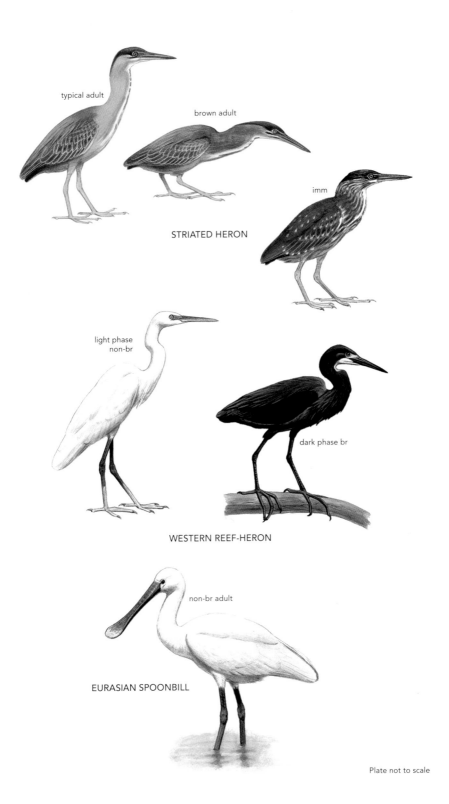

typical adult

brown adult

imm

STRIATED HERON

light phase
non-br

dark phase br

WESTERN REEF-HERON

non-br adult

EURASIAN SPOONBILL

Plate not to scale

**SPOTTED CRAKE** *Porzana porzana* 22–24cm (9.5–10in); 90g. **BEHAVIOR** Most active at dusk or after dark. **DESCRIPTION** Similar to Sora rail, but underparts flecked with white, undertail-coverts pale tan, and lacks black on face and throat. **FLIGHT** Shows large pale wing patches. **VOICE** Repeated high-pitched, sharp *we-eet* notes like a snapping whip. **STATUS AND RANGE** Vagrant to St Martin and Guadeloupe. **HABITAT** Edges of dense vegetation of ponds and marshes.

**COMMON RINGED PLOVER** *Charadrius hiaticula* 19cm (7.5in); 42–78g. Very similar to Semipalmated Plover, but broader black breast band, longer bill, and more pronounced white eyebrow stripe. Breast band less pronounced in non-breeding season. Best distinguished by voice. **VOICE** A melodious two-syllable whistle, *choo-ee*. **STATUS AND RANGE** Vagrant to Jamaica, Barbados, and Guadeloupe. Should be looked for on other islands. **HABITAT** Water edges. Primarily tidal mud flats, but also rocky shorelines or inland pond margins.

**PACIFIC GOLDEN-PLOVER** *Pluvialis fulva* 23–26cm (9–10.2in); 100–225g. **BEHAVIOR** Flocks. **DESCRIPTION** Fairly large; slender; long-legged. More slender and longer-legged than American Golden-Plover, also wings are shorter and do not project beyond tail as in latter. Golden cast (yellower than American Golden-Plover) on back, face, and eyebrow stripe; breast also yellower. **BREEDING** Black below; mottled black and yellowish-brown above. (Less white on neck than American Golden-Plover, but white band extends down sides and flanks to whitish undertail-coverts.) **STATUS AND RANGE** Vagrant, primarily on Barbados. **HABITAT** Fields and golf courses; also tidal flats.

**NORTHERN LAPWING** *Vanellus vanellus* 28–31cm (11–12in); 130–330g. Large, crested plover with broad black breast band, black on forehead extending to tip of crest, and dark, greenish upperparts. (Southern Lapwing has darker face, paler upperparts, and lacks black on crown and crest.) **FLIGHT** Wingbeats slow and floppy, with no white on upperwing. (Southern Lapwing displays broad white bars on upperwing and base of tail.) Underwing shows white wing lining. **IMMATURE** Crest and color pattern less conspicuous. **STATUS AND RANGE** Vagrant to West Indies. **HABITAT** Grasslands and tidal flats.

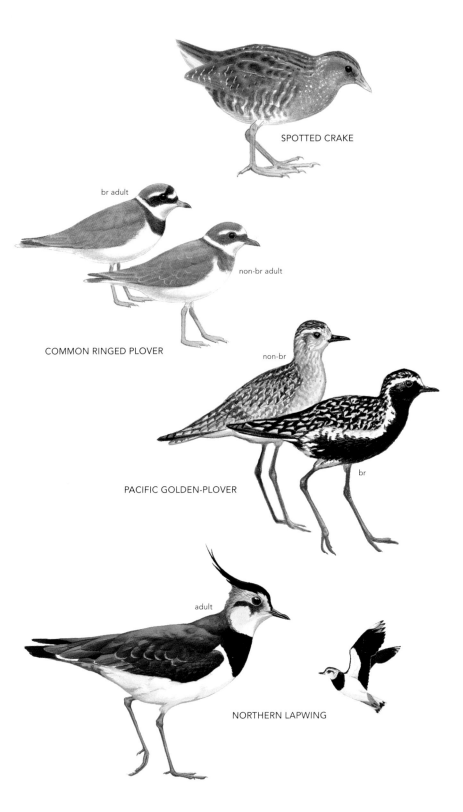

SPOTTED CRAKE

br adult

non-br adult

COMMON RINGED PLOVER

non-br

br

PACIFIC GOLDEN-PLOVER

adult

NORTHERN LAPWING

**LONG-BILLED CURLEW** *Numenius americanus* 51–66cm (20–26in); 450–980g. Large, with extremely long, down-curved bill. Mottled cinnamon-brown above, paler below; legs bluish. **FLIGHT** Cinnamon wing linings. **STATUS AND RANGE** Vagrant to West Indies. **HABITAT** Mud flats, lagoons, wetlands, sand bars, and shorelines.

**LITTLE STINT** *Calidris minuta* 12–14cm (4.5–5.5in); 17–44g. Smallest sandpiper, very similar to Semipalmated, but smaller; finer, straighter bill; paler ear-coverts and crown. Generally seen in non-breeding plumage. **VOICE** Clear *tip* or *tit*. **STATUS AND RANGE** Vagrant to Lesser Antilles. **HABITAT** Mud flats. Typically with other waders.

**SPOTTED REDSHANK** *Tringa erythropus* 29–32cm (11.5–12.5in); 100–230g. Red legs and base of lower mandible. **FLIGHT** Large white patch on lower back. **NON-BREEDING ADULT AND IMMATURE** Gray above, paler below; blackish lores, paler in immature; white eyebrow stripe. **BREEDING ADULT** Black, heavily spotted white. **STATUS AND RANGE** Vagrant to West Indies. **HABITAT** Shorelines, tide pools, marshes.

**TUNDRA SWAN** *Cygnus columbianus* 1.1–1.5m (3.6–4.9ft); wingspan 1.8m (5.5ft); 4–10kg. **BEHAVIOR** Surface feeder; flocks. **DESCRIPTION** Huge, with long neck and short legs. **ADULT** White; bill black, sometimes yellow on lores. **IMMATURE** Pale grayish-brown; bill pinkish. **STATUS AND RANGE** Vagrant to West Indies. **HABITAT** Shallow ponds and lagoons.

**ORINOCO GOOSE** *Neochen jubata* 61–67cm (24–26.5in); 1.5–2kg. **BEHAVIOR** Surface feeder, often grazes. **DESCRIPTION** Large, with pale gray head and neck. Reddish-brown body; dark wings with white speculum. **STATUS AND RANGE** Vagrant to West Indies. Recorded from Barbados and Jamaica. **HABITAT** Freshwater marshes and wet savannas.

**GREATER WHITE-FRONTED GOOSE** *Anser albifrons* 66–86cm (26–34in); 2–3.5kg. **BEHAVIOR** Surface feeder, often grazes; flocks. **DESCRIPTION** Medium-sized. **ADULT** Brownish-gray above; white rump; pink or orange bill with white edge; belly barred black. **IMMATURE** Uniform dark brown. **STATUS AND RANGE** Vagrant to West Indies. **HABITAT** Ponds and lagoons.

**BRANT** *Branta bernicla* 55–66cm (22–26in); wingspan 1.1–1.3m (3.6–4.3ft); 1–1.5kg. **BEHAVIOR** Surface feeder; flocks. **DESCRIPTION** A small goose with a black head, neck, and breast. (Canada Goose much larger, with white patch on face. Also a more terrestrial and freshwater bird.) **STATUS AND RANGE** Vagrant to West Indies. **HABITAT** Shallow bays and calm coastal waters.

LONG-BILLED CURLEW

adult

LITTLE STINT

br adult

non-br
adult

SPOTTED REDSHANK

non-br adult
& imm

TUNDRA SWAN

imm

adult

ORINOCO GOOSE

adult

imm

GREATER WHITE-FRONTED GOOSE

BRANT

adult *B. b hrota*

Plate not to scale

**CANVASBACK** *Aythya valisineria* 51–61cm (20–24in); 1–1.5kg. **BEHAVIOR** Dives, flocks. **DESCRIPTION** Sloping forehead profile. (Similarly patterned Redhead lacks sloping forehead.) **MALE** Reddish-brown head and neck. **FEMALE** Brown head and neck; less contrast in plumage. **FLIGHT** Elongated appearance. **FLYING MALE** White belly and underwings sandwiched between black breast and tail. **FLYING FEMALE** Whitish belly and underwings contrast with dark breast and tail. **STATUS AND RANGE** Vagrant in West Indies primarily October–March. **HABITAT** Large, deep lagoons.

**BUFFLEHEAD** *Bucephala albeola* 33–38cm (13–15in); 230–600g. **BEHAVIOR** Dives, flocks. **DESCRIPTION** Small. **MALE** Large white head patch; white forewing; plumage primarily white. **FEMALE** Much browner; white facial stripe. **FLYING MALE** White forewing and secondaries. **FLYING FEMALE** White secondaries. **STATUS AND RANGE** Vagrant in West Indies October–March. **HABITAT** Open bays.

**AMERICAN BLACK DUCK** *Anas rubripes* 53–64cm (21–25in); 0.7–1.7kg. **BEHAVIOR** Surface feeder. **DESCRIPTION** Dark brown with purple speculum. **MALE** Bill yellow. **FEMALE** Bill olive and mottled black. **FLIGHT** White underwings contrast with dark body; purple speculum. **STATUS AND RANGE** Vagrant to West Indies. **HABITAT** Shallow waters.

**TUFTED DUCK** *Aythya fuligula* 40–47cm (16–19in); 0.6–1kg. **BEHAVIOR** Dives. **MALE** Very similar to Ring-necked Duck, best distinguished by entirely white flanks (Ring-necked has only white vertical shoulder bar), long crest (not always visible), and absence of white ring on bill. **FEMALE** Similar to scaup and Ring-necked, but lacks eye-ring of latter and has smaller white facial shield than former. **STATUS AND RANGE** Vagrant to West Indies. Could occur on any island. **HABITAT** Primarily bodies of open fresh water.

**GARGANEY** *Spatula querquedula* 37–41cm (14.5–16in); 240–580g. **BEHAVIOR** Surface feeder. **FEMALE AND NON-BREEDING MALE** Very similar to Blue-winged and Green-winged Teal but facial markings more defined, especially whitish eyebrow stripe; crown darker; dark legs (Blue-winged are yellowish); dark undertail-coverts (Green-winged are white). **BREEDING MALE** Lengthy white eyebrow stripe. **STATUS AND RANGE** Vagrant to West Indies. Could occur on any island. **HABITAT** Shallow wetlands.

**WHITE-FACED WHISTLING-DUCK** *Dendrocygna viduata* 38–48cm (15–19in); 500–820g. **BEHAVIOR** Surface feeder, nocturnal, flocks. **ADULT** White face. **IMMATURE** Paler; face beige. **FLIGHT** Wings dark above and below; no white markings except on head. Head and feet droop; feet extend beyond tail. **VOICE** High-pitched three-note whistle. **STATUS AND RANGE** Vagrant to West Indies. Could occur on any island. **HABITAT** Open wetlands.

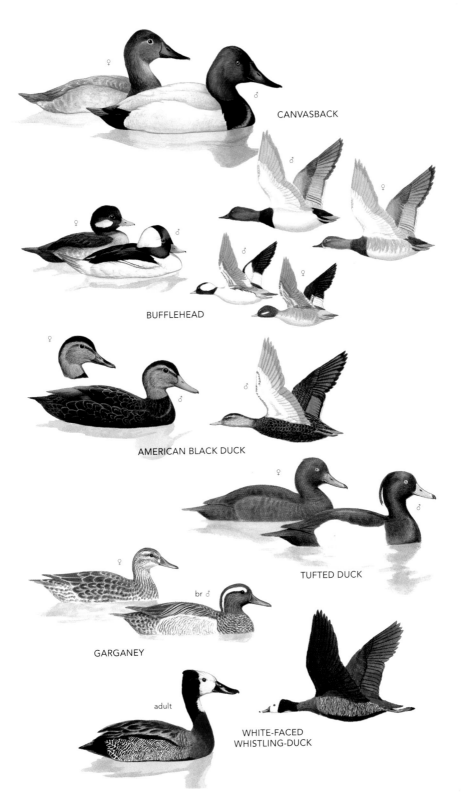

CANVASBACK

BUFFLEHEAD

AMERICAN BLACK DUCK

TUFTED DUCK

GARGANEY

adult

WHITE-FACED
WHISTLING-DUCK

**BALD EAGLE** *Haliaeetus leucocephalus* 70–102cm (28–40in); wingspan 1.8–2.3m (6–7.5ft); male 4.2kg, female 5.1kg. Very large. **ADULT** Primarily dark brown with white head and tail. **IMMATURE** Brown overall. Takes four to five years to acquire adult plumage. **FLIGHT** Soars with wings flat; wings and tail broad; immature displays mottled white on underwings and tail, which varies depending on age. **STATUS AND RANGE** Vagrant to West Indies. Most likely to occur in northern Bahamas and Cuba. Occurrence likely to increase with recovery of species in North America. **HABITAT** Near water bodies.

**EURASIAN KESTREL** *Falco tinnunculus* 27–35cm (10.5–13.8in); male 200g, female 260g. **BEHAVIOR** Perches on fence posts and electrical wires. **DESCRIPTION** A fairly large falcon. **MALE** Differs from American Kestrel by larger size, combination of bluish-gray head with reddish back and wings, and bluish-gray tail with black terminal band. **FEMALE** Larger size, more heavily striped underparts, and lack of facial stripe behind eye. **FLIGHT** Pointed wings; long, slender tail; hovers. **STATUS AND RANGE** Vagrant to West Indies. Could occur on any island. **HABITAT** Open country.

**WESTERN MARSH HARRIER** *Circus aeruginosus* 48–55cm (19–22in); wingspan 1.2–1.5m (3.8–4.8ft); male 560g, female 750g. Large; with long, slender wings and tail. Lacks white rump of Northern Harrier. **MALE** Brown overall, heavily striped below; pale gray wings and tail; rust-colored belly and abdomen; pale tan-colored head and breast. **FEMALE** Dark brown overall, lacks stripes; crown and throat whitish. **FLIGHT** Tilting glides low over ground with wings held in shallow "V." **FLIGHT MALE** Underwings pale gray with black tips, tail pale gray. **FLIGHT FEMALE** Wings brown, but leading edge of upperwing whitish. **VOICE** High-pitched *quee-a*. **STATUS AND RANGE** Vagrant to West Indies. Could occur on any island. **HABITAT** Marshes.

**BLACK KITE** *Milvus migrans* 55–60cm (22–24in); wingspan 1.2–1.5m (4–5ft); male 240g, female 320g. Variable coloration. Generally dark brown above, reddish-brown below with fine streaks, head and forewing variably pale gray to brown. Tail long and often slightly notched. **FLIGHT** Dark overall, with pale gray head and diagonal band crossing upper wing. Wings held flat; often twists tail. Frequently soars and glides. **VOICE** Very vocal. Shrill whistle and rapid whinnying call. **STATUS AND RANGE** Vagrant to West Indies. Could occur on any island. **HABITAT** Open or semi-open areas, usually near or over water.

BALD EAGLE

imm

adult

EURASIAN KESTREL

♀

♂

♀

♂

WESTERN MARSH HARRIER

♂

BLACK KITE

adult

Plate not to scale

**LEAST FLYCATCHER** *Empidonax minimus* 13cm (5.25in); 11g. White eye-ring; two white wing bars; white chin; pale yellow belly. Best distinguished from other *Empidonax* by voice. **VOICE** Distinctive, unmusical *che-bek* with accent on second syllable. Also sharp *weep* or *wit*, often repeated rapidly. **STATUS AND RANGE** Vagrant to West Indies, where recorded from Cuba and Grand Cayman (Cayman Islands). Likely occurs more regularly in western Cuba. **HABITAT** Brush and open woodland.

**EULER'S FLYCATCHER** *Lathrotriccus euleri* 13.5–14cm (5.25–5.5in); 9–14g. **BEHAVIOR** Sallies from low perch for insects. Flicks tail up and down with jerky motion. **DESCRIPTION** Pale tan or pale reddish-brown wing bars; underparts yellowish with grayish-olive breast band; whitish eye-ring. **VOICE** Murmuring *pee, de-dee-dee-dee-dee*, first note higher. **STATUS AND RANGE** Vagrant to Grenada. Believed to have formerly bred there. Not reported since 1955. **HABITAT** Primarily moist mountain forests.

**TROPICAL KINGBIRD** *Tyrannus melancholicus* 23cm (9in); 32–46g. Fairly large, with primarily yellow underparts, pale gray crown, greenish back, and gray facial mask. Crown patch usually concealed. (Western Kingbird smaller, with white in outertail feathers.) **VOICE** Similar to Gray Kingbird, but softer, less emphatic *pip-pri-pip-pri-pip-pri* ... **STATUS AND RANGE** Vagrant in West Indies. Formerly resident in Grenada, but absent since about 1940. **HABITAT** Open, semi-arid scrubland.

**TOWNSEND'S WARBLER** *Setophaga townsendi* 13cm (5in); 9g. Dark cheek ringed with yellow. **ADULT MALE** Black cheek, chin, throat, and side streaks; yellow lower breast and belly; white outertail feathers. **ADULT FEMALE** Slightly duller; yellow chin and throat; white belly. **IMMATURE** Paler. Cheeks olive-green; underparts may lack black or have only fine streaks. (Black-throated Green Warbler has paler, yellower cheeks; less yellow on breast. Blackburnian Warbler has striped back.) **STATUS AND RANGE** Vagrant to northern Bahamas and Cayman Islands. **HABITAT** Forests, primarily conifers.

LEAST FLYCATCHER

EULER'S FLYCATCHER

TROPICAL KINGBIRD

TOWNSEND'S WARBLER

adult ♂

imm

Plate not to scale

**ALPINE SWIFT** *Apus melba* 20–22cm (8–9in); 80–120g. **BEHAVIOR** Aerial, typically flocks. **DESCRIPTION** Large swift, grayish-brown above, whitish below; dark bar across breast. **FLIGHT** Fast and erratic flight propelled by shallow, rapid flapping on stiff, bow-shaped wings. **STATUS AND RANGE** Vagrant to West Indies. **HABITAT** Open areas and fields.

**COMMON HOUSE-MARTIN** *Delichon urbicum* 12.5–14cm (5–5.5in); 11–23g. **BEHAVIOR** Flocks; often perches on wires. **DESCRIPTION** Distinctive white rump; tail notched. **ADULT** White below. **IMMATURE** Grayish wash on breast and sides. **VOICE** Scratchy *prrit* or *chirrp*. **STATUS AND RANGE** Vagrant to West Indies (Barbados and Guadeloupe). Should be looked for on other islands. **HABITAT** Open areas, often near water.

**COMMON CUCKOO** *Cuculus canorus* 32–34cm (13–14in); 110–130g. Gray overall, belly and abdomen white-barred gray. **FEMALE** Usually like male, but also a less common red phase that is reddish-brown above, barred with black; and white below shading to pale rufous on breast and throat, underparts entirely barred. Uppertail flecked with white. **FLIGHT** Pointed wings, long tail, deep wingbeats, usually low over ground. **STATUS AND RANGE** Vagrant to Barbados. Should be looked for on other islands. **HABITAT** Primarily open country with bushes and trees.

**EASTERN BLUEBIRD** *Sialia sialis* 15–16.5cm (5.75–6.5in); 30g. **ADULT MALE** Bright blue upperparts including tail and wings; reddish throat, breast, sides, flanks, and upper belly; white lower belly and undertail-coverts. **ADULT FEMALE** Duller, with whitish eye-ring. **IMMATURE** Grayish-blue above flecked with white; breast and upper belly whitish with conspicuous gray ringlets. **VOICE** Clear whistle, *chur-lee*. **STATUS AND RANGE** Vagrant to Bahamas, western Cuba, and Virgin Islands. Should be looked for in northern Bahamas and western Cuba. **HABITAT** Field edges and open country with hedgerows.

**LAZULI BUNTING** *Passerina amoena* 14cm (5.5in); 16g. **NON-BREEDING MALE** Mottled brown and blue overall with orange breast and white wing bar. **FEMALE** Primarily brown with traces of blue on rump; pale wing bars. **BREEDING MALE** Blue head and upperparts; breast orange; belly, abdomen, and wing bar white. (Similar Eastern Bluebird has much finer bill and lacks white wing bar.) **STATUS AND RANGE** Vagrant to Cuba. May occur more frequently than recorded. **HABITAT** Primarily brushy areas.

ALPINE SWIFT

COMMON HOUSE-MARTIN

adult

adult

adult ♂

♀ red phase

COMMON CUCKOO

EASTERN BLUEBIRD

adult ♂

adult ♀

non-br ♂

♀

br ♂

LAZULI BUNTING

**HOODED ORIOLE** *Icterus cucullatus* 20cm (8in); 24g. ADULT MALE Orange-yellow with black throat, breast, wings, back, and tail; two white wing bars. ADULT FEMALE AND IMMATURE Olive-yellow overall; two white wing bars, lower less conspicuous. Longer, more slender, down-curved bill and longer tail than Orchard Oriole. STATUS AND RANGE Vagrant to Cuba. HABITAT Palms, woodlands, and thickets.

**EASTERN WHIP-POOR-WILL** *Antrostomus vociferus* 23–26cm (9–10in); 43–63g. BEHAVIOR Nocturnal. MALE Mottled grayish-brown; blackish throat; narrow white throat stripe; outertail feathers broadly tipped white. FEMALE Duller; throat stripe pale tan; outertail feathers narrowly tipped pale tan. VOICE Repeated *whip-poor-will*. Usually not vocal in West Indies. STATUS AND RANGE Vagrant to Bahamas, Cuba, and Jamaica. HABITAT Dry, open woodlands.

**GREATER ANI** *Crotophaga major* 46–49cm (18–19.3in); male 165g, female 140g. Large, glossy blue-black overall, with long tail, distinctive keel atop bill, and whitish eye. (Similar Smooth-billed Ani is smaller, has dark eye, and lacks bluish sheen.) STATUS AND RANGE Vagrant to West Indies. HABITAT Open woodlands, thickets, and forest edges, often near water.

**FISH CROW** *Corvus ossifragus* 36–40cm (14–16in); 260–300g. A small crow, entirely black with a short tail, best distinguished by voice. Much chunkier than all grackles and lacks long, wedge-shaped tail. VOICE A high-pitched nasal *ka* or *ka-ka*. STATUS AND RANGE Vagrant to Bahamas, primarily Grand Bahama. Appears to be occurring with increased regularity. HABITAT Primarily coastal marshes.

**HOUSE CROW** *Corvus splendens* 40–43cm (16–17in); 250–370g. A "two-toned" crow. The face, throat, forecrown, back, wings, and tail are black, while entire neck, hindcrown, and underparts are gray (sometimes dark beige). VOICE A harsh, flat *caaa-caaa*. STATUS AND RANGE Vagrant to West Indies (Cuba, Barbados). Likely arrive via ship transport. HABITAT Primarily around human habitations.

adult ♂

HOODED ORIOLE

adult ♀
& imm

EASTERN WHIP-POOR-WILL

GREATER ANI

FISH CROW
(not to scale)

HOUSE CROW
(not to scale)

**VESPER SPARROW** *Pooecetes gramineus* 14–18cm (5.5–7in); 20–28g. Chunky; barred below. Note white eye-ring and outertail feathers; ear patch usually bordered with white along bottom edge; rusty shoulder patch (not always visible); sometimes a faint whitish eyebrow stripe. (Savannah Sparrow has bold, often yellowish eyebrow stripe and lacks white outertail feathers.) **STATUS AND RANGE** Vagrant to West Indies, primarily Bahamas. **HABITAT** Open grassy, gravelly, or weedy fields.

**LARK SPARROW** *Chondestes grammacus* 14–18cm (5.5–7in); 25–33g. **ADULT** Bold head and facial pattern; black breast spot; large white patches on outer corners of tail. **IMMATURE** Head pattern less distinct; breast pale grayish and heavily streaked. **STATUS AND RANGE** Vagrant to northern Bahamas, Cuba, and Jamaica August–March. **HABITAT** Open semi-arid areas with scattered bushes.

**SWAMP SPARROW** *Melospiza georgiana* 12–15cm (4.75–6in); 13–24g. **NON-BREEDING ADULT** Gray central crown stripe, eyebrow stripe, cheek patch, and sides of neck; blackish mustache mark; white throat; breast grayish with a few blackish streaks. **IMMATURE** Similar, but breast and throat unstreaked gray; grayish cheek patch. **BREEDING ADULT** Crown reddish-brown. **STATUS AND RANGE** Vagrant to Bahamas. Occurs primarily November–May. **HABITAT** Marshes and brushy areas.

**DARK-EYED JUNCO** *Junco hyemalis* 13–17cm (5.25–6.75in); 15–25g. **BEHAVIOR** Flocks. **DESCRIPTION** Blackish-gray overall; white belly and outertail feathers; pink bill. **STATUS AND RANGE** Vagrant to northern Bahamas, Cuba, Jamaica, Puerto Rico, Virgin and Cayman Islands. **HABITAT** Cultivated areas, field edges, hedgerows, lawns, and roadsides.

**AMERICAN GOLDFINCH** *Spinus tristis* 11–12cm (4.25–4.75in); 13–20g. **BEHAVIOR** Flocks. **NON-BREEDING ADULT AND IMMATURE** Brownish or grayish above; black wings with white wing bars; light gray to whitish below; whitish rump; often some yellowish on face. **BREEDING MALE** Bright yellow overall with black cap, wings, and tail. **BREEDING FEMALE** Olive above, yellowish below; black wings with white wing bars and white rump. **STATUS AND RANGE** Vagrant to northern Bahamas and Cuba. Occurs mid-October through December, also April. **HABITAT** Weedy fields, roadsides, thickets, and second growth.

**HORNED LARK** *Eremophila alpestris* 18–20cm (7–8in); 30–40g. Brown upperparts, whitish below with faint striping on sides. Distinctive facial pattern: note black mark before and under eye; black bar across breast; yellowish eyebrow stripe. Chin and throat usually pale yellow. **VOICE** Very high-pitched *tsee-ti-ti*. **STATUS AND RANGE** Vagrant to Bahamas. **HABITAT** Sand dunes, dirt or gravel fields, airports.

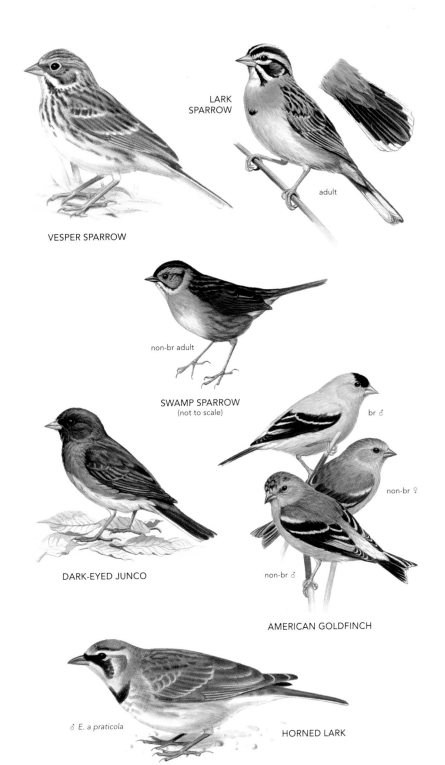

LARK
SPARROW

adult

VESPER SPARROW

non-br adult

SWAMP SPARROW
(not to scale)

br ♂

non-br ♀

DARK-EYED JUNCO

non-br ♂

AMERICAN GOLDFINCH

♂ E. a praticola

HORNED LARK

**J JAMAICAN PETREL** *Pterodroma caribbaea* 35–46cm (14–18in). **BEHAVIOR** Nocturnal when at nesting cliffs. **DESCRIPTION** Dark gray overall, except white rump and uppertail-coverts; legs and feet pinkish-white. **STATUS AND RANGE** Endemic to Jamaica, where believed extinct. Slim possibility it may persist in cliff faces of John Crow Mountains. **HABITAT** At sea except when breeding in cliffs.

**ESKIMO CURLEW** *Numenius borealis* 30–35cm (12–14in); 270–450g. Small curlew. Noticeably smaller than very similar Whimbrel and with shorter, straighter bill. **FLIGHT** Cinnamon-colored wing linings; dark, unbarred primaries. **STATUS AND RANGE** Vagrant to West Indies occurring most frequently in Barbados. Believed extinct since late 1980s. **HABITAT** Grasslands, plowed fields, sometimes mud flats.

**J JAMAICAN PAURAQUE (JAMAICAN POORWILL)** *Siphonorhis americana* 24cm (9.5in). **BEHAVIOR** Nocturnal. **DESCRIPTION** Small, mottled dark brown with narrow white chin band; reddish-brown hindneck spotted black and white. **MALE** Long tail tipped white. **FEMALE** Narrow tail markings pale tan. **STATUS AND RANGE** Endemic to Jamaica, where believed extinct. Genus endemic to West Indies. **HABITAT** Open forest in semi-arid lowlands such as Hellshire Hills.

**IVORY-BILLED WOODPECKER** *Campephilus principalis* 45–50cm (17.5–19.5in); 450–570g. By far the largest West Indian woodpecker. Crow-sized with prominent crest, black-and-white plumage, and large ivory-colored bill. **MALE** Red crest. **FEMALE** Black crest. **VOICE** Soft, toy trumpet–like call, *tut-tut-tut-tut*; unusual for the bird's large size. **STATUS AND RANGE** Formerly permanent resident in Cuba probably until early 2000s, but now believed extinct. May survive in the Cuchillas del Toa mountains or the Sierra Maestra. **HABITAT** Pine woods mixed with deciduous forests.

**BACHMAN'S WARBLER** *Vermivora bachmanii* 11–11.5cm (4.25–4.5in). Yellow eye-ring. **ADULT MALE** Large black patch on throat and breast; black patch on crown; yellow forehead, chin, and belly. **ADULT FEMALE** Duller; black on breast reduced to fine streaks or absent; crown and hindneck gray. **STATUS AND RANGE** Believed extinct. Formerly uncommon and local migrant and non-breeding resident in Cuba September–April. Last widely accepted record 1964; 1980 report dubious. **HABITAT** Undergrowth in moist woods, canebrakes, and forest edges bordering swamps.

**S SEMPER'S WARBLER** *Leucopeza semperi* 14.5cm (5.75in). **BEHAVIOR** Believed to forage on or close to ground. **DESCRIPTION** Long, pale legs; pale feet. **ADULT** Nearly uniform dark gray upperparts and whitish underparts. **IMMATURE** Upperparts including rump gray washed with olive-brown; brownish-gray below. **VOICE** Soft *tuck-tick-tick-tuck*. **STATUS AND RANGE** Endemic to St Lucia, where believed extinct. Last certain report 1961, but others until 1995. Most reports from ridge between Piton Flore and Piton Canaries. Genus also endemic to St Lucia. **HABITAT** Primary or secondary moist forests at mid-elevations with thick undergrowth, mountain thickets, and dwarf forests.

**S GRAND CAYMAN THRUSH** *Turdus ravidus* 27cm (10.5in). Gray with red bill, eye-ring, and legs. Abdomen and outertail feathers white. **VOICE** Quiet, prolonged series of warbling notes. **STATUS AND RANGE** Endemic to Grand Cayman, where believed extinct. Last confirmed report in 1938 at eastern end of island, but other reports up to 1965. **HABITAT** Dry limestone forests.

**S ST KITTS BULLFINCH** *Loxigilla grandis* 19cm (7.5in). Black with reddish-brown throat, undertail-coverts, and crown band. (Similar Lesser Antillean Bullfinch much smaller, with much less reddish-brown crown band and throat patch.) **STATUS AND RANGE** Endemic to St Kitts, where believed extinct. Specimens from early 1930s, but unconfirmed reports until late 1900s. Genus endemic to West Indies. **HABITAT** Mountain forests of Mt. Misery.

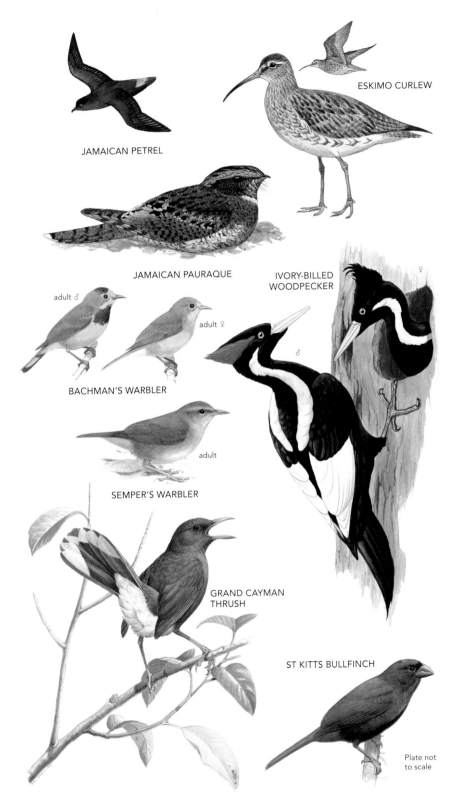

JAMAICAN PETREL

ESKIMO CURLEW

JAMAICAN PAURAQUE

IVORY-BILLED
WOODPECKER

♀

♂

adult ♂

adult ♀

BACHMAN'S WARBLER

adult

SEMPER'S WARBLER

GRAND CAYMAN
THRUSH

ST KITTS BULLFINCH

Plate not
to scale

*strepera* 78, 84
*Margarobyas lawrencii* 106
*Margarops fuscatus* 214
Martin, Caribbean 114
  Cuban 114
  Purple 114
Meadowlark, Eastern 222
*Megaceryle alcyon* 142
  *torquata* 142
*Megascops nudipes* 106
*Melanerpes herminieri* 144
  *portoricensis* 144
  *radiolatus* 144
  *striatus* 144
  *superciliaris* 142
*Melanospiza bicolor* 238
  *richardsoni* 236
*Mellisuga helenae* 134
  *minima* 134
*Melopsittacus undulatus* 152
*Melopyrrha nigra* 234
  *portoricensis* 234
  *taylori* 234
  *violacea* 234
*Melospiza georgiana* 274
  *lincolnii* 252
Merganser, Hooded 80, 86
  Red-breasted 80, 86
*Mergus serrator* 80, 86
Merlin 90
*Microligea palustris* 196
*Milvus migrans* 266
*Mimus gilvus* 212
  *gundlachii* 212
  *polyglottos* 212
*Mniotilta varia* 178
Mockingbird, Bahama 212
  Northern 212
  Tropical 212
*Molothrus ater* 226
  *bonariensis* 226
*Morus bassanus* 24
Munia, Chestnut 248
  Scaly-breasted 248
  Tricolored 248
  White-headed 248
*Myadestes elisabeth* 210
  *genibarbis* 210
*Mycteria americana* 44
*Myiarchus antillarum* 156
  *barbirostris* 156
  *crinitus* 158
  *nugator* 156
  *oberi* 156
  *sagrae* 156
  *stolidus* 156
  *validus* 158
*Myiopagis cotta* 162
*Myiopsitta monachus* 150

*Neochen jubata* 262
*Nesoctites micromegas* 144
*Nesophlox evelynae* 138
  *lyrura* 138
*Nesopsar nigerrimus* 226
*Nesospingus speculiferus* 220
Nighthawk, Antillean 110
  Common 110
Night-Heron, Black-crowned 42
  Yellow-crowned 42
Nightjar, Cuban 108, 110
  Greater Antillean 108
  Hispaniolan 108, 110
  Puerto Rican 108, 110
  Rufous 108, 110
  White-tailed 108, 110
Noddy, Black 254
  Brown 36
*Nomonyx dominicus* 82, 88
*Numenius americanus* 262
  *borealis* 276
  *phaeopus* 62
*Numida meleagris* 118
Nuthatch, Brown-headed 168
*Nyctanassa violacea* 42
*Nyctibius jamaicensis* 110
*Nycticorax nycticorax* 42
*Nymphicus hollandicus* 154

*Oceanites oceanicus* 22
*Oenanthe oenanthe* 210
*Onychoprion anaethetus* 36
  *fuscatus* 36
*Oporornis agilis* 188, 204
Orangequit 216
Oriole, Bahama 224
  Baltimore 222
  Black-cowled 224
  Cuban 224
  Hispaniolan 224
  Hooded 272
  Jamaican 222
  Martinique 224
  Montserrat 224
  Orchard 222
  Puerto Rican 224
  St Lucia 224
*Ortalis ruficauda* 118
*Orthorhyncus cristatus* 134
Osprey 98
Ovenbird 180
Owl, Ashy-faced 104
  Bare-legged 106
  Barn 104
  Burrowing 106
  Cuban Screech 106
  Jamaican 106
  Short-eared 104
  Stygian 104